T4-ATW-806

Revelatory Letters to Nina Cassian

Also by

Maurice Edwards

*How Music Grew in Brooklyn: A Biography
of the Brooklyn Philharmonic Orchestra*

Revelatory Letters to Nina Cassian

a memoir

by

Maurice Edwards

QCC ART GALLERY
The City University of New York

Copyright © 2011 by Maurice Edwards
QCC Art Gallery Press / Literary Series

All rights reserved. No part of this book may be reproduced or
transmitted in any form or by any means without the permission
in writing from the publisher, except by a reviewer who may
quote brief passages in review.

Disclaimer: The events recounted in the following memoir actually took place,
although occasionally the dating of a letter has been adjusted.

Library of Congress Cataloging-in-Publication Data

Edwards, Maurice, 1922-
  Revelatory letters to Nina Cassian : a memoir / by Maurice Edwards.
      p. 416   cm. 16.5 x 22.9
  Includes bibliographical references and index.
  ISBN 978-1-936658-08-4 (alk. paper)
1. Edwards, Maurice--Diaries. 2. Cassian, Nina. I. Title.
  PS3555.D9456Z46 2011
  812'.54--dc23
  [B]
                        2011045655

Design by Adrienne Davich
Cover by Mumtaz Hussain

QCC Art Gallery Press
222-05 56th Avenue
Bayside, NY 11364

I can hardly dedicate this book to my
Muse, Nina, since she's already in the
title — but I do so anyway! — as well
as to my family and the many friends and
colleagues who people it, just as they
once peopled my life.

"Live with your century but do not be its creature."
—Friedrich von Schiller

Dear Nina:

Be my muse—amuse me! Instead, your last note, about ending it all, sent shivers through my soul. Especially since this was not the first time you have raised that specter. Nor were these mere hints. No, they were quite unambiguous statements. You even showed me the little *étui* where you keep the magic deathly potion hidden from view. But how can you possibly revisit that earlier morbidity? Especially *now*, when life seems to have opened new doors for you; when you are accepted everywhere, welcomed by young and old alike; consulted, canvassed, honored, revered even? Could this be another facet of your *ewig weibliche*? Does the Janus face of death always force its way into your system when the face of life seems to be in the ascendancy? What can I do to detour these thoughts, to bring you around to your more positive Self?

Not surprisingly, the paradox of your present plight reminds me of the first time I myself contemplated ending it all. It also happened when I should have been full of *joie de vivre*. I was visiting the beautiful Ticino region of Switzerland, sight-seeing, walking along the shores of Lake Lugano on a hot day in June with the sun at its zenith, when I found myself high up on a promontory overlooking the lake—and all of a sudden froze on the spot, as if pinioned to some primordial rock. All I could do was stare down at the dark waters, where the shade of the promontory deadened the otherwise gorgeous blues of Lake Lugano. My short life reeled through my brain. I was a mere nineteen at the time, with no particular problem or gash tearing at me, surely no Promethean vulture feeding on my vitals! I felt a sudden anomie; a monotonous, post-adolescent melancholy; a stubborn questioning of all existence: what was I doing here? What was this rock to me, this lake, this country, this life? Slowly, gradually, I edged toward the brink from which I could have dived easily, or jumped. Whereupon, what seemed like an arrow—was it a beam of sunlight breaking through those mellifluous trees enveloping the rock—touched my forehead, shook me awake, and saved me from pointless self-immolation.

I was otherwise quite happy then, on leave from the American Army in Germany, here in a peaceful, unbloodied country, where I had just met a wonderful woman, a Neutral Swiss, but on our side; a doctor, but also a poet, somewhat older than me. Yet when you're young that's most appealing and often quite seductive. She was my guide in this new found land, clean, peaceful, untouched by war. Almost pristine.

Should I tell you more now about Toni, for that was her name, "my Swiss chaperone" whom I was to meet again, months later in Paris, where she had gone to do medical research? She, who had been a volunteer nurse to the Allied Armies right after their landing in Normandy? And who had worked farther west with the American naval forces that had landed in Brittany, from which adventure she had brought back a beautiful 11th- or 12th-century wooden Madonna, which came to adorn her little room in the former Cloister of St. Germain des Prés in modern Paris? She also brought memories of an American naval lieutenant whom she had fallen in love with on that tour of duty. Now a captain, he was my superior officer at AFN Bremen, where I had wound up after the war ended and had become part of the Army of Occupation. It was he who had sent me on leave as Mercury to his Diana in Switzerland.

But I'll go into all that in later letters that will describe my nine rather adventurous months in Paris. That's where I was demobilized, and lucky enough to begin the transition to civilian life, but not before enjoying the last few amenities of Army privileges the first few months of that stay. Yes, there's almost too much to tell. Where shall I begin?

Your loving servant,

M.

PS: Forgot to welcome in the new century! And to mark the birthday of my late beloved mother, whom I wish you could have known, who was actually born on the cusp of the last century, January 7, 1900. Little could she or anyone have guessed then that more of mankind was to be slaughtered during those hundred bloody years that followed than ever before recorded in *les annales tristes*. Let's turn a page in hope for a cleaner, better, more humane future this time around.

January 13th

Dear Muse:

Thanks for your encouraging words. And your reassurance that you've buried your dark thoughts in that *étui*. So you would like me to pick up the tale wherever memory may guide me? To recapture the past in pieces that do not flow sequentially? Like free association with a psychiatrist? Will you be my doctor, or my muse, perhaps both? Good! Chronology doesn't matter then. Did it ever?...

Now, where did we leave off? Demobilization in romantic Paris? Actually, it was a dark, damp, cold Paris that winter of 1945-46. I hadn't realized until then that Paris was geographically north of New York; hence the shorter days as one approached the solstice. Everything seemed so very gray—the monuments, the palaces, the official buildings, the art galleries. Even the people looked sallow and gray. Many from malnourishment. Food was scarce. Only the rich could splurge, or the Army!

Those first few months, before full demobilization, I was able to play Santa Claus, along with many another GI similarly stationed there, by bringing canned foods, candies and even some clothing to friends, and to my teachers as well. For, in my application to be discharged in Paris, I had applied for a scholarship, or *bourse*, as they call it, to study literature, music and dance in what many then considered the center of the intellectual and art world. I was fortunate to be awarded a small stipend, which enabled me to take voice lessons with Pierre Bernac (who, of course, certainly didn't need charity clothing, always being so nonchalantly chic) and another fascinating teacher who looked like a clerk out of Balzac, but whose name eludes my memory, for the moment. Let's call him Maestro X, in the meantime. A lifelong friend and disciple of Fauré, he invited me from time to time to dinner with his family and friends at his comfortable flat on comparatively luxurious Boulevard Arago. That's where I was first introduced to those charming, long, drawn-out French bourgeois dinners.

We'd start with drinks and *hors d'oeuvres* on the small balcony overlooking the Boulevard about 7:00 pm. By 7:30 we'd move back into the dining room, where the service would begin slowly, one dish promptly after another, often two potages, separate légumes, etc. Usually we did not get to dessert until 9:30 or 10:00 pm, at which time we'd move to the living room for *aperitifs*, more talk, and music-making. I often had to sing the latest Fauré or Debussy I had been working on with the Maestro, surely long before those struggling *essais* were really ready for "publication," as it were! I needn't have worried. My audience was predisposed to like an American paying homage to its favorite French composers of *chansons*. Besides, I was a pupil of their host. Those evenings never ended before 11:00 pm, often going on until near midnight. Of course, I'd feel guilty the next day when I'd see people lining up in the stores to buy the sparse food on the nearly bare shelves, though nothing like the lines I was to see many years later in Moscow and St. Petersburg (then called Leningrad), or the lines you or your family probably faced simultaneously in Bucharest?

Indeed, at times, one still felt in garrison. The war was not that distant. The effects of the shelling of Paris were still quite in evidence. Many buildings along the *quais* were pockmarked. Few repairs had started yet. Lighting was limited at night. And the vermin had become disquietingly bold. Occasionally, one would espy a large water rat perched on the railings of the Pont Neuf leading to the Ile de la Cité. Though I once saw a distant American cousin of that rat preening himself on a pedestal in front of a near abandoned apartment building on West 81st Street, across from the Museum of Natural History here in NYC, not too many years later. (That was when the West Side was quite run down, some years before Columbus Avenue gentrification had begun.)

Is all this too depressing? Probably I should go back a bit to tell you what I was demobilized from? No, I don't think you want to hear about the dreadful monotony of those mostly dreary Army days. I had no Dulcinea to whom I might address my fanciful moments, although there was Geraldine, whom I had left behind in Manhattan. She who was certainly my first love; she whose image managed to haunt my days and years long after she "broke me in" one night after a modern dance class given by her friend Jane McLean, a Martha Graham dancer, down on dingy but romantic Bleecker Street in the West Village of Manhattan.

I had met Geraldine two years earlier while attending the University of Wisconsin, in four lake clover Madison, one of the more beautiful cities of the Midwest, and at that time also noted for its experimental approach to education, as well as for harboring over a thousand student "refugees" from New York, most of them members of the ultra Left. Geraldine herself hailed from Washington DC (and, accordingly, not so far left!), where, orphaned at the age of five, she was taken in and raised by a *nouveau riche* family, the Loews, who ran one of the bigger movie theater chains in the East. They may have been originally, I now suspect, theatrical "gypsies" or possibly circus people before settling down to good, solid bourgeois business initiatives in the nation's capital and environs.

So, while only moderately leftist—she often reminded me she came from south of the Mason Dixon line, and somehow was never quite able, even though she was otherwise precociously matured, to shed some anti-black feeling—Geraldine was definitely different from most of the New York types I met in Madison.

One of these I shall never forget: a large, Mother Earth figure of a woman, dear old Becky. She seemed ancient to me then, though she was probably only about ten years older than me. She lured me to her apartment one night to preach the gospel of unadulterated Marx—to naive me! I was, after all, a rather shy young socialist, who had been converted to that more moderate faith some years earlier by the compelling oratory of the now legendary Norman Thomas, many time Socialist candidate for president, who I heard outdoors giving a campaign speech in a wheat field in northern Wisconsin. What I recall most was the beautiful simplicity and directness with which he spoke: no old-fashioned bombast or rhetoric, such as one might have expected in that non-auditorium of outdoor space. Ah, he was so profoundly sincere! Of course, what many leftist Europeans don't seem to know is that what was once radical socialism here was taken up gradually, small step by smaller step, by Roosevelt's New Deal and later by Johnson's Great Society, as it was gradually transformed into normal, everyday existence in America.

For Becky, socialism and its adherents were all too tame, too slow. She was an unabashed extremist who wanted action now, and found it, and more, with the Young Communist League (YCL). So I challenged her blind idealism with some of the facts that only a surprisingly few of us seemed to know at that time, and which most YCLers refused to believe, even when confronted with the evidence: the Moscow Trials (fully exposed several years earlier by the Dewey Report); the Nazi Soviet Pact, which had just been struck; or the writings of Victor Serge, who these eager young Communists totally disavowed; plus the many stories of undisguised tyranny that could be read between the lines of most newspaper reports. But Becky defended it all with the standard Popular Front cant of that period, which she sincerely believed: all critiques will be solved, nay resolved, by "the withering away of the dictatorship of the proletariat." It was a phase we all had to go through in order to reach the gates of Paradise. Alas, Becky still subscribed to this hogwash thirty or more years later when, to my great surprise, I ran into her one day walking down Riverside Drive in Manhattan. Neither the Hungarian Revolution nor the Czech Spring, which by that time had come and gone, were enough to disenchant her, wake her up, or bring her down to this good earth.

Back to Geraldine, my first love, who feared no competition from Becky, but who proved more elusive and harder to pin down than a Nabokovian butterfly. Our only near moment of romance back in Madison, before I was whisked away into the Army, came when we were improvising Wigman-ish dances one Saturday afternoon to early recordings of Tchaikovsky, Wagner, and Strauss on the large living room floor of a fancy sorority house to which one of her richer friends belonged. *Hélas*, those passionate writhings went unconsummated. That was Art! The other "art" had to wait until our meeting twelve months later in New York. Yet again, under the arc of dance?

Is that why Dance was to play such a big role in my aesthetic preoccupations after the war? Why I searched out the great Preobrajenskaya in Paris and took lessons with her, me the only adult, indeed the only male, in a class of eight- to ten-year-old female offspring of the White Russian colony in Paris, aspiring to replace the great so-called Baby Ballerinas—Toumanova, Baronova, Riabouschinskaya, and others—when they outgrew their thirty-two *fouettés*? I was already too old to even dream of becoming a *danseur noble* and surely too short! At most, I might have developed into a character dancer and/or choreographer.

Of course, had I been sensible and coldly calculating about it all, what I should have done was just observe the classes, learn what I could from them about the fundamentals of dance, and perhaps end up as a dance critic! That was the sage advice one of my more sane French male friends gave me at that time, and which, no doubt, I ought to have heeded. But I justified my perhaps overenthusiastic embrace of dance because (a) I loved doing it; (b) it would make me a better all-around performer, which was my more realistic long-range goal in theater; and (c) it brought me into a world of glamour far removed from the Army life I had just left. Besides which, my dear, it made me exercise every day; it kept me in shape. However, dear Muse, it was mighty hard work trying to catch up with a strict regimen of training that ideally I should have begun at least ten years earlier. Hence, I suffered many a stiff limb, several pulled muscles, plus a stretched tendon in the back pocket of my left thigh, leaving a little knot that took years to finally disappear; not to mention much chagrin and embarrassment at being this large, ungainly male swan (or drake?) prancing among these charming little *cygnettes.*

Perhaps the greatest lesson I learned from this experience is that when you undertake anything in the Arts, you have to go back to the fundamentals in every way, and every day. You must become like a child again and learn anew. Each essay (in the French sense of the word) in the arts is a fresh start, a new adventure. Then, there are always the ancillary rewards and pleasures. You certainly learn how to appreciate that art more from the inside out once you fully embrace it, dig in, and really work at it. In my case, after only a few months' study, supplementing my classes with the Russian children by private lessons with the tiny, wiry, hunchbacked (yes!) Preobra-jenskaya, Margot Fonteyn happpened to drop in one day to visit her old teacher while I was having such a class. There stood terrified, embarrassed me, struggling with exercises in elevation, and there was Mme. P. asking me to do an entrechat-six for our visitor, which I managed, *mirabile dictu*, to pull off with some aplomb. When la Fonteyn, who was always the most gracious of people (offstage as well as on), learned that I had been studying dance for only three months, she gave me a congratulatory hug and kiss I shall never forget! Which, of course, made me melt all the more whenever in later years I saw her dance on the stage, or even in film or on TV specials. Especially, watching that touching documentary about her retirement to her crippled husband's estate in Panama, where she cared for him until death took him away.

Then, there were other remarkable people I was lucky enough to meet and, in some cases, get to know better, during those short nine months in Paris. Among the most fascinating, of course, was that famed avant-garde American expatriate couple, Gertrude Stein and her beloved life-companion, Alice B. Toklas, to whom I was lucky enough to be introduced by one of my GI friends at Cité Universitaire where we soldiers in the process of being discharged in Paris were temporarily lodged. Gertrude, as you have probably already heard, always liked meeting American soldiers and talking to them, and much of what she gained from those talks went into her

16

book, *Brewsie and Willie*. (But not from me, I'm sorry to disappoint you: I think I met her after the book was already written, though not yet published.)

In any case, our "dormitory" while in Paris was the beautiful Swiss building, Pavillon Suisse, designed by Le Corbusier, my first experience at living in a thoroughly advanced modern building. Built between 1930 and 1932, its "hi-tech" structure, *avant la lettre* (of course, it was only fifteen to sixteen years old at that time) was elevated off the ground on a reinforced concrete platform, giving this comparatively small structure an almost regal entrance. Not without reason, Le Corbusier and his then-partner Pierre Jeanneret called it one of their *habitations de grandeur*. At first, it seemed a little cold and forbidding with its glass blocks and ferrovitreous windows, even though softened and mitigated by its elegant lines and the brilliant colors of its ceramic tiles. But, in time, it actually began to feel like home, and I would return to it at night with a real sense of belonging.

Being in Paris, I almost always would be "coming home" from older structures: withered old theaters; charming but dark, cold flats (heat was hard to come by in those first months after the war); or elegant boulevard mansions from the Baron de Haussmann days. Then there was the intimate, medieval room that Toni (remember her, the poet/doctor I had met earlier in Zurich, as per my first letter?) had been lucky enough to lease in the former nunnery of Saint Germain des Prés, which she shared with that genuine 11th-century, carved, wooden Virgin Mary she had brought back from Brittany, instead of me! (Needless to say, I was desperately jealous of that Madonna.)

Not to mention the widely disparate restaurants and bistros from which one returned late at night. Or the second- and third-floor studios of those ramshackle old buildings in Pigalle, where Egorova, Preobrajenskaya, and other Russian ballet teachers, as well as Leo Staats, the reigning French master known chiefly then for his ballet, "Les Deux Pigeons," with whom I also studied briefly, gave classes. (It was his charming lady assistant who took me to see the great Louis Jouvet and Marguerite Moreno in Giraudoux's deft but genial play, *La folle de Chaillot*. And also a brilliant revival of Cocteau's hot-house

Les Parents Terribles.) Ah yes, each place had its own special flavor and sense of history, its unique smell of having-lived-there-ness, to fall back upon the then-reigning existentialist lingo.

Was this where *L'Être et le Néant* belonged? Was it not in the very air Sartre breathed? Is that why *La Nausée* seemed so authentic when I was introduced to it back then? Sartre made that library where Roquentin worked and read, fairly breathe through my pores. Was that "Da-Sein in Paris"? (Somehow I didn't get around to the *echt* Master, Heidegger, until somewhat later.)

Yes, my dear, here I was, plunged willy-nilly into the birthplace of French Existentialism, and almost didn't need to read the texts. Though, of course, I was too curious not to do so. Besides, I was fortunate enough to meet one of the best of the younger female minds of that period, the philosopher essayist Claude-Edmonde Magny, who loved to go dancing at the Bal Nègre with this American soldier in uniform (which I didn't shed until after three months in Paris). It had its advantages. She could also talk literature and philosophy with me. How she loved our American novelists: Faulkner (with the accent on the last syllable, of course), Hemingway, Fitzgerald, and above all, to my amazement, Dashiel Hammet! Only years later did I begin to understand the extraordinary value the French— and other Europeans, including, of course, you Romanians, my dear Muse—put on these writers. Doesn't your literary weekly, *Dilema*, boast a motto by Faulkner?) In their eyes, these were the only true Americans. Along with our good old Western movie stars, especially Gary Cooper (pronounced Koo-pair), who became cult heroes there long before they attained that status here. Even more amazing, and most hilarious indeed, was to go to the French cinema and hear Mae West speaking French! For, back then, American movies were dubbed, not subtitled.

Surprisingly enough, in view of her precocious understanding of French and German philosophy—Heidegger, Husserl, Bergson, Marcel, Sartre, Merleau-Ponty, as well as other important figures I had never heard of, let alone studied or even read—Claude-Edmonde was strangely deficient in any comprehension of, or even acquaintance with, British and American philosophers, the logical positivists, pragmatists, et al. She didn't know Russell or Whitehead, but thought Charles Morgan important! Nor had she heard of our pioneer Americans—Peirce, Dewey, Santayana, or even William James. And Wittgenstein hadn't crossed the channel yet! Of course, like most Europeans, she esteemed Emerson enormously, and among the poets, Dickinson and Whitman. Oddly enough, I don't remember discussing Poe with her; for I've found down through the years that almost all European intellectuals rate Poe much higher than we do, including you, my dear. Didn't your father translate "The Raven" into Romanian?

One night, accompanying Claude-Edmonde on a walk, along with her very good friend, Marcelle Sibon, Stephen Spender's French translator, we stopped briefly at a restaurant where I was introduced to the Grande Dame of St. Germain des Prés, namely, Simone de Beauvoir, surprisingly gracious and attractively dressed. We spent a few minutes at her table in pointedly small talk—"don't you prefer the American accent to the British?"—and then moved on. Unfortunately, I never saw her again.

Reflecting back on this meeting, and other brief encounters with French artists and various members of their intelligentsia—Jean Paulhan, Maurice Blanchot, Picabia—I often wonder why they were so open and welcoming to me: a young, naive, discharged, non-commissioned soldier who had absolutely no claim to fame, who hadn't "done" anything yet, had made no special mark in their world (or any other world, for that matter). Was it simply because I was an American to whom, as one of their "liberators," they felt some obligation to be kind? Or could it be that they were pleased (and relieved) to find one of that tribe who shared their values or who seemed to understand them, and valued their work and its significance? I shall never know, since, alas, I was not to return to Paris until more than forty years later, except in my dreams!

How could I have stayed away so long from a place where I had felt so much at home? From people who seemed to appreciate me for myself alone, not for what I had done or might be about to do! Sometimes the mere thought of this *manqué* depresses me so. I try to bury the memory of it. But, of course, it won't go away, and comes back to haunt me often, perhaps for the better. For it was in Paris that I took my first giant steps toward maturity. Would I have matured faster had I remained there longer and become another World War II American expatriate? In any case, the long-delayed revisit was revelatory, and also essentially reassuring. Short as it was, and supplemented by an unexpected second return trip almost exactly one year later, it surely helped me see through to the heart of my French experience, its value and its limitations, at least for what I was to become—and am?

Ah, dear Muse, are you going to reprimand me now for dwelling so long on what might have been? How will this jibe with the psychological portrait you're no doubt in the process of drawing up of this prodigal son? Could that be one reason you agreed so readily to the idea of my writing these letters to you even when we're both in town, a process justified, of course, by the fact that I'm something of a *Tale of Two Cities* character with two addresses—one, my studio/office in Brooklyn and the other, our "*maison*" with you on Roosevelt Island? Well, all the more reason that you reassure me of your support to carry on this conceit, a sort of epistolary dance!

...Perhaps this letter exchange will not only fill you in about aspects of my life I somehow used to think wouldn't interest you, but will also help me come to a better understanding of why I did this instead of that in certain situations, and eventually lead to a better overall understanding of myself? A bonus would be, of course, that it would bring us closer together in our understanding of one another!

Hangdoggedly yours,
M.

Chère Madame:

Thanks for your prompt, positive response. I'm glad you agree with the idea of continuing this letter exchange whether in town or not! Of course, your advice as to how I should go about it is right on the button, and to the point! I must fill in the record now, come hell or high water: search each moment for what it meant to me then, what it came to mean later, and, if relevant, what it means to us now.

Certainly there can be no doubt that this less than a year in Paris matured me far more than a quick return to Academia in the States would have done. On the other hand, had I stayed on and become one of the expatriates, might I not have grown into something of a hybrid of two cultures? Probing back, I think that that fear haunted me then and there and was probably a major factor in my going back home, though, of course, the more obvious pressing factors were those of family ties and proper completion of my studies in America. I figured that I could always go back to Paris later for an advanced academic degree. Indeed, that might have been the wiser alternative. But Wilhelm Meister's *Theatralische Sendung* reared its tempting head, and that Drive or *Sendung* could only be realized in America first, or at most, in England. Yes, England probably was the place I should have moved to after that prelude in France.

However, more important than all these almost self-evident rationalizations and justifications for actions taken or not taken, there was the deeper, nagging question of finding out who I really am. Something in me said: you can only discover that back where your roots are. You shouldn't settle for a romantic, foreign solution. That would be superficial. It would, in any case, simply postpone the final reckoning. And what, in any case, is a final reckoning? Am I not, are not all of us, constantly reassessing ourselves? Shedding our skin every seven years like a snake? Do we not wake each morning to face a new weathering, a new film layer of comprehension, a new challenge and an ever new set of tests and checkups? As it says in the *Schulchan Aruch* (*Ethics of the Fathers*): "Arise each morning and face the day like a lion!" In that spirit, dear, patient Madame, let's move on to the next memory chip.

For example, what happened at Gertrude Stein's? Perhaps the most amusing, and for Alice B. Toklas, most touching incident, took place one winter morning when I arrived to find thin, wiry Alice in tears. Quite surprised, and worried by her discomposure, I sat her down to try to reason calmly with her, to find out discreetly what was wrong, and then to reassure her that all would be well, that things would work themselves out for the best. Never before had I seen Alice less than poised, alert, and indeed, somewhat formal. Finally, after some delicate, rather circuitous questioning to put her at ease, she told me what was amiss: Gertrude had insisted that morning that she get rid of their cat!

And why? Simply because Gertrude's beloved dog, Basket II, hated Alice's cat, or so Gertrude maintained. But Alice pleaded that they needed the cat to rid the house of the persistent mice. After all, it was a very old building they lived in. It had not been maintained at all as it should have been. Moreover, the city itself was teeming with vermin. Did I not note earlier seeing large water rats preening themselves from time to time on the railings of the bridge leading to Notre Dame?

But Reason could not prevail. Love for Basket II overturned that. Even poor Alice's overwhelming love for her cat went by the wayside, "And that was that was that!" Alice rose and wiped away her tears. We never heard another word about that episode; and we returned to the errands that had to be run that day to prepare for one of their bimonthly literary matinee salons, on Wednesdays, as I recall, at 4:00 p.m.

These were usually attended by leading lights of the Parisian and British literary and artistic worlds, who came to sit at Gertrude's feet. I was privileged to be allowed to "sit in" on several occasions. Among the "stars" who attended these often exhilarating sessions were Henri Michaux, Stephen Spender, and numerous lesser-known figures, at least, less known to unsophisticated me. Discussions were carried on primarily in English, though French was spoken from time to time. (By the way, Gertrude, in spite of living over forty years in France, spoke French with a shockingly thick American accent; Alice, less so.)

But Gertrude, seated exactly in the pose Picasso painted her in, in that great portrait of her now housed at the Metropolitan Museum of Art, dominated all discussions. The amazing thing about the portrait is how uncannily Picasso caught the timeless element in her. Painted at least thirty years before World War II, she looked to me exactly as she did in that portrait. She sat on the same sofa, her thick legs ensconced in similar knee-length, thick woolen stockings, hands and elbows resting on her thighs in almost the same posture. All that was missing from the Picasso portrait was the gray hair that had since accumulated and the dark moustache (although Alice's was even more pronounced, since she still had black hair, or did she dye it?). All in all, a formidable figure. The agelessness of the portrait was, of course, inherent because of the basic African mask Picasso finally used for her face, and only after that long struggle to finish the portrait, eighty-three or eighty-four sittings, wasn't it?

Gertrude, as might have been expected, had very pronounced views on America, which she had only revisited twice since starting her exile in France, once to receive a literary award and the other time to lecture on the American college circuit, at the same time promoting her not-so-recent opus, *The Autobiography of Alice B. Toklas* (though, of course, written by G.S.). She had also, on the occasion of one of these literary matinees, just returned from a visit to several American Army bases in Alsace Lorraine and Germany. Apparently, she had met some soldiers there who agreed with her strange views on how the Catholic Church was undoing America. While expostulating on this theme, she made some blatantly erroneous statements about Catholicism in the USA and also advanced some astounding, misleading generalizations about the country as a whole, so much so, that, humble me, I ventured to disagree by raising my hand to speak. At which point, I felt Alice hovering at my elbow, quietly offering me some of the delicious pastries Gertrude and I had picked up earlier that day on the Rue de Rivoli, and whispering, "We don't contradict Gertrude." Whereupon I fell silent, and munched away at a tiny Napoleon, feeling more defeated than N. himself must have felt after Waterloo.

However, on a one-to-one basis, Gertrude was easy to converse with, generous to other writers (although she hated Ezra Pound with a passion), concerned about the world around her, quite up on politics in general, and was basically a kind, warm human being. This seeming contradiction between her private and public demeanor reminds me now in some ways of the diverse aspects of Zero Mostel, another larger-than-life figure whom I came to know twenty-five years later when I played in the original production of *Fiddler on the Roof*.

Mostel, too, was warm, *simpatico*, comparably ample of girth, concerned about the well-being of everyone around him, most generous and supportive of his poor relatives, and whoever happened to be his listener at a particular moment. But the minute a third party intruded or "entered the scene," he would shift immediately into another gear: he'd be "on stage," giving a performance, even if only to the two or three in the party he was addressing. When I would talk with Zero backstage, or between breaks in rehearsal for *Fiddler*, or alone in his dressing room, he was seriousness incarnate. But back in rehearsal, he might kick me in the shins, since I was playing a beggar, and he was definitely "ruler of the Queen's Navee." Or in actual performance, when the men of the shtetl were lined up behind him as they confronted the town constable threatening a pogrom, he might be painfully twisting the wrist of the villager just behind him, trying to break him up as he was bearing down on the constable. Of course, this had nothing to do with the play, the script, or the scene in general. Yet the audience never guessed what that contrapuntal action might have meant, if indeed they ever perceived it through his clever, dexterous manipulations.

Only two weeks after *Fiddler* had opened, the Rabbi, who I was understudying (and who was played by Gluck Sandor, a noted pioneer Modern dancer and choreographer himself, one of Jerome Robbins's first dance teachers and an important influence on him), became violently ill. As his understudy, I had to step in for him at the last minute, without rehearsal. That night, as I was for the first time about to give the blessing over Mottl outside the moving circle of the Prologue, Zero was standing sagely nearby after introducing us, as was his wont, except that while I was uttering the blessing, under his breath he was doing the best he could to break me up and spoil the blessing. Fortunately, he did not succeed in this malicious maneuver! I outmaneuvered him that time.

Another time, however, when I took over the role of Avram, the Bookseller, whom I also understudied, I managed to get a laugh on a line that the actor playing the role regularly never got. But this laugh meant that the laugh Tevya (Zero) always got a few lines later on suffered slightly in intensity. Sure enough, during intermission I was summoned by the loudspeaker to Mostel's dressing room. Seated like a royal Wazir, with legs spread wide apart, almost identically the way Gertrude's used to be, he started off by assuring me how much he liked me, and how much he wanted me to succeed in show business, etc., etc. On he went, benevolently suggesting that I play the line more like my predecessor. "It makes more sense that way," he reassured me, "and will show you off better." What else could I do but agree, and thank him? Nevertheless I reported to the stage manager what had happened, and asked what he thought I should do about it. "Do just what he said," was his firm advice. "Even though your interpretation may be better, in my opinion. We can't upset the old boy."

Which reminded me, in turn, of a story which that fine comic actor and an old friend of Zero's, Jack Gilford, told me one day when I ran into him in Shubert Alley, shortly before we were to go into rehearsal with *Fiddler*. "Don't ever try to cross Zero," he warned. "When he and I were together in *A Funny Thing Happened on the Way to the Forum*, I had one line which Zero never let me finish, not during the entire run of the show, because he was afraid it would get a laugh. And that would cut down the laugh he hoped to get later, after what should have been mine. I tried every trick in the book"—and Gilford had plenty of vaudeville tricks and show biz experience up his sleeve—"but to no avail. In fact, that ordeal nearly broke up our long friendship."

But, of course, it didn't. For, in addition to their long, old ties of professional and personal friendship, they were partners political-ly, Zero, in particular, having suffered the slings and arrows of talking (or not talking?) to McCarthy's Congressional Committee. Indeed, politics almost kept Zero from taking on *Fiddler*. He had sworn he would never again work with Jerome Robbins, who was scheduled to direct the show, because Robbins had squealed and given names to the Committee. Thus several years before, when Robbins was called in by Hal Prince to "fix" *Funny Thing* on the road in Baltimore, Zero refused to talk to Robbins. Any notes Jerry had for him had to be given to Zero in writing. But at this point, somehow, time had smoothed the edges somewhat, and they did manage to communicate rather well, though coldly, and drily, during rehearsals for *Fiddler*.

As to Gilford, he was still an unrepentant Stalinist at that time, even after Hungary and the Prague Spring. I vividly remember him and his wife Madeline some years earlier, haranguing the cast of one of my first summer-stock experiences in Woodstock, back in 1951 or 1952, I believe. These *spiels* usually took place during lunch breaks, or at night in one of the local taverns. Of course, this was shortly before Hungary and long before Prague, indeed almost contempora-neous with the odious McCarthy hearings. (In fact, one day, during the Woodstock run of the play we were in, there was some sort of municipal rally near the theater involving protests about a proposed supermarket takeover of the theater grounds, during which I'm sure I detected one or two soberly dressed, unsmiling strangers whom I suspected may have been the FBI.)

Maybe that's why Gilford and his wife were so vocal about their position, etc., which mirrored exactly what the *Daily Worker* and *The Nation* were saying at that time. And I was the only member of that very young cast politically mature enough to dispute their stand. I could also call upon a background of European experience (especially in Germany with the Russians, when we had to hand over Saxony to them) to challenge the fallacies of their dictated party line arguments.

But, wait: do you really want me to go on with this? I know it's an especially touchy, possibly painful, subject for you, my dear

Muse. After all, you were in Eastern Europe at that very moment suffering under the boot of the Soviet colossus. Wasn't Georghiu Dej lording it over Romania in the early fifties? But, idealistically, you were hoping that the humane doctrine which helped launch that system might still manage to bring about the withering away of the dictatorship and the installation of a truly benevolent, fair and humane, socialist State. Where each would develop according to his own inherent abilities; where no one would starve; where all peoples and races would be treated equally; where the Greedy World of Capitalism would dissolve and Ethics and Socialist good will would reign supreme instead... Still, you didn't object to my description in an earlier letter of my first dialectical encounter with Becky Nathanson back at the University of Wisconsin, before I entered the Army and left for Europe, did you?

Well, I'm at a crossroads now. There's still so much to tell you along these lines: our division being the first to meet the Soviets at Torgau on the Elbe at the end of the war; subsequent experiences in Saxony, the province we turned over to them in the division of Berlin agreement; Olga, the beautiful Ukrainian/Polish underground DP, with whom I studied Russian, oh, too briefly, in Weissenfels (near Leipzig); vociferous discussions in Bremen with Germans unhappy that we hadn't turned around and pushed the Soviets back Eastward; meetings with leftists in Paris and many would-be ex-Resistance fighters; that extraordinary moment when I chanced by accident to come upon the German Communist Party Command Post Hdq. in Frankfurt (were they surprised!) as I was passing through that severely bombed railroad and financial center, while en route from Bremen to Paris (where I was to be demobilized), sightseeing among the ruins, looking for the place where Goethe once lived, *und so weiter*.

Are you curious? Does all this belong in these letters? I await your wise counsel, dear Lady Virgil, in guiding me through this modern Inferno of Realpolitik...

Until then, guardedly yours,

M.

27

June 25, 2000

Dearest Nina:

In the meantime, even before getting your reply to my last missive, I send you this extraordinary snippet (which I just ran across) from a posthumously published poem, out of the mouth of our reputedly most apolitical poet, Wallace Stevens:

>   The rape of the bourgeoisie accomplished, the men
>   Returned on board The Masculine. That night,
>   The captain said,
>   "The war between classes is
>   A preliminary, a provincial phase,
>   Of the war between individuals. In time,
>   When earth has become a paradise, it will be
>   A paradise full of assassins."

>   (from "Life on a Battleship")

Could Stevens have been thinking of the horrors perpetrated by the Hundred Flowers regime of Mao Tse-Tung? And the 30,000,000 more or less who starved from its ill-induced famine? And what about the assassins of poor Cambodia? And still more recently the absolutely incomprehensible slaughter in Rwanda? Not to mention Bosnia. And, now, even more inadmissably, Kosovo!

Which recalls a talk I had two years ago in Paris with a rather interesting writer whom our mutual friend Harriet Zinnes introduced me to in New York some years ago: Albert Russo, a man of many countries and allegiances. Trilingual at least, he wrote in English with what one might call an American accent, but primarily in French, and occasionally in Italian. (He had lived in all three countries.) Meeting once in his modest but comfortable studio apartment not far from the Arc de Triomphe, he showed me a shelf full of the many books he had knocked off in these several languages, mostly French, of course. (He has since written many more, if we're to believe Google, which claims he has published worldwide over 65 books of poetry, fiction and photography!) Part of his adolescence—the high school years, I believe—was spent near Lake Tanganyika in Rwanda. Now he was trying to interest publishers in his memoir of that epoch, thinking of course that the then-current tragedy would awaken public interest in what he had to say about pre-genocide Rwanda. How different and idyllic it sounded, recounting a period only about twenty years before the massacre!

That sudden shift, that slit of time, that crackle of the earth, between the calm and the storm, between tragedy and comedy, between sanity and madness, brings to mind many a mind-boggling paradox, from the Hermannsschlacht to Bosnia. And how often will that moment of insight be suddenly illuminated by a chance encounter with someone who "had been there," who knew what it was like before, as Russo from South Carolina/Tanganyika/Milan had? Or it could be even a taxi driver? I remember one such juncture that happened a few years ago, at the height of the Bosnian conflict, before the U.S. belatedly stepped in, when Sarajevo was most heavily besieged. I would often ask my taxi driver where he was from, especially when I couldn't tell for sure from his photo or identification plate. This particular driver turned out to have been born, and gone to school, in Sarajevo, and to have loved that remarkable city. His stories confirmed what I'd often heard, namely, that it was one of the most successfully "integrated" cosmopolitan cities in the world, where, according to him and others, Muslim, Serb, Croat, Turk, and Jew lived and worked easily and comfortably together on almost all levels. And all spoke the same language, Serbo-Croatian. Indeed, most of them looked pretty much alike....And then?

But here I move back into that difficult, often dirty, ugly realm of Realpolitik, even before getting your reply to my earlier note! Forgive my garrulousness. I shall now put down my pen (i.e., shut down the computer) and wait for what the Mailman bringeth forth.

Awaitingly yours,

M.

September 11, 2000

My prompt, dearest Muse:

Thanks for your quick, positive response to my last two missives! You say that you're curious to learn where the intertwining snake of consciousness and memory may lead me next? That is most tantalizing. It frees me to begin to reconstruct some of my more amorphous memories. Was it Jonathan Swift who wrote "When I rebuilt Rome in your mind, it was as though I walked those streets"? Or was it like Freud going back time and time again to that church in Rome to ponder and explore how to get under the marble skin of the Michelangelo Moses.

But for heaven's sake, you don't think I would even presume to emulate such eminences? I bring them up—or those memories erupt—to help me better understand this whole process. For it's still a mystery to even the most advanced neurology scientists of today (though they're supposedly making great strides) as to why memory zigzags in such unpredictable ways. Though obviously the clues to some associations are much easier to find than others.

For example, why does my mind now suddenly jump back in time to that hot July day in Upper Peninsula, Michigan, when my Father was trying to teach me—or to induce me—to swim in those still-ultra-cold waters of Lake Superior? How he walked me out to where the water came up to my neck, then picked me up in his arms and threw me a yard farther out, where the water would be over my head were I to try to stand, and where I had no other choice but to paddle like a dog desperately trying to stay afloat. And how well it worked! I simply had to paddle back to him, which I did, as he gradually backed farther and farther away from me, toward the shore, until I was at last able to stand up without drowning. But, of course, that experience didn't turn me into a tournament swimmer. Though oddly enough, it did not prevent me from becoming a pretty good fancy diver about ten years later in high school in Wisconsin, capable of competing in intramural athletic events.

And now I find myself a few years later crawling, face down, rifle in hand, with barbed wire stretched above my head, and blanks being fired over the field, as we soldier recruits are being broken in on an obstacle course in basic training on the hot sands of Camp Shelby in lower Mississippi, not far from Biloxi and the Gulf of Mexico. Then scrambling up a tall barrier, reaching the top almost out of breath, and slithering down a rope, only to encounter still more obstacles before reaching the final goal. Quite different from the reality of crawling a hundred yards under enemy fire nine or ten months later on the other side of the Atlantic, on the other side of the Rhine, in Germany!

Our division, the 69th, part of the First Army, operating directly north of Patton's 9th Army, was in pursuit of the retreating Germans, whose defense seemed to have collapsed almost totally once we crossed the Rhine at Remagen. For I was damned lucky to have missed the worst of the Battle of the Bulge. We were now covering twenty to thirty kilometers a day. The towns and villages would simply surrender as we passed through. Few of us, at least in our regiment, had encountered much opposition. In any case, being the tech sergeant of the quartermaster company of an infantry division, my duties were largely of a clerical nature, handling logistics and planning, and our company was almost always at least a mile or two behind the rest of the regiment, which meant, basically, fairly safe behind the lines. The Germans were dangling white banners, flags, towels, handkerchiefs—anything white would do—from their windows, and their mayors or equivalents were turning over the keys of the towns to us as we advanced through them. Our lieutenant colonel in charge of supplies for the division began to get careless and slaphappy with our success. But he was still itching to see battle! How he envied the officers of the combat companies in our regiment. He wanted to come out of the war a hero, with decorations like them, and promotion to at least a full colonel.

However, on one fateful day, about the third or fourth successive day of unchallenged advances, as we reached the edge of a town that had just succumbed like the others without a struggle, we were suddenly stopped by a young lieutenant of the tank corps of our division, which always preceded our infantry companies. Here we were, the colonel's small advance detail in two jeeps, four men to each jeep, being held up by a junior officer! Recklessly blinded by those easy advances, the colonel was furious, even after the lieutenant cautiously and respectfully explained to him how he and his men were quite sure there had to be some German soldiers not too far out in the fields ahead of us, about 800 to a thousand yards beyond the town. Indeed, that's what Intelligence had informed him of, and warned that it would be very dangerous for us, basically unarmed except for carbines and rifles, to go any further on our own. Moreover, he was under orders from his commanding officer not to let anyone through until the tank corps itself had probed and cleared the area first. But our obdurate colonel brusquely disregarded the warning and ordered us to move ahead on our own reconnaissance mission, with the explicit task of finding a site for setting up Division Supply Headquarters for the next day.

None of us eight men, other than the colonel, wanted to go any farther, but we had no choice, and so we drove past the temporarily stalled tank corps to carry out "Mission Impossible." The road we started riding down was one of those alley-like roadways you find depicted in many European landscape paintings, flanked on either side by rows of stately poplars or similar, tall thin trees. Fortunately, this road was also flanked on both sides with fairly capacious, deep ditches adjacent to its rows of trees.

The field stretched flat and bleak in front of us for a thousand or more yards at least. Besides the two parallel rows of trees, there was nothing special about the scene other than a generous clump of trees on the right side of the road, about 800 or 900 yards ahead. Yet the colonel continued to ignore the cautious lieutenant's warning, plus our own urgent seconding of that warning, namely, that some German soldiers could be hiding out there in that ominous clump, poised to ambush us. The Colonel ignored our warning as well. So onward we moved, albeit rather slowly.

We were about halfway between the tank corps waiting skeptically behind us, and that thick clump of trees ahead, when suddenly the Germans opened fire. I was in the seat behind the colonel, on the right side of the forward jeep, when this happened. He shouted to all to jump into the ditches on either side of us and return fire from there. We did so, in my case, landing directly behind the colonel on the right side of the road. Finally recognizing the great danger we were now in, he turned his head back toward me and ordered me to dash like hell back to the tank corps for help and reinforcement.

I didn't have time to be scared, though I took in some mighty big gulps of air, and started out pronto down that depressed ditch in a crouched run so that I would make a less visible target for the gunners shooting from that clump of trees. After covering about 100 yards that way, I gradually assumed more height, until fifty yards or so later I was running fully erect, and, accordingly, faster. I felt safer now, knowing that a moving target is much harder to hit and also that the accuracy of rifle fire diminishes proportionately the more distant the target.

By then I was moving so fast that before long I was within hailing distance of our tank corps. Some of them came out to meet me, so that I could tell them, breathlessly, what had happened, though, of course, they had already surmised as much, seeing me running toward them. Their lieutenant immediately gave the order to lob shells into that dangerous clump, which they did. There was no return fire, which meant that the German unit must have realized it was outnumbered, now that our tank corps was on the move, and had precipitously skedaddled away. Within a few minutes, our forward tank, on which I was precariously perched, had reached the site where the eight of us had been forced to debark from our jeeps.

I hopped off the tank when we reached our jeep and jumped down into the ditch, only to find the colonel lying there motionless: a bullet had pierced the left side of his helmet, gone through his head, and come out of the right side. The other six soldiers in our group were, thank god, unharmed.

I was stunned cold as I closed the Colonel's eyes and adjusted his limp, but heavy body, holding death in my arms for the first time in my life. But this was no time for tears or lamentation, yet only after that point was I able to calm down and relax somewhat. The lieutenant asked me to describe what had happened, which I proceeded to do. I was thanked by the comrades of my group for running back for help under fire, and congratulated by the tank corps men who ultimately saved all of us. Then the mood changed: it was time to move on with their mission. I was forgotten as they focused on the task ahead.

Whereupon a most peculiar thing happened. Almost as if in a trance, I accidentally pulled the trigger of the carbine I was carrying over my shoulder (fortunately pointed upward to heaven!) and a small shot rang out. So embarrassed I wanted to crawl under the tank, I was thoughtfully handed a drink by one of the men, and nothing more was said about that faux pas. Nor was anything more asked until later as to why the colonel led us out there into such an obvious ambush in the first place. They must have realized that mine was probably a delayed reaction to discovering my colonel dead, and to the cumulative anxiety I had suppressed in order to make that run and reach the tank corps. Indeed, it was then and there that I most forcibly learned that so-called bravery under fire is nothing more nor less than the 100 percent focus and concentration needed to accomplish the task ahead. Once you manage to do all that, you have no time to be scared—until afterwards!

But what am I saying here? All this sounds too much like an old soldier's tale, something I've generally tried to avoid telling all these years because I didn't want to be taken for a braggart, or a would-be "hero"; or a veteran trying to convince people he really saw battle. *Au contraire*, this was one of the few dangerous moments I faced during my comparatively short, relatively easy-going "Army career." (Except perhaps for the last days of the Bulge before we actually crossed the Rhine.) In fact, later I often felt guilty facing or dealing with soldiers who had been through much more than I and had endured real physical suffering and/or hugely terrifying confrontations.

I'll just wind up this account with its ironical, concluding aftermath: the lieutenant colonel was awarded a posthumous silver star for leading us into an ambush—and yours truly got the modest bronze star for helping us out of that ambush. Yet there were no hard feelings anywhere; and it was at least a minor consolation for the colonel's wife to think that her husband had died a true hero. Nor did she ever learn the whole story, as far as I am aware!

A little exhausted from this soldier's tale, which would need a Stravinsky to make more of it, *si ça vaut même pas la peine.* I'm going to sign off now and check out Spengler on *The Decline of the West* !

Militarily yours,

M.

December 5, 2000

My dear Ariadne:

I hope it wasn't too much to take, that rather protracted story? You say that you could stand even more war tales? Really? A description of the dead cows and horses passed when we joined our Army in Belgium as it emerged covered with mud and blood from the Battle of the Bulge? No, not yet. Maybe later. For now, guide me with your Minotaur string out of the Cretan labyrinth, the Cave of Machpelah, and/or any other grave sites to happier horizons for the nonce!

But before closing the book on this account, perhaps I should give the colonel credit where it was his due and which he deserved and, at the same time, put on record my gratitude to him for making my Army days (up to his tragic end) certainly more palatable and involving than they probably otherwise would have been. Realizing that our own regimental major was not too good at reading maps, nor plotting moves, nor even calculating elementary supply needs and the like (though he was a great womanizer, but there was little chance for that in the here and now), the colonel had me take over many of his duties on a come what may basis. In other words, he didn't tell the major "Go fuck yourself!" He simply had me read the maps for both of them.

Also, he would often take me to corps headquarters for strategy sessions, along with the handsome, silent major. I had become the colonel's de facto aide-de-camp, as it were. And since he knew that I had some facility with both French and German, I would often be brought into situations where a translator was needed. How else could I, a noncom, have gained such access to, and understanding of, how to run a division, or any large organization, for that matter, without this kind of experience? Thank you, dear late, lamented lieutenant colonel.

One incident, in particular, I shall never forget—partly because the odors associated with it were so strong! And you sometimes wonder about my olfactories? About two days before that fatal event, while we were still riding high, we had entered a very small village, filled with those inevitable and most welcome white surrender flags, around noon. Time for chow, and a brief respite. So the colonel had me stand up on the hood of his jeep and make a speech to the assembled town, for by now over a hundred villagers had gathered in that improvised small square.

Our unit was parked near a huge pile of still-moist manure; each of those villages had such fertilizer piles at nearly every bend of the road. I was told to let them know that we, the American Army, had now taken over their village officially; that we would need space in some of their barns for storage of vital supplies; that this village would be our link to the next quartermaster supply site; and that there would be serious recriminations if all of their arms were not surrendered then and there. So everybody had better follow the rules—or else.

As I started to explain these things and lay down the law to them in my hesitant, limited, nonidiomatic German, nowhere near as polished as that dreadful, impossible standard German officialese, the colonel exhorted me to get tough and scare the hell out of these people. "Let them know who's boss," he puffed. To my amazement, I—who a half hour earlier had marveled at the way little nine- and ten-year-old youngsters could rattle off those difficult, complex German box sentences without grunting or blinking an eyelid—found myself shouting warnings in apparently comprehensible German, using locutions I never knew I had under my belt, or at the tip of my tongue. Nor was I able to speak German that fluently again until some months later while in the Army of Occupation in Bremen. It was a most exciting sensation, but confusingly mingled with those almost overwhelming, near-alcoholic fumes emitted from that huge pile of manure next to me. Could it be that I was on a "manure high" when I barked out those orders and warnings to the humbled, frightened farmers of that tiny German hamlet?

Speaking other tongues, as you know, is subject to the most precarious variations. Each situation is unique. Remember my first visit with you to Bucharest where I met a number of your friends? How I became almost tongue-tied in front of them and forgot the little Romanian I had acquired in the laborious six weeks of cram sessions I went through with you before we took off for that Colloquium on the Diaspora of Romanian Language and Literature in that charming ex-resort, Neptune, on the shores of the Black Sea? The conference center and our hotel were right on the beach, remember? Going down to breakfast, I would enjoy greeting other attendees with *"Buna dimineața"*—good morning in Romanian. But I couldn't say much more if any one of them would be inclined to stop and talk. By the way, wasn't that near the luxury hotel that Ceaușescu usually favored?

Was I stumbling that way because I was afraid I might embarrass you in front of your friends with my bad grammar? For, later that same week, after we had settled in a modest hotel in downtown Bucharest, and as I wandered off during one of your daily naps

37

to a meeting I had with someone at the American Embassy, I found that I could ask for directions on the street in Romanian and make myself understood comparatively easily, considering my limited vocabulary and lack of practice. Or similarly, several months later when we were in Paris, there were occasions when French spilled out of my mouth with great ease; and other times when the words got stuck in my gullet, and just refused to emerge. Could this be a phenomenon by any chance also related to hormonal ups and downs one cannot always command at will, or certainly not willfully force, when they don't flow naturally?

But I promised to change the subject and also to change venues. High time I did so, right? Although, in a sense, I already have, what with those evocations of today's Bucharest and Paris! It's strange how, because of the romantic images we Americans seem to concoct whenever Paris is mentioned, or even that Little Paris, Bucharest, musings such as those above already seem to have taken on a premature sense of nostalgia, just a few years after they occurred!

Could this be related to that other seemingly universal phenomenon, the patina of age? What does it mean? You see how subtle it all becomes once you try to analyze it, how inconsistent in terms of age or timing, i.e., when does it start; when is a work of art, or a memory, subject to it, etc.; and why does it seem to vary so amazingly from venue to venue, from object to object, from period to period?

Thus, some of my memories are immediate, unclouded, unmediated, direct. Such as a boy shoveling a path to school way back there, eighty-some years ago, in the Upper Peninsula of Michigan (mentioned before, remember, when describing how my father tried to teach me to swim). Our winters would often end up with thirteen to fifteen feet of cumulative snow left on the morning after a long snowfall the whole night and day before. And it wouldn't have to be of blizzard proportions or necessarily need wild winds to build up such little mountains of snow.

Since the temperature would steadily hover around zero or below, any moisture in the air would turn to snow immediately. So it was not that unusual to wake up and realize that in just taking a few steps outdoors, one could be practically buried in snow, depending upon which way the wind had blown the drifts. It was much like Emerson put it in his poem "Snowstorm": "the mad wind's night-work, the frolic architecture of the snow." On such mornings we would have to either tunnel our way to school or else ski there or go by sled. The air on such occasions would be unbelievably fresh and pure. Breathing it, if the temperature did not sink too low, was utter joy. But we'd usually need at least an hour or more just to reach school, even though this was a tiny hamlet of only eight hundred souls, with the school just on the edge of town. Once we got there, we'd have to shed boots or overshoes, mittens, and scarves, then dry off and warm ourselves at the stoves. After all that, refreshed as we were, some of those delayed morning classes which by then had moved into the early afternoon would become surprisingly exciting and instructive, in the best sense: we probably learned more in those foreshortened sessions than during a standard full school day. Indeed, I've often opined that the distribution of school hours, not to mention factory hours and rehearsal hours for plays and concerts, are all too mechanically set up and determined.

For example, the standard seven- or eight-hour rehearsal day for a Broadway show tends to become quite unproductive by the time you reach the fifth or sixth hour. Of course, a good director usually has sense enough to move into another, contrasting scene or section of the play you're working on, or to shift to improvisations or try something totally different. And that helps. Even so, anyone's power of concentration diminishes greatly after five or six straight, uninterrupted hours of intense rehearsal or sustained work of almost any kind.

Writers and painters, who are essentially soloists—to carry on the theatrical/musical metaphor we've set up—can take a break almost any time they feel the need. But what about factory workers? I don't know the research, which I'm sure has been done in that field, but I suspect that some of the reforms recently instituted in the auto industry and other manufacturing milieus, often partly inspired by the Japanese, or even emulating them in the hope of achieving their astounding success, may be related to coming to terms with this problem, i.e., how best to increase productivity. Which means, in other words, getting the most out of every hour put in.

Certainly, the standard 9:00-to-5:00 working day needs re-thinking in almost all situations and milieus. Adjustments can always be made. Look what the Spaniards and Italians have done for centuries in adapting to their hot climates by instituting the mid-day siesta. The dynamics of any such regime should also be investigated. I'm sure we could all be more productive working under less strictly regulated schedules, with their artificial pressures, inhibiting customs, and work taboos.

Or look at the educational scene. Really good teachers know instinctively when to make breaks or changes or shifts of focus during a long day of classes. But more of them should. And those who don't ought to be taught how to make such adjustments. It would pay off. Why should college hours be so much more flexible and livable—and potentially more productive—than those on the high school and elementary school levels? Especially since we can absorb so much more during those three or four years preceding puberty, as, I believe, George Bernard Shaw preached in one of his Prefaces.

In any case, we learned a great deal on those foreshortened, snowbound days in that little schoolhouse way up in tiny Amasa, Michigan, on the edge of the huge evergreen fir forests of the Upper Peninsula, not far from the beautiful Porcupine Mountains (though technically speaking, merely very high hills!) and cold, majestic Lake Superior. (Wasn't that Longfellow's "Giche gume?")

I also acquired the fundamentals of skating and skiing during those wonderful childhood winters in upper Michigan. Skating ponds were all over the place. We made our own little ski jumps by adapting portions of the hill leading up to a mining site for such purposes.

And during the summers, what joy we had traversing that same terrain, now bereft of snow, green and glorious with grass, birds, and jutting rocks, in our cowboy and Indian games. Aided and abetted by the gray cement ruins and irregular remains of mining structures long since demolished: they became our Roman ruins one day, our Indian forts another.

But I also have the too-vivid memory of being "crucified" at play one afternoon on the slope of such a mining hill by my friends and classmates after they had tired of the usual cowboy-and-Indian repertoire. I, being the only Jew in town, was to be crucified (as one of the thieves?). They became the mob in Jerusalem leading Christ to Golgotha. "Hey, what are you doing?" I cried out. They were working out their revenge on me, the Jew, for having killed their Christ. Yes, little me. I was accused of perpetrating that enormous crime! These modern-day avengers were children of good, honest immigrant miners from Catholic Poland and Italy and Protestant Sweden and Finland. They were inspired by what they heard in their churches on Sundays or were taught in their Sunday School classes (or both). But, of course, they being my friends, my schoolmates, the ritual was done in play: the ropes were not pulled too tight. I was not physically stoned or punched, kicked or wounded, in any serious way, during the "reenactment." Except psychologically...

Again, I marvel, Ariadne, how memory skips about so unpredictably. Will I need your guiding string to bring me back in line? Or isn't that necessary? What did you do once you escaped from Crete to Naxos? Let me know by return mail or fax, or by one of your idiosyncratic drawings?

Curiously yours,

M.

Ides of March, 2001

Dear Nina:

Yes, you had every right to scold me for calling you Ariadne or anything else other than your own charming, most suitable name. But didn't you once tell me that Nina is really your pen name? That you were called something else as a child? Won't you refresh my memory on that score? Perhaps I was not so far off track in giving you a mythical name to fit the situation. Though you might rightfully argue that that famous Minotaur string or thread served a very specific purpose in a very concrete situation. After all, it did get Theseus out of the labyrinth. And it did save his life!

Again, hasn't the Memory game served you well? Could we be wrong in postulating that your memory thread kept you sane, especially during the early years here in America of your now over twenty year exile from Romania? Didn't you also keep a diary all those years, and the many years before, to give you something tangible to hang onto? In spite of your remarkable, almost photographic memory?

Unfortunately, I can't duplicate that gift. For I almost always find it difficult to recall the details of certain situations that seemed at the time so important to me, and to my future. Thus, now that I try to summon up the details of one such example, namely how, why, and when I severed relations with Alva, the singular girl I met in my symbolic logic class at NYU way back in the late Forties, after I returned from Europe, who seemed to be the center, or at least amorous focus, of my student period there, I find myself at almost a total loss. At least as to the ending phase. (Since you often ask about my previous loves, I'm trying to be totally open and honest!) Maybe I should, to paraphrase a line of Cavafy, "beg of you, O Memory, to be my best assistant!"

Yes, I do remember more of what led up to the start of our relationship, probably hurried along because Alva had a room in an interesting old building on the northeast corner of Washington Square, directly kitty-corner to our symbolic logic class. Wasn't it logical (if not symbolic) to retire to those comfortable quarters so nearby to help her with what to her were not the most logical assignments? Was I her Lewis Carroll and she my adult Alice? (Conveniently, she was quite small, about 5'1".)

Perhaps, yes, in a sense. But then I didn't have to worry about her being underage, did I? Yet, ironically enough, she retained a certain child-like innocence, especially when it came to logic and other intellectual matters, except perhaps for the abstract nature of her painting. So I tried the Alice approach in getting her to come to terms with the premises of symbolic logic, at least insofar as I myself had been able to master them up to that point. I had always enjoyed playing around with those kinds of quasimathematical relationships and was even able not much later to delve into the first pages of Whitehead and Russell's *Principia Mathematica* with a modest modicum of comprehension—and of vicarious pleasure.

Oddly enough, we didn't get to Wittgenstein in that particular class. (That surely would have been too much for poor Alva!) In fact, I didn't make that master philosopher's acquaintance until a year or so later, and then only via my own curiosity, picking up his Brown and Blue notebooks in the library—those invaluable transcriptions of some of his lecture notes—and only later dipping into language games, etc. This was before Wittgenstein became "fashionable" in this country. Instead, our professor, the eminent James Burnham, former Trotzkyite, author of the brilliant *Managerial Revolution* and soon to become leading spokesman for the new intellectual American Conservative movement (ancestors of our lamentable, warmongering neo-cons of today), ended this course with unexpected abruptness and launched us into a new course of his own devising, "Irrationalism," for the second semester. This turned out to be a quite fascinating series of adventures among the so-called irrational philosophies, a convenient all-embracing term for existentialism (then the rage) and what led up to it: Kierkegaard, Dostoevsky, Nietzsche, Freud, then, sidestepping Husserl, on to a tempting dash of Heidegger and maybe too much Sartre.

Now that I look back on this scene, didn't Burnham shortchange us a bit on both courses? For example, would it not have been wiser to have spent at least a full year with symbolic logic and another entire year with his irrationalist thinkers? Still, all that notwithstanding, both classes were certainly more exciting than most college courses. Though I was lucky to have also studied the English empiricists, Locke, Berkeley, and Hume with Suzanne Langer (her philosophy of art course came later at Columbia) and the philosophy of history with Sidney Hook during that same period. In fact, at the end of my term in that course, Hook invited me to go on and do graduate work with him in philosophy. More about those two re-markable personalities—and remarkable teachers—in another letter.

In any case, Alva did not choose to go on with the irratio-nalism course. Could that be one reason our friendship dwindled? Or was it that Reality hit us in the face with her becoming preg-nant unexpectedly, in spite of our precautions? And I having to help her get (and pay for) an abortion, even though she had rich parents. For, of course, we couldn't let them know about it! Not back then in 1948! Indeed, it was the last thing in the world to put on the table that night we were invited to a fancy dinner in her parents' deluxe, porch-windowed, high rise apartment on 4 Washington Square. I was treated royally, as if I were the Galahad guy they were counting on to finally bring their errant daughter back to her senses after ear-lier skirmishes and/or affairs with a number of bedraggled painter or sculptor friends. Little did they know me; was I really that different from those others? Or did I just look more bourgeois and respect-able? After all, to them wasn't I a nice "boychik," getting a degree at a prestigious school, NYU? Besides, there seems to be something about me that generally makes the average onlooker think of me as more bourgeois than I really am.

Well, Alva decided to get over the trauma of the abortion simply by escaping to Paris to join some of her artist friends then living there. She herself was something of an apprentice painter, hav-ing studied with Richard Poussette-Dart. Now, looking back, I'm not sure whether I ever got a letter from her during that sojourn of es-cape. I vaguely remember seeing her again briefly about a year later in the environs of NYU, when she brought me somewhat up-to-date on her comings and goings, after which it seems that she was ex-pecting to return to Paris again very soon. Also, tempted as I was to go along (and possibly resume our affair in Paris?), I very much suspected that she must have been already involved with someone else. Why else the long silence, especially after she returned to the

States? All she had to do was pick up a phone. But she never told me tales, nor gave me facts: she was always tantalizingly vague on such matters. (Actually, I think I remember having encountered one potential rival in her room months earlier.) In any event, I would not have been able to get away from New York at that time: I simply had to nail down that Bachelor of Arts, for which I needed only one more term. Besides, I was also seriously studying music, dance, and drama collaterally with going to college and beginning to get involved in a few professional theatrical and dance projects from time to time.

Was Alva testing me? She certainly knew how much I was drawn to Paris; I had often told her about my halcyon nine-month, post-war stay there. Who knows? As Fate would have it, I was punished in a most peculiar way for turning down that offer. For years I had a recurring dream about dallying away my time in Paris, meeting Alva and her circle there but never getting any work done; a most vivid dream, almost always winding up with me doing hasty, last minute packing, regretting not having looked up my old friends from that war weary, but oh-so-welcome 1946, missing an important concert or exhibit here or there, and then desperately trying in that pounding guilt-ridden dream to catch a train to the airport, also feeling great frustration because somehow I was never able to get around to revisiting the Louvre, the Tuilleries, or any of the countless sights I had missed on this return dream visit; finally, feeling empty, exhausted, and cheated. Or in another version of that dream, having been stuck in some Latin Quarter hovel, suffocating from an inexplicable inertia; indeed, not being able to budge out of that atelier or apartment which looked like a room from the French movie set for Gorky's *Lower Depths*; again feeling reams of guilt for wasting valuable time in beau Paris.

These dreams were, no doubt, on the one hand, guilt-ridden distortions of my inability to ever get back to Paris, and, on the other, of my failure to come to terms with myself over my vague feelings for Alva and/or her strange ambivalence toward me. Also, mixed into these memories was a blurring of Alva with Ann, my wife-to-be, both similar waif-like gamines, with a like penchant for odd silences.

Or, since these dreams continued to haunt me for many years after that episode, perhaps the "guilt over Paris" theme became a token, all-embracing symbol for those times when I felt a deeper-down guilt over not being sufficiently true to myself or to what I dimly sensed to be my truer destiny.

What is, was, or could be, that terrifying word? Do I, or any of us, have a defined Kismet? For example, was I really destined to write these confessional notes to you? Was I truly fated to meet you, my beloved Nina, in this twilight period of my life, indeed, of both our lives? Have we not often mutually marveled at this *rencontre tout-à-fait inattendue*? Were you actually wafted here by the Hand of Fate to help me find my way? Or am I handing you too much of a burden? If so, let me know, and we can then become more justifiably *giocoso*!

Apprehensively yours,

M.

November 3, 2001

My dear Nina:

Your response to that hyperbolic request in my last letter was somewhat chastening. I realize now that I got carried away with some of the tempting abracadabra of mysticism, the tantalizing strings of fate, and the dangers of over-explicit analyses of dreams, etc. Of course, I would never in my more sane moments ask such an impossible thing of you, even if it were possible! Maybe we should phone in Delmore Schwartz's short story, "In Dreams Begin Responsibilities" and call it a night! And, of course, beware and eschew the *giocoso*, as you so frequently and wisely admonish me to do. (Shades of the Jabberwocky's "Beware the jub-jub bird, my child!")

Whatever, your letter has certainly brought me back to my senses with a thud, and I shall try now to take up the knitting tapestry of memory and return to unraveling its threads one after another. The problem now is: which threads, where do I start?

Try pushing the obvious buttons? To recall my parents? Like Goethe in *Dichtung und Wahrheit* assigning his poetic fantasy to his mother and his organizational gift to his father? That wouldn't work for me. For starters, I'm certainly no Goethe. Nor, in any case, am I quite sure yet which parent gave me what! Besides, I'm hardly ready for that kind of wrangle.

So then, more about my childhood? But I've already touched on that several times, and certainly more such incidents will be creeping in from time to time in these letters as they relate to other stories and their related memories.

About my poor, departed, but hardly forgotten, Pirandello-like schizophrenic wife, Ann? Alas, I really don't know how to deal with those multifaceted, mercurial memories yet, some of them still so painful and numbing; others life affirming and touching; but most of them highly ambivalent and definitely depressing.

Still, starting to talk about Ann now suddenly brings to mind the image of a very positive person, one who knew, and empathized, with her, that extraordinary wizard of the Word, the Hungarian refugee graphologist, Klara G. Roman, for whom I worked part-time on and off for several years as a sort of secretary/amanuensis. But haven't I already told you a little about her, even before our various later Romanian/Hungarian *contretemps* and *malentendus*?

Anyway, I can't remember who first recommended me to Mme. Roman, although I think it may have been Geraldine, who always managed to discover interesting people—indeed, often actually sought them out! She once struck up an uninvited correspondence with T. S. Eliot and got herself invited to England to meet him. A similar letter to Louis Kronenberger led, I understand, to an interesting *amitié amicale* between the two of them, she being much the younger partner. And, *pièce de résistance*, she was for a time a mainstay of the oddly, but as it turned out, appropriately named "Hard to Find Employment Agency."

Be that as it may, Klara Roman was certainly one of Geraldine's best finds. A refugee from Hungary, in her mid-to-late seventies by the time I met her, she was working on a challenging, perhaps overly ambitious project, *The Encyclopedia of the Written Word* (from the graphological point of view). It was to be a sequel of sorts to her major opus in English (which, in turn, is a summary or compendium of her best works in Hungarian) called *Graphology: A Key to Personality.* She very much needed someone to help her put the new book together, to fix up the English of the myriad entries she had already started, and to help her write up new ones as needed. She intuited that my albeit limited knowledge of French and German might make up to some extent for my nil knowledge of Hungarian, so that when she had trouble finding the right expression in English, she could try a phrase or wording from one of those other languages to help cue me in as to whatever she had in mind. Then together we would somehow hit upon what she really wanted to say and recast it in viable English.

Actually, the first phase of this job had me helping her prepare a talk she was scheduled to give at The New School, where at that time she lectured on so-called scientific graphology. For she always insisted on differentiating her truly serious approach to, and knowledge of, that graphology from the cheap fortune-teller type so widespread in this country, as opposed to Europe, where educated and trained "scientific" graphologists are used by large industrial firms for guidance in hiring people, as consultants in psychological clinics, and as aids in comparable situations. Apropos the European respect for graphology, and it being taken seriously there, I just read the other day in Gershom Scholem's book on the remarkable critic Walter Benjamin that back in immediate post-World War I Germany, Benjamin had actually practiced graphology himself; and that he had probably been introduced to it by Ludwig Klages, an important psychologist of that period. But, of course, I knew about Klages through Roman, who used to invoke his authority, or, indeed, sometimes disagreed vociferously with him! Besides, didn't he descend into some sort of apologetic intellectual neo-Nazi?

Among other accomplishments, Roman herself had invented

the graphodyne, an ingenious device used to measure pressure exerted by the hand and fingers during the act of writing. Indeed, she was even able to detect an endocrine deficiency in adolescents via this method. Moreover, she had already published a number of studies and scholarly articles in various psychological journals in Europe on this subject and on other aspects of graphology—mostly in German—two or three of which had been translated and published in comparable journals here even before she arrived on these shores. This background, no doubt, led to Klara Roman being asked to teach at The New School, although that appointment may also have been facilitated by a recommendation from the influential Eugene Meyer family in Washington, DC, whom she knew, probably through mutual family connections. (I was never "in" on Klara's family politics.)

Work on that first lecture went so well that she hired me to help edit the *Encyclopedia* itself, for which labor she was only able to pay a modest hourly fee but which I needed at that time to supplement whatever I might be earning (or not earning) from an Off-Broadway show or a minor singing job.

Working on this *Encyclopedia* with Mme. Roman turned out to be a fascinating and, in unexpected ways, quite rewarding experience. I may indeed have learned more about the practical discipline of writing from her than I had from any of my college professors or literary friends—and this, despite her broken, highly accented, truly original English. We would work on an entry—say, a definition of pressure in handwriting—certainly not easy for anyone to define, a challenging test even for a learned, skilled professional encyclopedist! We would then redo her draft of that definition three or four times, by which time I might think it ready. But no, she would still be unhappy with some aspect of it. Whereupon I'd rework it again alone by myself and then again with her, until she was satisfied. The amazing thing is that, in spite of her limited English, her instinct as to the correctness of a particular definition, and its aptness of expression, was almost always right on the mark. Of course, part of the problem lay in the fact that she could not always make sufficiently clear to me early on, in her own terms, just what she was trying to say. Yet through trial and error we usually managed to get there. And, of course, by the time the galleys arrived, there was still more revision and refinement.

In a certain sense, this experience mirrored that earlier trial by error—studying ballet with Preobrajenskaya in a class with child would-be dancers—described in a previous letter. Both times I had to humble myself before masters of their subjects and learn to find my way from the simple to the complex in an almost ruthlessly demanding way. Ultimately, perhaps, I learned more through the process than through the subject or the technique itself.

Interestingly enough, I discovered halfway through my period with Mme. Roman that some years before, Ruth Herschberger, an excellent American poet whom I had met through my mentor, Joseph Frank (unique literary critic and author of a definitive five-volume biography of Dostoevsky, but more about him later), had tried to write up some of these definitions with her but had then quit quite abruptly. When I ran into her at some sort of literary party several years later, I naturally asked about her experience with la Roman. As I suspected, she had found the work too demanding and feared that it would take away too much from the concentration she needed for her own poetry and prose. But would it really have done so? I wonder. I think her exit from Roman was probably more due to a clash of two strong female personalities. And ambitions. Since I had no such literary pretensions, and probably also because being a male, it was easier for me to be neutral and noncompetitive, Mme. Roman did not need to worry about my wanting to "take over" in any way. Thus when I would hold up a choice and argue a point, she respected my objective stand regarding that point and would give it the full measure of her attention and consideration. Looking back at it from a comparative distance, I still marvel that we were able to work together so harmoniously, in spite of her strong temperament, a certain hauteur, and an often selfishly demanding manner. Could this Hungarian apprenticeship have been preparation for you, my Romanian princess, Mme. Nina de Cassian?

Of course, being continental, Mme. Roman was still, even at

her advanced age, also quite a charmer. One episode in particular comes to mind. Once, having worked very hard and almost without respite for about two weeks, with me coming in almost every day for several demanding hours, she suddenly decided that we both needed a rest, a change of pace. So she invited me for dinner the next night in her tiny apartment. A modest table was set, candles were lit, wine was served. She dressed specially for the occasion, even had her hair newly coiffed; and more perfume infused the air than it ever did during normal working hours. And she was much more relaxed and expansive than usual.

The thought could not help but enter my mind: was Mme. Roman possibly trying to seduce me, someone a third her age, and after all this time? Or did she just want to establish a nice, relaxed, friendly mood? Naturally, I tried to respond to the ambiguous situation by playing innocent, but at the same time not neglecting to compliment her on her appearance, sighing over the wine and the food, and maintaining a neutral brio as best I could. Until I made one fatal mistake...

It happened that I had once served a somewhat comparable role, while attending NYU some years earlier, for an older American woman writer on social studies, at that time engaged in compiling a book on Haiti. (Yes, Haiti has always had its WASP fans.) La Roman knew a little about this earlier assignment and had no reason not to take it in her stride. There had been no secrets, no intrigues! But somehow, during the latter half of the dinner, I happened to refer to Mrs. Wilson (for that was her name, mother of the then-famed novelist Sloan Wilson, author of *Gentlemen's Agreement*) as "that woman" I used to work for. And Klara was scandalized. To this day, I'm not sure exactly why but suspect it must have had something to do with what you, my dear Nina, so eloquently call the "cultural differences" between Americans and Europeans. In other words, it was probably not gallant of me to even mention another woman on this "romantic" occasion. And, above all, not to refer to her as "that woman"—possibly a fallen woman? Or in any case a potential rival?

Whatever the rationale, the spell was broken. The remainder of the evening passed in near total silence. It even hampered for awhile our subsequent working sessions, although gradually that pattern of our relationship soon returned to normal. Nor did she ever refer to that dinner again.

Does this not remind you a little of one or two occasions when you and I have had a somewhat similar *malentendu international*?

Graphologically yours,

M.

April 20, 2002

Dear Ninicuța:

Pleasantly surprised to read your mellow response to my last letter. And especially relieved to see that our relationship is not threatened by these recollections, stabs at memoirs, fragments of stories of the past, et al. Even more so, that you welcome them, and encourage me to carry on. But on to what? For, this somewhat free-association method that I have been following, and which has so far given these notes whatever rhyme or reason they may (I hope) have, sometimes deserts one when most needed.

Indeed, I seem to be at such an impasse now. And that impasse is made doubly threatening when I try to come to terms with the other problem that lurks ahead as I search to write down these memories of incidents in my past, snapping them up out of that maelstrom of *temps perdu*?

Namely, how do I deal with memories and incidents involving people still here in this world with us? When I write about Gertrude Stein or Klara Roman, for example, I don't have to worry about offending them so much as to bring on libel suits because they have already left this world, though, of course, I would never dream of tarnishing those accounts—or any others I've so far written about, or still to come—with anything other than honest recall and sincere surmise.

Still, just how does one deal with memories of friends, colleagues, and the like, who are still regnant, still alive and kicking on this oft-times hostile earth, some of whom could conceivably rise up and challenge such memories? For, what X may consider a totally unbiased account of an episode with Mrs. Y or Mme. Z, those two might very well deem damaging and unfair to them.

What do you advise? Of course, a few "living" ghosts have already been invoked in these letters. Even some references to you, my most vital living being! Come to think of it, could I have inadvertently offended you in any of these letters? Or misquoted any of the others? If so, by all means speak up! But it's time to move on. I'm confident that somehow I'll find a way out of this conundrum.

Perhaps I should start up again by telling you a little more about my late, ill-fated wife, Ann, than I've already done over dinner or wine. That's surely now a "safe" subject, since she's long settled in another abode outside of time; although her recently discovered sister (at least a new-found person to me!) might question some of the reportage, but that's another fascinating story in itself. In any case, I'm sure you will want to know more about Ann's long, hopeless struggle with coming to terms with reality. About whom, when I asked that doctor in the Kings County Hospital office adjoining the waiting room in which were gathered scores of other women also about to be "transported" to Pilgrim State Hospital, for a prognosis of her malady, he said, pointing to all of them, not just Ann, "There, but for the grace of God, go you and I. Only a thin film, a narrow escarpment, makes the crucial difference. Isn't this a cruel world we all live in? They do not want to live in it anymore. Rather than face the daily dosage of hard knocks, they withdraw from reality. And we, knowing so little about how to deal with them—or it?—we give them a daily dosage of something else, a pill that, in turn, may turn out to be nothing but a palliative or a pacifier."

"But, doctor, doesn't my wife suffer from what seems to me to be, according to what I've read on the subject, a classic case of paranoid schizophrenia?" "You said it," he replied. "Not I."

And so, poor Ann was then transferred to Pilgrim State Hospital for what turned out to be something like a seven-month stay. This was her second such hospitalization. But she was a clever woman, "one smart cookie" as one of the hospital personnel dubbed her and occasionally others like her. She had learned from her first hospital stay how to behave in such situations, and before long had managed to convince the doctors that she was cured, ready to go home!

Hence, one day when I was visiting Ann about two months into her first stay at Pilgrim State, she announced proudly that they were going to release her; that they thought she was ready to go home. "Isn't that wonderful?" she enthused. But I was skeptical. How could the turnaround be so quick? She still seemed somewhat spaced out to me. So I questioned her doctor. He told me that she was all right and that he had informed her she would be released soon. I was stunned. "What kind of tests have you given her?" I asked. "It took six or seven months at Rockland before they let her out of there. Of course, it would be wonderful if she really were cured. But are you quite sure she's stopped hallucinating? You know, she's quite clever at giving you—as she used to give me—the 'right' answers to make you think she's okay. So, I wonder... Do me a favor, Doctor, and put her alone in a room where you can listen in on her, without her knowing that you're doing so."

Which he did, and, lo and behold, he heard her talking a blue streak to herself, and to other people nowhere around but whom she thought to be there, and in the usual paranoid patterns, her talk studded with illusions, exaggerations, illogical sequences, etc. Accordingly, her stay was extended several more months and more attention paid to her case before they released her. But even after that, she wasn't really cured. No more than she had been "cured" after her first hospitalization at Rockland County where we had to take her after her first visible, acknowledgeable breakdown.

That came about in a touching manner, seemingly all of a sudden, but actually after a long prelude of intimations, warnings, and signals of which, in retrospect, I should have taken more cognizance. However, when one lives with such a situation day in, day out (night in, night out, as well!), the changes usually come and go so gradually and well-nigh imperceptibly, that a special twist or shocking turnabout is often needed to wake one up to a shift in personality, a truly changing front or unfamiliar mask, a bewildering unknown quotient.

So, when I returned home from work one fateful summer afternoon and found Ann crouched under our little baby grand piano, holding tight our five-year-old son, Jacob, and warning me that "they" were coming through the window, I should not have been shocked. Perhaps frightened, yes, but not surprised. For, as I said above, there had been ample warnings, now that I look back on even the short stretch of time that preceded it. Thus only a few weeks before, she had complained that the neighbors were always talking about her and mocking her. She could hear them through the walls, she claimed. "How do you know for sure what they're saying? They usually talk in Spanish amongst themselves, don't they?" I countered, trying to calm her down, to reassure her that it couldn't be as bad as she thought. (We were then living in a West Side Manhattan neighborhood that was gradually being taken over by the Latino community.) "Well, it sounded just like Yiddish, so I understood every word." While even Ann's Yiddish was far from fluent, as I recall, it certainly bore no relationship to Spanish, although, of course, Ladino, the Spanish/Sephardic counterpart of Yiddish, would have. But Ann didn't know a word of Ladino or anyone who spoke Ladino!

In fact, a few weeks earlier, she had insisted that I confront the nice, friendly middle-aged man who lived one flight above us and insist that he apologize and treat her more politely in the future. But when next I saw him, and broached the subject, I found Señor Ramon to be totally, sincerely unaware of any unpleasant encounter with Ann. Actually, he said, he hardly ever saw her anymore in the hallway or on the street in front of the house. Then he added that he missed running into her and hoped she was all right. Indeed, it had reached the point where Ann had become afraid to go shopping at the nearby supermarket. People pointed at her, she complained, as she passed by them with her pushcart.

What was more damaging in the long run, as proved to be the case, was the effect of this paranoia on our son, Jacob. For example, mornings I used to walk him to his kindergarten class only a few blocks away and would be surprised when he did not respond to the many cheerful "Hi's" and "Hello, Jacob's" that came from his little classmates as we passed them on the way to school. Apparently Ann's paranoid suspiciousness had begun to be imitated or taken on unconsciously by Jacob, and for totally unwarranted reasons. For he was actually quite popular with his schoolmates. He had been elected president of his kindergarten class only a few months before. But soon there began to be unpleasant little incidents at school, including temper tantrums and rollings on the floor. Before long, I was called in to discuss a fight he had had in class. Yet whenever I would confront Ann with such a puzzlement, she would always come up with a clever rationalization for justifying her—or our—son's behavior: he was defending himself; the kids were teasing him; he wasn't feeling well, etc.

However, this time she obviously had reached a breaking point, for she asked pitifully, as I pulled her and Jacob with difficulty out from under the piano, that I take her to the hospital. Would that she had been so willing to go in later years when comparable breakdowns occurred, and when she needed hospitalization much more than on this first occasion. But more about that fatal problem later.

So we brought her to the nearest hospital, from which she was then assigned to Rockland County, the state hospital that handled patients from our district of Manhattan. This was the first of four hospitalizations Ann was to undergo. The second, mentioned earlier above, was at Pilgrim State in Nassau County, as were the third and fourth, because in the meantime we had moved to Brooklyn. (And patients from Kings County, which is Brooklyn, went there.) There should have been at least a fifth hospitalization, but by then the State had passed that disastrous law whereby such hospitals could only accept patients if they themselves asked to be committed or consented to let their next of kin bring them there.

As you've only been in this country for the last twenty-plus years, you probably don't know about that fateful edict passed by our state legislature (and, alas, many others) some forty or so years ago, which half emptied all the state hospitals; nor about the enormous dearth of halfway houses for the mentally disturbed that existed then. Alas, that shortage still persists, when they are more needed than ever. Thus, most of those poor people who opted out could never "find" themselves again. Far too many ended up in the streets of New York and other cities all over the state. That's where poor Ann might well have been floundering about aimlessly had we not kept her safe at home, whatever the stress and strain.

And of that there was more than enough. But there was also the burden of guilt: had I been more alert to the warning signs and got Ann to a doctor earlier, could her mental deterioration have been stopped or, at least, mitigated or even held off? A moot question, especially when one realizes how little medicine knows about preventing mental breakdowns. Yet the question persists and nags at me, even to this day.

Or did I do right by her in day-to-day situations? Should I not have been there at her side more often when she may have called out for me? But in those first days, I had no idea how sick she really was. Was I perhaps too selfishly involved in my own busy life to notice? Could I have possibly discovered the illness sooner? There were many times when I could not come home for meals as often as I should have liked, or might not have been able to return until late at night, particularly when involved with a concert or a theater production. Though, again, I brought her to rehearsals whenever possible (and Jacob, too, when he was small), and even gave her a role in *Stacked Deck*—an electronic opera with character types such as the Green Lady, the Confidence Man, and the like. Ann played the Cabbage Woman, and quite well, too. There was another occasion when she and I did an exhibition ballroom dance sequence for a large benefit hotel dinner for the Brooklyn Philharmonic. She was a remarkably talented natural dancer (unlike her older sister, Tzivia, who struggled with floor technique in Martha Graham classes), and had done some professional ballroom partnering before I met her.

But I also look back to the time when she came home after her first hospitalization at Rockland and we started follow-up therapy for her and Jacob at the Lincoln Institute for Psychiatry. Shivers run down my spine even now as I recall that strangely cold, formal, uptight place and that even colder, stiff, upright doctor— let's call him Dr. Mabuse—to whom she was assigned. Was this kind of doctor right for her, poor Ann, basically a warm, unconventional and in some ways rebellious spirit? Wasn't Dr. Mabuse perhaps a little too righteous, too "square," too obtuse? The kind of "scientist" who went too much by the book? Who, moreover, had absolutely no sense of humor?

For example, he had little patience with me trying to fill in with what I thought would be helpful background about Ann; my attempts to explain how ultra sensitive she was to light, to sound (she had amazing hearing, almost as acute as a dog's), and, above all, to her extraordinary ESP. She probably could have made a living at reading tea leaves or palms, or like feats. Indeed, when I took her to a summer clinic set up by Duke University at Steinway Hall on 57th Street in Manhattan for dealing with studies of extrasensory perception, she did alarmingly well on the so-called envelope test. Given an envelope by the test doctor, a visiting eminence in that field, which contained short descriptions of his relatives in Finland, Ann was able to tell him what was in that envelope!

However, our uppity Dr. Mabuse was not interested in such data, nor did he, as far as I could tell, ever explore any such paths with her. Or any other approaches? Had he done so, might this not have led her to a greater trust in his treatment of her? Or should I have followed my instinct then and there and shopped around for another clinic, another doctor?

Or, many years and three hospitalizations later, when we were led to another doctor who indeed specialized in those new "scientific" diet/drug regimens, this well-meaning man prescribed one that proved almost impossible for her to follow consistently, what with one pill to be taken three times a day; another half a pill twice a day at different times than the first; a third to be alternated with the second; and a fourth only twice a day, etc., etc. I would have had to hire a part-time nurse to make sure she always took all those pills according to schedule, in the proper sequence, at the right time, and in the correct designated amounts. As it was, I made charts for her, fed her the morning doses, called her up whenever I could to remind her about the later ones, and, of course, always gave her the final doses at night. But how faithfully did she—or could she—follow that complex menu when I wasn't there? And even had she done so, would that have done the trick? *Ce que j'en doute beaucoup.* After all, that kind of drug therapy was only in its first stages anyway, and surely not tested enough.

Yes, the more I dealt with the various doctors and psychiatrists at the many different clinics, hospitals, and half way houses we visited, tried, haunted, and went through, the more I discovered how little anyone really knew then, or knows even now, about schizophrenia. Thus, for awhile there was great excitement over the new drugs. And these did indeed help a good deal with some cases (especially those more inclined to violence), but they did not cure. They also helped Ann expand from a size 6 dress to a size 22, the result of a combination of the drugs and carbohydrate-focused food served to patients at the state hospitals she attended, and resulting in an overweight burden that surely put a great stress on her heart.

Next there was a flurry over special diets. Then came the special wards. One saving grace: we had escaped the frontal lobotomy craze by the time she first entered a hospital. But all the rest proved in vain.

Yes! It pains me to recall those years. I had better sign off for awhile...

Be patient!

M.

PS: Amazingly enough, dear Nina, while on break in evolving this long, tough letter, I ran across the following headline in today's *Times*: "Evidence Mounting for Role of Fetal Damage in Schizophrenia," with a quite cogent summary of the nature of the disease: "A dramatic change is afoot in the scientific understanding of schizophrenia." How many times did I eagerly rush to read such articles in the past, hoping to find the answer! This one goes on: "The first symptoms usually appear when people are in their late twenties, but neuroscientists now believe that the seeds of the disorder are often sown during fetal development."

April 22nd

Dear patient Mme. Cassian:

This is a quick follow-up to yeaterday's long letter about Ann.

What about all the countless articles and theories that preceded that timely *Times* article, with their frequent exaggerated hopes and oversimplified panaceas, and the hundreds that will no doubt follow this latest one? For example, there was that amazing early-19th-century tract, *Psychology of Insanity*, I stumbled upon in my on and off research all through Ann's vagaries, which startlingly revealed how little we had moved in the last century and a half.

In any case, inherited genes have always seemed to me to be the most likely natural explanation, and, if so, what can be done about that? The die is surely cast before birth, even before the possible onset of fetal damage. Of course, the latter could exacerbate a planted condition. But now, with increased knowledge of genes and how to manipulate them, will there finally be hope of restacking or realigning the genes in sufficient time to prevent a disease, or at least mollify somewhat its threat or its effects?

As to backup for the gene theory as far as Ann is concerned, there is and was her family. It turns out that Ann's mother had been hospitalized for a considerable spell when Ann was a child, and she, along with her older sister and brother had been put in a foster home during that period. (I have subsequently learned that there was a third sister about whom neither Ann nor Tzivia nor their brother

Sidney ever breathed a word, mentioned briefly above. But more about that later—a bizarre subject that demands a letter in itself!) All this seemed to support the deep down feeling I always had that something inherited, some biological short-circuiting, must have been at the root of Ann's slow deterioration. For she was so healthy, happy, and buoyant in so many other respects, at least before the breakdowns began.

The article continues: "The basic flaw in the brains of many schizophrenics seems to be that certain nerve cells migrate to the wrong areas when the brain is first taking shape, leaving small regions of the brain permanently out of place or miswired. Such errors in neural architecture may have one or more causes, which remain to be discovered." Which leads to the formulation of this latest theory, and the conclusion that such brain misconnections might develop when the mother catches a virus early in pregnancy. "But that theory does not solve the entire puzzle," the article warns. "Schizophrenia is probably many different kinds of problems that converge on the same syndrome, not just a single disease."

How well I know...

Gradually, Ann grew worse and worse. The decline was slow and sporadic, but inevitable. Was this what Pirandello went through those twenty or more years with his wife, whom he only belatedly hospitalized? In those days at the end of the 19th and the beginning of the 20th centuries when there were fewer magic drugs and reinvented placebos?

But enough! The next time I write about Ann I want to tell you more about her non sick side, her more felicitous moments, her curious, special kind of intelligence; also about her special care and devotion to Jacob; and ponder what she might have done with her life and her many talents had this disease not turned her smile into a frown; her brisk, graceful walk into a premature waddle; her open spirit to a shut book.

Medically yours,

M.

Dear, sympathetic Nina:

Again, your patience gives me courage to go on a little more with other aspects of Ann's story before delving into different detours, alleyways, and bypasses in this nonlinear tale of moments that might interest you in this modest life of mine.

I think I may have touched on some of this back in the early stages of our own relationship, but perhaps the great irony of it all may now be more evident to you than it was then, namely, one of the main reasons why I fell in love with Ann (at least one of the more consciously self-understood or felt reasons) was that she seemed in the beginning to be the most natural, earthy, unneurotic woman I had up to then ever become involved with. I thought: great, just what I need! Of course, the earlier "neurotics" were almost always fascinating, interesting, sometimes seemingly "*misterioasa*" women, but ended up being less so once one got past the neurotic mask (or masks, in a few cases). The supreme irony is that this down-to-earth, seemingly unneurotic young woman, Ann, turned out to be my one truly psychotic companion!

Not that one or two other ladies lurking nearby down the corridors of life might not have qualified for that category! I'm thinking, for example, of the flamboyant Sandra Hochman, whom you met recently, and who practically threw us out of her expensive high-rise apartment on East 72nd Street near the East River in a fit of pique during her ill-fated Fourth of July roof party there, when you uttered something totally innocent that she misconstrued as anti-American! (How did the Fourth of July so warp her judgment that day?) And there was also that former literary editor of the old *Esquire* magazine I told you about some months ago, Alice McIntyre, she who claimed to have initiated featuring strong fiction by leading American writers in that heretofore dry, factual men's magazine, who also happened to be the aunt of a now-famous woman poet and is said to be somewhat manic. But sane enough to have made some of the best translations of Verlaine I've ever read. (I used to call her "Tiny Alice" in jest.)

Yet their abnormal manifestations, perhaps because they were both older women than certainly Ann was when I met her, and time and tide had stiffened their prides and prejudices into combative poses, were more blatantly evident. It does not take long to know where one is at with them, especially in a social situation involving three or more people. Interestingly enough, in tête-à-tête talks, those problems usually loom up less obviously. Probably because they no doubt feel more confident in their powers when confronting only one person.

To detour just for a brief moment. Similar aberrations in otherwise highly intelligent people bring to mind the interesting phenomenon that such behavior, when perpetrated by famous figures or recognized genius types, is usually excused and/or tolerated as just that—a minor aberration. I'm thinking of cases like, for example, that of the great English novelist who was also a competent philosopher, Iris Murdoch, and the antics that resulted from her affair(s) with the controversial, sadistic Bulgarian-born Nobel Prize Winner, Elias Canetti. And, of course, there are probably even more shocking cases we've never heard of, since their perpetrators have managed to avoid exposure. Or borderline cases such as Strindberg.

However, Ann's overt behavior in those first days I knew her was open, direct, friendly, and honest—diametrically the opposite of those famous eccentrics. She was working as an assistant to the director of a small exercise salon, which had been recommended to me as a good place to go for keeping in shape. This was some years before the mad explosion of Training Centers, weightlifting, jogging, and, later, of fancy "aerobics." It was run by a former minor-league weightlifting champion, but a man of somewhat unexpected culture and love of the arts (who also claimed to have successfully laid siege to Lana Turner, among other beauties). A number of dancers who didn't like the Pilates system went to him instead. It was probably through one of them that I discovered Harry. I had reached that stage in life where I neither had the time nor the need to continue dance classes or the like. Nor, by a long shot, did I ever want to become a body builder—in fact, just the opposite!

Fortunately, Harry seemed to have worked out a nice balance between those two disciplines. He even incorporated some ballet barre exercises into his workout regimen, doing kicks, for example, with a small weight attached to the foot, or arm exercises with smaller weights. These he supplemented with some of the standard calisthenic exercises: sit-ups, stand-ups, foot and leg work, abdominal and back strengtheners, etc. And a modest amount of light weights for the arms and the back, though I was much against going too far with any weights whatsoever, having seen how ugly those biceps and pectorals become when the lifter gets older or lessens his regimen, and muscles turn into blubber or fat. It was easy to make Harry understand that, and so he developed a modified program for me with few or no weights.

Going two or three times a week, I would naturally run into Ann fairly often. She was an affable assistant and took good care of H's "patients." Gradually I realized that she was giving me rather more attention than the others. (Looking back on it, this was a quite advanced salon in that it catered to both men and women, though naturally more to men. Yet, unusual at that early stage of today's ubiquitous exercise and diet epoch.)

At first, I was not inclined to pay too much heed to Ann's attentions, but not because I was not attracted to her. On the contrary, I found her most appealing from the start. But rather because I was under the impression that she was not just H's aide-de-camp but perhaps something more than that. So when occasionally we would go out after my workout for a coffee or a drink—provided she could manage to escape for a few minutes—I would probe her a bit on that subject. She was understandably a little coy in answering such queries and usually managed to provide me with some ambiguous explanations as to why she was working there, and for so little pay, it seemed. Some friends from her ballroom dancer days had apparently first directed her to H's studio. Then once when she fell short of enough money to continue the training, Harry offered her a part-time job assisting him with menial tasks such as cleaning the studio, helping with record keeping, etc. Eventually he also entrusted her to supervise workouts with some of the older clients.

In any case, before long, Ann and I had graduated to the roof for a little jogging. Then one late afternoon, while taking a break, seated near the ledge of the roof, it happened. We simply fell into each other's arms and melted into one another as if it were the most natural thing in the world.

No questions asked; no coquetries; no long courting; no embarrassment to be doing this (somewhat) in public. I had found my "natural" woman at last, a remarkable someone, in total contrast to the neurotic twistings and turnings, questionings and postpone-ments, rationalizations of irrationalities, et al, that complicated the lives of most of the other women I had known or become involved with up until then.

That night she came to my apartment. No more questions about Harry.

Yours transitorily,
M.

October 16, 2002

Dear Nina:

"What a large volume of adventures may be grasped within this little span of life by him who interests his heart in every thing, and who, having eyes to see, what time and chance are perpetually holding out to him as he journeyeth on his way, misses nothing he can fairly lay his hands on."

So "spaketh" Laurence Sterne in his nonsentimental *Sentimental Journey*; and so much did this passage intrigue me that I once toyed with the idea of letting it serve as a model, if not inspiration, or, at best, justification, for digging up these memories—a *Non-Committal Journey*, I fancied I could call it.

But then I demurred: Sterne would be too formidable, if not too "stern" a model!

For there are many, perhaps too many, times as I jot down these notes, when I ask myself "why?" Why am I doing this at all? Why should anyone except you, dearest Nina, be interested in what this basically unknown-to-the-world entity "me" thinks or thought of X, Y, or Z in situation A, B, or C? Or why the Rhine looked so grim when we crossed it at Remagen on that dash through Germany after the Battle of the Bulge, and was sorely disappointerd not to discover even one of the fabled Lorelei lying on any rocks midstream? Or why I did not find the Bois de Boulogne as magical as I had expected, but the enchanting little Cişmigiu Park in Bucharest did the trick for me? What happened to me on the Way to the Forum?

Still, I do recall, for example, how interested our mutual friend, Harriet Zinnes, would be, when at lunch or high tea with her upon a return from some trip or other, she'd ask what happened, what did I see, whom did I meet; she always seemed to marvel at the enthusiasm with which I would describe every detail of, say, trying to locate a music publisher in the Oxford Street section of London, only to discover that the street I was looking for changes its name three times within three winding blocks. And how relieved I was when at last I found it. Or how I admired London's geography in general, and was always amused at its citizens' sangfroid in giving directions on how to find one's way through its maze. How, after even the most complicated set of instructions, your informant would sum it up like this: "Just two doors down, turn to the right, then take three cross streets north, make a sharp twist to the left, but watch for the newsstand where you must turn right again..." And conclude inevitably with a jolly, friendly, encouraging, but always absolutely confident: "You cawn't miss it, dearie!"

Of course, every great city boasts its small charms and minor fascinations which are not necessarily to be found in the various and sundry Baedekers and guidebooks vended at their tourist centers, although I'm the last one to dismiss those usually helpful volumes of invariably awkward sizes or untenable hefts. Indeed, you need them—plus open eyes, ears, and nose—to discover the personality of a town. Other advice for the travel born: above all, always try to walk as much as possible, take buses rather than subways when traversing a manageable distance, talk to the "natives" if you know the language (or observe them if you don't), go into and explore shops even when you're not in the market for their goods. Sit down for a coffee or a drink, preferably at an outdoor table in front of whatever restaurant or tavern you choose, and savour the landscape of faces and movement of the crowd, plus the physiognomy of the local architecture. Not every building need be a masterpiece to be interesting. Try to pick up a local paper (and a different one each day to get a more varied sense of the city, the people, the politics, the day-to-day concerns), not necessarily literary ones, though you can take one of those back to the hotel or pension to read late at night. Moreover, nowadays you can get even more up-to-date ideas about a city or a country by scanning its TV shows. Thus, when last in Paris, I often took in a midnight talk show to help accelerate reaccustoming my ear to the spoken language. The next day I'd get along that much better on the quai or the boulevards when asking directions, etc., or striking up a conversation with someone on the street if he or she looked interesting. Or, as Sterne intriguingly noted, "by him who interests his heart in every thing."

I recall, for instance, a discussion (which turned at times into a heated argument) I had about forty years ago on the train going from Venice to Parma, with a militant young communist from Reggio Emilio. He was trying to bring me up to date on what was going on in Bologna (major city of that province), and why the then-current administration must be brought down. Of course, there had already been at least fifty-nine governments since WWII, and, more recently, a remarkable effort was being made to clean up bureaucratic headquarters and dethrone and prosecute corrupt politicans (some in the very highest positions). These varying efforts were met with varying degrees of success or disaster—unfortunately, probably, now almost all have been either abandoned or put on hold due to Berlusconi. On that occasion, however, my interlocutor shrugged his shoulders in disbelief when I questioned him about the problem of secret Mafia influence in the government. Wasn't that perhaps more damaging, with its labyrinthian miles of corruption, to the average Italian than pure capitalist greed? Especially if hitched to that greed, aiding and abetting it by polluting it further? I wonder what excuses that young Bolognese would make for the Party nowadays, or for whatever equivalent dogmatic sect he may have shifted to. Though, being much older, he may more likely have moved equidistant to the right—right into the arms of Berlusconi?

Later, after a short sojourn in Parma, arriving in Florence on Good Friday, it was remarkable what a pall that day put upon the city, which didn't lift, religiously enough, until Easter morning, when I found myself in the huge piazza in front of the Duomo, mobbed with all types of people, drawn from seemingly everywhere, and from all walks of life. Most touching was the sight of a young shepherd who must have wandered down from the hills above Florence, walking his little lamb through the Square, and then lifting it to his shoulder as he stopped in awe before the great Ghiberti carved panels in the center of the piazza.

Two days later, after more exhaustive sightseeing, visiting the obligatory churches, museums, gardens, squares, and even the unusual synagogue, I decided to go that night to a Maggio Musicale concert, which was to be conducted by the great and venerable Carlo Zecchi. So, with my usual over-confidence in finding places unaided and by myself, but having misplaced my trusty map, I had no choice but to ask directions to the concert hall. To my utter amazement, no one seemed to know anything about either the concert or the hall! Fortunately, I knew the general direction from having studied my map of Florence earlier, and so got off to a good start. Yet I must have questioned at least ten people before finally zeroing in on just how to traverse the last ten blocks to the site. What was especially surprising was to discover how few Florentines I asked even knew about the existence of that particular hall, let alone where it was, and fewer yet who had ever heard of the Maggio Musicale festival itself. (Would one find the same blankness in Manhattan? Possibly. Would the average Londoner be able to direct you to Covent Garden? A little more likely.)

But the concert was more than worth the trouble, as indeed was the whole process of asking people directions and finding one's way in a new city, frustrating as at times that was. Zecchi must have been in his late eighties by then, I think, or possibly even ninety, heavily arthritic-ridden, and seemingly helpless. He had to be practically carried to the podium, and then forced to hold onto the bars of his music stand from time to time in order to maintain his balance. (The concert management was wise enough to give him a very sturdy one.) But once he started conducting, one forgot about his pain, watched only the eloquent hands, and heard only the ensuing music. It was the most fulfilling Brahms I had heard in many years.

Luftpause! You're probably asking, my dear, how in the world did I just end up in Florence? By what circuitous, hidden agenda did my memory hop, skip, and jump from Remagen on the Rhine to London to Paris to Italy? What subterranean selective process chose just those fragments of reminiscence? For example, though indeed no Goethe, I could go on with my *Italienische Reise* for pages and pages, with a whole chapter devoted to the architecture of Venice alone, and a footnote on the incomprehensible Venetian dialect. But I'm not a John Ruskin with his great *Stones of Venice*, nor hardly a Mary McCarthy with her lesser *Venice Observed*, I'm sorry to say! Nor, enlightening and constantly absorbing as the trip proved to be, did it change my life as it seems to have Goethe's. Besides, I really don't want any of these letters to sound like a travel book.

Which brings me back to the question I raised at the start of this letter: why am I dredging up these seemingly unrelated mementos of my past? Is it to entertain you or to justify my existence—in your eyes, in the eyes of others, in my own eyes? Or is it to answer some higher order, some pressure of conscience? Possibly even a hitherto unrecognized teleological urge? No, nothing so grandiose!

I think it's simply that I'm trying to make sense of my life: finally to understand myself, arguably, as Socrates said, the most difficult of all endeavors.

Accordingly, I ask myself, who am I?

"I think, therefore I am," said Descartes, oh so simply, yet so profoundly. But, I naively add, I also feel, eat, drink, sleep, talk, read, and fornicate (though less frequently these days, being an octogenarian!)—all of which reinforces my "I am" consciousness. For, somehow or other I've always been sure that somewhere inside all those Peer Gynt onion peels of my being is a steadfast, basic core "I am" that no one can take away from "Me"—no, not all the assaults to the ego one suffers throughout life can remove that core. They may help my "I am" to develop new protective onion-skin layers, but my "Me" is still there holding fast to my ineffable, ultimately undefinable individuality. As another great French thinker, Diderot, asked, "And can I, if I am me, act other than myself? Can I be myself and at the same time someone else?" I don't think so; at least, I can't. I might try to be something more or less other than what deep down I am. But I can never truly succeed in doing so, even though I may temporarily make believe I do, or be deluded into believing that I have done so. Hmn... could all this be at the root of the histrionic urge almost all people have to some degree or other? (Are we harking back to Wilhelm Meister's *Theatralische Sendung* again?)

Yet Diderot may posit otherwise when he goes on to ask: "And has there been, since the time I have been in the world, even a single moment when this would not have been true?" No, not for me, myself, and "I am." And then there's that fascinating alter ego of still another Frenchman, Paul Valéry's Monsieur Teste, with his astute *"Je suis chez moi"*- I am at home in Myself! (Does that deserve another letter?)

Well, well, what am I doing here, dear Nina, getting sidetracked again into such ontological questions when all that I wanted to do when I started these letters was to entertain you. Nevertheless, I hope that in telling these tales, and by virtue of their mix, I may willy-nilly reveal more of the Me that is "I am" or the "I am" that is Me—with a wave to Thee, my wayward love!

Yet, if you get down to the bottom of it all, none of us can ever escape these eternal questions. Which is probably why, while I don't want to stop and wallow further in the self addictive mire of internal self-focus, I do want always to be honest with myself and true to my memories, even if a certain anecdote may on occasion offend one or more of the parties under discussion, whether still around or not. Of course, I would never offend for offending's sake! For there is an "I" and a "Thou" to any truly existential, "real" relationship in this world—or out of this world—*pace* Martin Buber, the sage who probably best explored that territory, or even Levinas, one of his leading disciples, as you are aware, who carried that rich vein of thought even further into the last century. Dare I broach it again in another letter, should the occasion call for it, or a related memory evoke it?

In the meantime, let me know your take on these matters. Though maybe I should go back to your poems for your answers? They often bear ontological fruit without consciously meaning to do so.

Ontologically yours,
M.

February 18, 2003

Dear supportive, inspiring Muse:

Yes, of course, you're right: "*Habe nun, ach, philosophie*"—enough already! But you do agree that it was worth getting such things off my chest to clear the air, and maybe thereby to help justify, if only for myself, my own *recherche du temps perdu*? Which, in turn, is surely one of the main goals of these letters between us (instead of, say, prolonged telephone calls), is it not? Thus, your auxiliary suggestion, that you'd like me to explore more deeply how or what I felt, or still feel, about a particular event, a random adventure, or a specific episode, is both to the point and challenging. You want me to be more concrete, don't you? You obviously want to know more about how each event affected me. You want me to not fear to tread where "angels may fear to," in spite of Rilke's warning "*Jeder Engel ist schrecklich!*" (Which makes me wonder what Pleshu, your most erudite Romanian editor of *Dilema*, has to say about Rilke in his recent book on angels!)

In any case, quite a daunting assignment! However, I'm a tad disappointed (as a wary Southerner might put it) to have to admit that I thought I was doing so all along, albeit in a more subtle, implicit way. For, as I think I explained earlier, I don't want to ape the confessional mode of Lowell, Sexton, Plath, and their ilk, powerful as much of their work hit us when it first came out, and as much of it may still do so. Even less did I ever dream of competing with St. Augustine, Boethius, or the paranoid Rousseau or any of their multitudinous progeny! Everyone seems to be writing memoirs these days (including your own admirable, three-volumed Romanian, *Memory: A Dowry*). Just check the book review sections of any of the major daily papers and the better literary weeklies.

In any case, I want always to remain as true to my own peculiar personality as I possibly can. And that prickly nature, as you know only too well from your encounters with it, is not given to overly explicit expression of emotion, except perhaps when it reaches the temper point and sometimes explodes! Is that kind of reserve, then, one of the protective onion skins I seem to have grown? Will I have to shed more of those skins, peel off more layers, dig down deeper to the aboriginal roots of my being to finally convince you that I did feel A, experience B, and suffer C? Besides, isn't there usually an amusing or even satirical side to almost every such episode A, B, or C—if we examine it dispassionately, or bring it closer to ourselves—that we wouldn't want to miss out on? In the final analysis, isn't it my own "I" that decides what to do in any specific situation?

Isn't it "enough to merely be!" to quote Whitman. "Enough to breathe! Joy! Joy! All over joy!"

*

Well, *que sera, sera*... From now on, I shall make every effort to give you more and more of the true Me, as far as I'm capable of doing so unselfconsciously. (Regardless of whatever animal personality you currently endow me with!)

Alors, humbly, consciously, and conscientiously yours?

M.

P.S. Of course, the various animal personalities you've endowed me with complicate things still further! Remember, first I was a squirrel, which you attributed to all of what you call my squirrelling around; moreover, squirrel sounds nice in Romanian: Veverița. But things began to get more complicated when suddenly you saw me as a koala, a sort of Australian teddy bear, I suppose. Then, as if that weren't complex enough, one day I became a penguin—because of my waddling walk? So what could you call me now? Simple: you took the initial letters from each of those three animals, incorporating ski from squirrel, pen from penguin, and ko from koala, and I became a unique, new animal species—a one and only SKIPENKO, with a Ukrainian sonority, to boot!

July 5, 2003

My most demanding Mistress!

"Enough philosophy!" you repeat, echoing Goethe, as I did in my last letter. Now you want blood? You ask me to pull out all stops and lay the refuse and spittle on the table. All right, lady, I'll try. But I'm warning you: it goes against the grain of yours truly.

Thus, in your verbal "guide to the perplexed," among other things, you urge me to describe my failures as well as my successes, which plunges us immediately into a puzzling conundrum of a paradox! For, just what is success? Don't we need a definition of terms? And who is to be the arbitrator of any such forums? Then there is also the situation to bear in mind—the what, where, when, and how of it all (not to mention the why)! As you know, timing is often everything. Plus which, one needs time to know what really matters. What may be a failure in the public eye might well be a success (or at least a satisfactory attempt) in the author's (or composer's) private eye. Indeed, he or she may even live to see that work vindicated. Think of such notorious cases as Verdi's *La Traviata* being vociferously booed at its premiere; early Wagner mostly misunderstood and reviled; the wild opening night of Stravinsky's *Rite of Spring*, half pro and half contra; and countless others. However, let's shy away from such fabled extremes and return to my more humble experiences, say, in the theater.

It turns out that there were indeed a number of plays and operas I directed—and was sure I had brought to life—which worked well for some and not so much for others. But most of these the press never got around to see! Does that mean they were failures? I think not. Not necessarily. (Yet *l'homme moyen* would most likely opt otherwise.) Of course, as we explore this issue, I suspect we may find that my greater mistake lay in not promoting my own work as aggressively as probably I should have, so that it could have been seen and judged more fairly and widely, or could, at least, have entered the public arena and been given a decent chance. Why, for example, after that laudatory article in *Newsweek*, where I was dubbed "the indefatigable Mr. Edwards" (a copy of which I once showed you), did I not push heaven and earth to get that short, provocative Joyce Carol Oates play I directed, *The Ontological Proof of My Existence*, which was duly praised in that review, moved to a better Off-Broadway site? And insist on an absolutely foolproof reproduction of the very successful mounting I had made of it at The Cubiculo, which, in turn, had led to that article? Also, at the same time, I should have energetically spread the word about my role in making and developing that remarkable "Cube of Energy and Innovation," which is how that *Newsweek* critic had generously dubbed "The Cubiculo"?

Indeed, why not? What held me back? Perhaps because it would have involved forfeiting other responsibilities. For example, it might have meant curtailing or even giving up my ongoing agenda at The Cubiculo, postponing or cancelling some of the dance concerts and other plays that were scheduled to be performed there in the next few months; also, taking time off from my other (and better paid) job at the Brooklyn Philharmonia; finally, delaying the transfer of my emotionally disturbed son from public to private schools. In other words, maybe I should simply have been more ruthlessly selfish in advancing my own private cause(s), not just the agenda of those others I worked for, and, above all, my family needs, which I was probably neglecting overly much already.

For, as I search my memory, this was a pattern that often repeated itself in my life, indeed, from time to time, long before the Oates play and its concomitant laudatory *Newsweek* article and numerous times after it. For example, I should have (I know that I could have) done more to make a run of one of my productions that was generally agreed to be a success by almost everyone, namely, my staging of Dostoevsky's *Notes from the Underground*, Part I performed verbatim, not a word cut or transposed, by a very good actor, Norman Sample, perfect for the part. An ex-philosophy student from NYU, who wandered the streets of the Village, growing and shaping his beard to duplicate Dostoevsky's, and living the life of, nay, virtually becoming, the protagonist of that extraordinary book, Sample had the same kind of intensity as Gerard Philippe. I had seen Philippe years before on the Paris stage in Camus's *Caligula* and, remarkably, also one night caught sight of him crossing a small street bridge on the way to his theater site, already totally immersed in the role, breathing the inner life of Caligula, though without his toga.

Norman, our Dostoevsky, got a great review from *The New York Times*, as did our production, which should have prompted and justified transfer to a larger venue. We were certainly tempted, and made numerous attempts to raise enough money to do so. But, of course, that was not going to be easy. It never is. Besides, who would invest in something so intellectual, so seemingly uncommercial?

That's what the naysayers claimed. We should have countered that our production proved the opposite, that *Notes* could be quite theatrical and intellectually stimulating at the same time, certainly more theatrical than most any layman (or even theater person) would have dreamed possible. As it was, it drew quite a wonderfully mixed audience, even without any extra promotion or advertising other than a single ad in the *Village Voice* and our standard mailing. But a full house and an extended run in the tiny Cubiculo was one thing; how could we expect five times as large an audience, nightly, in the larger-size house we would have had to move to? So, again, you're right: we should have persisted. We might well have found an in-between-sized theater; the cast was small—one person! The set was a shack of a room with broken-down furniture and cracked windows, in the slums of mid-19th-century St. Petersburg...

Yes, even now as I recount this lost opportunity, I chide myself for not having worked harder to make more of a production that should have been moved immediately after that review and the good word of mouth praise and rising audience interest it had stimulated. With it, moreover, I might have made the kind of mark I needed to put myself in the running as a director for outside projects. Instead, we took the safer route of trying to book it on the college circuit, and lined up only one repeat in some campus far from NYC. Even that outreach venture was not pursued as intensely as it might have been. After all, *Notes* was required reading in most colleges at that time. But we stalled, partly because I was carrying out other programs and mandatory projects already lined up for the Cubiculo and the Brooklyn Philharmonia (as it was then called), and Sample himself had neither the money nor the know-how to do so alone.

A similar strategy might have been attempted also with the Oates play referred to above, the one *Newsweek* covered. It was also quite Dostoievskian, as fate would have it. The protagonist was obviously modeled on that consummate nihilist, Piotr Verkovensky, from *The Possessed* (or *The Demons*, as it is sometimes also translated), but transposed into a modern American milieu. It was surely one of my best productions: how I wish you had been around then to see it! It, too, had a small cast—only three—and a single set. But it was a short play: it needed a companion piece. So why, for example, didn't we ask Oates to write one for us, and then mount the two of them together six or eight months later? Why not? Or why didn't we

76

later think of reviving the two of them and making a double bill of these Dostoievskian-related theater works? That could have made quite an evening.

Similarly, there were any number of other productions of mine that deserved more attention and, with clever promotion, might have sustained a longer stage life, such as my revivals of Massinger's *A New Way to Pay Old Debts* and Hugo's *Marie Tudor*. Yet, in all fairness to ourselves, there was so much activity Off-Off-Broadway during that period—literally hundreds of productions annually— that one could never be sure of getting any press coverage at all, even when mounting a premiere.

How different it is today, when a company such as the Pearl Theatre group, which pursues a rather similar repertoire to what we did (though generally less adventurous), now gets coverage for almost every production it mounts and, accordingly, more public support, and private backing than we were able to rack up. Nor is their programming quite as unique as was the Classic Theatre's, whose premise was to present those great plays from the past that have been neglected rather than the 86th mounting of Chekhov's *The Seagull* or the 57th production of Ibsen's *A Doll's House*. Thus we did Turgenev's rarely performed *The Bachelor*, instead of his *A Month in the Country*, which everyone does; or Ben Jonson's *Epicoene* (in his day, his most popular play), instead of the usual *Volpone* or *The Alchemist*; Euripides' *Alcestis*, instead of the perennial *Medea*, and so on.

In retrospect, as I try to make sense of all this for myself as well as for you, the pattern becomes clearer that obviously I could have used that extra dose of stubborn, persistent "chutzpah" which overcomes all such obstacles as those outlined above. Also, the dose of ruthlessness almost always required at one point or another in any push to commercial success. Something perhaps worth a paragraph or two of discussion later?

Didn't I once, during one of our earlier inquisitorial confrontations, with you seated across the sofa tea table from me in your living room, a Scotch in one hand and a Benson & Hedges ultra-lite in the other, zealously probing the hidden corners of my life, confess that in spite of all my outward worldly knowledge and apparent experience, I was still basically, *au fond*, an Innocent? That, moreover, I was brought up by two parents who were even more innocent and far less worldly than I: two honest, lovable people who somehow never taught me that the world is a Jungle, where often, indeed most of the time, one has to bare one's teeth and extend one's claws in order to survive, let alone prosper. Surprisingly, I don't think the need for such behavior ever crossed their minds, at least, not in those terms. In fact, I remember more than once, on visits back home to Wisconsin from the big city, trying to deal with this very subject and making a special effort to clarify for them what I meant by that language, but with little or no success. They never showed any sign that they may very well have had their own good reasons for not filling me in about Reality, or displayed even a kind of covert understanding that they might have had something they were trying to hide from me in order to protect me. No, I'm afraid they simply didn't catch on at all as to what I was trying to explain to them.

There is also, perhaps, another factor we should keep in mind. After all, as you know, I have been able to achieve some degree of so-called worldly success in some fields, though not always the kind of success I may have wanted. And even though I never sought "success" or fame or wealth, per se, it would have mattered only insofar as those so-called accomplishments might have enabled me to make more of my abilities and talents, i.e., to direct and produce more and better plays; to bring out the work of more and better writers, composers, dancers, actors; to help advance the art itself in more ways; maybe do some writing of my own, and so on. In other words, the "life" of the work, or the life-enhancing thrill of doing what one wants to do, whether the world accepts it or not, has been more important to me than that elusive but usually quite transitive phenomenon we might call "quantifiable success." Or, as Yeats put it:

> The intellect of man is forced to choose
> Perfection of the life or of the work.

To return to the main theme, surely one of my major handicaps was that having, as I do, a variety of talents and abilities, I was not able to focus as much as perhaps I should have on just one of them. Or, recognizing that problem, I did not more calculatedly determine which was the best path to pursue, that is, which of my varied abilities would more likely lead to that first level of "success" that might catapult me into a position where I could, in turn, proceed to cultivate those other talents. For, once accepted as X, people are more prone to give you a chance as Y and/or Z. But they are loathe to concede in advance that one might become X+Y+Z eventually. In other words, I did not realize until too late that the world is as suspicious of the poly-talented as it is scared of the polymath.

Interestingly enough, the Memorial Service I went to last Sunday while you were enjoying your daily, early-afternoon nap was for just such a polymath. You may recall that one reason I decided to go—for Stefan Bauer-Mengelberg, the honoree, was neither an old friend nor recent acquaintance, but rather a great friend of two friends of mine (which is no doubt why I was invited). Also, curiously enough, now that he was gone from this earth, I had begun to sense a belated, deep-seated kinship with the late Stefan, far more so than when he was alive! I now realized that he may have been regarded by some as a talented failure, in spite of his having achieved an enviable measure of temporary worldly success in two or more of his fields of endeavor. Moreover, probably because of that earlier success, and because he had also managed to impress people in each of the realms he subsequently entered, the word failure would hardly have been used, or consciously articulated as such. For example, Stefan was still even then a rather big name in some music circles, especially to those of a certain age and in the know. Some of them probably wondered why he had left that field so abruptly and did not capitalize more on the various lesser and greater breakthroughs of his multifaceted existence. That awareness led me, once ensconced rather skeptically at the Memorial, to listen all the more attentively to the various tributes made by, and reminiscences of, his longtime friends, relatives, and professional associates and/or clientele. I even found myself suddenly taking notes. Was I thinking I might find some clues to my own life story, which bore (or bears) at least certain superficial parallels to his, especially in its multifaceted nature? In any case, obviously something took root; for the notes began to fall automatically into a kind of ode or peroration, which I have since tried to shape a little more cohesively as such. Well, for better or for worse—and let me assure you, I don't aspire here to be a Pope or a Dryden—here's the result. Let's call it a

REPORT ON A CONSUMMATE POLYMATH
(Stefan Bauer Mengelberg Memorial Service)

Though I scarce knew you—
as I only surfacely ken this Beethoven *Andante*
now being essayed by your surviving friend, Mme. G---
upon the ill-tuned piano
in this scholastic, English club-like, NYU Legal Lounge
—where we, your motley destined friends, assemble today
as at the fabled Persian "Conference of the Birds,"
to pay, in our variegated plumage,
our diversified homage
to your multiple, compartmentalized existence
and multifold personalities
that plowed so many varied complex fields
of intellectual and artistic endeavor,
and brightened consanguineously
so many of our lives...
Now the Beethoven fades out
and the Bauer-Mengelberg eulogies begin:
we learn that, appropriately enough,
you once lived on 27 Mozart Strasse,
in Heidelberg, no less,
fountainhead, no doubt, of two of your
fecund fields of endeavor—
"*Habe nun, ach, Philosophie*" and "*An die Musik*"—

consummate polymath that you were,
Master of many disciplines,
yet Crown Prince of none,
though well you might have so become.
But, in the long haul, you preferred
the lottery of the Law—
to savor its give and take—
as did your forbears for some 200 years before...
       For, as they say, genes will always tell,
and gugal (10 to the 10th power) came in-between.
What could you do but give what
you wanted—the law of Gargantua Pantagruel?—
you who wouldn't have an answering machine
and eschewed indefinitely submitting bills
to your clientele.
                       Leaping, living higher,
jumping from one discipline to another,
O Pioneer of computerized music notation,
incipient piano virtuoso, but probably bored by practice,
eventually, impatiently, you grabbed a baton
and broke the back of the New York Philharmonic conducting
       obstreperous Stefan Volpe.
After which the West Coast beckoned, and you, giant stork,
flew back & forth intercontinentally for one whole year
       to conduct there and here, and here and there.
But then you couldn't stand the "business of music"—
       as you baptised it—any longer;
and sought refuge in Academia
by heading and reforming a music school
—since, then as always, you viewed the world,
as we've just been told, through aesthetic-tinted eyes...
       And now another surviving friend, Mr. B--- joins Mme. G---
to give us the *Andante* from Mozart's *Sonata in F Major
for Four Hands*—that your neighbors, unbeknownst to you,
used to enjoy listening in on surreptitiously...

Followed by still more ramifying reminiscences
from the many here who do not know each other,
but were brought together by their bond with you—
be it legal, educational, musical or even controversial—
and formalized through the fraternally embracing social graces
of your faithful, beyond-the-pale friend,
the ecumenical, ever practical, Rabbi Freedman.
How they loved you how we all loved
You
with the ebullient, vital face,
for whom the scars of War and Exile
did not seem to exist—
or were they subsumed beneath that open smile?—
having fled the Rheinland when only a 12-year-old boy
(and then only one-quarter Jewish), escaping
providentially with your beloved Mother, Kaethe,
three days before World War II erupted.
You
with your generous, nay overgenerous, kindness,
who, kinkily, would never let any of your
entourage—even when they numbered 20 or more—
foot any restaurant bill...
        Then we're told the incredible tale
of the 40 Ali Baba crates of wine you ordered
to stock your friends' cellars—
which took seven biblical days and nights
to sort out and distribute...
        Thus, as one friend after another mounts the podium,
your extraordinary chronicle unfolds in Paul Bunyan profusion:
How you brought civilization and symbolic logic
to Binghamton and Thunder Lake...
How you defied the IRS better than Edmund Wilson
because you did it kosher style,
legally reading the law more brilliantly
than its own reputedly by-the-book practitioners...

How you were beginning to master Chinese,
that monosyllabic language with its
complex polyphonic pictograms...
How you turned Law into a Game of Wit
and conquered It...
      Yes, we shall miss all the Stefans, even those
personae most of us never knew.
But we know now they were there
within, behind, and around you
and your male Mona Lisa smile,
when Death dismissed your class at midnight,
and met you on the stairwell.

*

Food for thought? Does it nourish my thesis? Back up somewhat my self-analysis? In any case, it has been a lesson in rhetoric. Let's talk about it and related matters when next we meet, which I hope will be very soon!

    Polymathically yours,
                M.

                               December 15th
My dear, also multifaceted Ninotchka:

O lmpw upi jave grpwm o, [atoemt—a jabberwocky sentence if ever there was one—though probably only pronounceable in Polish! (And reminiscent of your own invented language, Spargan.) The result of my having accidentally started this letter one set of keys too far to the right on the computer keyboard. So let's start all over.
    I know you have grown impatient over my not sending you a follow-up to that last letter with its over-lengthy ode, but which you thought—and I, too, thought—had finally broken my latest writing

83

block. It's not that I don't have any number of stories jostling about in the cerebellum, anxious to emerge and take over, but, rather, that I'm currently stuck as to which one fits this series as it is now proceeding. In simpler terms: which should come next? So, perhaps in the meantime, it would be better to record a few miscellaneous shorter notes or episodes, culled from free association, or struck off by physical memories, until the just-right, hopefully bigger/better, story falls in line?

For example, this morning as I was hurrying down 70th Street so as not to be late (that old bugaboo of mine, as you may painfully recall) for the weekly sabbath Synagogue Service I've been singing, lo, these many years as part of a professional male octet (no women being allowed to sing in an Orthodox temple, as you also are indignantly aware of, one of your chief complaints against Judaism, is it not?)—well, as I rushed along, I wondered what may have happened to Cecily Brown, that tall girl/woman, aspiring dancer, whom I used to pass occasionally, loping down this very street like a tall kangaroo. Indeed, the simile is not too far-fetched: I recall her singularly long legs, with their ample large thighs; her comparatively small chest thorax; her odd, almost tiny head which would suddenly grow considerably larger when she opened her large-toothed mouth to speak. Plus her relatively short, stub-like arms. All she needed was a little pouch in front! Indeed, once when her bag swung that way, I was momentarily alarmed that I might have to go into kangaroo talk.

Otherwise we would have little to say: our brief colloquies generally languished into the usual theater small talk: what are you up to? How's Anna (Cecily and I had met in a special workshop of Anna Sokolow's devised primarily for teaching movement—not pure dance—to actors). Actually, Cecily would not have been so bad looking, were she not so ungainly, what with those long legs and that incredibly heavy, quite garish makeup she wore, uncomfortably reminiscent of what the older, one-time divas, who used to haunt the lobby of the nearby Hotel Ansonia and adjacent Needle Park, still wore for their little sorties into this drab modern environment up until a few years ago. (Perhaps they still wear it wherever they are? Have they found a new spot to haunt? For the spacious, arcade-like new subway entrance at 72nd Street has changed the whole nature of that square.)

In fact, I used to feel sorry for poor Cecily, with all her valiant optimism, keeping up the fight for a part in a musical, since there was so little chance of her landing one in the thin/maigre-figured female world that has dominated the American dance scene these last forty to fifty years. But Fellini would have welcomed her to help people the cinematic beaches of his Rome or his Ravenna...

Her startling kangaroo resemblance reminds me of another friend, Tomi Romer, more of an actual friend than Cecily, who was (and remains?) basically only an acquaintance. I had met Tomi through Geraldine during those first years in New York after my return from post war Europe and that memorable year in Paris.

Tomi, an aspiring actress, hailed from Chicago, already something of a bond between us, since it meant we were both brought up in the Midwest and therefore had at least that much in common. For not totally acclimatized New Yorkers, who always seem to come from somewhere else, that usually serves as a starter. Somewhat intellectual, endowed with a more inquisitive intelligence than the average actress, and moderately good looking, though hardly a beauty, Tomi's chances in commercial theatre were limited; this was long before the prevalence of TV commercials could sometimes provide alternative work to such aspirants. However, she was smart enough to grasp that if she were to make a mark for herself anywhere, it would have to be through her wit rather than her physiognomy. So she turned to writing stories and sketches. The latter led to a few ill-fated attempts to become a stand-up comic, the former to her fiction, eliciting stories often rather wry and basically self-effacing.

Probably the best one turned out to be a charming, whimsical tale about a G.I. soldier stationed in Australia who married a kangaroo! Especially amusing was her account of the unusual couple's landing in San Francisco, after a very long, tempestuous crossing of the Pacific from Down Under, and the sensation the kangaroo bride caused as she walked down the plank at Golden Gate with her proudly beaming soldier husband!

Looking back on this period, I now think it a pity that Tomi did not go on with her writing. That kangaroo story, for example, was never published, so far as I know. She was to have given me a copy of it, but never did. In fact, I doubt whether she ever tried to market it. Maybe because, around this same time, her first real theater break suddenly came: she landed two small parts in the first season of John Houseman's brave attempt to establish and develop an American Shakespeare Repertory Company in Stratford, Connecticut. Her friends were all taken by surprise, for she had had no training or experience in classic theater, nor much in American vernacular repertoire either, yet somehow she managed to persuade Houseman to take her under his wing for that company's initial summer season. It was probably through a combination of feminine wiles (Houseman was susceptible), spiced by her quite different kind of wit. In any event, she performed several minor female roles creditably, though unfortunately not inspiredly enough to be noticed, except by her friends. So she wasn't asked back for the following season, after which I and other mutual friends seem to have lost touch with her. That is, until one day, Geraldine phoned to say that Tomi had died, still under the age of 30. None of us, except possibly G. herself, had had any inkling of her malady. It seems it was leukemia, and that, sadly, she had gone back to Chicago to die in the lap of her family.

Tomi's premature exit from this world reminded me of several other friends and fellow actors who died much too young. Tomi had been one of six women in my production of the first electronic opera, *Stacked Deck*, back in 1956, with its Dada/Surrealist-inspired "chance" text by Dick Higgins and pioneer electronic music by Richard Maxwell, which we first did at the 92nd Street Y on its Music for Our Time series, and, after a good reception and good reviews, we repeated the following year at Cooper Union. My own dear Ann was in it: she played the Cabbage Woman, as I told you earlier, remember? So was the very beautiful Ruth Sobotka, ex-dancer and costumier from the New York City Ballet, once married to the great film maker Stanley Kubrik and now trying to become an actress (we once acted together in a workshop production of a De Maupassant short story, directed by her then-amour, Dino Narizzano). She played the seductive Green Woman. Also in it was the plump, very serious, perpetually frowning Florence Tarlow, who later became one of the darlings of the Judson Theatre group and of the flourishing Happenings circles. Dick Higgins claims to have discovered her in the Circulation Room of the New York Public Library on 42nd Street, where she was working as a librarian (and probably very good at it). And now all four of these vastly different women—Tomi, Ann, Ruth and Florence—are gone from this earth. Indeed, the only female from that cast who survives is Alice Spivak, who played the Lady in Blue. She taught acting for years at the HB Studio (and may still be doing so), though I believe she has gone into individual coaching for actors, some directing, and casting.

Strangely enough, as far as I've been able to find out, all the male cast members of that *Stacked Deck* crew are still alive and kicking, two of them having gone on to become leading character actors on Broadway—the versatile, affable Richard Latessa and the ultra-serious, often dour David Margulies. And I think tall James Cahill was seen from time to time in Off-Broadway plays and probably did occasional TV and screen work, although I've heard nothing about or from him for a very long time. I wonder... One of the most interesting of the male cast, Francis Dux, seems to have disappeared somewhere in the wilds of England. And singer Martin Sameth (who was with me in *The Golden Apple*) shows up at places like La Mama periodically, usually sporting a long, terribly unruly, white beard and huge, bushy eyebrows. But composer Richard Maxwell died before any of the ladies did, and librettist Higgins obligingly later, after they did.

Probably the person who might have interested you most, dear Nina, out of this quite varied cornucopia of characters was Dick Higgins, who had, in the almost Everyman morality-coded text of his *Stacked Deck*, anticipated many of the theatrical devices (and cliches) of the Theatre of the Absurd, though I don't think he ever tuned in to Adamov or some of the other early absurdists in Paris. At least, he never mentioned them. More obvious were the blatant chance elements he

87

used. This came naturally to him, since he had studied with John Cage at the New School and was certainly a staunch disciple of that I Ching master manipulator. In fact, one could maintain that Higgins was something of a deconstructionist before the Word!

Nonetheless, the overall impact of *Stacked Deck* was quite original: one reason we all had great hopes for Higgins at that time. Geraldine had sort of taken him under her wing. Indeed, it was she who brought him to us. He did go on to become a superb publisher and promoter for the Dada/Surrealist/Gertrude Stein-inspired worlds of those involved with the Happenings and related fads of the late fifties and early sixties. (Higgins' library had all of Stein's writings, including a then rare text of *Tender Buttons*.)

He later spent some time in Germany with the Fluxus group and other avant-gardists and while there seems to have been inspired by closer exposure to the language to make a rather good translation of that beautiful Novalis long poem, "Night." He also managed to write some stimulating literary criticism during that period, which deserved a larger audience than it got. (Maybe I should suggest to his friend Richard Kostelanetz that he bring them out again.) Above all, Higgins rendered a great service by setting up his own independent printing house, The Something Else Press, for which he served as publisher, editor, and overall guru. Of course, coming from wealth, he never really had to worry about making a living (as far as I know); and, in spite of a long sojourn in a loft on what was then the edge of Soho Chinatown—the Chinese have since moved several blocks north of that apartment—living in seeming penury, and affecting a modern, Bohemian style, one was always somewhat aware of a suppressed patrician strain and a certain dry style. But talent and intellect were always there waiting to be tapped. Unfortunately, our paths rarely crossed in those later years, especially after he moved to upper Park Avenue; and when they did, each being so filled with the pressure of finishing a current project, we'd say we must get together soon. Instead, obviously, we both procrastinated too much. I would so much have liked you to have met and talked with Dick. He was also that rare thing, a good conversationalist.

Again, in this rueful mood, going back to Tomi's sad fate, her early death and unfulfilled talents (at least, Higgins lived longer, achieved maturity, made his mark), makes one wonder what may have happened to the scores of struggling actors, singers, and dancers one encountered during those early apprentice days in New York; plus the many would-be stars one worked with in Off- and Off-Off-Broadway plays; and what about the many musicians and singers one auditioned while running the Brooklyn Philharmonic? The vast majority seem to have sifted back into the everyday banalities of trying to earn a living in this often cruel metropolis. Very few went on to become stars; a relatively few managed to make something of a living in their chosen profession, while another group (probably the majority) carried on a double existence of part-time work in another profession to support occasional sorties in the theater. Worse yet, they almost all had to suffer the occasional disrespect shown the so-called unsuccessful actor in this country. All this, in such sharp contrast to the general reception of actors, singers, and dancers in Europe, who are treated with great respect by the ordinary public, even when they are not stars or headliners but simply "Artistes," as they call them, though that's beginning to change, as I understand it, with the overall general decline in governmental subsidy in both Western and Eastern Europe, where many a state supported theater is failing or curtailing production because of reduced subsidies.

Yes, art is cruel, as you well know. I was reminded of this, that afternoon of the last day of our last trip to Romania, when, as you may recall, I visited without you, I'm sorry to report, the now beautifully restored Bucharest National Museum of Arts. (You were tied up that afternoon with saying goodbyes to your multifold friends—remember?) Unlike London's great National Gallery, or the Louvre, where in most sections almost every work, or at least every other, is a true masterpiece, here one had to plow through many mediocrities. Or if not exactly that, then at least rather dull, or merely competent works. So that one Tintoretto was needed to light up a whole roomful of lesser-known coeval Italians. Three El Grecos had to do the same for the Spanish gallery, though a small, unusual Zurbaran challenged him.

Yet the lucky rooms devoted to the Flemish and German schools contained the powerful "Massacre of the Innocents" of Jan Breugel, the Younger, plus his stunning "Four Seasons"; an astonishing small Rubens ("Man Wrestling with a Lion"); and four or five remarkable canvasses by Teniers, the Younger.

The Museum also boasts a rare sculpture by Camille Claudel, the lesser-known sister of poet playwright Paul, in the French wing, next to two strange, very early "realistic" Monets and a Sisley, I believe. But one had to wade through many lesser lights to see these. Oddly enough, I shall probably carry away a unique memory of this museum: for there, not far from those Monets, hung a painting by Charles Chaplin (1793-1858)—a possible distant French relative of our great English/American Charlie Chaplin? (Or was Chaplin more likely a stage name?)

Of course, when we turn to a hypothetical, comparable museum of world music, how many moderately talented composers, even some who were once stellar figures, such as Heller, Raff, and Spohr, are now almost totally unknown or forgotten, their scores moldering in damp basements, dingy attics, and neglected libraries of Europe and America? Or if we consider the strange ups and downs in the reputations of such composers as Sibelius, Hindemith, and Milhaud? Or wonder why Mozart's *Cosi fan tutte* now rivals his *Figaro* and *Don Giovanni* in number of performances these days, when it was hardly ever done in the 19th or early 20th centuries?

And poets? Why, there's probably an even higher mortality rate for reputations among your fellow poets than among composers! Remember how shocked we were recently to find so few American poets whose names we recognized in that early 20th-century Oxford anthology of American verse edited by Ludwig Lewisohn that we found hiding away on one of your library shelves—and how little of the once highly regarded output of 19th-century American greats such as Bryant, Whittier, Longfellow, and Lowell, and their ilk, is even known today, let alone read?

But enough! I certainly didn't intend this letter to turn into either a polemic or a treatise. So, *la revedere*! I'd still like to hear your views on some of these matters, voiced in your delicious accent, and conjured up in your charming Romanian locutions...

Love,

M.

PS: Not wanting to be unfair to your worthy Bucharest Museum—so beautifully and lovingly restored from damage it suffered during that strange, short, ambiguous revolution of 1989—I hasten to add that the north wing galleries devoted to Romanian art are extraordinary, especially the icons and icon-derived works in the medieval and renaissance rooms, mounted and installed, as they are, in a work-enhancing state-of-the-art mode. They must be seen to be believed!

April 1, 2004

My dear, too-long absent Nina:

What did you make of that last missive? Did you actually manage to plow through it? So far, you've hardly commented on it, and I was looking forward to a little discussion or even debate! Then, again, maybe it doesn't need that kind of treatment. Some things, once said, are sufficient unto themselves. Others pass on.

Certainly, one wishes more of our so-called statesmen and politicos here in this country—and, I fear, also in your often ultra-verbal East European realms—would recognize that truth. On the contrary, these types seem to flourish on Repetition. Especially when wrong, and then they won't admit it. Which, of course, leads to the Big Lie. And that, in turn, engenders constant reiteration until it becomes part of the landscape, painfully difficult to amend, correct, cancel, or change—unless living history reveals the depth of the deception. Which perhaps we're beginning to see now, with people finally wondering what happened to the Emperor's (viz. Bush's) clothes...

In any case, I'm also writing this before getting any answer to that last letter—indeed, our letters may have crossed—to say that I'm more concerned these days about our verbal communication than these written notes, some of which almost seem to turn into essays. For, on occasion, your vocal tone has been so varied recently that I'm not always sure I'm talking to my beloved Nina, but rather to one one of those Mme. X's of *cinema noir*! Then there is always the problem of whether or not my dear Mme. Nina fully catches what I'm saying over the phone and is perhaps too proud to ask me to repeat it. In person, of course, I'm always more confident that she comprehends my English, even when I speed along, because now she can hear me clearer, she can read my lips, or she's more aware of the body language which always enhances the verbal.

Or could it simply be, dear Nina, that you (or a possible future reader) may be getting a little tired of this project? That perhaps you're beginning to suspect that it might not make any sense, since we're talking and seeing each other all the time anyway, so why go on with this written exchange? Even though up until now you have been the one to urge me on when I was depressed about continuing. That, indeed, you felt this writing was potentially of more importance to me than almost anything I had done heretofore in my life. That at least I should finally fulfill that aspect of my being which, as we both know, I have until now for the most part neglected. (And you also know that from the very beginning I've been more skeptical than you about that hypothesis.) Or could it simply be that I've inadvertently offended you in recent days, and you think I should know what went wrong and apologize for it? What is your verdict, dear Judge?

Curiously and anxiously yours,
M.

July 1, 2004
Dear unpredictable one:

Your verdict hasn't come in yet, and I really should be patient and wait for what you may have to say on the subject. But, forgive me, I

92

want to report briefly on the fascinating public forum to which I had invited you recently, but which you couldn't attend, about that singular new German writer, W. G. Sebald, now being praised so highly by almost everyone but who actually has been living and teaching in England for the last thirty years or more. Yet he writes in German, so he is no Conrad, although the hype has lifted him almost that high already. Why? The situation is quite reversed. Nevertheless, you and I should get to know his work. *The Emigrants*, his third book, but the first to be translated, consists of four different tales, none of which is either fact or fiction, yet each is definitely based on reality. What also gives it great individuality is that it is supplemented with photographs, 90 percent of which, according to Sebald, have a documentary kind of reality. Further paradoxes. It sounds like some sort of hybrid, but I'm anxious to read it as soon as possible. Especially after the discussion led by James Wood, that brilliant, young English literary critic, now resident in the USA, teaching at Harvard and writing for *The New Republic* and *The New Yorker*, as well as the comparable major British literary journals. At the end, Harriet Zinnes, who was there, and who, as you know, invited us, introduced me to Woods. A bit like my days in Paris, hobnobbing with the elite...

Interruptedly yours,
M.

Ides of October, 2004

My dear, wise, conciliatory Nina:

Yes, it was good to hear from you at long last, and you're quite right. I made too much of the situation. However, it is certainly reassuring that you're still "Gung Ho" with the project and want me to open up and be as free as possible from now on, as well as allow current happenings to stimulate the memory buds.

Took a long walk this morning—part of my new regimen, as you may recall my telling you earlier, to help steady the blood pressure—through Fort Greene, that part of Brooklyn where I park when not *chez toi* at Roosevelt Island (my studio, as it were), and then on up into adjacent Clinton Hill. Back in the 1890s and the early 1900s, these communities were the stylish part of Brooklyn. They had begun to displace or supplement the Heights in that respect. And, indeed, that's why the new Brooklyn Academy was built in Fort Greene on leafy, spacious Lafayette Avenue, instead of being rebuilt in the Heights, after the disastrous 1903 fire destroyed the old, hulking hall on Montague Street. Great trees still line Lafayette all the way from the Academy up to Pratt Institute at the summit of Clinton Hill, where that pioneer oil man, Henry Pratt, established that excellent college of design and engineering. Some of the mansions built during that era still stand, with the largest of them now being used by St. Joseph's College. Magnificent Morgan stained-glass windows were installed in the elegant Presbyterian church one passes en route.

One also crosses leafy Cumberland Street in Fort Greene, where our prim, echt American poet, Marianne Moore, passed most of her New York days, probably one reason she became a baseball fan of the now-vanished local Brooklyn Dodgers. You remember, I'm sure, the beautiful extension of those great trees on Portland Avenue, where your friends, the three J's (James, Jim, and Jay) live? But since we always visit them via taxi, we miss the beauty of the charming vicinity of their domicile, which includes historic Fort Greene Park, topped by its great lighthouse-like monument to the soldiers who died in the Revolutionary War (many of them buried beneath it), the last structure built by that great American architect Stanford White, shortly before he was murdered by his rival in a Mayerling-like love triangle that shook America in the early 1900s.

Actually, this area was the site of the Battle of Long Island, which the Americans were losing to superior British forces, until Washington's silent, secret transfer of his troops to Manhattan and thence on to New Jersey under cover of the moon one crucial night changed the course of that War. So there are many ghosts to contend with!

Ah, the walk also stirred up a strange mix of memories from

differing parts of my own past life. Somehow, in an almost premonitory way, I had become somewhat familiar with this section of Brooklyn, long before I ever thought I would one day work and live here or that I would ever become a Brooklynite!

Actually, my first taste of Brooklyn was the section just north of Clinton Hill, namely Williamsburg (a separate city until the middle of the 19th century), where during World War II I visited the Berezow family, whom I got to know through Rachel, wife of the great critic Joseph Frank—friends from my pre-war University of Wisconsin days in Madison. Rachel had wanted me to look them up when I was stationed briefly in Manhattan for that ASTP training period, where I was able to advance my knowledge of German language and culture. (The acronym, ASTP, stands for Army Special Training Program.) One of Rachel's younger sisters, Freda, though not as beautiful as Rachel, turned out to be a charming, cultivated, and well-read young woman, studiously pursuing music composition with a son-in-law of Schoenberg, Felix Greissle, I believe, at the 92nd Street Y Music School. Perhaps more about Freda later. I think she became somewhat smitten around that time with yours truly. And definitely more about Joe Frank and Rachel.

But, to get back to Fort Greene and Clinton Hill memories stirred up by my walk, there was first the Brooklyn Academy of Music itself (now better known by its acronym, BAM), certainly the major lure to Brooklyn of any follower of the performing arts. Because of my early interest in modern dance, I couldn't help but go to one or two concerts there while in New York. Indeed, it was at the Academy where I first saw Sophie Maslow and Pearl Lang and their modern dance companies (but oddly enough, not Anna Sokolow, under whom I was fated to work not too many years later in my first Broadway show.) Both were originally solo dancers with Martha Graham. Geraldine had by then put me in touch with still another, perhaps less noted Grahamite, Jane McClean, with whom I took my first lessons in modern dance during that special training period with the Army, as I told you in one of my first letters, although I had been "exposed" to modern dance theory, etc., at the University of Wisconsin through lectures given by that noted pioneer Margaret d'Houbler, who notoriously used an authentic, dangling skeleton in teaching movement technique!

We ASTP students were stationed at City University, about 20 blocks north of Columbia University, and had days packed full of classes in German history, geography, science, and culture and heavy sessions in conversational exercises. I remember especially a tall, quite beautiful blond teacher, Fräulein Trude Günther, who would end each of her classes with a famous quote from Goethe or Schiller or Rilke, such as that great moment in Faust when the bargain is made between the Devil and *Faust*: "*verweile doch, du bist so schőn.*" And there was also a wonderful, bubbly, plump historian who had fun demonstrating differences between German and Yiddish expressions, and whose name slips my mind, I'm sorry to say—he was a brilliant, important scholar (as were most of the instructors we had).

Yet, heavy as our schedule was, we were given great freedom at night to roam Manhattan, Brooklyn, and the closer suburbs. It was during that period, for example, that I had some of my first important concert and opera going experiences. (Though my first baptism of live opera was *Lohengrin*, performed in the huge Milwaukee Auditorium, to which I hitchhiked, 200 miles from tiny New London, at the age of 12 to attend—and thereby almost gave my mother a nervous breakdown! More on that period later.)

As luck would have it, one of my fellow students in ASTP had studied with Hindemith before enlisting in the Army, and he guided me to some first-rate concerts. That was how I got to hear the debut recital of the fabulous mezzo-soprano Jennie Tourel at Town Hall—a gala night, indeed. Being in uniform, we were given the best seats, which made it all the more exciting: I could see these great artists in close-up, as it were, something much rarer in those early pre-TV days. Now, close-ups of artists have become almost a commonplace, which sometimes, with singers, makes for some excruciating moments. Then, it was all glamour for me. Not only was Tourel a superb recitalist, she was perhaps even more important for introducing us to works from the Russian repertoire seldom heard in America back in those days (and still not often enough, in spite of the incredibly busy Gergiev). She also provided my first hearing of anything from Rossini's miraculous *Cenerentola*.

There were numerous other highlights from my visits during that period to the Metropolitan Opera, but I'll only note a few, since I know opera to be something of a bane to you. Perhaps the most perfect overall performance I took in, in that period, was Debussy's *Pelléas et Mélisande*, with the divine, petite Brazilian soprano Bidu Sayao and baritone Martial Singher in the leads; Lawrence Tibbett (whom I had heard and seen in the movies) as the villain, Golaud; and the superb, impeccable, penguin-shaped Pierre Monteux conducting. Yes, Nina, you would have loved that performance, since Bidu Sayao was totally believable as Mélisande; Singher was young and handsome enough then for Pelléas; and Tibbett, though older, still in good voice, looked the part of Golaud and certainly endowed it with just enough melodrama to maintain and enhance the fairy tale atmosphere earlier established by the two leads. You would not have had to close your eyes at that opera performance, as you say you usually do when fat sopranos and diminutive tenors take over an Italian opera.

Similarly, I'm sure you would also have enjoyed the remarkable *Marriage of Figaro* I heard next at the Met, with that charismatic *basso cantante* Ezio Pinzo as Figaro and Sayao again as a most delectable Susanna. But you probably would have had trouble with the Met's *Tristan und Isolde* performed during this same period with Melchior's and Helen Traubel's large stomachs constantly bumping into each other during that long love duet in Act II, magnificent as their singing was.

This Hindemith pupil, whose name, alas, I've also forgotten, happened to be a true poetry lover as well and took me to hear Muriel Rukuyser, to whom I believe he was related, read from her unusual—especially in those days—social protest poetry at the New York Public Library, which, remember, dear Nina, many years later honored you with its Golden Lion Award! Wasn't that the occasion that led to our own romantic union? Remember how we had met again at a party Harriet Zinnes had given to welcome her son's Romanian fiancée on her first visit to New York? And how Harriet invited you so that the guest of honor would have at least one Romanian-speaking person to converse with? (And you brought along another, the enigmatic painter, Yvonne Hasan.)

True, I had met you a few years earlier through our other mutual poet friend, Daniela Gioseffi; and it was Daniela who introduced me originally to Harriet. Then you and I lost touch with one another until the Harriet party. Remember also, how, before leaving it, you asked me if I had a tuxedo, and, if so, could I be your escort to this formal dinner presentation of the Golden Lion Awards, one of which you were scheduled to receive that evening. So I said that yes, of course I have a tuxedo, a must for the many concerts and special affairs I had to attend as part of my role as Executive Director of the orchestra (I think my title had finally reached that level at that point in our lives!). And added that if I were free, yes, I'd be delighted to take you. Well, it did happen, but perhaps we ought to go into more reminder details about that in another letter? Especially about that amazing postal card with twin dachshunds I sent you from Paris a month or so later, and which apparently set your heart aflutter? For it reminded you of your late pet dachshund, Molpedo. And up to that point, you had never told me a word about dear Molpedo.

Jumping Jehosophat! How did I bounce to 42nd Street, Bryant Park, in Manhattan from Clinton Hill, Brooklyn, and then end up at the salon of Mme. Zinnes across the street from MOMA? How amazingly and unpredictably intertwined memories become! But to get back to a few other very early Brooklyn experiences in the Fort Greene and Clinton Hill enclave. There was an interesting visit I paid in the late Forties to a Center for the Handicapped located only a block or so from what became my residence many years later on Lafayette Avenue. I had gone there with one of the strangest characters I got to know during those first years in Manhattan, a certain Wayne Murray (aka Birnbaum), who had been hired to produce an entertainment for the poor, suffering residents of that home, using their fellow inmates in the show he had concocted for them. What

I seem to remember most vividly at this great distance in time was the strange grayness of the street and the neighborhood, which, in retrospect, must have been due to the weather, a late spring dusk, probably the aftermath of a dank morning and a day deprived of sunshine, but which at that time I thought was gray, sad, uninviting Brooklyn! (A grayness remarkably resonant with that which greeted me in my Paris winter described several letters back.) Am I confusing you, dear Nina? Be patient...

But once we got into the building, and Wayne had plunged into a dress rehearsal with its inmate trainees, the lights went on both literally and emotionally. It was amazing what good performances he was able to draw forth from these untrained, inexperienced, handicapped amateurs. And how uplifting this was to us, the spectators. It also increased my respect for the often *louche* Mr. Murray: here he showed real depth and understanding of human nature, and a patience and generosity of spirit I had never before suspected him capable of (nor saw much demonstration of later on). Actually, it turned out to be a lesson for me as well, a key to working with an unfamiliar group of people or a different ethnic community that I was able to use in opening up doors to community concerts and events I was destined to produce at least thirty years later, when I was running the Brooklyn Philharmonic. Its headquarters, ironically enough, were located only several blocks from the site of Wayne's Center in the Fort Greene district of Brooklyn, in the shadow of that tall, obelisk-like Soldiers Monument mentioned earlier.

One example of this application was to take place another several blocks in the other direction within the oddly eclectic 19th century Episcopal Cathedral on Washington Avenue, off of Fulton Street. We were scheduled to do a short jazz Black Mass intro to a cut version of the *Messiah* there with the Brooklyn Philharmonic and invited topnotch jazz and percussion artists, all under the baton of the then quite young Cuban-born Tania León, the talented offspring of an incredible melange of black, Hispanic, and Chinese blood.

The church was interesting not only architecturally but even more so, perhaps, because it and its membership had also been the focal point and headquarters of a distinguished line of African Americans who had been freed several generations before the Civil War and had maintained a kind of patrician presence in that border-land between the Clinton Hill, Fort Greene, and Bedford Stuyvesant areas of Brooklyn ever since (and still do, to a lesser extent, I've been told, by community leaders).

Then there was another early Brooklyn experience, that is, before starting to come out daily for my part-time job at the Brooklyn Philharmonic and my eventual move to Brooklyn. That was my first attendance of an event in the large Opera House of the Academy. Those dance recitals I had gone to several years earlier all took place in the more intimate side theater to the big hall, the then very beautifully appointed Music Hall, with its exquisite wooden paneling, now, for better or worse, transmuted into the BAM Rose Cinema complex.

Moreover, this symphony/opera gala was also for me one of those remarkable "preview" or "prelude" events one occasionally ex-periences in this remarkable sojourn of ours on earth. Little did I dream when I went that night in 1948 to hear a new orchestra be-ing conducted by a Viennese refugee, Herbert Zipper, husband of my charming dance or movement instructor at Piscator's Work-shop, namely, the oddly christened Trudl Dubsky-Zipper, and end-ed perched high up in the second balcony of that historic hall, that merely seven or eight years later I'd be making hundreds of visits to this very same hall and would get to know it inside out, above and below. Yes, that night I do remember experiencing a strange excite-ment, which I then attributed variously to maybe the hubbub in the Academy, the musical highlights of the program, or to sitting so high up in the second balcony of this enormous edifice yet feeling so close to the stage. But perhaps there was also a mysterious, premonitional sensing of the future?

In any case, the shrewd Herr Zipper was smart enough to feature a work that New Yorkers had been dying to hear for more than fifty years, the last two acts of Verdi's heretofore un-performed-in-NYC masterpiece of an epic opera, *Don Carlo*. It boasted a stellar cast, of whom I remember now only the then young Regina Resnick, and, of course, the wondrous music which Zipper managed to evoke from what must have been a pick-up orchestra of some of New York's best freelancers, the pros and cons of dealing with I was to endure for many a year starting, as I said, about seven or eight years later.

Interestingly enough—to back up my previous hypothetical premonitional feeling—this orchestra was in a sense a preview guinea pig of the kind of orchestra out of which the Brooklyn Philharmonic was ultimately to develop. Unfortunately for Maestro Zipper, his poor wife Trudl, and the then well-meaning Director of the Brooklyn Academy of Music, Julius Bloom, this big, highly hyped event, so loaded with hope for the future, turned out to be a one-night stand. (I believe the Zippers ended up in the suburban Chicago area, where he taught in some music college and did occasional conducting.)

Also, as I later learned, this was not the first time Bloom had failed to establish a resident orchestra at the Academy. His most notorious default was the ill-fated, two-year stint with the great Sir Thomas Beecham during World War II, to which the old trouper was said to have contributed so much time, élan, and enthusiasm, that it should have worked. But probably the main lesson that Bloom could have garnered from that experience, as well as the Zipper one following it, not to mention several lesser let-downs even before the Beecham debacle, was that if one seriously expected such a commitment to take root, one had to come in armed with enough money to maintain a footing for several years. Only that way could one have time to find and develop the contacts and wherewithal to establish a strong Board of Directors, ideally guided and goaded by an imaginative, aggressive manager or executive, one foresighted enough to plant strong roots in the community and with the gumption to launch several seasons of programs. Then the obvious next step would be to find ways of building an audience for these events, at the same time financing the inevitable deficits of each concert (since non-profit programs like these very rarely, if ever, pay for themselves) through fundraising from both the private and public spheres.

No, my dear, not-too-worldly poet, I won't go on further into all that, since you probably already know more about how those worlds function from your brief years with me than you ever really wanted to, although, of course, you entered my life just as I was leaving that world. In any event, why repeat myself, since the gist of it is covered quite thoroughly in my book, *How Music Grew in Brooklyn: A Biography of the Brooklyn Philharmonic Orchestra*, the writing of which you suffered through during the first years of our marriage, and parts of which you read several times and enjoyed more than I expected?

Let's move on to other realms and other memories. Except to note that now you can understand why my memories of those earlier sallies into the "wilds of Brooklyn" often carry special overtones of auxiliary experiences to come.

Perhaps I also need a little snooze just to recover my equilibrium. In the next letter, I'll move back to the present to cover something you missed while you were away. *À tout à l'heure!*

Nostalgically,
M.

January 23, 2005

Chère Nina:

As I promised, a little news about the here and now, while you were off on your latest excursion to Romania, alas, the first such trip I could not share with you. I am saddened to have to report that your favorite little store on the Island, the fish market run by that odd Korean couple on our sole Main Street, was closed down by the inexorable bureaucracy that handles mercantile rentals on Roosevelt Island. So no more of their fresh fish, crabs, or mussels. Or their pungent Korean kim chi. Or their wonderfully prepared garlics. Nor my running out for last-minute fruit and vegetable supplements to our supermarket shopping at Gristedes.

What is worse is that the demise of this invaluable little store follows, as you know, the unfair shutting down of the pizza/pasta parlor next door to it, and the earlier lockout of that charming little Spanish bakery directly across the street from our one restaurant on the Island. I was so upset by all this that I wrote the following letter while you were gone to the editor of *The Wire*, the Island newspaper (which he published!). Here goes:

To the Editor:

Your last issue of The WIRE, brimful of news, facts, and theories about the woeful status of Roosevelt Island, proves without a shadow of doubt that the domino theory, to which our nearsighted management has subscribed since at least the late '90s, has taken over lock, stock, and barrel, ad infinitum, in the endless Cold War between the still behind-the-scenes powers that be and our poor, suffering Lilliputian public.

Most recently, and seemingly without warning, overnight capitulation of the totally defenseless Fresh Fish Store was the last to date in the domino series of falling Little Retailers on Main Street. The poor owners probably didn't even know at first what was hitting them, for the Brobdingnags forgot to bring along interpreters. Now we're all forced to fish elsewhere.

Before that domino fell, it was the friendly Pizza Parlor, with its quaint old wicker chairs, and once-convenient, adjacent space where one could get a great pasta carbonara, not to mention sizzling hotdogs and pizza when on the run, that was struck down. And some time before that cruel day of the domino, there befell the demise of the Little Bakery, which once offered an amazing array of fresh baked breads, cakes, flans, and auxiliary coffees and sweets when the Trellis Restaurant was too busy to pour, or didn't care. Maybe they needed a Don Quixote referee? (Note the possible ethnic overtones in each of these topplings.)

Years ago, when I first landed on this historic Island, there was even a tiny shoe-repair store to smell up the street. (Was it the first domino to fall?) So we were deprived of that convenient nook and now have to voyage to Queens or the Lower East Side for that lowly service. More recently, there was the scare over the card shop (still another ethnicity?). By some miracle, it has so far escaped the deluge, but will it be next? Or will that honor go to the quaint hardware/video potpourri emporium across the street, where one—with a little guidance and patience, to be sure—can find almost anything. Questioned about a possible pending debacle there, too, the poor Korean mistress of that pyramidal space could not hide her anxiety.

So one wonders. Why were these small, feisty enterprises denied occasional supportive loans or little subsidies when they were so needed, but that Gulliver-sized monster, Gristede's, was granted two years' tax abatement? For, as our Cassandra voiced Ellen Polivy has pointed out in your worthy gazette, "the residents of this Island are captives to the Decision Makers."

One could go on and explore the domino theory in reverse as it applies to the incremental rise of one new construction site after another, gobbling up ball fields, tennis courts, children's playgrounds, heavenly greenery, and surreptitious squirrel refuges: selfish enterprises granted scandalous bargain deals to erect huge, demonic dominos—octagons, hexagons, and flagrant trapezoids which, once filled, will so over-populate this poor little Island that we'll have to swim to Manhattan.

But I leave all that to the prescient spirit of Jonathan Swift. Consult his Tale of a Tub.

I signed it: "aka/Dr. Samuel Johnson & Mr. Houyhnhnm"!

*

So what do you think of this little satirical excursion, my dear? I'm sure you share these sentiments and laments over the loss of these little, so-convenient stores on Main Street. Shall we give it to the Island's archives? In retrospect, I wonder how many readers of that Island paper have ever read *Gulliver's Travels*? If not, they'll probably be stymied when they bump into Brobdingnab in the middle of the letter or Mr. Houyhnhnm at the end. More might have a nodding acquaintance with Dr. Samuel Johnson, one hopes!

In any case, it's unlikely the letter will do any good. One has to know someone in power to even begin to influence any kind of civic policy. Though now that we have a Democratic governor in Albany, there is cause for some optimism. As you may recall, Roosevelt Island is technically part of the State of New York, not the City, when it comes to legal and property matters. Already, I understand that the new appointee to head the Island is making encouraging waves. He will be calling a sort of town meeting in the church basement next door to us next week to which everyone on the Island is invited. Do you think you'll be strong enough to attend? It might give you a better idea of how democracy can still function at the grassroots level in good old America. (Though surely you've seen samples of these type of meetings on TV.) Besides, it is said that this new man will listen to, and may even heed, the *vox populi*.

But perhaps I should first let you catch up with your mail? Do pen me a note soon.

Curiously,

M.

April 17, 2005

Dear inquisitive Nina:

En route to a meeting with Charles Prince recently, I was walking across town on 57th Street to his temporary abode near Eighth Avenue, when I noticed that the venerable old Automat on 57th Street near Sixth Avenue had been demolished. True, it had already lost a lot of its old historic feeling when it was turned into a poor imitation of the popular old Stage Delicatessen on Seventh Avenue (still extant, I think), but the framework of its original, commercial pre-World War II version of Art Deco remained standing somewhat intact. So, since one could still see the skeleton, even though one lamented the changes, one could, to a degree, take it in stride. Yet to see that gaping hole there now was quite disturbing.

The skeleton had given way to the ghost of that once-vibrant cafeteria and incomparable Midtown meeting place. It brought back a flood of memories, especially of the period when I lived nearby for awhile, on West 58th Street during the Fifties, but also of even earlier bargain lunches gobbled down there in a hurry when in that area; of counting nickels to put in the various slots of the wall machines; or sometimes simply taking refuge in the Automat from a sudden rainfall or snow squall.

More important were the many memories of friends one used to meet there for a bite, for a catch-up on what was new, "any scandal on the Rialto?" It was, after all, an ideal, cheap, fairly comfortable, unpretentious space where one could visit with one's friends and/or relatives in Midtown, in the post-Depression era—and feel somewhat neutral about it all. Well-dressed, affluent business people could be eating or drinking next to you on one side of your table, while not so well-clad poorer specimens might be just as busy lunching or munching on the other side. Or simply biding their time: a sort of Midtown resting place.

Occasionally, stray celebrities might be seen downing quick coffees, cocoas, or teas. Even though one wasn't always quite sure who the imbibers were, somehow they often looked familiar—had one seen them in old movies, or on more recent TV shows? Then there were what looked like various circles or cliques of professional friends and colleagues who would almost always be there in mid or late afternoons more busy talking away than eating and drinking.

For example, I recall seeing from time to time the French-American composer Edgar Varèse holding forth at a table with what seemed to be colleague composer friends. However, much as I would have liked to go over and ask him a few questions about his unique music, I could never quite notch up enough nerve to do so. Why not, I wonder? For he was most friendly with his disciples; at least I presume that's who they were. Of course, years later, when I was running things at the Brooklyn orchestra, I would not have hesitated. In fact, I probably would have walked over and invited him to be the guest of honor on one of our programs, and would feature one or more of his works on our Moderns series—which we ultimately did anyway—but, alas, by that time he had passed away.

I believe I remember also seeing Alexander Calder there once with Varèse and his circle. Some time later, I was to find out why. Calder was doing the sets for *Happy as Larry*, my first Broadway show. It turned out that he was a great friend of Burgess Meredith, the director and star of that ill-fated play. And so, one day, all of us in the cast were invited up to Calder's studio, which was in a building a few doors east of the Automat on the southwest corner of 57th and 6th. This was a huge, cast-iron studio building, probably originally some sort of factory. It had been taken over largely by artists (and various kinds of artisans), during the late Forties and early Fifties, who needed high-ceilinged, large-sized studios, for what must have been bargain rentals.

Later, in that same building, I often visited the Hungarian-born (half Polish?) painter, Sari Dienes. (Her always-absent husband was a distinguished Hungarian refugee mathematician she left behind in England when she emigrated to the USA.) Her enormous studio on the fourth floor was a haven for poets and musicians as well as painters and sculptors. Among other things, Sari had been "into" making rubbings of sewer caps or covers when I first met her.

107

But more interesting were the beautiful sets of rubbings she had made years earlier of American Indian rock paintings and Rocky Mountain scratchings, which she had been commissioned to record by the federal government. She was also an inveterate collector of found objects, carrying on the Dada tradition, although her initial training and first important master teacher in Europe was Ozenfant. Her earlier works reflected that, and touches of it would sometimes creep into her later works. (To my eyes, often a welcome, unexpected relief.)

Around that time, she underwent a phase of constructing table sculptures and odd facades by artfully stacking and joining various shaped and colored bottles into various and sundry shaped forms. A number of these constructions were given to Merce Cunningham and John Cage, with whom she usually spent a great deal of time every summer in the New Jersey country colony where they all had bought little houses—I used to nickname them dachas—from which they would sally forth in their frequent mushroom hunts (or binges?).

It was also through Sari that I met the amazing Mura Dehn, whose amateur documentary films of early jazz dancing at the Savoy in Harlem now constitute an invaluable record of African American ballroom's shifting styles, all before rock and roll. Charleston. Big Apple. Jitterbug. And countless variations thereof. But more about Mura another time. (These pioneer films can be seen nowadays at the Lincoln Center Library for the Performing Arts.)

To get back to 57th Street... I shall never forget one mild dusk evening in early summer, when on the northwest corner of 57th and Sixth Avenue, then occupied by the famed Buckingham Drug Store (kitty-corner to the Calder-Dienes studio building), everyone suddenly stopped to look and see a beautiful woman emerge from the pharmacy en route to being picked up by a chauffeur and taken to some sort of affair—it was the divine Garbo. Chicly attired in a long black mink coat, she was made up to kill. This, in contrast to the times I used to pass her walking in Central Park, wearing old European-style dresses, or unpressed lanky slacks, all topped off by her unique floppy hat. And definitely no makeup. So that, as she would walk swiftly by (and she had a quite masculine stride), most people would fail to recognize her. This time, however, it was quite different, that night at the corner. Well accoutred, and with makeup, as I noted, and no doubt realizing she had an audience she could not escape, that profile extraordinaire lit up the sky, as it were. People literally stopped in their tracks, in awe. Then, as her limousine drew away, all fell back into normality. The effect of that remarkable face.

A friend of Tomi's—remember, the woman who wrote the kangaroo story—had been in the cast of *A Streetcar Named Desire*, in a small role, that of a friend of Stella's. This actress described how at the opening-night party for that play, to which Garbo had come, the same sort of thing happened when she left. Everyone stopped what he or she was doing or saying and ran to the window to gaze at her as she left, in awe similar to the Buckingham crowd above.

I don't think I ever told that story to Sari; it probably would not have interested her. In fact, she would most likely have mocked those people: "Oh, those simple, innocent, unsophisticated Americans. So childish they are!" For although she was too smart ever to really knock America, which, after all, had given her a pretty good welcome and far more scope to work than more insular England—at least the English artistic world of that period—she was also too much absorbed in her own self to grant even Garbo a nod.

Actually, as I look back on the scene now, I see that Sari acted at times as though she were the Queen of 57th Street, though there was another painter/photographer from England who shared that huge apartment with her, the lovely Stella Snead, who probably more deserved the title! But I hardly got to know Stella then; she seemed somehow to fade into the background as Sari held forth, when I would visit them in those days. It was only much later, when I ran into Stella again at one of Harriet Zinnes's somewhat rambunctious gatherings, that I belatedly realized what a rare person I had missed back then. Not only was Stella a great photographer—especially in recording the magic of India—she was, and is, until quite recently (I seem to have lost track of her), a highly respected pioneer surrealist painter! But, of course, with Sari at that time, surrealism was already old hat and all kinds of bottles were certainly "in."

Yes, memory, as you know, is often cruelly selective. For example, I believe that Sari thought more of Mura Dehn at that time than of Stella. Perhaps that was because they were so totally different. Of course, Mura, being a dancer and filmmaker, posed no challenge to Sari's position in the art world. Though, amazingly enough, I cannot remember now for sure just when and how I first met the ubiquitously cheerful Sari. I think it may have been while we were both out shopping in her neighborhood (for I was living then on West 58th Street). She invited me up to her phantasmagoria place for a drink, and I was won over. After all, it was the closest thing to the Paris atmosphere that I had had to forsake much too soon.

My wise, patient Muse, doesn't this last tale only emphasize anew how important timing is in all these matters? For example, in our own *rencontres*, why did meeting you again at Mme. Zinnes's fateful (for us) party precipitate our future relationship, when our two earlier meetings with Daniela hadn't? Surely it had nothing to do with our mutual horoscopes, though could it possibly have had something to do with the way the Parcae pulled their strings that season?

In any case, hoping these little stories have taken your mind off your poor teeth and suffering gums, as you recover from that horribly painful, but also painfully necessary, dental work you have just been through, I remain

your, as ever, faithful scribe,

M.

August 23, 2005

Ma très chère Nina:

As I noted in my last letter, Memory is often so arbitrary, and her *raisonnement* always so inscrutable, so unpredictable. Indeed, isn't

Memory one of the Muses? No? Wait a minute, while I look it up in my ancient *Smaller Classical Dictionary*. No, Memory, or Mnemosyne, her real name, was actually the Mother of all the Nine Muses (via Zeus, of course!). And daughter of Uranus... Or the Gertrude Stein/Virgil Thomson *Mother of Us All*?

In any case, my dear human Muse (were you the tenth daughter?), why do I suddenly recall that Easter (or post-Easter) gathering at the suburban home of one of your close Romanian friends, Ilinca, in upper New Jersey opposite the Riverdale area of Manhattan, during which I was introduced to many of her friends (most of whom were also your friends), as well as to the Romanian Easter ritual of colored eggs and lamb dishes (exotically delicious), plus a few folk songs and special holiday greetings? Where, as you'll surely recall, I met and talked to many of your friends, or friends of your hostess, one after another, most of whom, by the way, I never saw again? Fortunately, they all loved you so much that that love spilled over into their warm acceptance of me, a total stranger—and an American, to boot.

But what I remember most strikingly was the entrance shortly before we were about to sit down at long last to the dinner itself (by which time I had grown quite hungry from all the false starts and delays) of the son of an old, very special friend of yours from Romania whom you hadn't seen for years, and, in any case, did not know as well as his father. The son, when introduced to me, went into some kind of a trance: he was convinced that I was his and his father's old friend, Ali, sitting there, brought back to life! He claimed that I looked exactly like him, Ali, your late, beloved husband! After which, most of the others in the room looked me over again, and startlingly all agreed with him. But, of course, you had never mistaken me for Ali; nor did I look like any of the photos of him you had ever shown me. (Was this a Kafka moment in my life?)

On the contrary, haven't I, indeed, from the very start of our relationship, always encouraged you to maintain a full, comfortable place in your consciousness for your still-faithful, undying love for Ali? Haven't I constantly tried to be myself, totally different from him (as surely I am), certainly never even dreaming of competing with or "replacing" him?

What is also rather peculiar about this strange "penumbra" episode (could we call it that?) that seemed to fall over me, is why, prior to this young man's bizarre expostulation, none of the others present had even hazarded to note that maybe you were attracted to me because I might have resembled Ali slightly? But no, not a single person did so. Nor do I recall any of those people or others I met at the many other parties with your various cliques and collections of Romanian friends and fans that preceded this one, or followed it, ever remarking that maybe you saw something of Ali in me.

That is why the whole event still strikes me as singular. Could it have been due to the lighting in that house at that particular moment, falling on me at some strange angle; or could it have been whatever I may have been wearing, or the way I turned my head when I looked back at that man, the son of your dear friend, which resulted in this strange misidentification? Who can tell? But then, come to think of it, life is full of these, what we might call implausible, "mistakes." Could these, in turn, be related to what Proust deliciouly termed *memoire involontaire*?

Or to what Walter Benjamin, with more German pedantry, called the "phenomenon of aura" in a diary comment after seeing an unusually beautiful Cezanne in a museum: "It seemed to me that to the extent that one grasps a painting, one does not in any way enter into its space, rather, this space thrusts itself forward, especially in various very specific spots. It opens up to us in corners and angles in which we believe we can localize crucial experiences of the past; there is something inexplicably familiar about these spots." So that there may have been something "inexplicably familiar" in the penumbra that enveloped me that afternoon in the wilds of New Jersey, in an American house, and in a totally different era, whose spots seemed familiar to your friend's son and somehow homogenized into a portrait of your Ali superimposed upon poor, innocent me!

Parallel-wise, this odd phenomenon of the "inexplicably familiar" may also help explain those occasions when we are introduced to someone we are sure is a total stranger and yet are uncomfortably aware that on a certain level we're positive we have seen him or her somewhere before. Or perhaps this "involuntary memory" may also account for those other occasions when we take a completely arbitrary and unfair dislike to a person we are meeting for the first time, or to someone we observe across the aisle in the subway, or whom we bump into in a milling crowd in the theater?

Could we say he or she was enveloped by the wrong "spots"? Or that his or her spots unfairly drew up from the well of our memory some person in our past whom we never liked, or even hated? Or could all this be a manifestation of something even more unconscious and/or primitive, dredging memory from the womb of time?

But am I veering too far off course? Am I making too much of that particular incident? Let me know your "take" on all this possible "much ado about nothing."

In any case, surely these pranks of memory, these crossings of seemingly unrelated phenomena or experiences, these uncoverings of the unconscious levels of existence, these juxtapositions of opposites, are no strangers to you, my divine Poet! For, aren't they all basically the raw material of your art, your own profession? Didn't T. S. Eliot say in his pathbreaking essay on the Metaphysical Poets that "the poet's mind must be constantly amalgamating disparate experience," after quoting earlier that incredible passage from Dr. Johnson about such poets, how with them "the most heterogeneous ideas are yoked by violence together?" Years later, Eliot himself exemplified both "mottos" quite startlingly in "Burnt Norton," the first of his *Four Quartets*, with his reworking of Mallarmé's "*tonnere et rubis aux moyeux*" into "Garlic and sapphires in the mud/ Clot the bedded axle tree."

Don't you, too—doesn't any lively, resourceful poet—draw substance and challenge from such a process, or what one could also call an intellectual sleight of hand? Of course, poets have been doing this down through the ages, but clothing it in different language. For what could be less metaphysical than Shakespeare's Hotspur saying "I'd rather live with cheese and garlic/ in a Windmill"? Could that wonderful moment have somehow stuck in Eliot's mind, and unconsciouly got joined, and then transposed, into his "garlic and sapphires" image? But, of course, one never knows just where these joinings of disparate experiences start and/or end, or how they might resolve themselves into a revelatory new fusion. Thus, one wonders where Eliot came up with the idea of mud in this context. Well, it turns out that in another sonnet, "Le Tombeau de Charles Baudelaire," Mallarmé uses the phrase "*boue et rubis!*" Possible influence? Maybe, maybe not. And we could go on and on that way. Such "word" pursuits remind one of the commentaries upon commentaries the Rabbis made on scripture in their talmudic writings. Or Carlyle's philological suppositions in Lecture I of his *Heroes and Hero Worship*. Not to mention diverting, diversionary Derrida! Who, by the way, my dear, has written beautifully, and quite lucidly, on Celan and Levinas.

Speaking of strange happenings, I've just returned from a much-needed break (for you, as well?), during which I managed to glance through the latest issue of the *Times Literary Supplement* while simultaneously quaffing down a cup of tea with, appropriately, an English muffin. To my amazement, I opened to a review of an odd, new book called *Coconut Chaos*, about what happened to those of Captain Bligh's mutineers from the Bounty who, after their revolt, remained on Pitcairn Island. According to this writer, the whole event hung on the hook of Fletcher Christian's stealing a coconut, which some very serious historians actually hypothesize about as triggering that ill-fated mutiny. The author, a certain Ms. Diana Souhami, employs a simplifed version of Chaos Theory, which helps her explain, for example, "how a woman sneezing in China can cause a snowstorm in Alaska!" So that, according to the reviewer, Ms. Souhami becomes obsessed with what she calls "tangential associations" (letter written earlier!).

While I don't see you or me falling for her weird-sounding Chaos Theory, I rather like Souhami's phrasing—"tangential associations"—partly because it conveniently codifies for me the way these memories I'm writing up for you seem to be emerging from the well of my memory. It also helps account for that extra frisson we experience when a particularly fruitful or stunningly unexpected association hits the cerebellum. Or the awe we sense when an Eliot or a John Donne or a Hopkins strikes a metaphysical discord in a poem that produces in turn a brand new harmonium of understanding. Ironically enough, the "game" aspect of this series of tangential associations, juxtapositions, yokings of dialectical opposites, et al, is jovially exemplified in one of your favorite amusements, that "classic" surrealist game of "Exquisite Corpse." (Not to mention the byways, midways, and alleyways of John Cage's virtuoso use of the I Ching, which probably influenced more composers than was good for them!)

And, of course, contradictions, juxtapositions, clashings of opposites and contrarieties, antitheses and scaling the antipodes, obverse/inverse functions and contrapuntal techniques, all play similar roles in painting, sculpture, music, cinema, and the other arts. Isn't this especially true in our modern, eclectic era, when we have such a wealth of masterpieces to bounce off from? Look what Stravinsky drew out of Pergolesi or what Bach made out of a Vivaldi concerto. Or Picasso's coming back again and again with "deconstructions" of Velasquez, Rembrandt, Ingres, Goya, and other painters who inspired him! Or Luciano Berio's unexpectedly convincing "reconstruction" of Schubert's skeleton of a tenth symphony. Or the unexpected things our own dear, recently deceased Lukas Foss did to Scarlatti, Bach, and Handel in his *Baroque Variations*?

Coincidentally, I recently ran into some fascinating examples of this process in paintings on view at the Neue Galerie, that transformed mansion on the corner of 86th and Fifth Avenue now redone most elegantly (with good use of the Lauder family's cosmetic industry profits) and converted into a small museum (another variation?) devoted primarily to Austrian and German Expressionist art. That's where I had so much wanted you to join me before their most recent offering closed last week, a small, compact exhibit, with very few dull paintings, and not too many rooms to plow through, the kind of art show you prefer.

It featured about nine or ten great Van Gogh paintings and four or five of his etchings, along with obvious, and sometimes not so obvious, reworkings, variations, and transformations of them by leading German and Austrian Expressionists of the generation after Van Gogh, members of Die Brücke and the Blaue Reiter groups: Kandinsky, Nolde, Franz Marc, Kokoschka, Schiele, Schmitt Rotluff, and others, including your favorite, Klee. Their frequent take-offs from, and variations on, Van Gogh's use of color were, for the most part, wildly well done. Sometimes Kandinsky's most shocking, and purposely chosen, wrong colors for a peasant hovel in his early, expressionistic paintings, for example, would totally transform the canvas into a magic otherland, a deconstruction process clearly anticipating his later abstract, what I suppose one might call "particle," style. Or that Schmitt Rotluff self-portrait with so many layers of paint superimposed in thick Van Gogh strokes and fulsome dabs of paint that we have a hard time finding the painter himself on his canvas.

Whew! Time for another break, I fear. Scotch, perhaps? Or high tea? I really didn't expect to get carried away by so much theorizing. I know how much you prefer that I report concrete happenings, a specific life experience, or even on occasion a little "school for scandal." In the next letter, I promise that I'll go back to exhuming more moments from my past which might help you better understand me and my present self. Nevertheless, am I not also quite plausibly "me" in these musings, analyses, and commentaries? After all, they're mine. Didn't Valéry's M. Teste once call out *"Je suis chez moi"* ("I'm at home in myself")? Do reassure me...

Your devoted scribe, as ever,

M.

P.S. Apropos that last "me" point, I just ran across these lines by that often-incisive young poet, Franz Wright, son of the poet James Wright, whom I once met chez Daniela, you may recall: "It's true I write about myself. Who else do I know so well?"

December 13, 2005

My dear Muse, *chère Mme. Cassian*:

Isn't life constantly amazing? Here I was, in the last letter, going into a kind of exegesis about elements of chance, and concluding with an evocation of that supreme surrealist game, Exquisite Corpse, when, upon checking the quotes from T.S. Eliot and Mallarmé I used earlier in that letter, I found among my older books a slender volume I forgot I still possessed, an excellent Forties critique of middle-period Eliot, called *Four Quartets Rehearsed*, just what I needed to save me an extra trip to the big Circulation Library on 40th and Fifth Avenue. But, to my enormous surprise, and as an extra unexpected bonus, hidden within it were two delicately inscribed note pages, still in near-perfect condition, dating back to my post-war stay in Paris, penned by my beloved Swiss doctor Toni, handwriting so tiny I can hardly make it out now. Handwriting I haven't seen in over sixty years! (Because, alas, we lost touch after her move to Ann Arbor, Michigan, and her subsequent marriage to the eminent American literary critic, Professor Austin Warren.)

That, in itself, was enough to send memory tremors zigzagging through my body. I can just visualize Toni now seated at her desk in her special, private room in the cloister of St. Germain des Prés, next to the equisite wooden, medieval statue of the virgin she found in Bretagne, writing these two little poems, in quatrains of rhymed iambic verse in German, plus, in English, her humble excuse for them: "Can't help it. The thing just kept dripping out of my pencil. So, to get rid of it, off it goes through a pneumatic tube towards the fresh air of the University City. (By the way, thanks for the cash.) T." Fabulous! What could be more concrete, my dear Muse?

And, of course, you are acquainted with that wonderful system of pneumatiques that made Paris so unique—a sort of telephonic instant mail system! (Now superseded by our Email!) Interestingly enough, Toni entitled the longer poem "We, very old" and the shorter, "Variation on the theme, the sea is falling from the heavens." And what does she mean by University City? Well, remember, that was the place where we soldiers soon due to be demobilized were housed during my stay in Paris, but I think I used the French name, *Cité Universitaire* (located on the then-outer rim of Paris), when I described it to you in an earlier letter. That modern model city, where I was lucky enough to be assigned to a building designed by Le Corbusier. Where the paint hadn't yet begun to peel.

But the really strange thing about the discovery is this: I barely remember receiving that utterly charming note, so typical of Toni's verbal style, and her unexpected poems. It's the latter which I find particularly odd, since I do recall having tried so often before that—with no luck—to get her to show me samples of her book of poetry that she precociously wrote before she was twenty and which was, I think, published in Zurich. But I could never get her to do so; she'd always find one minor excuse or another to put it off. In fact, Toni never showed me any of her literary work but this. Nor did I ever see any sampling of the report she was writing up on the medical research she was doing at her Paris clinic. Yet how could I possibly have forgotten something I regarded as so important? Which brings to mind the wise Montaigne asking how we should regard those books we have read but have totally forgotten. And then takes forgetfulness one step further when he admits that people may sometimes quote passages to him from his own *Essays* that he can't recall having written! (Has this been a Montaigne moment for me?)

By now, you must be dying to see the poems. I'll xerox a copy and forward them to you or bring them along next weekend. In the meantime, here are the two quatrains of the shorter poem, "The sea is falling from the heavens," for the record, first in German:

> Vom Himmel auf die Erde fällt das Meer
> Die dürstend es und ewig neu empfängt.
> Sie atmet wieder, noch von Wassern schwer
> Und frei von Sonnenglut die sie bedrängt.
>
> Noch legt sich schon ein warm begieriger Wind
> Die Wasser heischend spielen um sie her

Und auf zum Himmel steigt, zumal gelind
Und immer dringender zurück das Meer.

And now, how's this for a quick English prose version of her German quatrains: "The Sea is falling from Heaven down to Earth, which thirstily and eternally welcomes it anew. She breathes again, still heavy with water, but free of the Sun's heat which oppresses her. Then a warm, eager Wind settles in and playfully but gently coaxes the waters up to Heaven, while smoothly but ever urgently pressing back the Sea."

Come to think of it, dear Nina, did you ever write any poems *auf Deutsch* or *en Français* in your earlier experimental periods? As you no doubt recall, both Rilke and Eliot wrote some pretty good poems in French. Celan wrote equally well in German, French, and Romanian, didn't he? And I'm sure there were many others.

To get back to those pages from Toni: why, or how, did they find their way into that particular book of mine? They certainly had nothing to do with either Eliot or his *Four Quartets*! Moreover, I'm pretty sure that I must have put them in there, not she. Or did I loan the book to her? She had been curious about Eliot. (Can anyone ever be truly sure about such matters?) I reckon that I probably picked up the little book itself—by the way, quite well written—in one of those second-hand book stalls near St. Martin's in London, adjacent to Trafalgar Square, during one of my short weekend-pass trips to London from Winchester, before being shipped off to Belgium, fortunately late enough, as I think I've written you earlier, to get in on only the tail end of the Battle of the Bulge. (But when we were shipped, they didn't know that the end of that battle was so near, nor did we! We were obviously being sent to bolster whatever forces were engaged in driving the Germans out of the muddy, bloody mess that was then the Ardennes.)

Or could it be that I acquired the book on the short return trip I made to England about midway through my nine-month stay in Paris?

I remember growing quite nostalgic around that time for

119

a taste of good old England. Besides, I had always said to myself I must see England in peacetime. And since, I reasoned, I would most likely be returning to America directly from Paris, it could be years before I'd see England again. (Alas, how true was that premonition.) So, I took leave of Paris for a week; it must have been in April, Eliot's "cruellest month" but a good time to visit, when there would be fewer tourists.

I needn't have worried: England's tourism had only just barely begun to start up by then. The country was too poor, too exhausted from the long, gruelling war to focus on reviving tourism. Not a major priority, to be sure. There were more important things crying out to be done. Remember that amusing British film with Maggie Smith about early ration-bound, post-war England—I think it was called *A Catered Affair*—in which someone's pet pig (and what a cute, intelligent pig it was) had to be sacrificed for a banquet the town was giving visiting bigwigs from the Labor regime? It was said that the pig was quite tasty and saved the day for the revellers! Prior to that, Ms. Smith used to run around the house, screaming, "Look, it's doing its business!"

So, having no agency to plot my trip, nor friends or relatives in England to house or advise me, I ended up devising my own personal itinerary. I decided that my first stop after London should be that wonderful old town in southern England where I had been stationed, Winchester, with its charming medieval High Street, its frequent touches of nobility—after all, it had been the capital of England long before London—and, above all, its solemn, magnificent cathedral, with its solid, thick walled basic Norman/Anglo Saxon structure (a variation of late Romanesque), dating from the late 11th, early 12th centuries, its crucial first builders having come from Normandy, I believe.

But not being an expert in architectural history and cathedral terminology, these are only the basic facts, as I recall. Back then in wartime, there were ministers and local architecture buffs who would identify and proudly point out various parts of the cathedral to us soldiers, acting, in effect, as amateur guides. Like almost all the cathedrals I was about to visit, Winchester had its many changes, accretions, added decorative motifs, revisions, and reconstructions over the centuries. Thus we were told that the original Norman structure was later topped by early Gothic features, such as transepts with enormous rib vaults, in the use of which Winchester supposedly led the way in England, and above all by its absolutely awesome, gloriously vaulted and proportioned High Gothic nave, begun in 1291, making it the longest Gothic church in Europe. Only St. Peter's in Rome is longer, they added.

On a smaller, more human scale, the cathedral also has a number of beautiful chantry chapels where Winchester's famed and often formidable bishops, including William of Wykeham, who supervised and paid for out of his own pocket the important 14th-century reconstruction work that was so badly needed, are buried. As are Izaak Walton and Jane Austen. But what I liked best and remember most, and the features that would probably please you most, my dear, are the beautiful choir stalls (where we soldiers used to be seated), with their extraordinary canopies, carved with flowers and plants, owls and monkeys, dragons, knights in armor, and green men! And done, of course, in a variety of late Gothic and early Renaissance styles. However motley the styles, they enchanted. And the overall structure is overwhelming: the cathedral stands like a huge crouching lion on the plain.

As soldiers, we knew it well, since we were required to attend services there every Sunday of our term at that base, unless we were lucky enough to draw a weekend furlough in London, where there was still the danger of V-rockets hitting the city. Still, in those days, as part of its goodwill policy, the Army wanted us to do as the English do. And, for the most part, I think our division comported itself quite well in Winchester. We fraternized freely: we were certainly partied enough! But what a hard time we had navigating the pitch black, curving streets at night in our return to barracks during those mandatory, strictly enforced blackouts. After all, Winchester is not that far from the English Channel.

Of course, that was where I first heard that ingenuous response one still gets in England (as I described in an earlier letter), when, after asking directions, and being given a winding, roundabout route, usually delivered at high speed in a thick, local, often incomprehensible accent, one is cheerfully reassured: "Yes, just follow your nose: you cawn't miss it!"

You can well imagine the waves of nostalgia I felt during this short, one-day visit as I relived my memories of comfortable, delightful Winchester, with its still-imposing cathedral, and a little stop-off at my favorite High Street pub before leaving town for the rest of my self-concocted itinerary. I wondered how the cathedrals I was going to visit could possibly compete for grandeur with this masterpiece I had in a sense lived with through those long, dark months (it was late fall, 1945, after all) of my Army stint in that beloved town.

You must be itching to interrupt at this point, and to ask: "Why this extreme love for, and curiosity about, cathedrals, those huge religious monuments? I always thought you were an agnostic, or possibly a Spinoza/Goethe kind of pantheist." Well, first of all, there is the immediate retort that if one were to follow the spurious line of reasoning that one needs to be religious to appreciate religious art, one would have to rule out over a thousand years of madonnas and other biblically inspired paintings, plus a large proportion of Western art. Besides, on a quick, almost crude level, one could also respond: Does one have to be a Buddhist to appreciate the countless, marvelous Buddha statues and paintings covering even more centuries? Or have to be a Mughal descendant to marvel at the Taj Mahal? And, my dear, what about your own early Romanian religious art, with its remarkable icons? Surely superior to most of its 19th- and 20th-century secular efforts.

Second, as to just how much the credential or "spiritual" level is involved versus the "aesthetic"—I'll try to go into that delicate, vexing matter at some point soon, particularly after guiding you through a few more cathedrals on my special route. But to hold for the moment, let me quote a most apropos opinion from Léon Brunschwig's *Introduction à la vie de l'esprit*: "A cathedral is a work of art when one no longer sees in it the instrument of salvation, the center of social life in a city; for the believer who sees it another way it is something else..." And perhaps even more pertinent: "The cathedrals of the Middle Ages...may have for some people a certain charm their authors did not suspect." Except that it must be far more than charm. For it is generally agreed that these extraordinary structures achieved an expressive power not seen in Western architecture since "the glory that was Greece and the grandeur that was Rome"! Finally, I might venture to add that, as with the glories of music, as you well know, it's never easy to translate those of architecture into words.

That sort of takes care of the aesthetic realm for the moment, don't you think? As for the "spiritual side," let me quote another sage, Erwin Panofsky, from one of his writings on the relationship between Gothic architecture and Scholasticism: "Both mysticism and nominalism end up with abolishing the borderline between the finite and the infinite." Could we say that in a Gothic cathedral all things merge? And that perhaps this interlude was serving as a stepping-off point to my future? Of course, one could counter all this with Abraham Heschel's eloquent summation of the Jewish position: "The Sabbaths are our great cathedrals; and our Holy of Holies is a shrine that neither the Romans nor the Germans were able to burn."

So getting back to the more immediate, mundane (?) reason for the English trip, I suppose I might add that I was disappointingly starved for that kind of architectural stimulus, because of the lottery of chance which shaped the path my Division took in Germany, and the locations of our stopovers, and the like; for there was nothing architecturally comparable or noteworthy left in the particular German towns we practically coasted through in our almost uninterrupted drive from the Ardennes to Leipzig and the Elbe. Thus, after we crossed the Rhine at Remagen, our route took us from considerably south of Cologne, with its great Dom (which, however, I heard had been seriously damaged when we bombed that city), along a latitude about equally north of Bamberg and the Baroque cathedrals of Bavaria (which had suffered much less damage, they said, and which I would have loved to have even glimpsed), as we moved eastward through Marburg and the Thüringian Wald, until we met the

Russians on the Elbe some twenty or so kilometers east of Leipzig. Thus there were also no major cities, other than Kassel, which we passed through. But even if there had been, there certainly wouldn't have been time to get out and ogle bombed-out buildings during that almost-mad push through Deutschland! Besides, we'd have run the risk of being shot at by stay-behind soldiers or resister snipers. All we could do was smell the terrain, squint at the ruins, and plow on. (Though I'll never forget that single cross hanging at a "cross-eyed angle" on the lonely, sole remaining wall of a certain bombed office building we passed as we traversed Kassel, nowadays probably most noted for its biannual Modern Art Dokumenta showings.)

Fortunately, Bach's St. Thomas Church in Leipzig had escaped bombing, but then it's hardly a standard cathedral, though it is surely the greatest "cathedral of music" ever. And since our division had settled in nearby Weissenfels until the Allies unwisely turned over the entire province of Saxony to the Russians, I was able to visit that great church several times. But what an irony it was, in approaching Bach's workplace, to find scattered on the sidewalks, streets, and byways of Leipzig hundreds of music scores (in various states of being, broken, split, ripped, burned, but, amazingly, more often than not in nearly 100 percent shape!) not only of Bach, but also of Schubert and most of the major composers published by C. F. Peters, whose headquarters, of course, were located in Leipzig. These scores had apparently been blown about after one or more of Peters's warehouses had been hit. (And the Germans had not yet begun one of their proverbially thorough cleanups there. I actually picked up at least five or six volumes of piano and vocal music still in near-perfect shape, some of which you and I have played from.) Luckily, Leipzig suffered nowhere near the damage of not-too-distant Dresden, about which I had already heard horrifying tales of woe, including reports of people having been buried up to their necks in the fallout from the bombing, from a goodly number of traumatized survivors and refugees of that terrible hellfire, who had settled temporarily in Weissenfels.

Later, in Bremen, where I was stationed next, and longer than anywhere else in Germany, the venerable, old Dom was badly damaged and had to be rebuilt. The only major historic structure left with some semblance of style and dignity was the sturdy, old, ruddy brick Rathaus, wounded, but still standing. And left totally undamaged, was a perky, plump, stone elephant in Bremen's small but delightful downtown municipal park, which I used to walk through on my way to see Ingeborg, but more about her and my stint on AFN (Armed Forces Network) Radio Bremen, in a future letter. Remind me...

And what about the great cathedrals of France—Amiens, Chartres, Rouen, Reims, and Notre Dame? Ah, that's still another story. Also to come later, I hope, a report on several fairy-tale-like chateaux encountered en route. (As in Marcel Carné's haunting film, *Les Visiteurs du Soir* with Arletty and those beautiful Prévert songs.) Oddly enough, I didn't get to do any French sight-seeing of that kind until after my English jaunt. There was still so much to see, and do, in Paris and its near environs.

This, too, is very important: English cathedrals, though of course enormously influenced by the ubiquitous European medieval style of cathedral building (it was, after all, a truly international style), present quite another phenomenon from the French or the German, or, for that matter, the Italian and Spanish variants. Maybe because at the height of this extraordinary furor of cathedral building (a big subject in itself, which I'd better leave to the art historians), England, as one critic put it, "had shown a tendency toward splendid isolation," and was in some respects a distant island. Well, whatever the reasons, the English certainly were not shy in developing their own signature art of cathedral building, though always open to, and subject to, changes coming in from the continent. Also, while an amateur like me might easily confuse one French cathedral with another, they being often very similar to the non-expert, each English cathedral I got to visit turned out to be quite stubbornly different from its brother (or sister)!

Looking this matter up in the library the other day to make sure I'm not talking out of my hat, dear Nina, I was pleased to find that it was generally agreed that English cathedrals definitely show more stylistic variations than the French, providing, as one historian remarked, "an unending variety of pleasure." In any case, these buildings are certainly the supreme expression of English architecture.

But it's time to return to the specifics of my vaunted English pilgrimage, don't you think? The next cathedral was in Salisbury, a totally different structure and a completely different experience from revisiting my "old friend" in Winchester—and only about thirty miles west of it. Truly another world! And who could say which was greater? Not I; I wouldn't even dare try to set one such wonder against the other. Besides which, I couldn't possibly be a fair judge, since I had only little more than half a day to give to Salisbury, whereas I used to see, when stationed there, at least part of the exterior of Winchester almost every morning for several months when I woke up: it had become a vital part of my first English landscape.

In any case, Salisbury's construction history was much simpler than Winchester's, and, accordingly, it presents a more unified appearance. They say that work on Salisbury was started about thirty or forty years after Winchester, and, unlike any other English cathedral, it was built without interruption (1220-1258). Its basic structure is compact, calm, and austere: a perfect monument to 13th-Century Early English Gothic. Moreover, the buildings of the close around it are also in the same style, giving an extraordinary sense of unity to the whole complex. The striking nave may seem longer than it actually is because of the way it blends right into the choir loft and thus extends to the end of the building. But it is probably the addition less than one hundred years later of its tall steeple, the loftiest in England, that makes Salisbury unique. Also, the fact that the cathedral sits on a flat space, a meadow-like open lawn, and is not hugged by the town, as is Winchester, nor on higher ground than the rest of the town, as I was soon to find out Lincoln Cathedral is, adds to its distinctiveness.

But, you might be wondering, how does Salisbury compare with either of these? That, I'm afraid, is a matter of taste. For example, that great eccentric, good old Ruskin, with his *Seven Lamps of Architecture* and other eloquent writings on English art, did not like Salisbury at all! While I'm pretty sure that you, dear Nina, would disagree with him. You'd probably love its almost fairy tale-like aura, never belied by its elegantly vigorous frame or the pure line of its uncluttered interior. Fortunately, Constable's famous sketches and paintings of Salisbury have immortalized it for a much larger audience than any other English cathedral except perhaps St. Paul's in London. Then there's also Turner's totally different view of the cathedral as seen through the windows of its cloister, an unusually humble and intimate work for a Turner.

However, what was not pointed out to me back then by any of the Salisbury locals during my lonely visit—strangely, I recall encountering hardly anyone else sightseeing at the cathedral that day—is that more ancient, prehistoric Stonehenge lay not too far distant, and I could probably have easily taken a bus to visit it! Imagine what a sobering and instructive contrast in ages, but possible similarity in vision, that would have afforded me. What a pity I missed that chance.

After the miracle of Salisbury, my next stop was Bath, with its large array of baths and mineral waters (naturally!), magnificent curved hotel structures, the still impressive, solemn Royal Crescent, and the overall imposing landscaping. But before going on further about my impressions of that long ago day, ought I not remind you that you, yourself, may very well have seen and experienced more of this unique city than I? For, back in the early nineties, didn't Brenda Walker, who had just translated and published some of your poems, schedule several poetry readings for you in southern England, one of which was at Bath, a few years before I met you? And isn't it possible that you may have stayed in one of its elegant hotels?

So, as you will no doubt recall, Bath had been the spa and pleasure city of Great Britain since the first centuries A.D. when those ubiquitous Romans occupied it, and, among other pastimes, indulged themselves in Bath's thermal springs (the only ones in the United Kingdom, I understand). What they probably didn't tell you is that, unfortunately, what once must have been some imposing Roman structures gradually fell apart after several centuries of changing hands from one conqueror to another. The old Anglo-Saxon poem "The Ruin" presumably describes Bath toward the end of that period: "Wondrous is this wall stone/ broken by fate, the castles have decayed / the work of giants is crumbling."

I don't know how and when Bath pulled itself back together, but it seems that by the 18th century this incredible place had regained its stature and become a popular resort for royalty, the aristocracy, and the nouveau riche, as well as a haven for gamblers, rakes, and beautiful bawds (the Las Vegas of its day?). In between taking the waters, I'm sure there was always plenty going on, on various and sundry levels, as evidenced by the marvelously ribald satires of Hogarth, Rowlandson, and other etcher/painters of that era. And didn't Jane Austen live there or nearby for awhile? Or at least must have visited it? Isn't *Northanger Abbey* set near Bath, with much of the action in Bath itself? And parts of other novels of hers as well?

No wonder Bath still exudes a kind of imperial splendor, even though, with the hardships of war and the declining English economy, much of what I saw back then was already looking rather shabby. Almost every building needed cleaning and/or a painting, if not a propping up. I'll wager it was quite prettified, and no doubt much of it rebuilt, by the time you visited Bath in the nineties.

Of course, strictly speaking, Bath didn't quite belong on this tour, since it boasts no great cathedral, only its not inconsiderable Bath Abbey, which certainly looked like a cathedral to me. Apparently, the term cathedral cannot be applied unless it serves as the administrative head of the church's districting (dioceses). Thus I think that nearby Wells Cathedral must have won out over Bath for that title. In any case, Bath Abbey's soaring high vaults in wholly Perpendicular style (the last phase of Gothic architecture in England) make for a fine, solid structure that has its own dignity and charm.

But we were told that behind this admirable abbey church lies a sad story of earlier destroyed abbeys and a half-finished church, which had been built on the foundations of Bath's original Norman church and was devastated by fire in 1137. Yet work on it continued, and a first revised version was completed about twenty years later. Then that structure began to fall into near ruin. And over the years a series of attempts were made to rebuild, although the new church was not finished until a few years before Henry VIII dissolved the monasteries. Fortunately, Bath's Abbey was spared; it is said that Queen Elizabeth I herself promoted its restoration. *Quelle histoire!*

Minor changes and adumbrations followed in the 17th and 18th centuries. Yet with all these ups and downs, it's a wonder that this Abbey/church survived at all and looks as good as it does today! Indeed, I rather think you'd probably prefer it to its larger, more monumental sisters coming up on my tour ahead. In any case, I soon bade Bath a fond farewell.

Exhausted from those three intense days of "cathedralizing," I was appalled to find that the next leg of my journey—from Bath to Lincoln—presented great logistical problems. Getting as far as Bath had been a cinch: there was a simple, almost straight, southwest headed, but direct, train line from London to Winchester to Salisbury, then a slight veering northwest to Bath. But there was certainly no easy diagonal or even curved connection directly to Lincoln. The trip involved several shifts and transfers from train routes to bus routes, and back and forth again, in order to make the right connections. It all took much longer than expected.

I didn't reach Lincoln until about 8:00 p.m., with the sun already set and near darkness setting in. That was a bad time, as you can well imagine, to arrive midweek, unscheduled, in a small English town, now rather undistinguished except for its most impressive cathedral. People looked at me askance: "What's this sole American soldier (I still wore the uniform) doing here at this ungodly hour?" was what I read on some of their faces. "What do we do with him? The only hotel is filled to the brim. And he doesn't seem to know anyone in town. Not a soldier looking for an old girlfriend. Oh dear, oh dear." Well, somehow or other a room was found. And since there wasn't a single open restaurant in sight, my kind, puzzled landlady for the night came to the rescue with a sandwich she had concocted and, of course, English tea.

All this notwithstanding, I awoke somewhat refreshed and found my way easily, unguided, up a wide hill or mount, to the massive, magnificent west front entrance to Lincoln Cathedral with its three enormous towers, dominating the town and the countryside around it for several miles. It is more bulky and solid looking even than Winchester because of its more square like proportions and design, though Winchester has a longer nave. Work on Lincoln seems to have been started about the same time as Winchester, in the last decade of the 12th century, after a fire, as in Bath, had burned down its first attempt at a cathedral. Then the next version was destroyed by an earthquake forty years later! What amazing histories these buildings have; what ups and downs; disasters; fires; political changes—but behind them all lay always the stubborn will of the people to build, complete, and cherish their own holy home.

We must not forget that for medieval man, a cathedral was indeed God's house on earth. Hence one was ennobled simply to step inside it! Moreover, their spiritual guides taught that beautiful buildings had the power to improve us morally and spiritually, that mankind could be more effectively shaped by architecture than by scripture.

Its third version, I was told by the friendly Dean within, was begun by St. Hugh of Lincoln, who hailed from Avalon, France, and whose rebuilding began at the east end of the cathedral with the apse and five small radiating chapels. This drama is beautifully rendered, I subsequently discovered, in a long Latin poem, probably composed around the time St. Hugh was canonized. I quote: "With wonderful art he built the work that is the cathedral church....The old mass of masonry was completely demolished and a new one rose. Its state as it rose fitly expressed the form of a cross. By arduous labour its three parts are integrated into one. The very solid mass of the foundation goes up from the middle, the wall carries the roof high in the air. The foundation is thus buried in the bowels of the earth, but wall and roof lie open, as with proud boldness the wall soars up towards the clouds, and the roof towards the stars."

Said to be the first to create a building in which the pointed arch was allowed full play, St. Hugh was probably responsible for the earliest form of pure English Gothic. For which he was memorialized in Lincoln's renowned rose window, called "The Dean's Eye," and the great Angel Choir with its beautifully carved angels in the spandrels, each playing a different musical instrument. The famous Lincoln Imp—perhaps first carved as a mischievous joke by one of the sculptors—is to be found here amongst the angels! A juxtaposition, which, my dear, exhausted lady, I'm sure would have tickled your "fantasy" and helped you proceed through the rest of the cathedral had you been there with me to experience it.

The central nave followed, with its soaring columns of Purbeck marble (black stonework), still in Early English Gothic style, but subsequent additions and accretions were made in the most advanced styles of their periods—pointed arches, flying buttresses, and the ribbed vaulting which allowed for the creation of Lincoln's enormous windows.

It struck me then that perhaps in order to compensate for all this grandeur, and to bring the cathedral down closer to the common man, the builders and/or the reigning clergy came up with colorful names for many of the cathedral's features, as we have seen, including its huge bells, one of which was called Great Tom of Lincoln, while the window opposite the Dean's Eye was known as the Bishop's Eye. Though, of course, we must remember that all those saints, prophets, and religious symbols were undoubtedly quite familiar and meaningful to even the most illiterate parishioner: as I noted earlier, the Bible was made more alive to them by their cathedral. May I call on again that poem attributed to St. Hugh to reinforce this argument? "The two windows that offer a circular light are the two Eyes of the cathedral; and rightly the greater of these is seen to be the bishop and the lesser the dean. For north represents the devil, and south the Holy Spirit and it is in these directions that the two Eyes look. The bishop faces the south in order to invite in, and the dean the north in order to avoid; the one takes care to be saved, the other takes care not to perish. With these eyes the Cathedral's face is on the watch for the candelabra of heaven and the darkness of Lethe."

Our modern Dean, in a more materialistic spirit, did not fail to boast to us that Lincoln's third tower is the tallest medieval tower in Europe, and also, for good measure, higher than the Great Pyramid of Giza! The beautiful geometrical, flowing tracery of its late 13th-century windows, however, and the 14th-century, eccentric Gothic choir stalls counteract what could otherwise have been heavy or lugubrious. So in spite of this glorious *embarras de richesses*, you end up simply overwhelmed by this enormous, yet prodigious, building, the largest in Lincolnshire.

Ruskin, who didn't like Salisbury, as I mentioned above, held that "the cathedral of Lincoln is out and out the most precious piece of architecture in the British Isles and roughly speaking worth any two other cathedrals we have." Well, I wouldn't go quite so far as that, but on the other hand, it would be presumptuous of me not to heed that master's words. After all, Ruskin certainly knew his cathedrals far more intimately than I or, indeed, almost anyone else, except possibly a Pevsner or a Panofsky. Assuredly, no one else has written as sensitively as he about them. Ruskin practically lived in the Cathedral of Amiens when he wrote his great study of that masterpiece, the one Proust was proud to translate into French, work on which no doubt vastly influenced Proust's own nascent, developing writing style. In fact, it's a good thing I wrote my above impressions of Lincoln first before recalling him and finding that extraordinary St. Hugh poem. Otherwise I'd have been humbled out of expressing any opinion of my own: one must bow before the divine Ruskin and that architectural genius, St. Hugh!

But just what does Ruskin mean by a "precious" piece of architecture? Does he, as I suspect he does, embrace both the spiritual and aesthetic realms with that multivalent word precious? Because when I tried earlier in this letter to answer your hypothetical query as to whether religion fitted into my seeming need to "experience" a cathedral, I think it safe to say that it goes back to that Spinoza/Goethe affiliation you suspected in me, that need to confront the unknowable. Yes, we all have some spiritual hunger; we all question why we're planted on this planet. As that crabby German dramatist,

Grabbe, had his Hannibal say: *"wir sind einmal in der Welt hineinge-worfen, wie können wir heraus?"* Moreover, with most of us, especially in our Western secular age, that mystery seems to be more easily approached via the aesthetic path. Didn't our ancestors instinctively realize this, which may be why they built their "palaces in time," as someone, I can't remember who, put it?

Come to think of it, my dear, isn't the great Mayan pyramid at Chichen Itza, which you so much admire and which you watched me climb when we visited Yucatan, also primarily a temple? And what about that incredible melange of temples and related buildings that is Angkor Vat in Cambodia, or Luxor in Egypt? Or---? One could go on and on. In any event, ascending Chichen Itza's pyramid can give you some of the same inner thrill as that experienced in traversing the nave of a cathedral: one thrives on the inner splendor of such physical-neural excitation. Of course, there are other paths and perhaps less noble choices, such as that famed skeptic's (possibly Voltaire?) caustic put down of "churches built to please the priests."

Perhaps I should call on Proust via Ruskin for some more refined illumination here? I ran across a book the other day on the shelves at the 40th Street branch of the New York Public Library with translations into English of Proust's prefaces and notes to his two translations of Ruskin into French. An extraordinary, most timely find, especially just now as I'm writing this missive to you. One of the two is Ruskin's famed book about the Amiens Cathedral—*La Bible d'Amiens*! Here's what Proust noted in his preface to that revelatory opus (in English translation, of course): "But it is time to arrive at what Ruskin refers to in particular as the Bible of Amiens, the West Porch....This porch of Amiens is not merely a stone book, a stone Bible. It is `the Bible' in stone. When you see the Western facade of Amiens for the first time, blue in the mist, brilliant in the morning, sunsoaked and sumptuously gilded in the afternoon, rosy and already softly nocturnal at sunset....where this creation of man reveals its very life, yet which nature has reclaimed by enveloping it, a cathedral, whose life, like that of the earth in its double revolution, unfolds down the centuries while renewing itself and maturing daily—at that moment, if you release it from the changing colors in which nature clothes it, you will receive in front of this facade a confused but powerful impression."

Then Proust almost outdoes Ruskin and our earlier architect/poet St. Hugh in this eloquent evocation (with echoes also of Shakespeare's great "this England" soliloquy): "Upon seeing this colossal and lacelike swarming of human figures in stone which rise skyward, holding their crosses in their hands, their banderoles or scepters, this company of saints, these generations of prophets, this train of apostles, this host of kings, this line of sinners, this assembly of judges, this flight of angels, side by side, one above the other, standing near the door and looking down at the city from the niches high above or from the ledge of the even higher galleries, receiving only the vague and dazzled looks of the men at the foot of the towers, you feel, at the ringing out of the bells, and no doubt in the warmth of your emotion, that this magnificent pile, motionless and thrilling, is a stirring sight. But a cathedral is not only a beauty to be felt. Even if it is no longer for you a teaching to be followed, it is at least still a book to be understood. The porch of a Gothic cathedral, and more particularly the porch of Amiens, the Gothic cathedral par excellence, is the Bible."

And then Proust goes on to quote specific passages from Ruskin that show how Ruskin personalized every inch of that extraordinary West Porch. I wish he had done the same for Lincoln!

Certainly, among other feelings and sensations, at least you know you've been through history, as well as touched the lives of the saints, as you emerge exhausted from Lincoln Cathedral. Though the dull, gray, dismal buildings that greeted me that day (at least that's what I felt over sixty years ago) and which seem to make up the town's center were a far cry from what must have been a busy, thriving, important mid-England commercial and cultural center back in the Middle Ages.

You breathe a questioning sigh as you turn back for a last look: does anyone still believe in gargoyles anymore (or their progeny)? Ho hum! It's time to return to earth and resume our special tour...

You'll be relieved to know, dear Nina, that getting from Lincoln to York was, thank God, much less difficult than on that previous expedition, getting to Lincoln itself. (Ah, how easily we evoke Him!) While York is certainly a more exciting town than modern Lincoln, its Cathedral, also known as the York Minster, physically imposing as it is, disappoints. I was told that it was started a little later than Lincoln and Winchester, which would account perhaps for its greater proportion of Early English Gothic, though, in this case, more influenced by the French version. Remarkably, while it took two-and-one-half centuries to build, and spans all phases of English Gothic, the York Minster seems to show more stylistic unity than any of the other cathedrals I visited except for Salisbury. Yet even with the stunning High Gothic Perpendicular nave, the great painted glass East window, or *grisaille* (said to rank with Chartres), the intricately carved canopy stalls and other felicities, and its enormous bulk—we visitors were proudly informed that it was the biggest cathedral in England after St. Paul's, making it the largest of all English Gothic cathedrals— somehow I didn't warm to this building as I did to the others on the trip. Maybe that's why? Too big? Too pretentious? (To be fair to York, I learned, in consulting the library, that it was given a most extensive cathedral rescue operation in the late 1960s and early 1970s, and probably looks much better today than it did back then!)

Actually, I must confess, dear Nina, I found the town, with its abundant remainders of a Roman wall and other structures, more interesting. After all, York is one of the most ancient sites in England, rivalling Winchester in the south. It was the chief military town of the Romans in 2nd-century Britain; Constantine was proclaimed Caesar here in 306 A.D. Medieval chroniclers claimed that it was founded about the time "King David ruled Judea"! (Did they make this claim before or after their horrific Massacre of the Jews in 1190?)

Still, it's a shame that we weren't able during the Lancaster Poetry Festival, where you read about seven years ago, to have slipped away cross-country for a day to "do" not too distant York together. You may also recall that York was where Auden came from, not to mention the perhaps overly maligned

Richard the Third. So why not say Amen and Godspeed to York with Auden's wry comment:

> Cathedrals,
> Luxury liners laden with souls,
> Holding to the East their hulls of stone.

But was I tiring of cathedrals already? Had I satiated those various hungers of mine in trying to cram too much viewing into too short a time? No, I don't think so. Because I found the last one on my junket, Ely (if we don't count St. Paul's in London as the final specimen), quite fascinating, and, in a strangely different way, fulfilling. It was certainly the most eccentric, and hence probably most "English" of the six I had seen. Indeed, with its large, sprawling, castellated exterior rising out of the flatlands of the surrounding Fens, from some vantage points, Ely looks more like a monastery, or even a castle—or, possibly, in the old days before those marshes were drained, a great ship—than a temple of worship. Parts of it are individually somewhat gauche. Maybe it's that combination, and the occasional clash of effects, that makes it ultimately homely and endearing?

They say that work on Ely was begun possibly even before Winchester and Lincoln, or certainly around the same time, for we know that one of the first builders of Winchester was called to Ely to help with its presbytery. In any case, to my unpracticed eye the basic overall structure looks more purely Norman than the other cathedrals I visited, especially its very long nave, which has been hardly altered down through the years, although Ely, like all our cathedrals, suffered many later accretions, some of which looked as though they could have been influenced by Lincoln. For example, I found the high, narrow entrance to the extraordinarily wide Lady Chapel, and the chapel itself, with its decorated arcades and quaint, nodding ogees, quite stunning. But surely the crowning glory of Ely is the famed Octagon lantern tower built to replace the original Norman tower which collapsed in the early 14th century; they say there's nothing more daring engineer-wise in Gothic architecture. You see eight huge pillars, from which the marvelous lantern rises up on corner posts, each cut from a massive oak tree. Even you, my dear Nina, would be dazzled.

Finally, the setting of this large cathedral and its various annexes in that small rural town of Ely, magically placed above the Fens—almost like a movie set for a medieval village—gives it a very special presence. It seems truly rooted there.

Enfin, back to London and St. Paul's for a glorious feast finale to this, my surely unique, Cathedral Pilgrimage: a long-looked-forward-to moment. For, we soldiers hadn't been permitted near St. Paul's on those London jaunts we took before leaving England for France, Belgium, and then Germany. It was considered too dangerous, what with the bombings, and V rockets probably aimed at it—at what some people called the big Onion! But to begin to describe St. Paul's to you now, my dear (and the original church upon which it was built) would surely be too much cathedral for one letter, don't you think? I've probably already more than over-stretched your patience on that score, what with all my preceding glosses and side comments. Besides, it's a totally different kind of cathedral, of much later provenance than any other on the trip. I'll just note that fortunately there was a little time left while in London, after going through St. Paul's (a viewing which hardly sufficed, and which I would have to make up for many years later), and before returning to Paris, for me to quick-visit a few of the less damaged Wren churches in the adjacent area.

Of course, you might well ask at this point: "What about beautiful Westminster? How could you skip that?" Well, because I had already visited that more accessible cathedral several times during my weekend "pass" trips to London before going overseas. As to those remarkable Wren gems which are, of course, a total contrast to the cathedrals, it wasn't until years later, on a much-too-belated return trip to London, that I was able at last to get a real taste of Wren, what with the tremendous repairs, restoration work, and tidying up that was done in London during that long interlude between my visits. But here again, dear Nina, you probably would have felt more at home in a Wren church than in any cathedral, no matter how great or significant.

Well, it was an exhausting, but exhilarating, eight or nine days—my Cathedral Tour—overall, a wonderful experience. It turned out to be a near-perfect itinerary for me, providing a most unusual and variegated panorama of England, touching highways and byways that most tourists would never see—and not just churches! Indeed, when I got back to Paris, several of my friends there suggested that I try to market the idea for others to pursue!

Well, first of all, as you well know, Nina, I'm not a business man. Moreover, I wasn't then, and certainly am not now, really that knowledgeable about the cathedrals of England, nor their multifold environs. Experts might wonder why I left out Wells, or Canterbury, or Durham, for example, or whichever other cathedral might happen to be that person's favorite! Or why I didn't start with York and move south? And so on...

Actually, the only thing I sometimes regret is that I didn't make this quixotic journey as a civilian rather than ostensibly as a soldier, for, though recently discharged, I still wore my uniform, thinking it might have some advantages in dealing with my English hosts. In a few instances, it probably did. However, it may have been more challenging to experience firsthand British treatment of a non-military American immediately after the War, a species about whom, I understand, there was often a wide range of opinion in and around highly civilized Great Britain back in cold, gray 1946.

In any event, I was luckily spared anything negative of that nature. On the contrary, I was treated like a special guest, maybe because the English are so proud of their cathedrals and were pleased that a lonely American would want to partake of that heritage? Indeed, some were probably amused at the sight of this odd duck of an American soldier coming back to their cherished land (whose integrity many felt we Americans had violated in occupying some of their homes, villages, parks, estates, and farms) just to see their old cathedrals. Though, again, others may even have admired me for doing so. Hence it was with some regret that I said goodbye to England again, took the train to Dover, and crossed that challenging Channel—this time, rather turbulent, as I recall—and jumped on another train that sped me back to *la vie en rose* in Paris. Or was it really so? Sometimes, on rainy wintry days, it seemed more like *une vie en gris.* But then there were all those wonderful Juan Gris paintings on Gertrude Stein's walls for me to drop in on and stare at, so many friends to revisit, Toni to court, plays to see, classes to take, lectures to hear, galleries galore, delicious meals to devour—a city to adore.

I shouldn't complain. Here I was, still a totally free being, out of the Army, moving easily between countries, satisfying my varied hungers for the various arts, going back to a pleasant temporary home where, indeed, I did feel pretty much "at home." But, for the first time since my demobilization, and probably because this English interruption of my French idyll brought back intimations of my own mortality, I began to wonder what really was home for me (that is, other than my interior, *je suis moi-même*)?

Thus, there were moments when I questioned what I was doing there, in Paris, in France, a stranger in another land. Was I seeing these people through colored glasses? Weren't they being perhaps too friendly at times, too hospitable? Did they all really love America and Americans so much? Why were so many so anxious to assure me that they had been part of the *Résistance*? Whereas in Germany nobody knew what the Nazis had been doing, here in France everyone presumably challenged the Nazis the best he or she could, some even achieving "hero" rank—or so they said. Almost everyone claimed to have been either part of the Resistance or having worked with it!

Yet, as I think back upon that time, why were certain subjects not brought up in conversation unless I raised them? Even with Gertrude and Alice! For example, I could never get these two to focus on what happened to them during the Occupation, or what they thought of the Holocaust. Or how they were able to survive so comfortably in the Vichy area throughout the war? They complained only of shortages; but not a word was uttered about people being transported out of France under their very noses. Nor any acknowledgement that they were lucky to have escaped that same fate. Nor how. Nor who shielded them? Who kept them from being hauled away? During such talks, it often felt eerily as if they had long ago convinced themselves they weren't Jewish at all. (It's only in the last few years that we have learned the truth about their fate, and how compromised in some respects they were.)

Of course, I myself was still woefully innocent of the scope of these matters; the full horror of which was yet to be revealed, although with each week, each month, more and more was gradually being made known, much of it published in the French press for the first time—all of which I tried to keep up with as best I could. It wasn't until somewhat later that those first terrifying documentary films of the camps were made, and that Kogon's and other writings began to appear.

Thus, to take a glaring case, while I had known that Celine was an open anti-Semite, I had no idea then of the depth of his commitment to that dark area, nor about his collaboration record with the Nazis. Indeed, it was not until much later, long after I had returned to America, that the French (or, indeed, the world) began to learn the full scope of the Vichy betrayal(s), but also that much of the Parisian intellectual and artistic community had collaborated to one degree or another with both Vichy and the Germans, one critic recently terming Paris the major "hotbed of collaboration!" (But wasn't this just as true of Romania, where, as you well know, my dear Nina, Holocaust denial still, to this day, continues to be endemic? Where your Iron Guard survivors pretend total innocence? And true of most other East European countries as well, I am sure?)

Of course, the majority of the people I met and dealt with in Paris, especially artists, writers, musicians, and dancers, were for the most part the genuine article, and, in any case, seldom had been in positions of power. Yet there were occasions when I'd sense that one of them might be pulling the wool over my eyes, that things were not always so black and white as they were being painted, when, indeed, they were most likely gray. Which, aptly enough, is the color I unconsciously used at the top of this section about my returning to Paris, isn't it?

Surely, my dear suffering Muse, doesn't a similar gray still hit you when you return to visit your beloved Bucharest? It does me, though I did not live there, and you did. But I put myself in your shoes! Why does so much of that period still seem a mystery to most Romanians? Why, for example, did it take so many years before the journals of Mihael Sebastian, with their revelations about the Iron Guard and its leading intellectuals—Eliade, Cioran, and their philosopher mentor, the anti-Semitic Nae Ionescu—were finally published and released? And, even then, somewhat begrudgingly admired and reluctantly accepted?

But to go back to the start of my little meditation on "home," there was first the natural inclination to think of my family, with whom, of course, I had been keeping up a fairly regular correspondence all through my Army stint via the very efficient Army APO. They were so anxious to see me again, to catch up with the past. After all, counting my two-and-a-half years at the university and three years in the Army, I'd been gone a very long time. We'd have to get reacquainted...

Yet how could I go back there to Madison, Wisconsin, to live, there where my parents and younger brother had settled down (partly at my recommendation, to be sure)? No, I'm afraid I had outgrown them (true, with some pangs of regret), as well as the more recent, cherished lake period at Madison. (Recall my telling you how beautifully situated that city is between four lakes?) What should my next step be? It had to be New York, where I could continue to be that citizen of the world I felt I had now become (although actually I had begun to feel that way even earlier). Surely, I would be able to transfer my credits from the University of Wisconsin to one of New York's great colleges and pursue my study of theater, dance, and music simultaneously there, along with obtaining a college degree. In any event, an inkling of my future path was beginning to reveal itself to me on that train ride from Le Havre to Paris. Was I growing up all over again? Or was this simply reaching a higher level, a new plateau?

So what memory do you want me to concentrate on in my next letter—this missive being already almost too thick for the mail—my dear, ever-patient muse, Mme. Nina Cassian?

Your loving scribe,

M.

May 5, 2006

Ma chère Muse:

Yes, *hélas*, you're no doubt right to complain that my last letter was perhaps a little too long, and, at times, *troppo pesante*; but it was difficult to break off in the middle of that trip to those six or seven cathedrals—and which ones could I leave out? Plus which, don't you agree that the letters covered a lot more ground than just those cathedrals and their sites? For, as in other situations, one memory "begat" another; one story spawned still another story. And, indeed, as you will recall, I was tempted several times to go even further afield with still another side trip or two but decided I had to get back to the cathedral tales then and there, or we'd never finish that, for me, strangely compelling, and, in some ways, maturing journey. Indeed, it had something of that drive that makes us climb mountains or search out new planets—"because it's there!"

For example, on the Army's diversionary swing into Germany, to Leipzig and Bremen, I could have gone into much further detail with each of those milieus but hesitated, since, as you'll recall, I've already covered many of those war memories in earlier letters. Also, I don't want these letters to go too far overboard with any single memory, unless you, my dear, ask for more details.

Thus, when I was discussing the architectural ruins of Bremen, I recalled strolling with Ingeborg through that little park with the elephant statue but decided it would be better to come back to her and Bremen later. Mention of her now also stirs up related memories of those months stationed there: one of my more pleasureable periods in the Army, perhaps the most. The War was over, Peace reigned. The Army ruled the roost. But not oppressively. And, having been given that assignment to work at Armed Forces Network (AFN) Bremen, I no longer had to rise at dawn, answer a roll call, or suffer the countless, monotonous conventions of military discipline, though that sort of routine had already begun to be more relaxed immediately at the war's end, and bit by bit while we were still in Saxony. For example, one day I was able to clear enough time to make a little trip back to Weissenfels to pick up some of the music I had "confiscated" from the streets of Leipzig and which I'd left with my voice teacher there. By the way, I don't recall ever mentioning her before in any of our conversations about that period. Nor do I remember covering her in any of these letters. Her name was Agnes König. Surprisingly, though a late starter as a singer, she had quickly become a leading Lieder soloist in East Germany (of course, not called that until later in history).

So, winging a little detour from Bremen, we've landed in Weissenfels. What about those music scores? Did I dare go back to retrieve them? We had turned the town over to the Russians about ten days earlier. Could we risk it? Would we have to get special permission from headquarters? For I remember quite well that first day when we met the Soviets at Torgau on the Elbe, how we all rejoiced, Russians and Americans alike. It was "Tovaritsch" all the way, all the day and into the night! Before long everyone was drowned in drink. And I, being one of the few in the company who spoke some German, and "*nyemnoshka po Russky*," was called upon to serve as the goodwill interpreter between the Russian officers and ours. (In fact, I was the only noncom in that special group.) But, of course, I also remember only too well how the very next day, while we continued to welcome their soldiers on our side of the Elbe, we were not allowed to set foot on their side. This standoff was maintained until our eventual, unfortunate capitulation of turning that entire territory, which was the historic German province of Saxony, over to the Soviets.

Before that, the only exception to that rule came when they needed us to help transport hundreds of thousands of Central and

Eastern European DPs (displaced persons) from Vichy France, the Lowland countries, and West Germany, where they had been drafted by the Germans to work for them during the War, back to their homes in Poland, the Ukraine, and Russia. To me and my fellow soldiers, it was an insult that our American headquarters had authorized and allowed the Russians (a) to bring these poor people back without examination, without protocol, without any human rights guarantees, and (b) to do so at our expense in our trucks! I remember how it took ages for them to pass just through Weissenfels. The line of trucks seemed endless...

And therein lies another tale, which will keep us away from Bremen for another moment or two. Is that okay, dear Nina? I think I may have told you once not only about my studying voice with Agnes K. in Weissenfels but that I also took Russian lessons from a still-quite-young Ukrainian woman, twice a week, at her rented room there in that same town. This is not so far-fetched as it might appear to be, since I had started to learn Russian back in Madison, Wisconsin, and already knew the Cyrillic alphabet and the basics of Russian grammar. In fact, just before I was drafted, our class at the university had begun working on Tolstoy's wonderful stories for children. And, of course, being starved since England of any contact with *das ewig Weibliche*, I was naturally only too ready to fall in love with this Olga. Even if not starved, I most likely would have done so anyway, as she was not only beautiful but high-spirited and intelligent, with a touch of Nastasya Filipovna temmperament thrown in for good measure. Plus a mystery element, that was soon to be partially resolved (or enhanced?) by the sudden appearance of her Polish Underground friend (or consort?), Kasimier. (Fulfilling a fateful pattern which over the years seems to have more than once throttled a potential romance I thought was in the making.)

Thus, a mere seven or eight weeks later, other aspects of Olga's hidden past were to unfold rapidly on the day of that shameful parade of American Army trucks, loaded with over 900,000 Eastern- European-born DPs, rolled traumatically through Weissenfels. (Tolstoy's nephew in England was later to vociferously criticize in the British press this ignominious episode in the history of the Allied Forces.) Olga and I, along with hundreds of others, watched together as the trucks rumbled by. When, lo and behold, in the midst of that long file of anonymous vehicles, Olga suddenly recognized her mother standing at the barrier railing on the back opening of one of them, searching the horizon. Olga yelled out her name, waved to her, and threw her some flowers (could she have known Mama would be on one of those trucks?) which missed the truck, although we thought her mother may have waved back. After which I led a weeping, much shaken Nastasya/Olga back to her little rooming house in Weissenfels, in then disputed Saxony.

Yet, the next morning when I went there for my previously scheduled lesson, Olga had disappeared! The landlady thought she might have left the place with Kasimier around midnight. (Strangely enough, K., a thin, wiry, haggard-looking Polish resistance veteran, whom I had met only the day before, had not been there watching that truck procession with us, at least as far as I was aware. Could he have been lurking behind us somewhere?) Wondering why Olga had fled—"and Kasimier, too?" I asked—that shrewd woman wagered that she may have been spotted by the OGPU (predecessor of the NKVD). "And someone also could have recognized K., don't you think?" Obviously, her landlady knew more about such political intrigues than did innocent me. Though, in retrospect, I realized that Olga had let drop a few hints about having done some underground work in Paris. This was even before K. showed up on the scene.

An intriguing story, for which I never found the ending, and about which I often vainly hoped and fancied I might learn more from Olga herself when I got back to America. For I had earlier left her my address in Wisconsin, and she had promised to write once the war was over. Her English was certainly good enough for her to have done so. (Could she have had special training in the Polish Ukrainian Underground during those couple of years she claimed to have spent in Paris?) Of course, like most of the bright young people I met in those early post-war days, and she was no doubt what the boys in our company would have called "one smart cookie," she, too, was hoping to end up in America, and would, no doubt, when the time came, have asked for leads and contacts. Sad to say, I'm afraid she may rather have ended up in a far less promising place, from which no messages could be sent.

What I learned during those five or six incredible weeks in Weissenfels, the central part of Saxony, was that, among other things, we were sitting on a potentially explosive situation, poised as we were at the end of the American lines, confronting the Soviets, not knowing what the Germans would do next. And what would happen once the Germans were finally knocked out everywhere, and surrendered? We now know that further military confrontations were stymied, or put on hold, by dividing Germany into four zones and making Berlin a four power shared capital. A tenuous solution or a postponement of future conflict?

To get back to what was happening then and there to us. That scene with her mother, and her subsequent disappearance or abduction (was she actually picked up by the Soviets, or did she and K. manipulate a very hasty exit from that danger?) happened so fast I could hardly catch my breath, let alone come to a satisfactory understanding of what was what. I do know that Olga was obviously on what one might call the "idealist" socialist Left, not the communist version. For she, as a Ukrainian, would naturally hate almost any Russian, especially after the way they let the Ukrainians starve by the millions in the thirties. Moreover, that hatred went further back than this century. Just like their hatred for the Jews, which she explained to me was due primarily to two causes: (1) the long history of the middle class Jews who collected taxes for their Polish aristocrat overlords during the late Middle Ages, when the Poles were a power to reckon with, and later as well, and (2) because so many officers in the modern Soviet Army were, or were presumed to be, Jewish. She herself seems to have risen above all this. Perhaps her two or three years in the West had matured her and widened her horizons. I only wish she had told me more about the Polish Underground, and what must have been an extraordinary life. Would she have done so had she not been whisked away—or whisked herself away—so swiftly and so unceremoniously? Or was she forbidden to do so? Was it too dangerous for her to talk turkey and/or identify herself in any way?

Voilà, another detour, my dear, but I hope, an interesting one for you. Did you not meet similar cases during your youth in Romania? Weren't you still in the equivalent of a Gymnasium or a Lycée at that time? And wasn't it basically a ghetto-like school with only Jewish students, taught by only Jewish professors, where, as you once said, you had the cream of the crop for teachers (high-level teachers, scholars, and intellects tossed out of the university and assigned to you youngsters)? But what about two or three years before the war when you were coming of age and were attracted to various idealistic solutions to global problems, somewhat as I had been more or less simultaneously in America? And you settled for Communism instead of one of the various Israeli radical movements which also tempted you at that time, so that you could remain in Romania, help solve its problems, and bring what you thought would be justice and equality to your own country?

Also, I might note, and you might elucidate it further for me: how strange that during this immediate post-war period when I was there in different parts of Germany, I never encountered any Romanian or Hungarian DPs, especially amongst the many other nationality DPs (Russians, Poles, Ukrainians, Czechs, Slovaks, those of the Baltic nations) whom we in the Army had to deal with? Could that have been due to the special relationships your wily leaders had with the Germans even though those soon came crashing down? But probably not in time to set up a flow of workers from your countries to the West?

In any case, let us now get back at last to my "illegal" foray into Weissenfels to pick up the music I had left behind at Frau Agnes's place. As I said above, because of my translator work and other unusual jobs I had to undertake for headquarters, I was tacitly accorded a sort of special standing during our brief sojourn there. Though only a Technical Sergeant, I was often granted certain officer privileges, among them being assigned a jeep that I could use from time to time.

So one balmy summer night, knowing we'd soon have to pull out of Saxony for good (alas!), I hopped into that jeep with only my corporal aide at my side and took off secretly for Weissenfels, probably about 15 to 20 kilometers away from our temporary encampment. The countryside was beautiful. The trees, hieratically lined up in parallel rows on either side of the road in typical Continental fashion, were in full bloom. The farmers, their helpers, and their families were preparing for the coming harvest. A true rustic scene. And the chickens, ducks, and geese were having a grand time monopolizing the narrow country roadway. This was by no means one of those over-hyped German superhighways!

En route, Corporal Martin and I had to get out of the jeep twice to shoo away those boisterous, squawking creatures. But, of course, they understood neither Deutsch nor Englisch. And before we had a chance to make a third plea in an improvised goose dialect, I discovered that I had unknowingly and unfortunately run over a handsome gander, knocking him for a fatal loop. The farmers shook their fists at us. Their wives hissed. The children giggled. And we jumped back into the jeep and sped on to Weissenfels. Yet I was strangely shaken by this unpremeditated murder on my part, so much so that on our return trip, I turned the wheel over to Corporal Martin, and had him drive this repentant "killer" back to our camp. Somehow this traumatic experience persuaded me, from that time on, that the German version of the Parcae had decreed that I should never again drive a car! The Vengeance of Weissenfels, I now call it.

Nevertheless, not long after that still-lamented slaughter, like Wallenstein, we entered a strangely different town from the once-happy *Stadt* we had left behind. For, within those few weeks since our turning Weissenfels over to the Russians, it had changed into a drab, dull, passive, ruled-by-the-book municipality. Curfew warnings were posted everywhere. People had to be off the streets at a certain time. Noise had to be curtailed. Soviet flags had to be flown. There was no sign saying "Don't have Fun," but there might as well have been. Dry, curt but intimidating announcements were made every hour over harsh sounding loudspeakers. Several watchtowers had been erected or improvised out of other structures. Police were plentiful, both civilian and Soviet. Unsmiling. Not at all simpatico.

Before long, understandably, we began to have serious misgivings that we might be spotted by the Russkies and picked up, and returned to our Camp Headquarters in disgrace. So we took off our GI caps and ties, rolled up our sleeves, and tried to look as sloppy, civilian-like and German as possible. That many of the locals were wearing parts of discarded or stolen GI uniforms (as was now universal practice in occupied Germany), made this partial disguise feasible. Then we hurried on to Agnes's little house, with its tiny, delightful garden, and its cherry tree, whose trunk she had taught me how to hold while performing the special breathing exercises she had devised for singers. (They still hold me in good stead, though I have a hard time finding the proper substitute trees!)

Agnes looked tired, wan, and distressed when we found her. But upon seeing us, she immediately turned back into her usual *gemütlich* self, ushered us quickly into her house, and firmly shut the door on her now-sad hometown. She didn't have to explain why, or much else. She recognized that we knew what she was going through. But she also realized that we were potentially in danger. And so, aware that a long visit was now impossible, she quickly put together the music scores I had salvaged from Leipzig and temporarily left there with her, packed them neatly in one of her few containers (paper shortages were enormous then), gave me a notebook with her unique voice exercises, and loaded us with tasty sandwiches and salads for the trip back. Then came a tearful farewell. In that short time, Agnes had become almost like family, one of the really "good" Germans I had so far encountered.

And one of the few people from that period who ever followed up on a promise to write after I left Germany, and actually did so. Here are a couple of short passages from one such eight-page letter: "And for January, I have two new singing students....As to the Russians, I have nothing to do with them. They commandeered the house of the Klagroth family next door for five months from the middle of July until November, including the room where we used

149

to sing. Ach, it was terrible!....However, for several weeks now, I've been able to rent a piano for my room—which is very good for me. And I don't need to go out in bad weather, thanks to helpful neighbors. Now I can practice often and sing whatever I choose. Recently I started working on Brahms Lieder, Vol. II....

"Yet once the Russians pull out of here, it would be such a relief. But what will become of Silesia, of Liegnitz? When will we be able to get back into our own homes? Or will we even be allowed to do so? What'll we find when we do? Everything destroyed—all finished?" And so on. Clearly life's adjustments were not easy for her under that new dictatorial regime.

Before closing the Agnes "account," I must briefly relate how I once made this sober, serious, modest bourgeois creature break up, lose control, and giggle like a schoolgirl. We were working on that charming song Schubert set to Goethe's poem, "Heidenröslein." As you'll recall, since I'm sure you know this Lied by heart, the word *Röslein* appears in the very first line. But no sooner had I sung it, than Agnes burst into laughter. "Nein, nein, lieber Herr. Not '*Rösslein*,' but '*Röslein*'! With a z sound, not a double ss. You sang 'little horse' not 'little rose'—which is what Goethe wrote!" Then she had me try it out several times before I was finally able to make those two only slightly different words sound like they should in German. Finally, the horse turned back into a rose, and suddenly all was right with the world! But as a result of this episode, I can never start singing that song without first breaking up myself—over sixty years later! The other residue: it made me wonder what other linguistic gaffes I may have made—and would no doubt continue to make—in my German conversations, past or future. (As to my more frequent gaffes in Romanian, you point them out as fast as they leave my mouth!)

Which, in a way, brings us back to Bremen, where I had to do a lot of talking (though not always in German), and where, luckily, I discovered quite a few more "good" Germans. I'm thinking especially of the Franken family, which used to hold weekly musicals in its charming low-lying townhouse that had somehow miraculously escaped bombardment, even though it was only a few blocks away from one of those boulevards which had been thoroughly firebombed. By that, I mean that the insides of all the buildings in a row might be totally burned out, but the frameworks of almost all of them would remain standing and, from a distance, look undamaged. So that one could be driving along one of these avenues, say, in the dim light of dusk, and not even be aware that they had been bombed: the remains were so remarkably extant. This was especially true in the more once-affluent sections of Bremen, whose *haute bourgeois* mansions were made of such strong stonework and concrete, with unusually bolstered frameworks, that they stood up to firebombing, although they might not have withstood a Dresden-sized bombing. But, again, dear Nina, I'm far from an expert on these technical matters.

At these modest little musicales, we would be treated sometimes to Lieder, at other times to chamber music, but more often to excerpts from operas. For the Frankens were trying to help the then-conductor of the Bremen Philharmonic revive both the orchestra and the Bremen Opera (for which the orchestra also played). Of course, it was premature for America to get involved in helping finance these projects, other than to encourage their leaders and to clear the way for them to use such public facilities as were still viable until rebuilding of symphonic halls and opera houses could get underway. But first, our forces had to concentrate on restoring civil order; to proceed with de-Nazification; to supervise intercity, interprovince, and international traffic; and to get the de-Nazified Germans to focus on restoring their badly damaged infrastructure.

So all I could do at this point was to help build up morale by attending such functions as the Frankens and other like-minded Bremen opera buffs and symphony lovers were giving, and by talking about these events and previewing their larger plans on my weekly music program over AFN Radio Bremen, which, fortunately, I was now able to do. Of course, I would also bring along to these gatherings plenty of canned goods, as well as gobs of cookies and candies for which they had been starved for years. So much so, that I came to be christened "Candy" by the Frankens and their guests. This was the family who, I believe I once told you, dear Nina, buried its *verboten* books in the garden at the rear of their house in order to evade Nazi searches and confiscations. I was shown the troughs where they had lain. Not only music lovers (their Mendelssohn scores had to be hidden as well), they were also sophisticated readers, though not at all avant-garde in their tastes. For example, Sternheim, Brecht, or Wedekind were never mentioned, although they did read Thomas Mann and Rilke and Stefan Georg. And Hauptmann was a revered figure. But a remarkable, good, generous family they were indeed: this was their "land of the heart." And when I returned to the States, they put me in touch with a branch of their family who lived in one of the more elegant apartment buildings on lower Fifth Avenue, not far from your beloved Washington Square and nearby NYU, where I was most cordially received—and thanked.

Now, as to my job at AFN Bremen, I was part of a team of seven or eight guys, GIs, Yanks, soldiers from varying walks of life—we were given such monikers by our own troops, and probably less flattering ones by the Germans. But what really made our situation unique is that, as I think I may have hinted at before, we were all working as an independent unit and were not subject to ordinary Army barracks discipline. In fact, while most of us were Army members, we had a certain crossover from the various other units of the armed forces, which was a rather healthy setup and led to better discussions, as well as fostering among us a greater competitive mettle. It's probably also the reason why it was called the Armed Forces Network. How else could our chief officer have been a Navy captain, that fine fellow whom I think I told you about briefly in my very first letter? The American whom Toni had met while serving as a nurse in Brittany at the end of the War? He was then a lieutenant and had obviously been promoted to captain on taking this position at Radio Bremen. It was he who sent me to her in Zurich on my furlough, knowing that she would be a good guide for Switzerland. Which, of course, she certainly turned out to be!

It was AFN's function to be the voice of America in Germany and other countries in Europe. If I'm not mistaken, the original "Voice of

America" broadcasts grew out of our pioneering AFN work, immediately post-war. We were there to sponsor good will, improve the image of America, and serve as an independent news source for those Germans who could speak or understand English. But obviously we could reach even more Germans, and other Europeans as well, through the universal language of music—classical, jazz, pop, folk, and native idioms. So there was naturally more music than talk on AFN Bremen, and it fell upon me to help organize and run that programming, in addition to my weekly talk show, somewhat in the style of *The New Yorker* "Talk of the Town" section. For my weekly symphonic program, I took on the pen name of Scribonius; I based my comments on the music to be performed, along with amusing anecdotes, etc., modeled somewhat on the radio talks of Deems Taylor, who had been the dean of music commentators back in the States before I left. Our news reporting and analysis were indebted more to H. V. Kaltenborn, another major, serious radio figure back home. But being young and rebellious, we never slavishly imitated either of these masters; in fact, we sometimes actually did caricatures of them as well.

Frank Mankiewicz, son of Herman Mankiewicz, who coauthored Orson Welles's masterpiece, *Citizen Kane*, and nephew of the great film director, Joseph Mankiewicz, was one of our best reporters. He ended up, in effect, as our news chief. After the war, he was to first achieve national recognition as press secretary to Senator Robert Kennedy and went on to become campaign director for George McGovern's run for President; he was also regional director for the Peace Corps in Latin America for a time and eventually took over as president of National Public Radio (NPR)—a fitting climax for a veteran of the Armed Forces Network (AFN) Bremen, don't you think?

Would life have been easier for me had I pursued similar lines? I often wonder. I was tempted at times to do so and auditioned successfully for WNYC when I first settled down in Manhattan but then never followed that up. (Actually, my radio experience predated the Army, for I had worked on some University of Wisconsin radio programs in Madison). I guess

I was just too curious about too many things to go into radio full-time. But, of course, as in Mankiewicz's case, had I done so, it might have served as an entrée to further contacts; but then again, we can't rule out that Frank's eminent father and uncle surely helped launch him in his beginning phases. There was another member of our staff whose name eludes me at the moment whom I would often bump into when in the Broadway theater area. He had become a very successful big-time radio announcer but apparently had no other ambitions. My last memory of him, after our talking a spell over his favorite Guinness, was a long, languid yawn as he opined that he thought it was about time for him to retire from radio!

To get back to Bremen. Though I might occasionally have mocked him, I looked up to Deems Taylor, as America's preeminent public music critic but also as a respectable, though not brilliant, American composer. In the backwater region of Wisconsin where I grew up, far from the music scene of New York, I had followed his radio programs religiously, as well as the weekly broadcasts of the Metropolitan Opera. (Remember my telling you of my hitchhiking two hundred miles, at the age of twelve, to Milwaukee to hear my first opera, *Lohengrin*, with Flagstad, René Maison, and Alexander Kipnis?) Yet strangely enough, once here in New York, I found that most people, even some of the more musically sophisticated, did not know Taylor's own music at all. Indeed, it wasn't until I programmed him many years later with the BPO (Brooklyn Philharmonic) that I got to appreciate the range of his oeuvre, though, unfortunately, one had to realize finally that his pretensions to greatness had hardly been fulfilled. Still, he did produce a few charming works, such as "Through the Looking Glass Suite," and some dance scores. But his two operas, *The King's Henchman* (with a libretto by Edna St. Vincent Millay) and *Peter Tibbetson*, both commissioned by the Met, and which were apparently well received by the press in the 1920s, didn't catch on with the general public and were soon dropped from the Met's repertoire. Nor do they hold up today: they seem quite wooden and devoid of real genius.

Of course, it was on this AFN Bremen program that I could help my newly found German friends and artists promote their drive to rebuild Bremen's orchestra and its opera. Fortunately, they moved so fast in this direction that we were able to broadcast their first symphonic program about six weeks after we opened the station; and shortly thereafter I went to see their first opera production in an improvised modest theater in the shell of some partially bombed-out building. It was *Frau Schmetterling*—which is what, as you're aware, *Madama Butterfly* is called in German! It was, indeed, my first experience at hearing Puccini sung in German, and was, I must admit, a dubious pleasure. Partly perhaps because the cast and orchestra were not yet up to its demands, but also because of the strange tonal texture of that Germanic vowel sound, so different from the Italianate. Nevertheless, as the evening wore on, I began to get somewhat used to it.

However, more important, perhaps, is that it also made me realize why European countries do operas in their own languages: the public always wants to know what that drama going on up there on the stage is all about (doesn't your Romanian public relish opera in its own language?) It strengthened my resolve, when I got back to the States, to try to promote a return to opera in English. After all, it was done that way in early 19th-century New York and is being done again that way in this century by the English National Opera at the London Colosseum—and used to be done that way quite successfully at the New York City Opera. For example, at their production of *Die Meistersinger*, sung in English some thirty years ago, it was the first time I heard and witnessed an audience realize it was a comedy they were experiencing, something they could laugh at and not sit on their hands! So whenever I got involved with opera workshops or experimental productions, I always opted for English versions if at all possible. But it's still an uphill battle, I'm afraid. The purists, who want all opera sung in the original tongue, have the upper hand, which has been very much strengthened since the almost universal use now of projections of simultaneous translations into English of what is being sung in French, German, or Italian. The same holds true for video broadcasts of the same. And, in the long run, I suppose understanding the lyrics is what matters. Certainly, opera is gaining considerable ground with the American public, while the symphonic sphere is losing customers, cutting down its seasons, often going bankrupt, I'm afraid. (As you know, we're all very worried now whether the Brooklyn Philharmonic will survive: they've already cancelled their May 9th concert, which was to have ended the season with a bang.)

Before leaving Bremen, isn't there still a little more you want to hear about, something about which, no doubt, you're a little curious yourself? For example, what happened to Ingeborg, whose story I've twice postponed writing about? Well, as you've no doubt suspected, she was a charming, young, aspiring cabaret singer—weren't we all young then and aspiring?—whom I met one night when a couple of us "guys" went slumming in the few nightspots that had so far reopened in Bremen. You probably won't believe this, but she actually looked very much like a younger version of Marlene Dietrich, though not quite as *saftig* as she was in *The Blue Angel*. Naturally, I fell for this enticing creature: my *solace* after losing Olga to the Polish Underground (or to the Soviets?).

Fortunately, there was reciprocation. In fact, it was on one of those walks with her past the elephant I described earlier that we had our first *malentendu*, or as Ingeborg would have said, *Missverständnis*. Something must have happened during that walk; suddenly, she began to act a little cold; and when we reached her place, she let me in almost unwillingly. Indeed, by this time, she didn't seem to want to talk at all. "Why so tongue-tied?" I asked. At first, she refused to answer. But I kept plying her with more questions: "What's wrong? Why the strange frown? Did I say something to offend you? Do you want me to leave?" Finally, Ingeborg blurted out: "But I thought you loved me; that I was your best friend in Bremen. *Und dann sagst du Sie zu mir*? How could you? And you kept on talking that damned language of Lessing." This was a blow, because one of my more precious memories of her during the first stages of our friendship was how she'd smile and say how she loved the way *"du sprichst die Sprache von Lessing!"* Now she twisted that around and accused me of being too formal, talking the language of Lessing! What before had charmed her now seemed to turn her off. Obviously that *Sie* was too formal now.

I immediately understood, of course, that I must have blundered into that unforgiveable mistake during our conversation while we were walking past the elephant, which for some reason or other had turned to general, serious topics; we had moved from greeting and kissing one another, I thought, to other realms. Especially since we were out in the world, walking in public. But then I realized that during that more "weighty" talk, I had most likely shifted unconsciously to using the formal second person plural, <u>Sie</u>, when otherwise I always used the intimate <u>du</u> form with <u>her</u>.

Well, I practically had to go down on my hands and knees to beg her forgiveness, and naturally tried to smooth it over by explaining that we don't make that distinction in English, that our du form is outdated, going back to thou in Milton and Shakespeare; that, moreover, when I would be talking about non-intimate subjects, it would naturally revert to the formal. It took a while, but she finally came around to understanding that I loved her whether she was a *du* or a *Sie*, and that we were a <u>wir</u>; she began gradually to trust me again. Though a slight distance was maintained on and off for a day or two following this little *malentendu*, before long it disappeared.

Of course, I could have complained to her then and there about something I had discovered shortly before this episode, namely, that she was also seeing my nemesis, the major! In other words, dear Ninicuṭa, and don't be shocked, I found to my dismay that I was sharing my Ingeborg with my major, that handsome ladies' man, who was still the second head of my regiment, next to the colonel, and who thought himself more important than ever since the death of our first colonel. (You no doubt remember that earlier letter in which I described what happened to him.)

Yet I never let Ingeborg know that I knew about her and the major. Yes, I was finally growing up, facing the realities of this new playing field that was Germany, and probably would soon be the world, in peacetime. Why create a melodrama, especially since he ranked so high above me and could potentially do me great harm? Besides, Ingeborg was a real charmer, and great fun; and though not too experienced a singer, made up for her lack of technique with her natural warmth and ebullience, plus plenty of that blonde, German sex appeal. She was also a good cook!

Then there was a quite different experience I had with the poor Latvian tenor who served as our regiment's barber, and whom almost everyone took for just an ordinary DP who'd escaped getting sent back to Eastern Europe but who actually had survived at least four different concentration camps. His name was Zladek something or other; we called him Izzy, for short. He seemed to have taken a sort of attachment to me, which I at first attributed to his realization that I esteemed him more highly than my fellow soldiers for having been a leading tenor in the Riga Opera; that he felt more at home with me, since I was probably more "European" or "International" than my *confrères*; and, above all, that I was more appalled and horrified than they seemed to be by his camp history. Indeed, his terrible experiences probably hit home more for me than the others, since I was also something of a *Landsmann* of his (my father having come from Lithuania, as you know, next door to Latvia). Thus, just this man's presence inevitably reminded me of my cousin Abraham, who, along with his mother and family, I had tried to get our family and those of his three other uncles in America to squirrel out of Europe before the war but had collectively failed to do so. My guilt over this, which grew every time I heard another report about the camps—and that terrible news was out there in black and white for anyone who kept his eyes and ears open, though admittedly not told as plainly, frequently, and alarm-warningly as it should have been— was now heightened even more when I looked into the eyes of this poor fellow man who had survived not one, but several camps; then intensified still further by urgent letters from my family, my father especially, grasping at the vain hope that this God-sent Latvian escapee would be able to help us find out what happened to our family. Of course, Zladek could do nothing but sympathize and empathize with our loss. He was pretty sure, first of all, that none of our relatives could have escaped their fellow Lithuanians, most of whom turned against their Jewish neighbors the minute the Nazis invaded Lithuania or were forced at gunpoint by the Nazis to do their killing for them (as did also his fellow Latvians and Esthonians); and second, even if, say, they had eluded them and joined that long forced march of multiple thousands of Lithuanians deeper into Russia, of which we had heard terrifying rumors, there was very little chance any of them could have survived that horror.

Nevertheless, I did sound out for my family, and for my own peace of mind, the few resources the Army had at that point; made further inquiries when in Paris; and later, when finally back in the USA, pursued any records available through the various Jewish and humanitarian agencies who dealt with such matters. Predictably, all without results. My mother and father later pursued other leads in the USSR, again to no avail. The family had at first naively hoped I could get to Russian-occupied Lithuania after the war ended. But my limited experience with the Soviet regime at Torgau, and later in Weissenfels, was enough to explode that dream, even had I been able to get leave from the Army to make such an expedition with that whole area in turmoil!

Which reminds me of one other episode from the Weissenfels period I missed in the account above, and which I think might touch you. During the single occasion we were allowed to cross the Elbe into the Soviet side of Saxony, which was to help guide a few truckloads of "leftover DPs" into that zone, we were stunned to encounter a small group of haggard, young Hungarian Jewish women who had been housed by the Nazis in cramped quarters, in a forlorn, narrow building not far from the Elbe in anticipation of being sent on to Auschwitz but who were luckily saved in the nick of time when the Russian forces reached that part of Saxony before they could be moved. Alas, we had to leave those poor girls (teenagers, or in their early twenties, most of them) there with the Russians, who were ostensibly legally in charge of the house and its inhabitants at that point. Let us hope and pray they were treated well, regained their health and strength, and subsequently found refuge elsewhere. Many years later I met a Hungarian woman who had survived one of those last-minute rescues in that part of Saxony, but she couldn't identify exactly where. Could it have been that lonely house?

To get back to Zladek/Izzy: had he not by some miracle been able to cut hair like an expert barber (which trade he hardly learned singing in *The Barber of Seville*, since Figaro, the barber, as you know, is a baritone role, and Zladek, of course, took the Count's part, a tenor), he would never have been able to survive not just one, but several camps.

Yet, while grateful to have found in me an "Amerikan" whom he could talk to—and we did talk, switching back and forth between several languages—and who was also able to find extra jobs for him, it turned out that, unfortunately, his affection for me was of a different nature. The minute I recognized this new complication, and the potential problems it could create, I warned him not to talk to anyone about it, and that from that moment on he must be more formal and discrete when visiting the station, or working in its environs. For I certainly didn't want him to suffer anything on that account. Hadn't he been through enough already?

Well, I suppose I shouldn't have worried. Izzy was obviously a pretty tough operator. How else could he, a Latvian Jew, have survived as long as he did in hostile, chaotic Mittel Europa and end up a free man in Bremen? And, judging from the few times I was able to let him sing on the air, it was clear that he must also have been a top-notch tenor in the Baltic states. But talent or no talent, to move up that high in the very competitive world of opera also takes a lot of chutzpah. To survive in the camp world took more than chutzpah and luck; it often demanded deceit, cunning, and, dare we say it, cruel amorality as well ("you die or I die"). After the war, that remarkable Polish non-Jewish poet/survivor of Buchenwald and Dachau, Tadeusz Borowski, was accused of immorality by the new Communist press for daring to suggest that anyone might have been more focused on survival in those camps than on good deeds. So I was pretty sure that our wily Izzy would manage to ride over this minor crisis.

Amazingly enough, twenty or so years later I ran into him, by that time grown rather plump and almost bald, peddling cheap rings and watches on Fifth Avenue, Manhattan, near the "Kosher" diamond district (47th Street)! Happy and relieved that he had found his way to America, I wanted to help him as best I could, this time, by recommending him as a cantor to a synagogue. However, it turned out that he had already lined up a High Holiday singing job somewhere in Queens. He was now too old and broken to even attempt to get back into opera, although I suspect he may have tried in vain to do so when he first reached these shores. In any case, I gave him my card but never heard from him again.

You see, my dear letter recipient, how each little story seems to evoke another tale. But I suspect you may have already heard enough about AFN Bremen, unless, wait... Let me just quote a paragraph or two from one of my weekly commentaries à la *The New Yorker* "Talk of the Town" columns for your edification—I hope!—after which we'll move on to other realms. The program was called "The Magic Pitcher," for which I served as a hybrid mix of master of ceremonies, disc jockey, and general overseer, and even participant in little sketches we sometimes introduced between a wide range of music recordings which were, after all, the main substance of these programs.

From "Magic Pitcher 5":

> We were wandering the streets of Bremen pondering what we could possibly discover among all its luscious ruins, which might conceivably interest you, dear audience, on this our fifth outpouring of "The Magic Pitcher." There were any number of things that hit us smack in the face, such as that peculiar Bremen atmospheric pallor, and those much too frequent spurts and spoutings of rain; then we'll never forget the time we nearly lost our balance going over the Weser Moat as they blasted out the remains of the Hillman Hotel—they say that even

161

Das Haus des Reichs shivered a little that day. We also got ourselves ferried across the Weser once when we got lost among the ruins of the old main city, looking for rats and bootleggers. But perhaps the most interesting objects on the landscape are the amazing dogs one meets. They are of all shapes and sizes and are apparently quite international, barking in English, Russian, French, and Polish. They seem to use German only when they get ferociously mad, which is very seldom, because, of course, we treat them much too well. Then we began to drool nostalgically back over the ocean, trying to remember what the hounds, mutts, and spaniels back in the States looked like. It was a most pleasant revery, since dogs always smell better in the imagination than they do in the flesh. They also taste good in song, and no one can express this more charmingly than Lena Horne... Listen now as she and the Phil Moore Four dialogue on the tune "I Want a Little Doggie."

Or perhaps you'd like this one from "Magic Pitcher 6" better:

In getting together this, our sixth edition of "The Magic Pitcher," we suddenly got the tremors: were we really doing right by you, dear audience? We had discussed at one time or another practically everything under the sun except the Southern Cross and Ex-Lax! But when we stopped to reflect, extract, retract, and deduce, why, deuce it, we were stumped by that very simple question: what does it all mean? In vain, we flitted through one tome after another, lexicon upon hexagon, Aragon, paragon, Trianon—hmn. Where are we? Chicago? Oh yes, to make a long story short: we concluded after all that research, that our contribution to society was absolutely and definitively NOTHING. So we decided right then and there that we'd have to reform. We looked up at the sky, sniffed the air, then contemplated our navels, and came to the brilliant conclusion that all we lacked was Purpose! For we supposed that according to Hegel, purpose gives it a point, point gives it a meaning, and meaning makes you happy. In other words, we decided that our purpose is—the Pursuit of Happiness. Which should make you, Hegel, and all the other philosophers happy...

Now that we've got that off our chests, we can proceed unburdened on our new path of Virtue and Purpose. And we propose to start off the new era gaily and trippingly with some scintillating jazz by the only Frenchmen who really know how to swing it. Yes, we've invited up the famed quintet, *Hot Club de France*, to do one of their finest numbers, "Swing Guitars." That's two-fingered, gypsy-blooded Django Reinhardt you'll hear snapping the strings of his guitar, and Stephan Grappelli doing the equivalent of hot licks on his violin.

After which, of course, we immediately broadcast their wonderful version of "Swing Guitars," which we're sure Bremen audiences never heard during the war years.

*

Well, there are many other memories from those fascinating months in Bremen that seem to bubble up, but perhaps the most apt one is what happened when I was transferred from Bremen to Paris, where I would finally be discharged from the Army. I had been able to get Captain Davis to swing a deal for me whereby I could live and study in Paris for a half year or so and then return to the USA. Which is roughly more or less what happened.

The first leg of this journey to Paris had an unusual twist to it, which I think you, dear Nina, will find particularly interesting in view of our various political discussions over the years and our sometimes conflicting points of view *über Welt Politik*. What happened is the following. I took the train (by this time, German rail lines were beginning to function fairly well) from Bremen to Frankfurt, where I needed to transfer to the Paris express. The first link of the trip southward along the Rhine was pleasant enough, though not nearly as delightful as the train ride you and I took from Frankfurt to Cologne up the Rhine some fifty years later. Yes, the train was quite comfortable, but, of course, could offer no amenities yet. However, since trains were also more scarce, I had to suffer a long stopover until the next Paris train came in. So I used that time to explore Frankfurt a little.

What a shock it was, when I emerged from the relatively unharmed railway station and walked into the utterly deserted, bombed-out, leveled-flat, downtown heart of Frankfurt. It was far more severely damaged than Bremen, which, in turn, had been far more damaged than Leipzig, as you may recall my telling you. I imagine its flattened blocks must have been more like those of Dresden. Tadeusz Borowski, that controversial Polish poet/survivor I quoted above, had an understandably much more bitter view of this. Talking about walking across parts of Deutschland in prison stripes, in one of his early post-war letters, he wrote: "The beauty of an enemy land? We developed our own criteria for beauty: the most beautiful city? Frankfurt reduced to rubble."

There was little activity that afternoon, hardly any traffic, vehicular or pedestrian. By chance, I had found an old map of Frankfurt in the station lobby; using it, I tried to trace a path to where Goethe once lived. Luckily, another lonely walker appeared on the horizon and showed me what he was pretty sure was the site. (Years later, on our German trip, remember, we visited the restored building, now an efficient, *echt* Goethe House Museum on that very spot.) Then, as I wandered further out from the center, a few more half-destroyed buildings seemed to spring up, but there was little of much interest, human or architectural, left to observe.

What I found quite extraordinary that day was when two of the few people still moving about those wide, empty stretches of rubble, in turn stopped me and asked for directions—in German. They apparently assumed that, as a uniformed person, I would know how to get around bombed out Frankfurt! Or was it perhaps my glasses, and the somewhat professorial look I seem sometimes unconsciously to exude? Fortunately, to my own surprise, with the help of that map I had picked up earlier in the station, I was able to guide each of them to where they wanted to go! Well, my dear, ever since that epoch-making moment, people, strangers, sightseers, lost children anywhere and everywhere continue to stop me to ask directions, where to change money, what restaurant I'd recommend, not only here in New York, but also in almost every state or country I visit! It even happened to me once in Bucharest while strolling down Blvd. Stefan cel Mare.

In any case, after that unexpected encounter, I turned around, moved right, made a half circle, and walked back to what I deemed would be more or less the same latitude as the railroad station and where the Paris train would soon be arriving. Suddenly, I found myself in front of one of the few solid buildings left standing in that desert-like area, what must have once been a modest store with offices above it. I moved in closer and could sense that there was activity astir within. After a few moments, I mustered up intrepidity enough to knock on the only door I could find. Lo and behold, it opened, and I was greeted with polite, though suspicion-lined glances. "What can we do for you?" And, in my now relatively more fluent German, I told them who I was, where I had come from, a little about my work at AFN Bremen, and that I was on my way to Paris. They relaxed a little, enough for me to quiz them in turn for awhile. To my amazement, I discovered that I had stumbled upon the German Communist Party Headquarters!

Whereupon we exchanged a little politically neutral small talk: "So how do you like Deutschland? How are things up there in Bremen? You like German girls? But you'll have more fun in Paris, *nicht wahr*?" Though one of them, looking out the window and pointing to the desert of broken stone and brick that was now downtown Frankfurt (all wood or lumber, of course, having been long swept, and/or stolen, away by now), grew serious for a moment and mused, "You see, we've got a lot of work ahead, but who's going to lead us out of this mess?" I answered, "The German people!" And, of course, they loved that.

Yet underneath that seeming amiability, there was a subtle jousting for position, the nature of which is caught rather shrewdly in an exchange (quoted in the Sam Tanenhaus biography of that controversial American writer and politico, Whittaker Chambers, I once showed you) between Chambers himself, then editor of *The Daily Worker*, and John Sherman of his staff, who reputedly helped draft Chambers into the Communist movement in the USA: "You're in the underground now," Sherman said gaily, "where I ask questions, but don't answer them, and you answer questions, but don't ask them." (Oddly enough, this conversation could have taken place around the same time as my unimportant but curious meeting with the German Communist Party.)

We never got that far, of course, for soon it was time for me to get back to the station. Yet I'm sure I left that CP group wondering how or why a stray American Army bloke was able to locate them, especially a non-com like me. Of course, the irony was that I wasn't out looking for them or anyone in particular! In any case, the terrain was so bare that I would have seen anyone following me, and they, in turn, could have phoned ahead to a possible comrade in the station, to watch if I really took that train. But—and I'm sorry to disappoint you, dear Nina, for I know how much you like mysteries—I very much doubt that I had them really worried! After a quarter of an hour, they probably changed the subject, forgot about me, and went back to the German equivalent of poker. And I went on my way, having soon forgotten them as well, with great anticipation of reaching that fabled city as I boarded the express to Paris. The ride was quite uneventful: I probably slept most of the way.

Has this letter gone on too long? A little thinner than the last, but we covered a lot of territory didn't we? And there'll soon be more on the way!

Chérie, je t'adore!

M.

October 17, 2006

My devoted *lectrice*:

Welcomed back to Paris by Toni and my various teachers; by Marcelle Sibon and Georges, her amiable sidekick; by faithful Madeleine (Léo Staat's always helpful assistant); and even by my local newsstand operator, I found them all avidly eager to learn about my trip. Rather touched that they even noticed I had been absent (not more than nine or ten days, wasn't it?), I was only too glad to regale them with tales from that exhausting but edifying itinerary. Even Gertrude Stein and Alice Toklas were curious, though the news from that quarter was otherwise disquieting.

Alice had already warned me that Gertrude had been ailing. Well, this time I saw her in the hospital, accompanying Alice on one of her daily visits. Gertrude had had a very serious operation (though I was never told just what kind; one didn't ask those questions of either of those ladies unless they gave some hint that it was a possible subject for discussion). By the time I saw her, Gertrude was able to sit up in bed, was apparently eating well, and sounded pretty much on the mend. Yet, as you probably know, she didn't last much longer after her return home, although she was still alive when I left for the States.

What a difference, I mused, from that brisk morning a couple of months back, when Gertrude, to all appearances in good health, cavalierly drove her Model A Ford over the bridge to Rue Rivoli, taking me along to help her shop for the patisseries she was to serve at her next matinée gathering of artists and writers. I believe it was during that trip that she told me how she had been asked by the then-young and most promising English choreographer Frederick Ashton to write another ballet scenario for him and the Sadler Wells Ballet. Their previous one, "Wedding Bouquet," had been a big success.

But why call on me? Well, knowing of my interest in and enthusiasm for the dance, and having enjoyed my blow-by-blow account of seeing Jean Babilée, France's answer to Nijinsky, leap through "Spectre de la Rose," with the Roland Petit Ballet at the huge but still-elegant *Théatre Champs Elysée* recently, she seemed curious as to what I thought would make a good subject for a new ballet, and how it should differ from "Wedding Bouquet!" Stunned (and cautiously flattered) that she would ask humble me to advise her, I stumbled about, improvising a couple of possible plots. (It happened that I had been talking scenarios with Léo Staats a few days before!) Which she took quite seriously, making mental notes, I am sure. Whether she ever used bits of any of them, however, or whether she ever finished that new scenario, I'm far from sure. Certainly Ashton never did another Stein ballet after that. But I'm glad she did stoop to ask my advice. It gave me some insight into how Stein worked on a project that involved other artists. I gather that she often sounded out other people about such things; just like she would examine a room; or a landscape—or a rose is a rose is a rose? Or listening to the tales of us American soldiers for her *Brewsie and Willie* book? (Was this her style of research?)

How sad that I never saw dear Gertrude again. Nor poor Alice, who, as you probably know, outlived Gertrude by several decades, though hardly long enough, of course, for me to introduce you to her when we visited Paris about ten years ago. Remember my pointing out the site of Sylvia Beach's famous bookstore to you on that trip? Enterprising Sylvia, who really did not like Gertrude (and vice versa), as I discovered when I visited her briefly back then, and who ended up talking mostly about Valéry and his wife. Little could I have guessed then what a story she could have told me about how she stood up to the Nazis when they tried to con-fiscate her books and take over her shop; and how she ended up in some kind of jail. But fortunately the war ended in time to save her. Modest, brave Sylvia Beach.

One surprise that greeted me upon my return was a long awaited letter from Geraldine, whom, as you may recall, I left try-ing to make a go of her life in New York rather than Washington. I was worried that with my exiting the Army, I'd have trouble receiv-ing any Army mail forwarded from Bremen to Cité Universitaire. I needn't have. The French postal system proved to be very efficient.

In fact, I was lucky that I was allowed to continue to live there after my discharge. Perhaps my *bourse* arrangement with the Sorbonne covered such matters? And Geraldine's letter did come via Bremen, as I recall.

After all that anticipation, however, the letter turned out to be a bit of a disappointment, as often happens, you know, when one's hopes are set too high. She had written quite long letters to me while I was sweating through training in Army camps in California and Mississippi; now, being 3,000 miles away overseas and accordingly more anxious for news about her and what she was up to, all I got were a few small crumbs of sentences. This was when I would have relished her take on what was happening in New York and Washington (she tended to shift back and forth between those two cities, Washington being her *cité natale*). Well, of course, with this paucity of news, my first natural reaction was to worry about whether she had found a new love and/or was simply too busy and distracted to write more about what she was up to! I began to imagine all kinds of scenarios, concluding that I shouldn't expect to see too much of her when I returned to America. Clearly, I was jealous in advance, even though, strictly speaking, I had no right to be, especially considering the fact that I myself had hardly been "faithful" to her, and that, moreover, neither of us had ever made any claims of eternal love and passion to each other, though I remember calling her my "poor wounded bird" in one of those earlier missives, possibly while still waiting in England to be shipped out to France.

But then I reread her letter and discovered she had found a very demanding new job with a major Madison Avenue agency. She also apologized for having to be so short-winded. Talk about that particular job, it so happens, turned out to be true: she had begun to work for the highly regarded Ben Sonnenberg, one of the master PR people of that era. In fact, many claimed that he had invented PR. Unfortunately, I never met him, for by the time I got back to the States, Geraldine had moved on to another job. Ironically, many years later, she did manage to introduce me to his talented son, Ben Sonnenberg, Jr., who, in turn, made a totally different kind of name for himself as the founder and editor of that first-rate, short-lived literary quarterly, *Grand Street*. Now defunct, unfortunately, it was just as iconoclastic a literary journal, though in quite different ways, as *Parnassus*. Your article on Celan appeared in the latter, as you will surely recall, as well as the one on modern Romanian poetry. But, strangely, none of your poems. *Parnassus* also closed shop this past season. Fortunately, *The New Yorker* did publish many of your poems, obviously a more important site for them. Pity I didn't think of it before, but young Sonnenberg might well have liked some of your poems for his *Grand Street* journal while he was still editing it. Perhaps I should try to get back in touch with him, and reminisce about Geraldine...

Now that I think of it, it is certainly possible that it was her tutelage under the elder Sonnenberg that helped train Geraldine's fine-tuned nose for what was "in" at the moment—an innate sense of what was important and trend-setting in the intellectual and art worlds. Somehow, she just felt that she belonged there among the elite and instinctively knew how to communicate with them. Accordingly, for the rest of her life, she would continue to pursue them and was often rather bold, original, and uninhibited in doing so.

Thus, on her first trip to England, she somehow managed to introduce herself to T. S. Eliot by calling on him at his office, although I'm sure she set up that *coup* with a series of flattering letters *en avant*. Similarly, on her first trip to Ireland, she met Yeats's widow through the auspices of Frank O'Connor, whom she had met in her effort to promote a play by his friend Padraic Colum, whom she also met here in the States. He was then a neighbor of a friend of hers on Riverside Drive.

And quite a few years later (for she never lost that talent), she wrangled an "audience" with the great Buckminster Fuller, in a period when she wasn't employed by anyone important and thus could not call on her job or employer as an agent for entrée. That idiosyncratic and hermetic architect surprisingly responded to what was probably a very clever letter of self introduction, wherein she displayed a great appreciation of his genius and may have hinted at the possibility of doing a book on him—and that probably did the trick. I don't recall why she took me along for that meeting. Perhaps because she was meeting him with his wife?

These were all amazing feats, considering that Geraldine was not well-connected socially, never finished college, and while quite well-read had many gaps in her self-education. But obviously she had a "smell" for what was unique and important and for the true innovators, and she knew how to fashion her intuitions in an uncannily clever way. But, alas, underneath all that flash and brilliance lay an emotionally bruised little orphan girl who had lost both parents in a terrible house fire and was later adopted and brought up by some well-meaning bourgeois family, who tried to give her the love she needed but with whom she never felt fully at home or truly wanted, and, as a result, she was never fully healed.

Oh, there is much more to tell about Geraldine Lust—whom I once christened *la belle Dame sans merci*—and the rest of our later, almost lifetime, Platonic relationship. For, after my return from Europe, though we didn't resume our earlier romance (something had broken the original spell), we still loved one another in one way or another and were proverbially fond of telling each other that we were sure to marry one of these days, i.e., when both of us would be free to do so! This illusion lasted with gradually diminishing force until, totally unexpected by her friends, she went into a full retreat from New York and her whole past life, several years before dying prematurely at the age of sixty-seven in a retirement community near beautiful, historic Lenox, Massachusetts, amidst the ghosts of Edith Wharton, Melville, and Hawthorne and so many others. And forbade all friends, of whom she still had many, to come and visit her—including yours truly!

I only worry, when it comes to writing about Geraldine, that I may have already told you earlier in conversation what I'm about to write you; nevertheless, by all means remind me to be sure not to leave out the story of perhaps her greatest *coup*, achieved when she was older, less attractive, and almost penniless, namely, getting Jean Genet's great play, *The Blacks*, produced successfully Off-Broadway, thereby unknowingly launching the careers of six or seven important African American actors (then called, more appropriately for that play, "Black"), including James Earl Jones and Cicely Tyson.

Obviously Geraldine was a very intelligent woman, in answer to the question you once posed as to who was the most intelligent woman I ever met. Impossible to answer! How could I, or anyone, determine the "most"? Just what is intelligence, anyway, and how does one measure it, outside of the infamous IQ tests, which tell you well nigh nothing about well-rounded, all-purpose intelligence, nor how it is to be judged or evaluated?

Thus you, my dearly beloved, are also a very intelligent woman, but your intelligence is of an entirely different nature than was Geraldine's. While you two would have recognized the intelligence in the other, your two types of intelligence probably would not have meshed. The same holds true for our modest, but brilliant, Swiss doctor Toni, though you two, with your Continental backgrounds, probably would have had more in common and got along on some levels. Similarly with the Hungarian graphologist, Klara Roman, with your Balkan background in common. So, too, possibly for the iconoclastic, questioning intelligence of the similar sounding Tomi from Chicago, who died so shockingly young. And how would you classify Faye's cool intelligence, which so far you have found somewhat off-putting—whom we have yet to talk about in these letters? Or that of writer/composer Doris Schwerin, whom you met briefly at our Geraldine memorial breakfast meeting a couple of years ago? And what about that very good, very pert, math teacher I had at NYU, who just bubbled forth that kind of intelligence? Or my severe, dour, rarely smiling philosophy mentor, Suzanne K. Langer, under whom I studied at both NYU and Columbia?

Then there are the great, fabled female figures of history, art, and literature—Nefertiti, Cleopatra, Theodora, Mme. Nehru, Golda Meier, Susan Sontag, Hannah Arendt, Hildegarde von Bingen, Catherine the Great, Jane Austen, George Eliot, Mme. Curie, Simone de Beauvoir, Simone Weil, Queen Cristina, Sor Juana Inez de la Cruz, Lady Murasaki, and on and on and on, not to mention

Gertrude Stein—what a spectacular array of superior intelligences! But it would be impossible to even begin to rank them. And where would you place that very special, clairvoyant intelligence of dear Emily Dickinson, whom you so adore? Or the critic Harold Bloom's hypothetical female author of much of Genesis? And what about Mae West, who wrote all the plays and movie scripts she starred in, except for *My Little Chickadee*, which she co-authored with her co-star W. C. Fields?

So let's forget about rankings—one would run into the same problems dealing with male intelligences, of course. What about the differences between male and female intelligences? That would make a fascinating essay in itself. A subject for a modern Montaigne, wouldn't you say? So, with a Rabelaisan grin, I say, *à la prochaine fois*.

M.

January 7, 2007

Meine liebe Nina:

I address you thus because somehow my thoughts go back again to that turbulent year I spent in Germany where so much happened in such a short time, from the last days of the Battle of the Bulge to crossing the Rhine at Remagen to meeting the Russians at Torgau to a somewhat idyllic *Luftpause* in Weissenfels and finally to those hectic months of music and talk at AFN Radio Bremen and that Alice in Wonderland exit via Frankfurt-am-Main en route to Paris...

But what continues to haunt me is what I so far have not managed to properly express in these letters, though there were places in some of the episodes I described where I touched upon that so difficult a subject, namely, just how did I feel about the Germans? Plus the obvious corollary: how was I able to deal with them civilly, they, the enemy, the destroyers of Europe, the extinguishers of the Jews and the Gypsies and whoever else did not fit their mold? They, the would-be masters of the world?

There is, of course, no one simple answer. First of all, I was, perforce, there where it happened (thank God, not when). So I couldn't say, as many of my friends and relatives back home said then, and some still say, "I would never step on German soil. I'd never, ever, go to Germany, even if you paid me. They should all roast in Hell!" But as I just noted, I was there, had to be there, although fortunately when the worst was over and post-war Hell was perhaps in the process of devolving upward into becoming more like Purgatory. Second, I had to learn how to deal with each person or situation as it arose, or for what it was—and also for what I am. Thus, I think I was incapable of a general, all-encompassing HATRED. Though, of course, I had every reason for a Specific Hatred for those who wiped out what was left of my own family in Europe, who exterminated millions of my fellow Jews, not to mention my brother Gypsies, and my already cursed, feeble-minded, aged, and crippled fellow men and women.

But even so, granted I could have hated that way, at whom was I to direct that hatred, and what good would it have done if I had? Was I to see a Killer in every German I met on the street? And what was I to do then? Kill him or them in Revenge? Was I to stalk the highway for stray Nazis like a Hollywood film avenger and then maybe eliminate an innocent DP instead? The problem was less severe, less specific, when one was still at war, in battle, or roaring headlong through Germany because one was part of a team, what many called a war machine, and hence didn't have to personalize each action. Nevertheless, when I had to give that admonitory talk on top of that manure pile in that quaint little German village (described to you in an earlier letter), I had to be firm and tough and had to demand everyone's obedience—all of which, to my utter surprise, I managed to do quite effectively.

Strange how my hardbitten, headstrong colonel, whose dead head I was later to hold in my hands, intuited that I could do so. In retrospect, maybe I underestimated him? Did I want to murder or maim the youngsters who ran up to me afterwards at that site? No, of course not! Nor would it have made any sense. Or the poor, old women sweeping the manure into piles?

Later on, when the war was finally over and we had set up our headquarters on the outskirts of Weissenfels, taking over a few buildings from which to administer the town and adjacent territory, of course it was still imperative to be stern and firm, but obviously with less urgency than before. Nevertheless, in the first phase of our Occupation, it was difficult to deal fairly and squarely with people such as those town leaders and bureaucrats whom you were sure had been faithful, submissive, automaton Nazis, and who'd just as soon turn on you and throw you out of their town, their province, and their country without the slightest compulsion, if they could. But you had to suppress such instincts and try to produce a sane, workable, and practical understanding between former enemies—a *modus vivendi* that would work fairly for both sides.

Yes, there were many situations in which it was almost impossible not to feel hatred, contempt, disdain, impatience with these often stubborn, gullible people. It was especially aggravating, for example, to discover that in Weissenfels, which is not that far from one of the less horrible concentration camps, Buchenwald (if one can even conceive of such a distinction, it being a major receiving center and transfer point to Auschwitz, I believe), forty-nine out of fifty people would tell you, assuming the most innocent faces you can imagine, that no, they had never heard of the place. And those few who had heard of it didn't believe any extermination ever took place there. "No, not there! Maybe elsewhere in Germany, but not there, not near us!" So what was I to do? Pull out their hair or pull out mine? How many degrees difference was this stance from the universal excuse of someone you know to be an anti-Semite: "Oh, no, some of my best friends are Jews."

In the second phase of the Occupation, which was, at least as far as my personal calendar was concerned, when I was transferred to AFN Bremen, time had already begun to gradually heal some of those wounds, suspicions, second thoughts, hesitations, distrust. And then you'd say to yourself, "Oh what the hell, let's go ahead. We've got work to do." Besides, the majority of the German people were so 100 percent occupied with restoring their cities, their businesses, their schools, their arts, *und so weiter*, they couldn't waste time on brooding over their losses. In general, one could say, as Czeslaw Milosz put it in *The Captive Mind*, that in the American Zone "people of all nationalities and social positions, ex-Nazis, ex-prisoners, the German bourgeoisie [were] baffled by what had happened." Yes, and most American soldiers and officers as well...

In any event, since all of us at AFN Bremen were so intensely involved in trying to build up our radio center and make it work, we, too, did not have time to dream about or think about Revenge. Hence, there developed a kind of cooperative trust between us and the immediate German staff we had to deal with. Then this began slowly to penetrate into the town itself, where I don't remember any revolts, any work sabotage, or any major complaints on the part of any of the local population during the months I was there.

Of course, the Army treated that population quite well. We didn't impose curfews, set up watchtowers, or harass them like the Soviets did in Weissenfels; remember my account of that trip back there? And I'm sure it paid off. But this may be a somewhat prejudiced view, since, being isolated from the problems of running a city, I would not have been aware when something went off kilter, unless it was a major goof or misstep. I did keep my ear to the ground as much as I could, however; and those at the station who were more directly involved with reporting the news would have caught anything serious, and then the rest of us on the staff would have learned of it from them, if not from listening to our own broadcasts!

Yet there was one constant, almost universal lament I would hear from the ordinary man on the street, both back in Weissenfels, and again later in Bremen, and that was: "Why did you stop? Why didn't you push the Russians back into Poland? We would have helped you do it. We wanted to. We still want to. Trust us, the Communists are dangerous. They're the real menace. There's big trouble ahead!"

Well, as history has shown, they were partially right. Stopping the Russians was accomplished *ipso facto* by meeting them in Germany. Except that we should have remained at the Elbe and not pulled back in handing over Saxony to them; also, we probably should have simply pushed further south and southeastward and taken Prague before the Soviets got there. Which we could have! The Ninth Army was itching to do just that, until reined in by that unfortunate Eisenhower deal. And this is not just me talking: most historians agree.

But nothing so simple as what those off the field quarterbacks advised would have been even half feasible. Besides, the German war machine was finished. What help could it have been then? Indeed, during those last months of the war, the Germans were so desperate they had to recruit teenagers and boys into the once mighty *Wehrmacht*—like the young Günter Grass, as we have subsequently learned. We saw this already in that rapid traversal of Germany we made after the Battle of the Bulge.

Oh my, I'm beginning to sound almost like one of those German barroom strategists I've just been criticizing. Of course, it was all much more complex than any of us in the lower echelons could have imagined. Witness the widely differing interpretations since advanced in the innumerable books and articles about that controversial corner of a much bigger conflict. Only this past summer there has been a spate of reviews of Norman Davies's latest book, *No Simple Victory: World War II in Europe, 1939-1945*, with special emphasis on what happened in Poland (his specialty) and other Eastern European countries before the eventually-to-be-raised Iron Curtain. One of his major contentions is that far more people know about the Nazi persecution of the Jews than about the Soviet persecution of the Poles, and he's trying to straighten that out. Of course, in doing so, he steps on many toes because he tends to equate them as two equal Holocausts, and, terrible and unforgiveable as the Soviet terror was, it was still far different from that of the Nazis, much more complicated and extensive, also longer-lasting. The two simply cannot be judged by the same terms. Also, in building his case, Davies tends to soft-pedal such things as the Polish government's policies toward Jews during the interwar period, and its

177

undeniable ethnic cleansing of Germans and Ukrainians after the war! Nevertheless, we should still seriously reckon with what Davies has to say.

Another recent revisionist voice is that of Janet Malcolm in her book on Gertrude Stein, in which she delves deeper into what really happened to Gertrude and Alice during the Vichy regime, protected, as it seems they were, by a highly placed French anti-Semite and collaborator—and it's not an edifying story. But not totally unexpected. Didn't I register in one of my earlier letters how I wondered why I could never get either of them to talk about that period, or find out what happened to their Jewish friends or acquaintances? And not only them. If the full truth had been told more universally, I fear it would have resulted in a veritable sea of shaved heads, *hélas*...

Dolorously yours,
M.

The Ides of March, 2007
Dear Nina:

Still somewhat doleful after that last letter, but for an entirely different reason. I just discovered via Google what happened to our beloved Stella Snead. Remember when I told you about that odd letter from her, a sort of form letter to her friends, inviting us to come in for a last visit and choose whatever books we would like from her library, which, she said, it was time to disperse among those younger than she. "After all, I'm in my nineties, I won't be here much longer." I wrote her a note to please hang on, that I'd try to drop by as soon as I could. Alas, I'm afraid that I procrastinated too long, for when I called two or three months later to decide on a good day to drop in, the phone had been disconnected, and I could get no further information from the phone company. Later, I called Harriet Zinnes, who, as you may recall, brought all three of us together again a couple of years ago, when we went to an exhibition of Stella's recent surrealist paintings, plus some of her very youthful ones, down in Tribeca. For I had lost touch with her after the death of Sari.

Well, Harriet had no idea where she could be. She hadn't talked to her for awhile. Again, last week, when I phoned Harriet to tell her about your upcoming reading at Barnes and Noble for the 15th Anniversary Celebration of "Poetry in Motion" (their project of putting poems in subway ad space, including yours about giving that seat to an elderly person), she still hadn't found Stella. So I consulted Mr. Google, and, sure enough, Stella had predicted her own demise. She died last spring "of natural causes at the Jewish Home and Hospital in Manhattan," the *Times* obit said. (Was Stella Jewish? I had seen no sign of it ever.) I was really very saddened at this news. Stella was one of the few "good" souls still around; she reminded me in some ways of dear Agnes in Weissenfels. She was certainly more kind, generous, and giving than her one-time soulmate, Sari. Surely more modest. I remember how at Sari's gatherings Stella would sort of shrink into the furniture.

Yet what a remarkable life she had led! You no doubt recall those early, nocturnal, dreamlike landscapes of hers populated by equally dreamy and fantasy-derived animals and semi-human figures. One could see the influences of Tanguy and Max Ernst, and others. In fact, I thought I discerned touches of early English primitive painting here and there. But then, after the beginnings of some recognition, such as being included in the Carnegie International exhibition in Pittsburgh, she suddenly abandoned painting and became a far more successful (at least in worldly terms) photographer, having moved to India where she lived for some years, photographing street life, nature and, above all, Hindu sculpture. These resulted in eight beautiful volumes. Then, after returning to the States, and a few other trips (I believe she made one to the Andes), and, probably under the influence of Sari, she began making collages from cut up pieces of her own photographs! Then, *mirabile dictu*, in the late Eighties, Stella began painting again. With that, recognition in the art world also returned to her in those last few years. Last season, for example, one of her paintings from the Forties was included in "Surrealism USA" at the National Academy Museum here in New York City. So the circle was completed. I only wish we could have seen her one last time before she stepped out of the circle and off of the globe.

Talk of Stella reminds me of another remarkable woman I met through the "auspices" of Sari, who certainly had a genius for bringing unusual people together; indeed, she could well have been dubbed "La Mama of 57th Street," for she shared that particular talent with Ellen Stewart of East 4th Street, the bustling hub of Off-Off-Broadway. Too bad that, as far as I'm aware, those two amazing ladies never met. In any case, the remarkable woman I refer to, and whom I believe I've already mentioned once or twice in earlier letters, was Mura Dehn Thomas—she, who introduced Sari and me to Gospel churches in Harlem quite some time before Gospel became the rage, and long before it began to be over-commercialized. Those were wonderful excursions: Gospel then was so pure that it made your hair stand on end, as you sat at the edge of a hard pew bench in a small, old church off one of the main avenues of Harlem. For Mura, that had long been a given; for us, it was a great, fresh discovery.

However, Mura's primary interest in Harlem was Dance! And, of course, that's where she made her mark. Her documentation of Afro-American ballroom dancing during its heyday at the Savoy Ballroom is now one of the treasures of the Dance Section of the Library of the Performing Arts at Lincoln Center. Yet at the time I met her, she was only beginning to put those films together and needed help in organizing them, not to mention making the most of her considerable talents. Naturally, I wanted to help her cause, even though I knew little about film and even less about the Savoy. But Mura knew that I was already producing things at Cooper Union, such as staged concert readings of neglected classic plays as well as occasional off-beat modern novelties. Why not come up with a project to help put Mura's research on the map? (Yes, dear Nina, my Cooper Union venture actually started as a joint project of Geraldine's and mine; we later invited my actor friend, Norman Shelly, to participate, with me handling the production aspects and G. and N. directing. We did some very interesting things there, such as D. H. Lawrence's little-known, but very beautiful, biblical play, *David*. But I'll go into that later.)

This collaboration led to other projects, of course. Among these was a unique evening of African American ballroom dancing, which I put on with Mura and technical know-how from Norman. For I think that by this time Geraldine had tired of these free productions, which, after all, take a lot of time and energy and bring in no cash! Anyway, she and Mura would never have been able to work together, not those two quite independent female superegos!

That memorable evening, which we called "Kaleidoscope of Vaudeville," took place Friday night, February 9, 1962, in the Great Hall of Cooper Union and featured the Mura Dehn Jazz Dance Theatre. This was not an ongoing company of hers but rather a convenient and suitable name for the extraordinary group of mostly middle-aged and older, very seasoned jazz ballroom dancers, tap-dancers, and ex-vaudeville comics, some of whom had been professional headliners back in the late Thirties and early Forties in Harlem, and others who had been part of an earlier traditional jazz dance company of hers. Mura was able to call on all of them just for this very special event, for they trusted her, and knew she knew her stuff. Plus which, she had the invaluable aid and advice of old-timer James Berry in putting on the actual show. She also drew upon her vast knowledge of the forebears of jazz dance—the minstrel shows of the 19th and early 20th centuries, early ragtime, one-step, two-step, the Charleston, and other later dances. She had already lived some of this repertoire.

The opening number—and what a spectacle it turned out to be!—was a marvelous Grand Parade and Bally-Hoo modelled on the old minstrel tradition, during which the whole cast stomped its way down the aisles of that venerable old Great Hall in the basement of Cooper Union, a veritable amphitheatre, that lends itself well to such excursions. (I may have told you before, about two years ago, when you read there at Daniela's special poetry reading for her anthology, *Women Writers on War*, that this hall was the site of some of the historic Lincoln-Douglass debates.) The parade was followed by Grand Dad, a number by a comedian, then a banjo solo and a blues vocal. Next came an evocation of the ragtime-cakewalk era up to the one-step and two-step and Charleston period, using a very talented group of natural dancers, trained by Elaine Johnson and Mura herself. After that, we saw Baby Lawrence do his muted, sophisticated tap-dancing; and then we marveled at that great old-timer and droll comic Johnny Hudgins, with his huge over-sized shoes that looked somewhat like snowshoes, in which he slid, skated, and glided round and about the narrow but long Cooper Union stage, while monologuing freely and breaking us up with almost every phrase he uttered. His humor was somewhat akin to that of his contemporary, the marvelous comedienne Moms Mabley. And for the finale of the first half, we had the exuberant Kodax group. All these artists were aided and abetted—and inspired—by a wonderful group of old jazz musicians brought together by David Martin, and seemed to know each other and the older dancers as kith and kin, brothers and sisters. Martin also featured individual star players in the independent music numbers as well.

The second half of the program started with the Tiger Rag, followed by a saxophone solo. Next came Buster Brown and Stomp Cross, two great old-time tapdancers. Then Top Cast, Mable Lee, and Bert Gibson. After them, music from the Thirties—vocal and instrumental. Then more tapdancing. All of it capped by a finale featuring chronologically the various dances originating at the Savoy (most of which Mura had already filmed back during their heyday)—the Big Apple, Lindy Hop, Boogie-woogie, Shimmy, Snake Hips, Savoy, Blues—up to and including Bebop and Rock and Roll.

Though "Kaleidoscope" proved a huge success with the public, we had been unable to get any significant dance or music critics to cover the show. How different it would have been almost anytime in the last decade or two! But back then, the public was not yet ready for the revival of these dances, not even tap dance. Think back to those movie musicals you loved as a young girl in Romania, with Astaire and Rogers, and Shirley Temple dancing with the great Bojangles, who in his youth was said by some to have possibly been an even greater tapdancer than Astaire. Remember also that during that period almost every Broadway musical featured tapdancers. That's where, indeed, Astaire took his first steps with his sister, Adele. But Agnes De Mille choreographing *Oklahoma* spelled the beginning of the end for the standard Broadway dance show. Dances now had to advance the plot of the playbook of any musical, so that by the late Forties and early Fifties, tap dance was totally out. That's why we were able to get Afro-American star dancers to join us in our non-profit program: they were dying for a chance just to perform again before an audience.

Yes, the more sophisticated black (excuse my sometimes using the non-PC term, since I often find the longer, more complicated Afro- or African American nomer a little awkward to use and also a little self-conscious) rising middle class of the late Fifties and the Sixties, even into the Seventies, did not want to be reminded of anything that smacked of Jim Crowism. They weren't yet ready for Mura's glorification of early Negro minstrelsy, later ragtime, or early jazz, nor the growing diversity and creativity of the black ballroom dancer. But, glory be, they can now at last afford to agree with her that minstrelsy represented the first signifcant interpenetration of European and African heritage into American theater, creating such an enthusiastic response that it was at one time called an "infatuation." Indeed, by the mid-19th century the minstrel craze had achieved a world-wide scale. Now forgotten or looked down upon by most, in its time, that craze was as sweeping as jazz in the first half of the 20th century. So that nowadays, the curious younger African American is hungry to know more about his forebears because that gives him a greater sense of his own worth; and he can now look back and better appreciate the originality of his parents and grandparents, and be proud of them and the significance of what they created.

It's interesting, dear Nina, to note how something comparable happens with other minority groups. Take the great resistance of American Jewry during the late forties and fifties and even into the early sixties of anything that smacked of the Jewish *shtetl*. I remember producer Hal Prince telling us at our first rehearsal that *Fiddler on the Roof* had been making the rounds of Broadway producers for over ten years and had had at least ten or eleven options, which were all dropped because these would-be producers couldn't raise enough money to launch a production—not until daring, young Prince himself faced up to the challenge. And, of course, the rest is history. But that was also because by the time *Fiddler* hit the boards, younger sophisticated Jews felt they could afford to be nostalgic about their ancestors. Similar things happened with Italian communities and the Irish (the latter now being sometimes carried to almost embarrassing extremes with such spectacles as those big TV Celtic nights on Public Television). Once a group feels it has been fully accepted by American society, it dares go back to its roots, and to honor and remember them. Look at the Greeks!

Yes, my dear, as I look back on it now—that "Kaleidoscope" took place fifty-five years ago!—it's amazing what a wealth and variety of talent, and what a range in age of the participants, Mura was able to bring together in such a short time. Of course, it was the pay-off of years of working with, following the careers of, and, perhaps in some cases, studying specific dances with many of these people. Then, too, as I pointed out earlier, most of them had no place else to perform anymore. Vaudeville, both white and black, was finished to all intents and purposes. Old-timers like the incredible Johnny Hudgins could only be seen occasionally on a variety TV show that dared to bring in artists known to black but not to white audiences. Most tapdancers had no work at all, except possibly in exclusively African American nightclubs or on community and church festive occasions. The younger black dancers, of course, were busy learning ballet, modern dance, and Michael Kidd and Bob Fosse steps and quirks, in addition to developing their own more modern versions of Lindy Hop and other old-time dances, though some of them also perfected their skills in performing the originals. Bringing them in helped make our show a more genuine picture of the world of black dance. Yet, weren't we, in turn, strangely neglecting their own pioneers in studying, absorbing, and incorporating the movements of African dance in the Caribbean and Africa itself, such as the beautiful, mesmerizing Katherine Dunham, whom I saw in her heyday, Pearl Primus, and Asadata Dafora, among others?

Mura was indefatigable. She was probably about fifty-five years old then, and had already accomplished the major part of her goals, namely, the actual filming of those dances. But, as I noted above, she still had to edit and catalogue them properly for Lincoln Center. Yet she felt she needed to do more to save the dances than just film them for posterity. Accordingly, her new, major long-range goal was to found and develop an Academy for such dance so that it could be kept alive and passed down from one generation to another. That's another place where she called on me to help, in such things as writing up grant requests for the establishment of an Afro-American Folk Dance Center, and the like. As she pointed out, "Almost every ethnic group at present has a folk-dance group representing it, supported by its government or some other cultural organization. [For example, the Ukrainian Dance Center near Cooper Union is backed by its Church. Remember their remarkable cathedral two blocks away that I pointed out to you one day as we passed by in a taxi en route to C.U.?] Only the Afro-American folk dance, in spite of its global following, has no focal point, no organized group of its own. Otherwise," she rightly argued, "much of that tradition will be lost forever."

So, to that end, Mura proposed the establishment of a school, and along with it, an authentic professional performing group steeped in that tradition, a sort of living archive—plus, of course, a documentary film library. As to her existing film, she was naturally anxious to bring that documentation up to date. The same is true of the music. Unfortunately, our efforts got nowhere: Mura was too far ahead of her time. Lincoln Center is only now beginning to fulfill part of that vision, fifty years on, with its admirable Jazz Center. It has probably already documented the various music styles of the past century, but I doubt whether anyone is carrying on a comparable documentation for each succeeding style of dance today. Not even the Alvin Ailey school, I'll wager, though it does incorporate admirably some aspects of the African American infusion into our Modern Dance tradition. However, with the advances in TV, the overabundance of dance commercials, more sophisticated video techniques, and the like, we shall have snippets of Hip Hop and everything else thrown into the pot for the immediate future.

But will these give us a truly objective, systematic documentation of these day-to-day phenomena? It's dangerous to depend on just commercial manifestations. These seldom employ the original or genuine "folk" or natural versions of such dances. The films of the Savoy that Mura made give one a much more authentic feel for the period and its dances than do the commercial and albeit-artistic, professional versions that showed up from time to time on the screen, like the famed-for-their-splits Nicholas Brothers, for instance. As she notes in her proposal: "The twentieth century makes it possible for the first time in the history of dance—thanks to films, dance Labanotation, and the unique historical moment—to observe and record a new folk dance creating itself. The possibility of retaining a full picture of this development must be realized." In addition to all this, she was eager to finish a history of minstrelsy that she had been working on.

Unfortunately, Mura had to slow down during the next decade or two for health reasons, so that she was unable to muster up enough energy to push her proposal as much as it needed. Nor could I take more time from my other work to help her go full speed ahead with her project. Nevertheless, ultimately she obviously was able to organize and to incorporate almost all of the footage she had shot during those eventful years at the Savoy, with the help of the Lincoln Center library staff no doubt, into a five-hour-long documentary about the overall evolution of black dance styles in urban America from the early 1900s to the 1950s—what the center calls a "unique visual record of vernacular jazz dancing," and here they coin a strange expression, "that *exuberated* [my italics] the heritage of movement that shaped the way we dance, on and off stage."

Highlights of this footage were later incorporated into a video that, amazingly, can now be obtained through the Internet, called "The Spirit Moves: A History of Black Social Dance, Part 1 and 2," which apparently happened shortly before she died. Part 1 covers dances from 1900 to the 1940s. Part 2 was filmed during the last years of the Savoy, the 1950s. Also, remarkably, and luckily, two enterprising ladies, Louise Ghertler and Pamela Katz, made a short film, "In a Jazz Way: A Portrait of Mura Dehn," that was shown at the Film Forum in 1987, along with a cut version of "The Spirit Moves." (Was Mura by this time too old and feeble to invite her friends to this showing? Or even to let us know it was happening?)

Whatever, let us be grateful that there is a visual record of this quixotic lady herself wherein she utters some of her unique insights into this extraordinary art to which she literally devoted her life. Thus, in her psychological analysis of social dancing, she maintained that the essential art of it is learning "how to hold your body and how to let it go." Or take her quite acute observation that these dances "chronicle a time of pre-war optimism for blacks (with the Lindy Hop and related subsequent dances) to the pessimism and disaffiliation of post-war be-bop and rock and roll." Or what perhaps are her most illuminating insights on that influence, and here I quote from her unpublished essay on minstrelsy (and which I helped her formulate): "In minstrelsy, it was the white man acquiring the character of the Negro. In jazz, it was the Negro assimilating the European form and recreating it into the rhythms of our era....In rock and roll, the Negro turned his back on all he learned from the white man. He now turned inward, and drew from inside....Whites are able to follow him and to master this form so completely alien to our culture....In rock and roll dance, the Negro and white are not to be distinguished, both deriving ecstatic satisfaction from it." ...Amen.

But as for her larger ambition, founding a folk dance academy and all that would go along with it, that plan really went nowhere. In fact, I'm probably one of the few who knew anything about it! I sometimes wonder now why she did not enlist the aid of two of her friends from their days and nights together in the Vienna Opera Ballet, namely, the wife of Rudolf Bing, then head of the Met Opera, and Mme. Piscator, still working in the States after her husband, Erwin Piscator, the great German stage director, the master of epic theatre, and a coeval of Brecht, had returned

187

to resume his directing career in Germany. Together they might have been able to reach other sources of backing that Mura could not reach on her own. Or was she too proud and independent to ask anything of them?

Unfortunately, I did not learn or find out about Mura's friendship with these potentially influential ladies until too late. It wasn't until the early Seventies that I got a call from Mura, whom I hadn't seen for awhile, to be her guest at the Met in Mrs. Bing's box. And there I found Mme. Piscator, with whom I had also worked, and about whom I shall soon tell you more, seated with Mme. Bing. I believe the opera was *Tales of Hoffmann*, but I doubt whether the ladies heard much of it. They had so much catching up to do. Alas, it was too late in the game to bring up Mura's grand project, and besides, Mme. Piscator had her own ambitious teaching and directing projects to carry out, as well as some writing to do, parts of which I had worked on with her in the past, never knowing that she knew Mura. But Mme. Bing? Lost opportunity, I fear...

So who was Mura Dehn (Thomas) and where did she come from, you are probably asking yourself. She was born and raised in Russia, and came of age shortly after the Revolution. While there, like a good, well-brought-up bourgeois girl (which she was), she was trained in ballet, but she was also exposed to other kinds of dance, including jazz, though strangely enough, she did not fall under its spell at that time. Rather, she was more spellbound by the great Isadora Duncan, then living in Russia, the *amour* of the avant-garde poet, Yevgeny Yesenin. But life soon proved too difficult in Russia, so Mura embarked first for Vienna, where she danced in the Opera ballet and where, as we have seen, she ended up in the same company with Mmes. Bing and Piscator.

But before long, she began to tire of the ballet and decided to try out Paris, which was then the big magnet center of everything new in the arts. There she met Josephine Baker and instantly became her fan, and a fan of jazz as well. Baker opened her eyes to what jazz was all about. So by 1930, after traipsing around Europe with a solo dance show she had worked up with the American husband she had acquired en route—the interesting satirical painter, Adolf Dehn—she was ready to emigrate with him to New York, where one night she stumbled upon that great dance hall, the Savoy, an event which was to permanently change her life. We have seen something of what it did for her, although before she reached that stage, there was a period of poverty which apparently led to an eventual breakup of that marriage. Some years later she was to marry another American, a Merchant Marine captain, Herman Thomas, seemingly of Danish origin. That's where the name "Thomas" came from, of course. He turned out to be quite an atypical seaman, had great patience with his temperamental wife, and actually encouraged her filming of dance aspirations.

Does the Mura story, I hope, make a little more sense to you now? Surely, you must have been wondering, my dear Ninotchka, how this beautiful, tall Russian Jewess became a sort of unacknowledged priestess of American Jazz. While you were just an innnocent little girl skating down the streets of Brasov and/or Bucharest, Mura was being converted to the West! You were no doubt too young to have seen her dance in Bucharest if, indeed, her tours in the late Twenties ever brought her there. But before taking leave of Mura, I should point out that underneath a sometimes off-putting bravado and hauteur, there was a warm, sympathetic human being and a true friend, someone you wouldn't be afraid to ask a favor of. Thus, for example, she was one of the few professional friends I had during that period who was at all understanding and considerate of my poor wife, Ann, and her problems, certainly one of the few I could be quite open with about them. She was also fond of, and playful with, our son, Jacob.

Similarly, I'm quite sure that she helped out a number of her Afro-American artist friends financially when they ran short. She also had a great deal of patience and forbearance dealing with some of their drinking and related problems. Finally, of this group of lady artists I've been describing in the last two letters, I think you might have been most at home with Mura, maybe even more so than with Stella, her English reserve being so at odds with your

189

warmhearted Romanian openness...

So with a Russian bear hug and a Romanian duple kiss, I bid you *la revedere!*

M.

October 15, 2007

My dear Nina:

Bringing up Mme. Piscator in the last letter naturally led to a number of memories springing up of her husband, Erwin Piscator, intrepid begetter of Epic theater and one of the theatrical giants of the Weimar Republic period, which, short as it was, produced a wealth of art that at times almost eclipsed whatever else happened during the first twenty years of the 20th century. As you Romanians know, great strides were made there in theater, architecture, painting, music, dance—not to mention science!

Fortunately, The New School had taken Piscator in—along with an extraordinary galaxy of major European, mostly German, refugee scientists, sociologists, economists, historians, and other great scholars (Adorno, Marcuse, Horkheimer, Arnheim, Arendt, et al)—to teach theater and to establish a drama school which was started up under the School's auspices back in 1940. I don't know the full history of just how this all came about, but by the time I arrived in New York after my "Paris period," Piscator's Dramatic Workshop was a busy, thriving, enterprise, helped no doubt by the GI Bill, which paid the tuition of most of its male students, and to which it was able to attract some of the best American acting teachers and theater people. These were supplemented—and enhanced—by a very good staff of German and Austrian theatrical refugees, among whom, of course, was Piscator's beautiful wife, the dancer Maria Ley, although, in the first years, I'm told, she taught less and organized more. In fact, before long, Mme. Ley-Piscator herself brought a great deal of money onto the scene through her charm and connections, having been married to one of the leading German Jewish business tycoons of that period, Frank Deutsch (who, earlier, had taken his life in Paris), and having intimate connections with the international elite.

Among the Workshop's lesser-known European teachers, one of the most popular, was that modest Viennese woman with the incredible name, Trudl Dubsky-Zipper, who taught "movement for actors"—not dance per se, though, of course, it usually verged closer into some sort of modern Wigmanish dance. You may remember my mentioning her in an earlier letter, the one discussing her husband, Herbert Zipper, and his sadly failed attempt to establish an orchestra at the Brooklyn Academy of Music. Trudl was a fine teacher, and a good, up-to-date "Hausfrau"; together they made a delightful, charming Viennese couple.

But, more importantly for a dramatic workshop, there were a number of excellent acting teachers, both American and European, among whom the one I probably learned the most from was the diminutive Raiken Ben-Ami, a veteran of Habimah's famed production of *The Dybbuk*, I believe. By the time I attended The Dramatic Workshop, after graduating from NYU, he was very much involved in handling the still-ongoing repertory theater seasons which Piscator had started some years earlier during the heyday of The Workshop. Under this plan, a season of plays embracing both modern and classic repertoire was presented annually at the small President Theater on West 48th Street, next to that noisy Italian tourist restaurant at the corner of Eighth Avenue (the upper floors of which housed the Academy), and was repeated downtown (or sometimes vice versa, or alternately) in the superbly equipped Rooftop Theater of that historic, old Yiddish Theater vaudeville palace, Minsky's—back then, still on Houston Street at the foot of Second Avenue. Now, alas, the whole building has been demolished and replaced by an anoydne, expensive apartment house. In any case, it was during that year that I had my first and only real repertory experience, playing everything from Malvolio in *Twelfth Night* to Dr. Einstein in *Arsenic and Old Lace*! It was wonderful to have people you didn't know stop you on Second Avenue and compliment you on a performance they saw last night or last week at the Rooftop and ask what role you'd be playing next. (Though in summer stock that happens all the time.)

Of course, these were modest, low-budget shows, not to be compared with the larger-scaled productions (often approaching spectacles) Piscator put on during the three or four years, immediately after the end of World War II, at the President, unfortunately cut back a year or so before I joined the Workshop. Perhaps the most exciting of these theater works was Piscator's take on Sartre's *The Flies* (the first Sartre done in New York); Piscator's famed adaptation of Tolstoy's *War and Peace*, scaled down to one evening, of course, and revised somewhat for American audiences; and the one most of us thought should have been transferred to Broadway, his powerful stage adaptation of Robert Penn Warren's great novel, *All the King's Men*, much more effective than either of the two later film versions.

Yet personally I found Piscator's inventive and moving staging of the German poet/playwright Wolfgang Borchert's expressionist post-war play, *Outside the Door*, possibly the most impressive of them all, and the one that our European-born teachers assured me was closest in spirit to his landmark 1920s productions in Berlin. It was certainly more in Piscator's epic style and used all kinds of technical devices, projections, etc., including an incredible rippling lightshow-like flooding of the entire proscenium for the monologue scene of the River Elbe, stunningly portrayed by the African American actress, Vinnette Carroll. Indomitable Vinnette went on to found and run the Urban Art Corps, whose production of *Don't Bother Me, I Can't Cope* moved to Broadway and ran for over a thousand performances. But before that transformation, I managed to persuade her to essay Cleopatra in a staged concert reading of Dryden's *All for Love*, which I put on for a "one-night stand" at Cooper Union in the spring of 1960, a year or two before Mura Dehn's "Kaleidoscope" described earlier. (Unfortunately, all our Cooper Union productions had to be one-night stands.)

When I came to the Workshop, after getting my BA from NYU, people were saying that it was already on the decline, that Piscator had lost interest in it, and that with the supply of Army veterans all but used up, it was now on quite shaky financial grounds. Nevertheless, I found it an exciting place to study theater and practice it, certainly more all-encompassing than those more insular acting classes I had been taking at night while still studying at NYU during the day. Besides, it was stimulating to walk and work in the same rooms that housed, trained, and graduated such future stars as the very talented Elaine Stritch, Bea Arthur, Ben Gazzara, Gene Saks, Walter Matthau, Tony Curtis, Harry Belafonte, and many a lesser light, and to hear stories, for example, when I was doing Malvolio there in *Twelfth Night*, about what a sensational Viola Stritch was when Piscator first staged his cut version of that play four or five years earlier, and how great Bea Arthur was in *The Flies*, and comparable tales about other actors.

Of course, the faculty missed them, though by the time I got there, most of the better American teachers had already resigned to form their own schools, the most noteworthy being the Stella Adler Studio, of course. I believe she first had Marlon Brando as a pupil in one of her original classes at The Workshop. (I was to take classes some years later with Stella and also to play four roles in her production of Kurt Weill's *Johnny Johnson* Off-Broadway, which Brando helped back.) An amusing sidelight to the *Twelfth Night* I did there was that as Malvolio I had three or four Violas (not Stritch, unfortunately, since she had by then long graduated into stardom), one of whom was the clever, spirited Elaine Dundy, who later moved to England where she met and married that caustic but generally very astute British theater critic, Kenneth Tynan, and who years later gained literary fame herself with her book about their tempestuous marriage and the British theater scene, *The Dud Avocado*.

Certainly, the level of teaching at The Dramatic Workshop was still quite high when I was there. The dogmatic, though often brilliant, Lee Strasberg himself gave an advanced class in directing, the one I mentioned Geraldine taking along with me. There was also a loquacious, but amusing, and very competent voice teacher, whose name eludes me now, who had the dubious distinction of training Hitler how to speak before his star pupil left Vienna for

193

riper grounds in Bavaria and ultimately Berlin and the Reichstag. I still do some of that teacher's voice exercises when I feel a bit rusty, or before going on stage, which reminds me of a delightful story about the great American comedienne, Ina Claire.

So forgive me for taking a little detour to some ten to twelve years after leaving the Workshop, when I was playing Tubal, Shylock's friend and confidant, in an Off-Broadway production of *The Merchant of Venice* at the Gate Theatre on Second Avenue, and also serving as assistant director to Boris Tumarin, who both played Shylock and directed the play. Bassanio was portrayed by Douglas Watson, once a promising young leading man on Broadway who somehow never achieved real stardom and, sadly, died too young to grow into the important character actor he might have become. Doug was a good sport, and once related to us during a rehearsal break how several years earlier, when he was featured with Ina Claire and Claude Rains in the Broadway premiere of T. S. Eliot's last play, *The Confidential Clerk*, he remembered Rains grumbling that he wasn't able to project that night, and Ina Claire scolding him, saying, "That's because you're not doing your voice exercises before the show, dear!" with the implication that, of course, she was. (A consummate actress, you will remember her, dear Nina, as the Grand Duchess in the Garbo film, *Ninotchka*.) I can still recall Ina Claire landing three laughs and a tear on one of her longer speeches in that Eliot play the night I saw her in it on Broadway. But she was getting older, and Doug revealed that she had to have certain cues and tricky phrases pasted on her tea cup or other props as memory guides. Of course, no audience would ever have detected such a ruse; she was much too skillful to betray anything but complete mastery while on stage. And Doug assured us that she did those voice exercises every night before the show.

To get back to Piscator and his Dramatic Workshop, the prize experience there always was to work with the "grand old man" himself, the Maestro, with his long white hair, impeccably combed back, and his formidable German preacher manner. I had the good fortune to do so when, to the other faculty members' surprise, he took over the reins of one of our Workshop productions, that of a lesser-known classic, Calderon de la Barca's long one-act play, *The Great Theater of the World*, similar to our English *Everyman*. Better known in Europe, that play as translated and revised by von Hofmannsthal, is still done every year at the Salzburg Festival, I think. As you can well imagine, this was a far from easy play to do. It needed a strong directorial hand, which, of course, is why I'm sure Piscator deigned to work with us younger students on it. It was a real challenge, which he met with what surprised me as being the most simple, natural, and theatrically logical means.

I can't remember any specific, special maneuvers of the kind for which he was famous, it being some sixty years ago; but somehow he helped each of us make our particular characters both uniquely ourselves and universal at the same time—which is very difficult to do, since, in this style of theater, and as written by Calderon, each character is basically a stock character or universal prototype. Yet this being theater, Piscator made sure that we were also real and believable personnages, within the epic framework. In fact, I think this is where he differed somewhat from Brecht over the latter's *Verfremdung* effect theory. Of course, that was part of Piscator's genius: he could plan his entire production moving little tin soldiers around on a facsimile chessboard set, and yet help the actors achieve verisimilitude, once he moved from soldiers to people.

Alas, shortly after working with us on the Calderon—I think we were his last set of American tin soldiers—he returned to Germany. Had to return, as I'm told by some sources! Disappointed, I'm sure, that Broadway had never really welcomed him, as he had expected, and certainly felt he deserved, though there had been various attempts over the years, especially after his *succes d'estime* producing Lessing's *Nathan the Wise* with Herbert Berghof as Nathan on Broadway in 1942. It's our great loss that none of these materialized during the next nine or ten years.

However, it wasn't long before Piscator reestablished himself in Berlin. As a *Times* article reported, when he premiered Peter Weiss's *The Investigation* back in the early Sixties, he was still in there punching: "A producer who considers a season wasted if he fails to shock half the town and outrage the rest, has done it again," turning that production into one of the theatrical events of the year in Europe. During this "return engagement," Piscator also premiered important works by Hochhut and Kipphardt. As Piscator himself used to put it, in his politics, he "always stood on the Left, where the heart is." You see, my dear, what we lost when he had to return to Germany. Of course, just why is still disputed, but there's no doubt that political pressure from Washington played an important role in that drama.

Yes, there were no doubt other reasons besides his being on the Left why America did not take to Piscator as much as he would have liked, and as much as you and I might wish it had. For our theater could have used more infusions of his know-how, his unique style, his stunning innovations, and his serious commitment to the art of theater. Primarily, I think it was because sometimes his work could be perhaps a little too didactic, a quality which is far from the American spirit, though his personality was actually more didactic than his directing! After all, he was a descendant of the famed 17th-century Protestant theologian and translator of the Bible, Johannes Piscator. Then, too, we were in the pre-McCarthy era: anti-Left suspicion and paranoia were already in the air. Had Piscator stayed in America, he probably would have had to go through what happened to Brecht and Eisler here, even though he had abandoned the Communist Party after his unhappy Moscow experiences in the late Thirties trying to make a film there. Now that I ponder the question, it's certainly possible that he sensed what was coming and decided to go while the going was good.

His was a more rigid personality than, say, that of a fellow German transplant to America, Billy Wilder. Unlike the latter, Piscator was never really comfortable with American gregariousness. From my limited time working under him, I think one could safely say that he never felt fully at home here. One must also bear in mind that foreign film directors in Hollywood have always been more successful than foreign stage directors on Broadway. The language problem is easier to surmount in the cinema, where dialogue is more limited, many takes can be made of a scene, and speech coaches are always standing by. Besides, any number of other factors can help carry a scene.

Now his elegant spouse, Mme. Maria Ley-Piscator (in the beginning, she was probably more famed than he as the dancer, Maria Ley)—who didn't follow the Maestro back to Berlin—was more flexible. Indeed, she went through many metamorphoses in her amazing one hundred years on this earth! One could almost say that if anyone had nine lives, she did. She was born Friederike Czada in 1899, daughter of a Hungarian architect and an Austrian concert pianist. Actually, one was never quite sure just who she was: A theater scholar? After all, she always called herself Dr. Piscator; it seems that she somehow managed to achieve a doctorate in literature at the Sorbonne after leaving Germany and settling in Paris for a spell, well before arriving on these shores. Or a dancer? We've seen that she performed as Maria Ley in the Vienna Opera Ballet along with Mura Dehn and Mme. Bing. One obituary called her a *Solotänzerin*, while her credits claimed that she helped Reinhardt stage his famed *A Midsummer Night's Dream* (though not the film). So was she also a choreographer? And a historian? She wrote a book about Piscator's theater, which was basically a redoing of his work *Das Politische Theater* into English. Or a writer? She managed to finish her autobiography at the age of eighty-nine (parts of which I had helped her with twenty years earlier). I think there was also a novel or two somewhere along the way. Or the supreme courtesan? She was, after all, a real beauty. It is said that she had any number of interesting lovers besides her three husbands, one of whom was the very wealthy Frank Deutsch, mentioned above, for whom she presumably converted to Judaism.

Ah yes, quite a remarkable woman, who played tennis well into her eighties. Who owned a large, handsome brownstone (that looked more like a "whitestone") on East 76th Street between Madison and Fifth Avenues. Who managed to teach and promulgate Piscator's epic, political theater for the last forty-five years of her life (but which also gave her academic standing and a *raison d'être*). Who gave a coherent press interview with a journalist for German radio at the ripe old age of ninety-eight from her perch in a select Jewish Home for the Aged. "Her German was perfect," the reporter marvelled.

What can one say? A chameleon-like *femme du monde*? She certainly knew how to dazzle men. I remember once sitting in on one of her matinee teas, observing a sophisticated critic from the German weekly *Aufbau* and some professor of drama from NYU as they sat at her feet in her elegant living room/salon, with its creaky old harp that she claimed was Mozart's, while she went on and on with tales about her beloved Piscator. But I never guessed that she was at least ten years older than I thought at that time, and twenty years older than those gentlemen could have imagined, agreeing amiably with whatever *mot* she might be trying out on them. (Come to think of it, Capek could have cast her in his play *The Makropolous Secret*.)

Well, my dear Nina, as you can see, it's obvious that my feelings about la Piscator are mixed. I started off trying to be as neutral and fair as I could in portraying her, nevertheless, somehow, irony, disbelief, skepticism have crept in—as they did in real life. Actually, my old friend, Anneliese Gellhorn (cousin of the pioneer feminist, journalist Martha Gellhorn, about whom I must tell you more later), when recommending me to Mme. P. as a part-time secretary/editor a few years after my Dramatic Workshop period, warned me that while all charm on the surface, she could be difficult, demanding, sometimes even duplicitous, and that I should always try to maintain a certain distance and objectivity. And Anneliese was dead right. Indeed, I didn't stay long on that first assignment; fortunately, a show came along, giving me a good excuse to quit, for I had begun to feel uneasy, uncomfortable at times.

Another interesting sidelight: Mme. P. didn't seem to remember me at all from the Workshop days. Of course, when I was there, the only play I recall her directing was a prettified *Romeo and Juliet*. Moreover, she was given few classes to teach and few plays to direct.

Instead, she could be seen more often going in and out of the executive offices with visiting VIPs, which once, I recall, included Dietrich. In fact, most of us students thought Mme. Maria Piscator wasn't the least interested in us, or in what we thought she thought of our tawdry, unimportant productions—unless she was the director.

So it wasn't until almost some twenty years later when I was running The Cubiculo that our paths crossed again. She had come to us with a project, an "epic happening" conceived and directed by her, called *The Debate*, a long one-act based on the famous "Speech on the Theatre" of the Commune in Paris, 1871. She had first put it on during the May 1970 student riots on the campus of Southern Illinois University, Carbondale, Illinois, where she was artist-in-residence at the time; and she wanted to revive it now for the 100th anniversary of that speech by bringing her student production to New York. The cost of transporting the students (there was no set, just lecterns and lighting) and housing them in NYC would be born by the University and her Piscator Foundation.

Well, you can see how I couldn't help but be interested in such a Project—so timely, somewhat experimental, and ideally suited to The Cubiculo. Moreover, the student actors didn't need to be paid. Besides, this time around I found her quite businesslike, serious, cooperative, and a little more likable. Of course, I realize now that this was part of her great skill—adapting her current behavior to her immediate needs. I was now in a position to do something for her. Hence the revised approach.

In any case, all this led to her hiring me to help her remount *The Debate* at Southern Illinois—a strange, forlorn site for a university—where, remarkably, she had been able to set up a library for Piscator's epic theater material, and where she also served as visiting professor of drama. It was an interesting campus experience, similar in some ways, and differing in so many others, from my days at NYU and Columbia. To my surprise, in view of their recently won "status" from the student riot period, the students were unexpectedly compatible, cooperative, and anxious to follow direction. Yes, they were actually quite serious about theater and wanted to learn as much as

Clockwise: nephew Glen, son Jacob, father, mother; meeting the Russians at Torgau on the Elbe in Germany, May 1945; my father, my son, in Madison, Wisconsin.

Clockwise: wife Ann, son Jacob; wife and son in Central Park; rowing a boat with Jacob; Jacob as a teenager at a boarding school near Hyde Park.

Clockwise: *The Drunkard* (Gate Theater); Marston's *Malcontent* (Classic Theater) with Denise Assante as the Duchess and me as the malcontent Duke; two scenes from *The Golden Apple* (Alvin Theater), as Nestor, one of Ulysses's men.

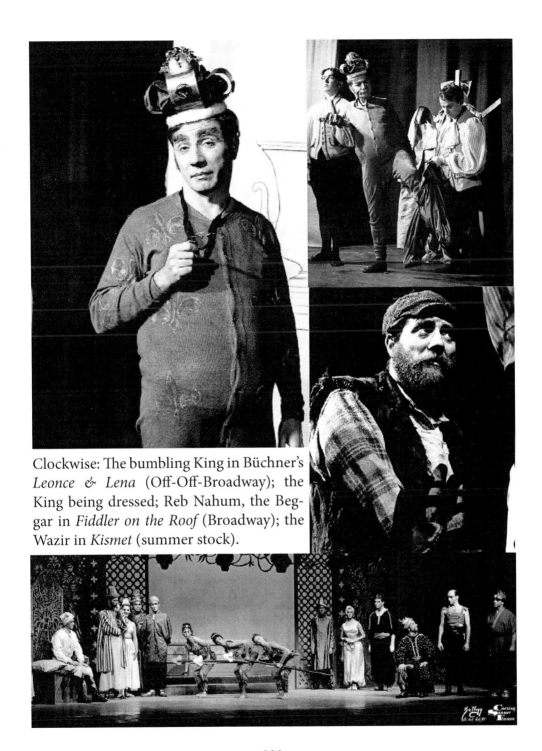

Clockwise: The bumbling King in Büchner's *Leonce & Lena* (Off-Off-Broadway); the King being dressed; Reb Nahum, the Beggar in *Fiddler on the Roof* (Broadway); the Wazir in *Kismet* (summer stock).

Clockwise: outside the Sullivan Street Theatre, home of *The Fantasticks*; the *Catered Cabaret* in a transplanted Lighthouse in Amagansett; the Girl's Father in *The Fantasticks* (Sullivan St. Theatre).

By Sam Siegel

Maurice Edwards, Royce Lenelle, and George Riddle in a scene from 'The Fantasticks,' which recently became the fourth longest running musical, passing 'South Pacific' (1,694 perform- ances) and gaining on 'Oklahoma!' 'The Threepenny Opera,' and 'My Fair Lady' (2,717 performances). 'The Fantasticks' is at the Sullivan Street Playhouse in New York.

NEW MR. PEACHUM
... Maurice Edwards tonight replaces Emil Renan as Mr. Peachum in the long-running "The Threepenny Opera." It's at Theatre de Lys.

As Mr. Peachum in the Kurt Weill/Bertolt Brecht *Threepenny Opera* (Theatre De Lys); upper right corner, arguing with daughter Polly and Mrs. Peachum getting drunk; at the outside wall of the DeLys (now called the Lucille Lortel Theatre).

At Cubiculo, Artist 'Can Try Anything'

Motto and byword of The Cubiculo Art Center (419 West 51st Street, Manhattan); The Cubiculo's four-sided cubic symbol.

the Classic Theatre

Executive Director
Nicholas John Stathis

Artistic Director
Maurice Edwards

presents

NORMAN SAMPLE

in DOSTOYEVSKY'S

NOTES FROM UNDERGROUND

PART I

Translation by—MIRRA GINSBURG
Producer—NICHOLAS JOHN STATHIS
Director—MAURICE EDWARDS

Clockwise: Portion of the poster for Classic Theatre production of Dostoevsky's *Notes from the Underground*, Part I (Classic Theatre); as director of *Notes*; Norman Sample as the Underground Man; with Marion Brasch, in the cabaret, *Songs of Love & Money.*

the Classic Theatre

PRESENTS

Songs of Love and Money

KURT WEILL & BERTOLT BRECHT AND THEIR PROGENY

with

MARION BRASCH and MAURICE EDWARDS

HARRY HUFF at the Piano

PART ONE

1. TANGO BALLADE from Threepenny Opera by Bertolt Brecht and Kurt Weill
(English Version by Marc Blitzstein)
MARION BRASCH & MAURICE EDWARDS

2. THE LOVE MARKET from Roundheads and Peakheads by Brecht and Eisler
(English Version by Eric Bentley)
Ms. BRASCH

3. NOTHING QUITE LIKE MONEY from Roundheads and Peakheads by Brecht and Eisler
Mr. EDWARDS

4. PIRATE JENNY from Threepenny Opera by Brecht and Weill
Ms. BRASCH

5. BALLAD OF THE JEWISH WHORE, MARIE SANDERS by Brecht and Eisler
(English Version by Eric Bentley)
Mr. EDWARDS

6. ON SUICIDE by Brecht and Eisler
(English Version by Eric Bentley)
Ms. BRASCH

7. MADELON OF PARIS from Johnny Johnson by Paul Green and Kurt Weill
Mr. EDWARDS

TOMI/Terrace Theatre
23 West 73rd St., NYC

208

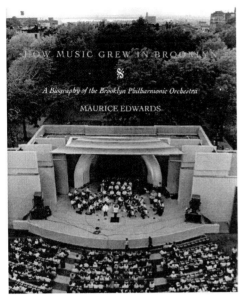

Clockwise: From the Brooklyn Philharmonic period: the orchestra in the old shell in Prospect Park, Brooklyn; at an outdoor rehearsal; narrating with the orchestra in the Cathedral of St. John the Divine.

Top to bottom: toasting the new year with
Nina Cassian; a drawing by first wife, Ann;
Nina at a reception for a poetry reading.

they could. And thrilled that they would be able to perform in New York! So they were rewarded with three nights at The Cubiculo at 414 West 51st Street, where they were able to repeat their Southern Illinois staging with minor adjustments to the new space, only a few blocks away from their long-dreamed-of goal, Broadway. Of course, we had planned it that way, and Mme. P. was able to add another production to her c.v.

Following this success, I was given the VIP treatment, taken to fashionable restaurants, invited to her summer home on Long Island, near SUNY Stony Brook, for swimming—where she also had her own cabana, of course—and began to be introduced to her more influential friends and colleagues. Things went "swimmingly," one could say, until one day she showed her true colors. In return for the advice I had given her on various projects and her attempts at writing her memoirs, for which I was not paid as handsomely as one might expect, she feigned an interest in my Classic Theatre productions, so much so that she led me to believe she would help back our next one, which was my revival of the Austrian master comic playwright Nestroy's *Love Affairs and Wedding Bells*, a delightful mid-19th-century farce. Being by her country's master comic playwright, one was quite confident it would appeal to her.

After all, another farce of Nestroy's had been turned by Thornton Wilder into his *Merchant of Yonkers*, which later became his Broadway success, *The Matchmaker*, which, in turn, was transformed into the international hit *Hello Dolly*. Little did I guess that this little request would someday backfire.

Well, dear Nina, knowing how much you dislike business matters, I don't want to burden you with the laborious details of what I went through trying to get Mme. P. to live up to her pledge. Suffice it to say that after four or five subtle reminders that we were due some money, I finally had to ask her for it outright, several unpaid bills having in the meantime begun to accumulate. Whereupon she curtly denied ever having promised us anything! Needless to say, I walked out of that fancy drawing room empty-handed and chose never to return (which may have been unwise in the long run). *Et voilà: fini Maria!*

Oh my Lord, I just got a call from Brooklyn Hospital. They want me to go there immediately. I'll phone you when I get back...

Worriedly yours,

M.

October 18, 2007

Dear patient Ninicuța:

I'm afraid I'll have to stay here in Brooklyn for the next day or two trying to clean out the apartment of our absent, so suddenly departed-from-the-world, son Jacob, on South Elliot Place, just around the corner from where I used to live on Lafayette Avenue. Remember the dark, dismal, crowded second-floor apartment you climbed up to, when you visited me there one fall day some ten years ago, and upon seeing it said quickly, "Oh no, let's go back to my place on Roosevelt Island."

Well, Jacob's place was perhaps even more dismal, though it was on the first floor of a small, probably once-handsome, turn-of-the-century apartment building, right next to that huge but excellent school Brooklyn Tech, half a block from beautiful Fort Greene Park with its tall lighthouse tower monument to the soldiers of the Revolutionary War. But I never took you to Jacob's domicile because you wouldn't have been able to navigate its small space, so covered with video games, comic books, computer parts and pieces of equipment, stray pots and pans, all sorts of odds and ends scattered helter-skelter, a tall bookcase with a strange array of books ranging from histories of warfare to workbooks on computer functions, to the latest science fiction to catalogues of comic books to stacks of menus from nearby international restaurants on Myrtle, DeKalb, and Lafayette Avenues. It was darker than it needed to be because he had thrown a large black blanket over its wide front window: he didn't want people looking in on his little empire from the street. Nor did he want the landlord, super, or any other inhabitants of his building to know what a hoarded mess he and his cat moved around in. Had we visited him then, the cat would have been called Ralph, a gift from Daniela Gioseffi for his babysitting for her. But these days a lithe, black Mr. Kit-Kat was reigning over the space, and only reluctantly let me enter when, holding my breath, I opened the door yesterday...

What I've been somehow describing to you was what it was like there eight or nine years ago. However, it gradually got worse, the piles of magazines and books grew, the miscellany multiplied; no wonder Jacob could never find anything whenever he really needed it. He simply could not throw away a single object. After awhile, I couldn't bear going there to see him and his mounting progeny, which in time would have consumed the room and all in it, as in that absurdist French play by Boris Vian, *The Empire Builders*, where the ever-expanding furniture finally forces the family out into the street.

Now, alas, after Jacob's most untimely death, I had to face this cumulative behemoth, as you know from my phone calls to you from Brooklyn Hospital, the Emergency Room of which he had been taken to by ambulance after collapsing in mid-afternoon on Fourth Avenue, on his way to his monthly checkup at a different site, Long Island College Hospital! But, alas, by the time I got to Brooklyn Hospital, he had left this world, felled by sudden cardiac arrest. The young, forlorn receiving doctor who had treated him painstakingly described to me how they had tried for forty-five minutes to resuscitate Jacob. In vain. The tragedy was totally unexpected, as you know. After all, as I just noted, he was having some sort of physical checkup every month in order to maintain his disability insurance. And it seemed as though his mild type of diabetes (treated by pills, not insulin) had abated considerably; his blood pressure was supposedly back to normal; he was steadily losing a little weight (this was ascertainable as his pants visibly grew looser and baggier).

However, as I now know, after piecing together various reports and evidence, it turns out that he had had an earlier collapse the night before, right in front of his apartment door. Fellow tenants found him there on the floor and called an ambulance, which took him to Long Island College Hospital, his monthly checkup site, and where they should certainly have had his medical records. If only the emergency doctor on duty that night had been able to detect something askew, or had at least kept him there longer for a more thorough examination instead of releasing him the next morning! (His friends say that I should sue the hospital.) Even when I phoned Jacob that morning, he said nothing about this. For, as he told his dear friend Claire Freeman, his kind neighbor from across the street, whose cats he used to babysit and whom he accompanied on her weekly shopping trips to New Jersey, he didn't want to worry me!

True, he had complained to me that Sunday night, and the Monday morning before, about feeling dehydrated, and you will no doubt remember how puzzled we both were by that assessment. How could he, who ordinarily drank gobs of water and soda whenever he crossed my threshold at Clinton Avenue or our joint threshold on Roosevelt Island—how could our Jacob possibly be dehydrated? Surely the first emergency room doctor should have followed up that hint better on Monday night before releasing him? Just as surely should I have been more alert and persistent in following up that strange complaint of his, something he had never complained of before.

Also, when I talked to Jacob Tuesday morning, he sounded groggy but said he felt less dehydrated (and, of course, said nothing about the overnight stay). I had phoned to remind him that he had an appointment to see the social worker at that very same hospital at 3:00pm. And he reassured me that he would go. Nevertheless, fearing that he might fall asleep and miss the meeting, I called again at 2:00. He said he was okay, and would soon be on his way.

Two-and-one-half hours later, I get a call from Brooklyn Hospital (actually closer to his place and mine than Long Island College), asking me to come down there immediately. When I arrived, I was informed by the admitting doctor to the Emergency Room that as they were examining and questioning him, he suddenly stopped talking and never talked again, even after those forty-five minutes of intense attempted resuscitation as described above.

Well, I couldn't believe it! So they put me, stunned, and a little wobbly, into a kind of waiting room for relatives of patients. A very sympathetic African American woman social worker tried to make me understand what had happened. Gradually I began to accept the unwelcome news, though it came across first as a kind of Nothingness: I couldn't fully grasp it, it was truly elusive... until the young doctor who had tended Jacob and tried to save him came and took me to the room where his body lay, and of course there he was, absolutely still, and looking so strangely serene.

So different from my poor brother Lester's tortured face after his terrible double heart attack twenty years ago in Toronto, to which hospital I had flown but arrived too late. A totally distinct scenario from that of Jacob's, Lester had had some warnings. Yet there he was, on a mission of mercy, showing his troubled nephew, Glen, the sights of Canada, Lake Erie, and for him, ill-omened Toronto. But more about brother Lester another time; I can't quite bear to recount another death at this juncture.

Stunned, I can't say more right now.

Sorrowfully yours,

M.

P.S. Further details about this episode to follow shortly.

All Saints Day, 2007

Cara Nina simpatica:

Ironically enough, I'm writing this right after a visit to that same nephew, Glen, now ensconced in a cold building at Kings County Psychiatric Center, who wanted to know all about Jacob and his fate. Remember, they wouldn't let him out to come to that little memorial service we put together for Jacob. Even when his healthy brother,

Allen, had flown up from Baltimore and had gone all the long way out to Kings County to take Glen to our service and back.

But the Center wouldn't permit it. So I felt I owed Glen that attention. Poor soul.

The Center is like a jail. First you have to go through a heavily guarded gate. After which you're given a pass. Then you cross a parking lot to the low-lying building they tell you is the Center. But when you get in you're hostilely told to sit down and wait until visiting hours start. (I happened to be four minutes early for a change!) However, they take their time. First, you have to sign in. Then you show them what you're carrying in the shopping bag of magazines you're bringing the patient. Then you pass through an electronic test arch, just like at the airport. Plus which they pass a searching wand over you. Finally you're allowed in. But they haven't advised you where to go or where the reception room is. So you stand perplexed in a small square of a hall when you get off the elevator, surrounded by six locked doors. There are no signs. Ah, a hospital aide appears out of nowhere. You ask him directions. "No, go to the second floor." A similar square-ish hallway greets you, although one door seems to lead to where you think the room might be. But it, too, is locked. Fortunately, another visitor who knows his way around the place shows up and gets it opened for you.

There you see emaciated Glen, his sharp features now softened by a wispy, whitish beard, sitting at a table, with his copy of a bilingual Torah opened before him. He has returned to Judaism after a bout with the New Testament. But he's calmer. He's not about to strike anyone as he had raged and threatened to do last year when I saw him at a different, less disciplined, center. Let us hope (and pray?) that this new phase will last. He tells me his new doctor is trying to find the right halfway house for him to be sent to. He seems strangely—for him—optimistic. I try to engage him in some sort of discussion. But he, who a few years earlier was aware of what's going on in the world, is now dulled. The drugs? So I'm reduced to asking him how the food is, what the room he sleeps in is like, who are the people he has to live with. Finally, as I begin to take my leave, a sudden spark is lit. He weeps: "But will I ever be able to have sex again?"

What a contrast to his younger brother, Allen, whom you got to know a little better at our modest memorial evening for Jacob that we hastily set up for his friends, our relatives, and those of my friends who had known Jacob, as well as your friends who had met him at some point. There we heard stories, reminiscences, and even some amusing anecdotes involving him from the surprising number of his friends in attendance that night. Wasn't it something of a relief to realize that at least his burdened life had given him some pleasures, some real friendships, possibly some joy amidst his sleepless nights, his demeaning self-deprecation, his inability to part with anything?

To get back to that critical moment at Brooklyn Hospital, where what they had informed me about Jacob was confirmed only too vividly. After which I was taken along a cold corridor to that warmer reception room, where that most accommodating lady set up an appointment for me the next morning with their staff cleric, who turned out to be an orthodox Chassidic rabbi! When I met with him, I was already under pressure to conform to the rules and regulations of the hospital, and about how and when Jacob's body would have to be removed and taken to some sort of funeral home that deals with such matters.

It was a difficult scene. Here I was inquiring about how we could have the body reduced to ashes, which could be sent to, or taken to, the cemetery in Madison, Wisconsin, where my parents are buried and where my brother Lester's ashes are interred between them, and which I thought would be the proper place for Jacob's ashes. The Rabbi was shocked: that's against the rules of Judaism in these matters. In fact, the body was already almost overdue to be treated. Burials, especially among the Orthodox, take place the next day or the following day at the latest. Nevertheless, at first the Rabbi went along with the idea and phoned the cemetery in Madison, but it turned out to be a very complicated and expensive process, although at this point I no longer have to worry about money, since what I had been setting aside in a trust fund for Jacob once I passed away, so that he'd be prepared to function in this life without me, as I had been warning him quite recently could happen soon, I am now free to use.

Both the Rabbi and I sat there a few moments, silently, looking at one another, perplexed as to what to do next. Whereupon I belatedly realized that the simplest, and, probably in the long run, best thing to do would be to abandon the cremation idea and put Jacob in the Long Island cemetery where his mother, Ann, lies buried. So, dragging up my memory, the word "Wellwood" came to mind, even if it sounded like coming out of Evelyn Waugh, and we discovered that there is indeed such a cemetery in mid-Island. We phoned them immediately and said that we thought there was a family plot for the Alperts, Ann's family name. Yes, there was one such plot, but it was already filled, and there was no space next to it. Fortunately, however, they were able to find a plot close to his mother's, which solved that problem.

From that point on, it was mostly a question of mechanics, logistics, and routine, the details and minutiae of which the Rabbi from years of practice knew inside out. He proceeded to line up the right "Kosher" funeral home, and got them to take Jacob's body to their place and prepare him for a modest burial the next day at Wellwood.

My dear Nina, I won't bother you with the countless, wearying, sometimes difficult, unpleasant details that preceded the burial, such as having to identify Jacob again at the Bureau of Health before he could be taken to the funeral home, and related matters. But the funeral home staff themselves, *Chasidim* without the *paias* (curls), proved to be most efficient and accommodating except in the matter of timing. Because, alas, the day before, after visiting the Rabbi at his office in the hospital to work out these details, I had to have a back molar tooth pulled. Remember my anxiety, dear, during that hectic period, when I kept trying to keep you abreast on the phone of one mad move after another.

The burial itself was almost Beckett-like in its stark simplicity and loneliness. Of course, there was hardly time to have a proper funeral ceremony, and that's why, as you know, I arranged for that memorial service in Manhattan about ten days later for his friends, and for those of mine who knew Jacob somewhat.

So there we were, the emissary from the funeral home, who had driven the coffin to Wellwood and who now doubled as the Rabbi, reading the beautiful burial service poems in Hebrew before the coffin was lowered into the grave, and then again after it was covered—and myself. The two of us started the process by shoveling the requisite sand and gravel over the coffin.

After which, the emissary drove me back to my Brooklyn hideout, and en route I learned how he, a young Chasid—from Israel, no less—had moved to America; set up his family here; was making adjustments to some of our Western ways wherever he could, without breaking any of the 617 biblical laws; had been taking intensive English classes; and was now studying how to be an insurance agent! But, as to his religio-philosophical background, it turned out to be very limited, once one passed the learned routines and dogma. Thus, he had never heard the name Martin Buber, knew none of his *Chasidic Tales*, certainly he didn't know what "I and Thou" meant, or, more seriously, led to. Never even heard of Gershom Scholem and his history of the Kabbalah. Indeed, had only an elementary conception of what the Kabbalah might be, except for a vague sense that the hierarchy frowned on its people studying it. And just simply the name, Emmanuel Levinas, bewildered him.

However, he was able to repeat from the Funeral Service for the Burial of the Dead (echoes of which I found later in certain passages from the opening of the Amidah in the Morning Service): "In Thy great Love, O Lord, Thou givest life to the dead, keeping faith with them who sleep in the dust. Who is like unto Thee, Lord of power... who sends death, and in the flowering of Thy saving power gives life?"—A way to find some light in death's darkness?

And I was grateful to him for that, and for bringing me back home, that is, my Brooklyn home, the place I let Jacob use whenever I was with you at Roosevelt Island or we were both off together to one of your poetry festivals in Europe, or visiting your homeland,

Romania, or on our one beloved cruise of the Caribbean. Yes, it was his second home; and it was where his little club met monthly. It will seem very empty for some time now, won't it?

With irrepressible sadness,

M.

Dear consolatory Nina:

Yes, our little talks have been helpful, and I appreciate how well you have stood by me throughout this totally unexpected drama. I'm also thankful that our modest memorial service for Jacob gave you a more rounded picture of his troubled, but not always unhappy, soul...

Not surprisingly, all this travail has brought back memories of my first, often rather lonely, days, weeks, and months in Manhattan, when I first came to anchor down here upon my return from Europe and the war, and after a short stay with the family in Wisconsin, far too short, indeed, for them. After all, they had been counting on me finishing my college courses at the university there, getting a degree, and living with or near them in Madison, that beautiful city built between a four-leaf clover of gorgeous lakes, to which the family had moved (upon my advice), while I was overseas. Yes, they were much happier there than in dull, flat New London, with its sluggish Wolf River and run-down town center and a similarly dull, mostly conservative, reactionary citizenry. So it certainly was very painful saying goodbye to Mother and Dad so soon following my Army/ European absence. After all, they had waited years for the Return of their Prodigal! And they had justifiably hoped to have me around with them for much more of their later years. Fortunately, they had my younger brother, Lester, still living with them there, to fill the gap for a short while, and who, once he left the nest, was able to fly home more often than yours truly. Then there was my sister, Millicent, who had left during the war years for Chicago and soon married and settled there, which meant she was only a couple of hours away from the family by train, bus, or auto.

So, you can see, dear Nina, with all these changes of milieu, work patterns, lifestyles, and related concerns, how lonely I felt during those first months of readjustment to civilian life, to a different college, and to this huge, often unwelcoming jungle of a city—good old New York. Occasionally, I'd subway to the tip of Manhattan, near the Staten Island Ferry, sit down on a stump or random bench, look out over the wide, quiet harbor, and simply muse.

Perched there thus, alone, I would sometimes feel adrift on a wavering raft in a sometimes, but not necessarily always, threatening sea. And when I'd turn around, I'd see only the fascinating but essentially intimidating skyscrapers glowering down at me. Yes, in such moments I was really alone. Outside of Geraldine, who alternated unpredictably living here or in Washington, and who herself had only a few friends in this megacity, where could I turn? In any case, most of them proved ephemeral.

Though there was one character who, when he blew into town, could be stimulating and fun—the Byron-like Herbie Benjamin, whom I'd first met briefly through Geraldine's auspices on campus in Madison before joining the Army. Odd, how only now do I wonder why he wasn't drafted, or what ruse he might have used to escape that fate. It was rambunctious Herbie, who, when he learned from G. that I'd be returning soon to the States, had her write and ask me to smuggle into NYC for him a copy of Henry Miller's *Tropic of Cancer*, which was easy to pick up in Paris but prohibited here. (Little did I know or suspect then what a cult figure Miller would become; nowadays, in some circles he seems to have assumed the status once accorded D. H. Lawrence, a far greater writer.)

Indeed, for that favor, I almost got penalized upon re-entering the country and had to do some fast talking at U.S. Customs to get by. Yes, Herbie was diverting, but almost always on the run, wandering here and there, and seldom to be found in his Greenwich Village sanctuary on Cornelia Street. The few times I visited him there, I kept my eyes open in the hope of catching sight of Auden, who at that time lived in the same apartment complex. Then there was Herbie's pleasant but somewhat diffident brother, Allen, who would not be moving to New York until many years later, whereupon he became a much trusted, close confidant of Geraldine's (though never a lover).

Nor should I forget to tell you that I actually had a smattering of family and close relatives scattered here and there in the Metropolitan area. Most accessible and always in town, unlike friends Geraldine and Herbie, was one of my favorite cousins, the beautiful but enigmatic spinster, Lee, who once worked at *The New York Times*, although by then had become a trusted saleslady in a fragrant-smelling Cuban cigar shop not far from the *Times* Building. Possessed of a natural, pleasant, though untutored soprano, she used to sing occasionally at Christian Science church services here and there in Greater New York. To my surprise, her joining that church had somewhat shocked my quixotic, but now quite old uncle Zavel, a confirmed agnostic, and an anarchist/socialist to boot. Once a personal disciple of the indomitable Eugene Debs from his old Chicago union days back in the early Twenties, dear gruff Zavel could talk about him, his hero, for what seemed like hours, when I'd visit him occasionally in his Parkchester retreat. Indeed, it was Uncle Z. who took me at the age of sixteen, when I had hitchhiked to New York, as I think I told you earlier, for the 1939 World's Fair, to a huge gathering of people, some sort of peaceful mob, in normally quiet Washington Heights. For I was staying with him and his family then, while they still lived near the Cloisters on Riverside Drive. It's a shame I can't recall exactly what that particular rally was all about, although I'm sure it was political, must have involved the Labor Unions, and possibly sounded warnings about the rising menace of Nazi Germany. Whatever, I remember saying to myself at the time, surrounded as I was by a sea of Jews, both at the rally and probably also on the block where I was staying: "Are these my brethren?" Quite different in its outspokenness from 98 percent Christian Wisconsin, whose pristine atmosphere and undemonstrative style I had imbibed for sixteen years.

Don't forget, dear Nina, that I was brought up in Amasa, Michigan, a hamlet of about eight hundred people in the Upper Peninsula, where we, my family and I, were the only Jews. A little mining spot, with a mostly immigrant working population, fifty-percent Finnish and the rest mixed Central European with a few upper-class Wasps running the town. Quite a contrast to where we moved, south into Wisconsin, during the worst days of the Great Depression, first to almost monochromatic little Elroy for a year or two; then a few years later, settling down in somewhat larger, but hardly cosmopolitan, plain, dull New London, a town of about 5,000, the site from which I had hitchhiked. At least New London had two other Jewish families, one running the local furniture emporium, and the other, wealthier, a fur dealer who ran a large farm, or little estate (?), some ten miles out in the country, conveniently away from the town, and whom we rarely saw. We were probably looked down upon as if we were their poor relatives (which, of course, we certainly weren't). Gogol would have enjoyed caricaturing this strange set-up, with its pretensions and inherent snobbery.

So, as you can well imagine, dear Nina, this assemblage in New York was quite something for your young Squirrel to witness! (Comparable to your first view of Bucharest when you moved there from calm Brasov, perhaps?) It also gave me a little scare: I had just finished reading Mother's copy of that prescient book, *Vienna: City without Jews*. But by now—that is, the time of my ending up, post-war, in New York—Zavel's family had spread out, with him domiciled in the Bronx, Cousin Lee in Manhattan, and her properly named younger sister, Belle (for she, too, though plump, was also a beauty), settled down across the Hudson in suburban New Jersey. Yet that was still fairly close to civilization, as we used to call it. Belle was just as independent a soul as Lee; after all, she disappointed even her ostensibly open-minded father (whom she loved very much) by marrying a Christian, a "capitalist" who worked for General Electric and whose "sales territory" was middle and north New Jersey, where he had purchased a smart ranch-like house in one of the more affluent suburbs. (In retrospect, I don't know whether Zavel was more bothered by her marrying a Christian or by the fact that he was a damned capitalist!)

Much further away, both geographically and politically, was the totally apolitical younger brother, Carl, who had settled in Detroit and whom I had met briefly a couple of years earlier when on furlough from the Army and been welcomed as a family "hero," while the eldest of Zavel's quartet of children, Walter, had broken almost completely away from the family when he married a pretty Italian girl and set himself up as an accountant in Poughkeepsie. She was reputedly a great cook, but I only remember visiting them once, talking with him and his neighbors on his friendly porch, and unfortunately can't vouch for the cuisine! Though I do recall having to make and endure some boring suburban small talk about people I didn't know for two long hours or so.

Finally, there were a few relatives on Mother's side of the family, who hailed from Milwaukee. It was this branch with whom I stayed, the wealthy Rotters, with their eight children in their ten-room mansion, founders of the big Rotter Baking Co., when I hitch-hiked years earlier to Milwaukee to see and hear *Lohengrin*. Their second-eldest daughter, the very intelligent and affable Bernice, with her husband and two children, was now comfortably ensconced in Baldwin, Long Island, where I used to be invited once a year for Thanksgiving dinner and, again, mostly dull small talk, which occasionally got heated up and even exciting when I would manage to get cousin Bernice to let David Sigman, her husband, who had been a brilliant union leader in the Midwest, hold forth and reminisce about his struggles and rise up the ladder in the then much more influential, but very tough, often violent, Union world of New York. It was during one of his tours as a national union officer that he met Bernice in Milwaukee. Come to think of it, it would have been great to have brought him and Uncle Zavel together in the same room, but that would have proven logistically too intricate, and possibly presumptuous, for me to have arranged it in those days.

Yes, you might well ask, with such a plethora of family nearby, why should I have complained? You're right: probably I ought not have. They were good, kind people, some of them even quite accomplished. Except that they were all at least a generation or two older than I was and moved in rather tedious circles. Moreover, they had by this time in their lives pretty much settled into their own private routines: they didn't need this grubby cousin from rural, upper Wisconsin, now humbly housed in some Manhattan ex-slum site, to complicate their lives. I, in turn, ended up dubbing them my Holiday Relatives (though, of course, they weren't aware of that.) Still, to their credit, later when I'd get involved in a play or a concert, they might show up for an opening. But there was little, if any, day-to-day contact. Even when I might run short of money, I was too proud to ask any of them for a loan. Though I'm sure most would have obliged.

That's why I reiterate that, in a certain sense, during those first few months in the wilds of Manhattan, I was basically alone. I knew no one. It was like starting school all over again. I was the new child on the block. It would take time to make new friends, not just mere acquaintances, on the campus at NYU. Thank God, I was usually too busy with lectures, homework, and a succession of mostly boring part-time jobs (except for Klara Roman, the graphologist), to keep me financially on an even keel. The GI Bill paid only my tuition at NYU, nothing else, and so I had to earn my own way while carrying a full load of classes. In addition to which, not long after matriculating, getting credit for my two-and-a-half years at the Univerity of Wisconsin, and acclimatizing myself to historic Washington Square and the NYU campus housed around its southeastern rim, I began to look for the right acting, voice, and dance teachers to carry on where I had left off with that training in Paris.

But here again I didn't really have the connections for locating the very best teachers, who, surprisingly enough, I was able to find so much more easily in Paris. Why? Probably because Paris is smaller and more centralized and its artistic community more compact; and because I, being an American, an ex-soldier and a guest in their country, may have inspired some of the people I met to look after me somewhat. Nevertheless, although it may have taken a little longer than overseas, finally I didn't do so badly in New York, after all. For example, a little "research" led me to the excellent Herbert Berghof studio, where I studied with Berghof's wife, the late revered, American master actress, Uta Hagen.

I took her special Shakespeare class where, among other exercises, one had to improvise in iambic pentameter in case one ever forgot a passage on stage! Jack Lemmon, then a comparative unknown, though one sensed he was already landing potentially lucrative jobs, also frequented the class; as Uta pointed out, if you can do Shakespeare right, you can do anything! Thus what Uta at this stage of her teaching career wanted most—later she would become more "Method"-focused in her approach—was spontaneity and a down-to-earthness with Shakespeare. No awe, no British-ism, no holding back. I'll never forget how one day in class she lost patience with my partner and me while we were doing the famous "Kate the curst" scene from *Taming of the Shrew* that she had assigned us. My student actress Kate was being much too tentative and weak in her repartee with my not-too-worldly Petruchio. Uta wanted her to shoot Kate's tart retorts out like gunshots. But the poor girl couldn't quite manage that, although she tried gallantly. Finally, exasperated, Uta ran onto the acting space (there was no stage), pushed that Kate off my thigh where, seated on a chair, I had been holding her down, jumped on my lap herself, and proceeded to practically pull my hair out as we battled back and forth. "If I be waspish best beware my sting," she hissed at me. And of course Uta was right! I remembered this exercise vividly when forty-five years later I directed with great relish a *Shrew* for the National Shakespeare Summer Conservatory project up in the Catskills with young students and somewhat older apprentice actors.

Yes, the real Uta Hagen was quite different from the delicate Desdemona I had seen her play a couple of years earlier on tour with Paul Robeson as Othello; or her fragile Blanche several years later in *A Streetcar Named Desire*, when she replaced Jessica Tandy. Moreover, I always felt somewhat at home in Uta's class, probably more so than I would have with almost any other teacher at that point in my life, because I had known both her parents: her father, the extraordinary art historian, Oscar F.L. Hagen, with whom I took an unforgettable course in Spanish art history back at the University of Wisconsin; and her stepmother, whom I sang next to in a performance of Handel's *Messiah* by the University Chorus in Madison, at Christmas time, 1942—both before enlisting in the Army in March 1943. (Nor did I know then what I later learned, that Frau Hagen had been a leading lyric soprano back in Deutschland.)

Oscar Hagen himself was a truly great teacher, one of the best I ever had, on a par with Suzanne Langer and Sidney Hook. Among other highlights of his course on Spanish art, such as demonstrating with slides the capacious range of Zurbaran or his insights about El Greco, I shall never forget his lecture on Velasquez, which he began by reading the Preface to *Don Quixote*—what better intro could one have had to that master? What better advice could a student get than this admonition of Cervantes in that incomparable Preface:

> You have no need to go begging sentences of Philosophers, Passages out of Holy Writ, Poetical Fables, Rhetorical Orations, or Miracles of Saints. Do but take care to express your self in a plain, easy Manner, in well-chosen, significant and decent Terms; and to give an harmonious and pleasing Turn to your Periods: Study to explain your Thoughts, and set them in the truest Light... Let your diverting Stories be express'd in diverting Terms, to kindle Mirth in the Melancholick, and heighten it in the Gay: ...keeping your eye still fix'd on the principal End of your Project... and your Business is done.

Nor was Spanish art Hagen's main specialty. Actually, he was probably best known at that time (at least in this country) for his monumental work on the history of American painting! All the more remarkable, as I learned subsequently, since he had started off in Germany first as a composer, having studied with Humperdinck, and had later launched the first great 20th-century revival of Handel's operas in those Goettingen Festivals of the early 1920s. What satisfaction it would have brought him had he lived long enough—although I'm sure he saw it coming—to have witnessed so many of Handel's operas now entering the repertoire of almost every major opera company in the world! So that his coming to America, long before Hitler, must have marked a total change of life for him, but one which he handled with great aplomb. That double life deserves a book in itself, don't you think, dear Nina? But I'm certainly too old to be the one to pursue that gambit now.

Of course, Uta, his daughter, whom they brought here as a child, was completely bilingual. In fact, the most natural and spontaneous performance of hers I ever attended was her Gretchen in a revival of *Faust, Part I*, performed in German, her Muttersprache, in the early Fifties by the Deutsches Theater of New York at that little theater then housed in the Barbizon Plaza Hotel on 58th Street and Sixth Avenue, with that incomparable character actor, the eighty-year-old Albert Bassermann as the Devil, and the future *Hogan's Heroes* veteran, actor Leon Askin, as Faust. After that, I usually found Uta's English acting, except in *Who's Afraid of Virginia Woolf*, just a bit studied, or somehow plotted, not quite spontaneous enough, not as natural sounding as her German acting. Later, I was lucky to see Hagen and Bassermann together again in Ibsen's *The Master Builder* (in German, of course) at that same intimate theater, where again Uta fared better, in my opinion, *auf Deutsch*. The following season, Deutsches Theater had Herbert Berghof—whose portrayal of Nathan the Wise I noted earlier in the letter about Piscator's Dramatic Workshop—essay quite convincingly the role of the tortured Orestes in Goethe's *Iphigenie in Tauris*, also in German.

But the real revelation of that production was the magical Iphigenie of Elisabeth Bergner (both Berghof and Bergner were Austrian, and veterans of Reinhardt productions in Vienna). If Uta's Gretchen was, say, 75 percent better than her Shavian St. Joan, then Bergner's Iphigenie in German, her native language, was 300 percent better than her valiant try at playing the duchess of Malfi in her heavily accented English! The difference being, of course, that

Hagen learned English as a child, Bergner as an adult. From the very first gorgeous, blank verse lines of Goethe that Bergman uttered, in her sweet, though firm voice, we knew we were already in Winkelmann's Greece, and she never once broke the illusion. Ah, what great theater—and seen by so few! Yes, dear Nina, you would have cherished those performances even more than me because your German is so much more fluent.

Later, I was to take acting classes with the extraordinary, unique Stella Adler; dance with Mme. Anderson-Ivantzova, a Russian-Swedish ballerina who had come over to America with the revue *The Black Cat*; and voice with her husband Ivantzov, a Russian baritone who had sung with Chaliapin and often beguiled us with tales about that fabulous figure. (How, for example, when given a song by some women's music club in New York to sing for them, he turned them down, saying he'd need a year to absorb it. He'd rather spit first!) Then, after graduating from NYU, I took classes of all kinds—acting, directing, speech, movement—at Piscator's Dramatic Workshop, sponsored by The New School (described in an earlier letter). But I'll get to these in due time, since each has its own story that I think might interest you.

Yes! You see, by attacking this period head on, I'm actually getting to understand some aspects of myself better retroactively than back then in the midst of the scene—or multifold scenes—in which I was participating. Indeed, I see now more clearly than before how I had been somewhat spoiled in Paris, and by Paris. Some things may have come too easily for me there. Also, and that's a most important point, when there, I didn't have to worry about earning my daily bread. It was much easier simply to pick up a baguette at the local bakery! Moreover, getting that small *bourse* from the French government, and the fact that I could still poach half of my meals at Army canteens when short of funds, made the Paris sojourn comparable in some respects to a vacation. Rather similar to how I felt, many years later, for example, when I was lucky enough to be invited to Venice to advise and work with a theater group there in its production of one of Mario Fratti's plays

I had premiered several years earlier at The Cubiculo, in NYC.

Again, even though I was actually at work, i.e., following rehearsals in rapidly spoken Italian, I felt suspended in a semi-dreamland, what one might call a vacation in Paradiso. Oh, I must move to Venice, I'd say to myself: what a paradise! But then, observing tense people in restaurants, harried workers in the street, ragged beggars in tourist sites, and diligent tourists themselves wandering through the various squares, their noses in their guide books, I realized that it wouldn't be so simple and easy, if I were to settle down, set up shop and try to make a living far away in *bella, povera Italia*. There was, however, another sort of "social" problem that bothered me a great deal during those first years back in America while I was trying to find my bearings, so to speak, and that was the different attitude here from that in Europe toward artists, writers, and other independent types. Over there, just being an *artiste, ein Künstler,* and you automatically had status. People looked up to you, or at least accepted you, whether you were a star or not. It wasn't necessary to be a "name" figure or a "big success" to be taken seriously and treated with respect. Of course, artists in Europe also have to face varying levels of acceptance. To belong to, or move with the elite naturally depends upon a certain measure of accomplishment, or at least strong signs of potential success. Networking and party crashing certainly exist there as well. In my case, being a soldier did give me a limited entree, I'm sure, to a number of thresholds which, had I been an ordinary civilian, I might otherwise not have been able to cross.

Nevertheless, back here in the States, having been exposed to a fairly wide range of social levels through the part-time jobs I had to work at while going to NYU, I was able to observe differences in response according to the backgrounds of my employers. Thus, when I helped edit and compose the correspondence and sometimes legal briefs of that fascinating but also somewhat baffling international Dutch lawyer, Edward van Saher, he and his second wife, Desirée Halban (by some strange serendipity a few years later I was to work for Saher's first wife, who called herself Lilla van Saher!) would occasionally invite me to dinner parties given at their Plandome mansion on Long Island. There, I first tasted that delicious, tangy genuine Dutch Indonesian cuisine (a mélange of the best from those two quite different food cultures, I presume) served on a large, elegant glass table, which our proud host, van Saher himself, had designed.

Of course, the fact that Desi, as she was usually called, was the daughter of the great Viennese coloratura, Selma Kurz, and had herself recorded Mahler's *Fourth* under Bruno Walter, and that, moreover, she knew I was a struggling young student of the arts, increased my options. Moreover, I had been recommended to them by Klara Roman, the graphologist I told you about in an earlier letter, whom they held in high esteem. But with our very liberal aristocratic WASP lady, Ruth Danenhower Wilson—remember my note above about her—whom I assisted in writing a book on her travels and social work in Haiti (of all places), I might be invited to tea after a working session, where we would sometimes be joined by her protegée, Selma Burke, the talented African American sculptor, but never to any of the larger-attended evening dinners in her charming Georgian townhouse on Washington Place in the Village.

An interesting postscript to this story of dear, well-meaning Ruth D. Wilson, is the strange ephiphany she seemed to have experienced when the long time tenant of her spacious, well-appointed basement apartment, a pleasant, rather well-off, homosexual Wall Street type, who had resided there for over twenty years with his genial companion whom we all liked, suddenly announced that he was moving to Brazil with his new wife (!) whom he had met on vacation in Rio. After which, Mrs. Wilson managed to give him only a modest, but intimate, stuffy farewell party, to which this time I was invited.

Naturally, in the theatrical world, social barriers were less strict and more flexible, though there again, unless you were working together in the same show, your social rating also depended to a large degree on your "success." Similarly, in the academic world: some professors were more democratic, shall we say, than others. Some were more curious to meet especially those students interested in the arts. Thus Frau Professor Pekary of the NYU German department would throw open her fairly comfortable flat, practically on campus, to students once a month for the German equivalent of "high tea," to visit, mingle, and meet other students and faculty with whom she was on good terms. And, of course, she ate up my stories about post-war Germany.

An avid music lover, for many years Pekary had been an American fan and friend of the great Norwegian dramatic soprano, Kirsten Flagstad, who, as you probably know, went back to Quisling Norway during the war to be with her businessman husband—although Pekary always assured me that Flagstad hated the Nazis and spent a most unhappy four years there. Fortunately, after the war ended, England proved more understanding and definitely more hospitable than our uptight USA, forgave her, and welcomed her back almost immediately post-war. So the English public was able to enjoy that fabulous voice for another ten years. Alas, it wasn't until the mid-Fifties that the Met finally weakened and brought Flagstad back to America to launch its way-overdue premiere of Gluck's *Alcestis*—about 190 years late! (Not quite as shocking as the Met's 200-year-delayed premiere this season of Gluck's *Iphigénie en Tauride*.)

What an experience was that *Alcestis*—hearing this unique singer, near the end of her career, her voice still rich, sumptuous, *sans* any *tremolo,* sing this very difficult role *auf Englisch,* and make every word understood, unamplified in that huge auditorium! I was lucky to have been invited to the final dress rehearsal (this was at the old Met), where Flagstad astounded everyone by singing full voice at 9:00 in the morning. The whole thing was especially moving for me, because, as you'll recall, she was the Elsa I heard in my first live opera, *Lohengrin*, that time I hitchhiked to Milwaukee at the age of twelve. Of course, Pekary loved that story, too! Alas, dear soul, she did not live to see or hear Flagstad's glorious return to the Met.

To get back to those early jobs, there was also a part-time stint I did down on Wall Street for a top-notch broker. Can you believe it? He actually wanted me to quit NYU and join the firm as his personal secretary and assistant! Imagine me navigating that feral jungle. But, under his tutelage, might I have become rich?

However, I shouldn't complain. Gradually, I got to know more and more people. I developed friends of various colored skins, types, and sexes through my classes at NYU (one of whom was *la petite* Alva, as you will recall from an earlier letter), other friends through my various acting and dance classes, and then, of course, more social acquaintances through the divers connections of Geraldine and her tribe.

Because, of course, it always takes connections to connect! Thus, I met that fine historian Henry Bamford Parkes, author of *Marxism: An Autopsy*, a book way ahead of its time, and his quite articulate wife, through Joseph Frank's recommendation, and was accordingly invited to their table. But probably because I was much younger, and hadn't yet "made" it, I wasn't invited to their parties. Although, some years later, running into Parkes on Upper Broadway, that hospitable West Side writers' enclave, he gave me a warm introduction to the intense, very serious Hannah Arendt, with whom he was strolling down the avenue. Upon his telling her that I had written a good master's thesis for Columbia on Christian Dietrich Grabbe, the crabby, eccentric 19th-century German anticipator of the school of the Absurd with his precocious comedy *Jest, Satire, Irony and Deeper Significance* (which I had also translated), Arendt answered back somewhat mock-indignantly, "But why Grabbe? You should be translating Büchner, young man. A much more important writer!"

To which I replied, "Well, his few plays have already been translated. Though I did do some of his wonderful letters for the Tulane Drama Review." "Fine! But what about `*Der Hessische Landbote*?'" she retorted. (She was referring to "The Hessian Messenger," the amazing political letter/manifesto Büchner wrote at the age of twenty-one, which probably led to his early exile.) In retrospect, why didn't she ask about his remarkable narrative, "Lenz"? Anyway, after a polite exchange of bows, the two of them proceeded down Broadway. (Could Parkes have been courting her?)

Unfortunately, I never saw Arendt again, although narrowly

missed doing so another time at one of Shirley Broughton's "Theatre for Ideas" evenings, for which I had staged that almost surrealistic Brecht one-act play, *The Elephant Calf* (in Eric Bentley's translation), which Brecht sometimes used as an interlude to be performed between acts of his longer play *Man Is Man*, with its striking anticipations of *Threepenny Opera*, (especially the ubiquitous Brecht/Weill male quartet which shows up also in *Mahagonny* and again much later in *Seven Deadly Sins*). Arendt was expected to attend, but couldn't make it at the last minute for some reason or other. Too bad, for it was a *Lustspiel*, which I think would have appealed to her sometimes off-beat nature, especially when it came to the arts, and where she was not so solemn as usual. Especially when we remember Brecht's subtitle to the *Calf*: "Or the Provability of Any and Every Contention."

Which brings me to another crossroads—as so often happens in these letters when I'm tempted to go into further detail about one or two related issues, as I am here—instead of proceeding with the main theme of the letter or at least the one with which I started! But then didn't Sterne backtrack and shift milieux all the time in his *Tristram Shandy*?

Well, let's start with Brecht... My exposure to him actually goes back to my early Army days in that Army Special Training Program (ASTP) in Manhattan I told you about a few letters back, where we had intensive, concentrated daily sessions in German language, history and culture (Spring, 1944). That's where I memorized a very early Rilke poem, *"Ich war ein Kind und träumte viel/ und hatte noch nicht Mai"* which later I had to translate for the class as an exercise. We had a remarkably expert and able group of German intelligentsia and scholars who served as our guides and teachers, one of whom, the tall blonde Trude Günther I believe I already mentioned (not to be confused with my post-war Ingeborg from Bremen), would utter famous lines of German poetry from time to time to illustrate a point or an argument, or just for the fun and relief of it, such as the crucial Faust/Devil challenge, *"Verweile doch, du bist so schön,"* or Heine's *"Was ist in deiner Stimme das mich so tief erschüttert?"*

In addition to working all day with us, six days a week, these teachers would sometimes also take us to certain concerts or programs they felt would enhance our appreciation and understanding of things German. Among these, one highlight was a powerful performance by Herbert Berghof at The New School of Lessing's *Nathan the Wise*, actually the best thing I ever saw him do in English; although some years later I was almost as impressed with his German rendition of Orestes in Goethe's *Iphigenie auf Tauris*, next to the divine Elisabeth Bergner, as noted earlier. As I discovered recently, this production was probably a short revival for The New School of what had been done on Broadway the year before—Piscator's one partial success on the Great White Way.

A week or so later, we were taken to another special evening of theater, a private showing of Brecht's *The Private Life of the Master Race* in one of the larger meeting rooms of the Empire Hotel, next to what is now Lincoln Center. I don't think there were any stars in it, although there may well have been some very good character actors whom I wouldn't have known or seen, since I hailed from provincial Wisconsin and by that time had only attended a few Broadway shows. It was, in any case, a strange, unique experience for me, to see a play performed in the round in a flat, monochromatic hotel room, without any of the technical devices even our college theater at the University of Wisconsin had, and which the New School's Lessing play must have had. (I was later to realize that our University theater was better equipped than most Broadway theaters. Thus, I recall that when Helen Hayes visited it while touring her *Twelfth Night* company with Maurice Evans as Malvolio through Madison, she commented that it was too modern and well-equipped, and would surely spoil us student actors.)

Well, frankly, that hotel Brecht production looked like a rehearsal to young, naïve me. And, of course, the Brecht idiom was totally new to me, even though that particular play is less didactic, and less "alienating" in its effect, than most Brecht. So that it wasn't until two-and-a-half years later when I saw *Mutter Courage* in Zurich that I felt I had seen an authentic Brecht production. Nonetheless, it wasn't a bad start for my long acquaintance with Brecht—*nicht wahr*? And this early exposure to different kinds of theater was to serve me well in the future. Besides which, it gave all us soldiers a much richer feel for German culture, which I'm sure was the main reason our ASTP teachers took us to these events.

My next Brecht encounter, other than reading Bentley's ground-breaking translations of *The Caucasian Chalk Circle* and *The Good Woman of Setzuan*, which I believe came out while I was overseas but which I didn't get to read until 1947 or 1948, was when, to my great surprise and pleasure, I encountered both his work and his translator, Bentley himself, after appearing in the Interplayers' (that important pioneer Off-Broadway company) production of O'Casey's *The Silver Tassie* in Carnegie Recital Hall (now called the Weill Hall). This enterprising group, which spawned Gene Saks, Bea Arthur, and Ben Gazzara, among other stars, had turned that small auditorium into a pretty workable little theater. Jack Palance, then in the early stages of his stardom, played the lead and did a damned good job of it. Anne Meara, then young, naïve, and quite beautiful, was his Irish lassie. I had a minor role, that of the Major in the big symbolic fantasy scene, but for a beginner it was a good breakthrough, and I learned a great deal in this, my first professional appearance. (I also chanted various Latinate settings from the Catholic service for background music to some of the scenes.)

This led to my being cast as one of the three satirical, mocking Gods in *Good Woman*, which was to be the Interplayers' next production. Bentley, who had just returned from working with Brecht in Munich, was on hand to advise and to make changes during rehearsals as we worked on the play. Unfortunately, that much-looked-forward-to opening night never materialized. Instead, the very first morning of rehearsal, the Interplayers received a cable from the great, but greedy, Brecht forbidding us to go ahead with his play. "I want a Broadway production!" was in essence what he insisted upon. And here we were in small Carnegie Recital Hall on 57th Street: good enough for a well-received production of E. E. Cummings' *him*, a noncommercial avantgarde opus if there ever

236

was one; and a quite professional mounting of another difficult, also noncommercial play, Sean O'Casey's *The Silver Tassie*; but, ironically, not good enough for that great Leveller, that preacher of equal rights for all, that anti-Capitalist par excellence, Bertolt Brecht! Didn't he know that Carnegie Hall is only one short block from Broadway?

Well, you can imagine, my dear Nina, how discombobulating this was for the poor, now-left-stranded Interplayers. It meant having to come up with a substitute play, casting it immediately, and going into rehearsal for it the very next day. Also, how disappointing for us actors, especially for those of us, a surprising number of the cast, who were eager to perform Brecht—including, of course, yours truly.

The Interplayers management turned to Bentley for advice. Could he think of an avant-garde play somewhat like E. E. Cummings' *him*, or at least in that genre, since *him* had been a big success? That, and their production the year before of Gertrude Stein's *Yes is for a very young man* had really put the Interplayers on the map. So they naturally wanted to do something in the same vein, if possible, to take the place of the cancelled *Good Woman*. But the only thing Eric Bentley could come up with on such short notice was the totally unknown (to any of us) Grabbe play, *Jest, Satire, Irony and Deeper Significance*, which apparently Charles Laughton had once recommended to him as being an extraordinary, early 19th-century precursor of the Theatre of the Absurd. Laughton, in turn, must have learned of it from one of the exiled German colony in Hollywood, with whom he was on very good terms.

So Eric, who by that time had somehow learned that I knew some German, turned to me and said, "Why don't you translate it for us?" That's how I was introduced to Grabbe, and why I eventually ended up doing my Master's thesis on him at Columbia. (As Parkes told Arendt, remember above?) But even had I been completely bilingual, which I certainly was not then and am not now, nor ever claimed to be, it would have been impossible to translate that odd, difficult piece in time for the Interplayers to produce that summer. They needed a viable playwright then and there to put into rehearsal at once. Unfortunately, I forget what they ended up doing, but it certainly wasn't at all of either the Cummings or the Grabbe ilk.

Nevertheless, this whole episode was important in that it introduced me to that amazing, crabby, unpleasant, in some respects obnoxious, genius, Christian Dietrich Grabbe, but also fostered my friendship with the very helpful and encouraging Eric Bentley, who included my eventually finished translation of that Grabbe play in the second volume of his anthology series, *From the Modern Repertoire, Series II.* He also steered me to several future translation projects, which I'll tell you about in another letter. And to my appearing about ten years later in a double role (Wang & Solly Schmidt) in Eric's translation of Brecht's *A Man's a Man,* Off-Broadway on West 42nd Street, as well as my staging *The Elephant Calf* for the Theatre for Ideas, using the same excellent professional cast of the larger play. This was only appropriate, since, as we pointed out earlier, Brecht often featured *Elephant Calf* as an interlude between acts of the longer play to be played in the lobby! Fortunately, you can hear me as Solly Schmidt singing some of the superb songs from that production. They were recorded by Smithsonian Folkway Records and can also be heard nowadays in our age of technical miracles on i-tunes!

Well, my dear, skeptical, intelligent Nina, you are no doubt wondering how in the world I ever managed that fiendishly difficult Grabbe translation over fifty years ago, especially since I didn't have you to help me handle the first rough draft as you have done recently with my translation of Thomas Bernhard's *Der Weltverbesserer.* Obviously, Bentley must have presumed that I knew more German than I did. And though I had just been through a few German literature courses at NYU under Professor Pekary and others, I knew I would need to check out my first drafts with several German experts. Yet I couldn't very well ask my former professors to do the "dirty work," i.e., to follow along the German text as I read aloud my translation to spot any errors. They would probably have thought it beneath them, or, more likely, be upset and wonder why they weren't asked to do the translating instead. Fortunately I had a number of authentic German-speaking refugee friends at that time to call upon for help.

One of them was that wonderful little lady, Leni Seligson, who gave us those pre-World War II books about the Rhine to take along on our visit to Frankfurt and Cologne seven years ago. Remember her? Well, she was my major "coach" in this process, ably abetted by her talented younger sister, Ilse Sass, who was my music coach for Lieder and other songs back in those days, and a fine chamber music pianist as well. Ilse was perhaps better at making sure we got the right tone for a particular passage, while Leni was more of an exacting word-for-word, phrase-for-phrase stickler for accuracy. And though hardly a scholar, Leni turned out to have read a great deal in early 19th-century German literature; after all, Grabbe wrote that incredible play way back in 1819. But this predecessor of Jarry and the turn-of-the-century French avant-garde was new to her and Ilse (as he was likewise to most any German you would encounter, except a specialist). Jarry had actually translated some Grabbe into French (from *Napoleon, oder die hundert Tage*), though Grabbe fit perhaps even better than he into the international theater of the Absurd movement of the Fifties and Sixties.

In any case, if there was a particular older "period" idiomatic phraseology my two aides didn't recognize or couldn't figure out for sure, Leni would pick up the phone and call one or another of her friends for his or her interpretation. So that by the time I showed Pekary an early draft of the manuscript, it was already accurate and viable. Moreover, she was usually able to help solve those passages Leni's and Ilse's friends disagreed over. (Sadly, Pekary did not live to see my Grabbe translation in its final published form; something I really regretted.) A footnote to all this: sometimes my theatrical instinct helped me to "get" the drift of certain passages my German friends continued to puzzle over.

This translation baptism by fire stood me in good stead when some years later I was asked to translate two German expressionist plays for Walter Sokel's *Anthology of German Expressionist Drama*, to be published by Doubleday Anchor, namely, *The Strongbox* by Carl Sternheim and *Cry in the Street* by Rolf Lauckner. Of course, it was Eric Bentley who had recommended me to Sokel.

For these particular translations, however, I thought it best to do them collaboratively, especially since there was an early deadline and working with the Leni/Ilse team would take too long.

So my partner in crime turned out to be one Valerie Reich, that interesting woman I once told you about, whose apartment was a labyrinth of books and newspapers, through which one had to wind carefully in and out, in order to reach a writing desk with a spot of light. Back in Vienna, she had been a private secretary and aide to the *Weltberühmte* psychoanalyst, Alfred Adler, in those days usually ranked just below Freud and Jung in prestige and influence in the psychiatric realm. She still did some independent consulting here in the States about him and his system, and was certainly more learned and well-read than either Ilse or Leni, though not necessarily better at translating dialogue. Where she was perhaps superior was in helping me with another translation I undertook for myself during that period, namely, Grabbe's one pugnacious prose piece, "On the Shakespeare Mania." Even so, later at Sokel's behest, I went through our joint effort with the Lauckner and the Sternheim with a third party, a friend of his, the beautiful Frau Walter Taussig, spouse of one of the leading singer coaches and assistant conductors at the Met Opera, who also served as prompter in its Wagnerian and Strauss repertoire. But even that was not the end of it, for it turned out that Frau Taussig was Viennese, which meant that we both had to call on an *echt* Berliner to interpret a few of the more elusive passages in Berlin dialect. Then there was the proofreading, at which stage of the game you always find a few other passages that still don't make total dramatic sense. That's when you finally have to trust your own instinct as to just what the author was trying to say—or, rather, to have his characters say!

I'm sorry to report a tragic postscriptum to the Valerie Reich part of this story, however. Several years later, she was found murdered in her apartment, amongst that plethora of books, old magazines, and dated newspapers. And the perpetrator turned out to be her own apartment-house super, a Balkan immigrant whom she had once introduced to me as her friend. Nor could I get the coroner or morgue people downtown to let me rescue the manuscript of that Grabbe "Shakespeare Mania" translation we had also worked on. (Though I later found my working copy.) And Valerie was such a good, trusting soul. *Sic transit Gloria mundi...*

Well, my dear, this translation business is probably all "old hat" to you, an expert in transforming French and German poetry into Romanian, not to mention the expert versions of *Hamlet*, *The Tempest*, and the *Dream* you made for Liviu Ciulei's productions of those plays. I still hope you'll reconsider and do the *Lear*, which Ciulei and the Romanians have been asking of you. (And we really should try to get these three Shakespeare translations published.) Nor can we forget the huge challenge you once met of translating many of your friend Paul Celan's German poems into Romanian. (And more recently his Romanian poems into English!) Plus your Ritsos translations and your Brecht? Didn't we go through this same torture when you helped me translate the "Stalks" section of Celan's *Poppy and Memory* into viable English, where we tried to capture as much as possible of Celan's unique tonality? He, who, as you'll surely recall, was such a marvellous translator himself, especially of Mandelstam and Arghezi, into beautiful German. It seems he also translated some Emily Dickinson, as an exercise, or a challenge—who knows?

Ah, yes, translation seems to be one of those things one says one isn't ever going to do again and yet somehow ends up tempted to try once more. I suppose it's because one usually feels there is something in the original that should be made available to the English-speaking world; and also, perhaps, because facing a tough translation, has something of the irrational daring of climbing an impossible mountain...

With untranslatable love,

M.

February 8, 2008

My dear, multilingual Nina:

Am still haunted *dîn când în când*—"from time to time" as you say with comparable succinctness in Romanian—by unexpected memory jolts about my poor, departed Jacob. Today, for example, I suddenly realized that his one remaining aunt, Frieda, the painter from Fresno, Ann's "unknown" sister who didn't appear on our relative screen until about seven years ago—that this strange, elusive, dare we say mysterious(?) woman has neither called nor written to console us about the untimely demise of the nephew she never met. True, I was a little late in informing her about the tragedy, but still, it's been over six weeks since I did so. And not a word from her yet—neither spoken nor written. Also, come to think of it, she never acknowledged receipt of the several of Jacob's drawings I had mailed her this summer to look over, and because I felt they would remind her of her late sister from whom Jacob no doubt inherited that drawing talent. Certainly not from me!

In any event, I checked my computer for letters I had written her since her locating us. Apparently she had heard that I was associated with the Brooklyn Academy of Music, and that's why she contacted them about help in finding me. Although the Brooklyn Philharmonic administrative office had long since left the Academy building, the orchestra was still giving concerts there. So they had no trouble locating me and putting me in touch with her. After which I wrote the following (I quote this letter because it sums up the situation quite succinctly, and will refresh your memory):

Dear Long-Lost Relatives! — Freda (Friede?) and Vernon— M. & Mme. Zimmermann:

I'm still bowled over by the discovery that Ann had a younger sister or, indeed, any other sister than that humorless elder sister, Tzivia! How was it possible that she never told me about you? Nor did your brother (and

242

her brother) Sidney, whom we saw far more often than Tzivia? And why did Ann never write you in Europe or elsewhere? But, by the same token, why did you—at least as far as I am aware—never write her during all these 45 years? I also checked with our son, Jacob, last night to find out whether Ann perchance had ever told him about you when he was a little boy. No. He was as amazed as I that you even existed...

In any case, it all sounds like something out of *Great Expectations* or *Barnaby Rudge*! Nevertheless, I think we should all make the most of it and be happy that we've found each other at long last.

Most curiously yours.   /s/ Maurice

*

Well, as you know, Frieda never did clear up that mystery for us, not even during the day or two we visited her twice at her handsome, almost luxurious, ranch house in Fresno, which, strangely, large as it was, did not have a little spare room for us to sleep overnight in! Yes, there was indeed something enigmatic about both her and her tall, wizened husband; he was transparently a species of con man or what one might call a mandrake type. Also, remember how, in that very first meeting, Frieda had a few violent swings of mood and emotion, which seemed to upset even their dog? Indeed, he proved to be more hospitable than either half of this strange couple. Remember, too, when a couple of months later, we got a phone call saying that she was putting us in her will, donating the house to us, and making me the administrator of her paintings and little sculptures? Then about a year after this unexpected bonanza, which to tell the truth, as you may recall, we didn't take too seriously, we got a report that their nephew, to whom they had entrusted most of their business matters during the last few years, had rooked them out of two-thirds of their estate.

So somehow the will was never mentioned again. Nor did Frieda ever respond to my letter telling her that we needed nothing from her, but suggesting that she might leave something for Jacob. Of course, we both tried to console her when her Vernon passed away two years ago. No doubt his absence has only accentuated her peculiarities. They seemed in some respects to act as though they were two against the world. Hence, she is probably more alone now than ever, having dismissed the very capable woman who had tried to keep things in order for her, including organizing and cataloguing her prints, drawings, paintings and sculptures. At least, there's no denying she was a very good painter!

It will be interesting to see how, and if, she responds to the loss of Jacob. Actually it might be a relief if she doesn't, because what is one to say to her now? Except that it would be a fitting close to this episode in our lives if we learned from the Delphic Oracle the reason for that long silence before she emerged from the Shades. Oh yes, I did note in my last letter to her that Jacob is buried near his mother—her sister, Ann—in lovely Wellwood Cemetery on Long Island. You'd think that that alone would have provoked some comment from his bereaved aunt? But perhaps not. Is it not more in line with the fact that she did not contact me, or worse yet, her supposedly beloved sister, during that long period of Ann's mental travail, about which she surely must have heard something from Tzivia, whom she had apparently been in touch with from time to time during all those years? Obviously, she did not want to become involved. It would have been too troubling: Ann might have become an unwelcome burden. But even after her death? Still a puzzlement. So let's forget those hidden relatives (could there be others?): it might be wiser then that if so, they remain in the closet.

Yet perhaps I should not be too hard on Ann's maverick, younger sister. After all, her older sister, Tzivia, who was residing on East 60th Street across from Bloomingdale's during all those years of Ann's suffering, was far more guilty of neglect, being only a half-hour subway ride distant from Ann. Can you imagine, dear Nina, that this well-educated, much more sophisticated sister, married

244

to a Columbia University physics professor, never once visited her younger, mentally ailing sister when she was in the hospital, not even to one of her four incarcerations! (Well, maybe once she went out to Pilgrim State, I'm not quite sure.) Nor did she ever cross the East River to see Ann when she was still at home with Jacob and me in Brooklyn to find out whether she needed help, advice, moral support, etc. Indeed, I wonder if Tzivia ever deigned to phone Ann when she knew I wasn't around?

Oh yes, while we were invited once to dinner at her apartment across from Bloomingdales' during the first year of our marriage, we were never invited back. Not even after Ann's returns from her various hospitalizations, when such a gesture might have been most helpful. Was she afraid Ann would have a fit or a spasm in her small apartment? That she might knock over and break some precious glassware? Nor did Tzivia ever phone me to find out how Ann was doing, progressing or failing. Or to ask for a prognosis as to when she might return from the hospital. Or how Jacob was handling boarding school? (Did she even know about Green Chimneys?) Or just to say: how are you?

In sharp contrast, Ann's brother Sydney, his wife, and family were more sympathetic and understanding in the beginning phases of the problem era and certainly showed more concern over Ann's well-being than Tzivia ever evinced. Sydney actually visited her at least once at Pilgrim State Hospital. In fact, during those first years, before she grew more deeply disturbed, and even sometimes when she would be back from the hospital for a spell, he and his wife would invite us—that is, Ann, Jacob and me—to holiday dinners in their modest but comfortable home in the flatlands of monotonous Canarsie. They even kept independently in touch with Jacob for a brief period after Ann died. Then they disappeared. It was only from others that I learned two or three years later that Sydney had also died of a heart attack, a cardiac arrest failure probably similar to what happened to both Jacob and Ann. (Was it in the genes?) But no word about where his wife and daughters had moved. They left no new phone number, no forwarding address. Not even after several vain attempts to locate them. For I had wanted to keep in touch with them, especially for Jacob's sake, so that he would have some relatives to fall back on after I'd be gone from the scene, but with no luck. That chapter has been closed for some time now...

Ironically enough, some of my friends were actually more helpful and concerned about Ann's welfare, and certainly about how Jacob was being taken care of, than her own family. One such friend was the charming, helpful Kathleen Costello, who had once been on the staff of the Advertising Council. Not a bad writer, and a great music and theater lover, she had been very close to the highly esteemed, once very successful, leading American dramatist, Elmer Rice, though only in his late, declining years, when she served as a kind of combined Muse and practical secretary to him. You probably saw several of Rice's better plays in Romania, such as *Street Scene* and *Counsellor at Law*, maybe also the innovative, expressionistic *Adding Machine* (of which I saw a very good production starring Fiona Shaw in London at the National, a year or so before I met you); or more likely you may have seen movie versions of one or more of those plays. Very intelligent, quite good looking, with a quirky Irish wit and sensibility, Kathleen and I had met through Geraldine's friend Bob Pace. Among other things, she would frequently help out as a babysitter for Jacob during those periods when Ann was in the hospital and I couldn't find anyone else at the last minute.

Recently, I ran across a "fun" letter (in the wrong file, of course) from Kathleen sent during the period when she was working briefly for UNESCO in Paris in which she reported that "the Living Theater was a resounding success—including their *In the Jungle of Cities*, which I found so painfully, badly staged and excruciatingly acted that I walked out on it. A UNESCO American from whom I have some hopes of getting another temporary job when this one ends turned out to be giving up on it, too—so we had a couple of beers together." Unfortunately, with her growing and gradually unstoppable addiction to drink, well-meaning Kathleen lost one good job after another (though she was otherwise eminently well-qualified) and finally returned, I think, to the bosom of her family in the heart of the Midwest. We all missed her terribly—Geraldine, Bob Pace, myself, and Jacob!—not to mention the bevy of friends she had accumulated in advertising and writing circles over the years.

Of course, once we were able to place Jacob in a very good boarding school for emotionally troubled children known as Green Chimneys up in Brewster (in a far-flung corner of Westchester County close to the Connecticut border), babysitting was no longer a problem. Well, my dear Nina, you can imagine what a relief this was on one level, but what a financial burden on another. His doctors and teachers at the excellent Pride of Judea elementary school, however, where we had enrolled him after Ann's first hospitalization, had both felt that with his mother's condition getting progressively worse, it was not good for the boy to be alone with her in the house so much of the time.

Interestingly enough, Jacob himself was usually the first to sense when Ann was going to be seriously "off," whereupon he would sound the alarm: "I think, Daddy, it's time for Mommy to go back to the hospital." The doctors agreed that this uncertain and unpredictable behavior of Ann's was too much of a burden for the boy to bear and would, in turn, negate whatever progress he might be making at school in those special classes he was taking and in the intense therapy he was getting. So they, too, recommended Green Chimneys as the right place for him after he finished Pride of Judea. With only five or six children in a class, and with constant supervision, Jacob could flourish there, it was hoped by all concerned.

Green Chimneys, with its wonderful playground slides and other facilities, its little ponies for the children to ride, all set amongst beautiful tall pines, only a short distance from Brewster, was like a luxury resort in some respects. Though, of course, the interior architecture and furnishings were simple and austere, and strong discipline was mandatory in order to handle the wide range of troubled youth it housed.

When Ann was not hospitalized, I would take her up there for the monthly visits we were allowed. But with her hair turning prematurely white, the children thought she was Jacob's grandmother and

247

I, his father. Haply, due to her troubled state, Ann was completely unaware of their innocent misapprehension. For the only thing she could focus on outside of herself during that period was Jacob. Indeed, when at times she'd even lose sight of him, that was one of the signals Jacob recognized which would lead him to warn me.

Those years were obviously very difficult, my dear Ninicuța, as you can well imagine. Moreover, because of the tremendous cost of Green Chimneys, I had no choice but to stick to my part-time Brooklyn Philharmonic job. I could not count on notoriously unsteady theater work to sustain such a budget. Unfortunately, I didn't have the knack of going the commercial route (that is, doing such things as voice-over for TV ads, and the like) nor the requisite chutzpah to keep at it if, as on rare occasions, I did make a little breakthrough in that field. For example, Doris and Jules Schwerin once introduced me to Eleanor Marx, the daughter of Chico, who happened to be an agent for commercials, and that led to her sending me out to a couple of auditions, one of which led to a small job. But I foolishly failed to "court" this smart lady after that with the flowers and flattery obviously needed to stay on her call list. Thus, years later I ran into an actor I had met at one of her auditions, who had been smart enough to do just that. He was eventually able to retire to a little cottage near Woodstock on the earnings she had led him to.

Ironically, this was after my being cast in *The Golden Apple*, a musicalized version of Homer's *Odyssey* transposed into post-Civil War America, and I should have known better. In any case, *Apple* was an artistic and a critical success and probably could have run longer had it stayed down on Second Avenue, where we had opened in what had formerly been a Yiddish theater (I remember having seen those great Yiddish actors, Menashe Skulnik and Molly Picon there during the War). But once *Apple* moved uptown to Broadway, it closed after a couple of months. Its sometimes cloying mix of nostalgic charm and sophisticated humor was not quite right for the average tired business man. And while it was good for me to have appeared in it, and I learned a great deal from doing it, it was only a step or two beyond being in a chorus. Yet, at least each of us soldiers had an identity; for example, I was Nestor, one of the Greek "heroes" under Ulysses. True, it gave me a handle of some sort to hang onto for a characterization. But not enough for it to become a stepping stone or serve as a commercial showcase that might lead to my being cast in future similar, more important roles.

In fact, it was shortly after *Apple* closed that Siegfried Landau offered me that part-time job at the then just-formed Brooklyn Philharmonia (Spring 1955). He needed someone like me, he said, to help launch that ambitious project; he also knew I needed steady work, our son Jacob having arrived that summer somewhat prematurely. So our needs coincided. What I remember most vividly from that incredible period—it was during the run of the *Apple* that I finished my Master's thesis on Grabbe, among other things—was my first visit to Bellevue Hospital to see little Jacob. The minute I entered the room with the premature babies lined up in their "breathing tents," a cheerful, friendly nurse led me to one of them, and pointing to a very tiny baby lying therein, said: "Put a pair of glasses on that one, and he'll look exactly like you!" Ironically, as I think I've told you a number of times already, when Jacob grew into adulthood, he ended up looking much more like my more portly younger brother, Lester, than me, his rather wan father.

To return to the casting problem. Even though still young, at that stage of my life I often could, and did, play older roles Off-Broadway; indeed, I was usually cast in such mature parts as Peachum in *Threepenny Opera*; an Army officer, such as the Major in *Home of the Brave*; or Roebuck Ramsden in Shaw's *Man and Superman*. But when submitted for similar roles uptown, on Broadway, while many directors and producers would usually like my auditions, sometimes even applaud them, they had plenty of older actors, the right age, to choose from. Thus once, after trying out for the touring road company of that charming, inscoucient musical, *Irma la Douce*, directed by the famed Peter Brook, having been submitted by an agent who had seen me downtown as Peachum, I was cast in just such a good, mature part, only to be told the next day that they had decided to give it instead to a much older character actor who was not only the right age but also the right size and shape for the costume of the man playing it at that time on Broadway, whom he or I was to replace! Of course, they would save money if the replacement could use the same costume. So they took him. (I got a surreptitious minor revenge of some sort on this fiasco when a couple years later I played Bob, an even better role in that play, in summer stock.)

Indeed, I think it may have been that experience, or any number of similar irrational, but expedient-for-the-producer, experiences that led my then eccentric but wise agent, Barna Ostertag, to predict: "In twenty years you'll be ripe for the picking!" Alas, she was right, except that twenty years later I was too busy directing my own Off-Off-Broadway Classic Theatre and running the Brooklyn Philharmonic to run after roles for which by then I might very well have been the right age. (But the right size? Not necessarily.) Perhaps I should have shifted gears right then and there and gone after those roles? Who knows? But directing lesser known classics, like the nowadays almost unfamiliar Ben Jonson comedy, *Epicoene*, or *The Silent Woman* (although in the 17th and 18th centuries it was his most popular play and may well have been the ancestress of *Charley's Aunt!*); and Euripides' little-known *Alcestis* and *Helen* (although Gluck made a great opera of the first, and the second was used by Strauss and Arnold Zweig for their opera, *The Egyptian Helen*); or a new play by Joyce Carol Oates—all seemed at that time a more engaging, more challenging, more satisfying alternative. Moreover, the Brooklyn Philharmonic job had its other kinds of challenges to whet my appetite and my interests. But having already written so much about the latter in my history of the orchestra, I needn't burden you with that now.

Besides, back then, my dear, again before the *Golden Apple* period, I was chiefly involved with the kind of experimental theater that didn't pay and usually ended up leaving the participant having to dig into his own pockets, such as that production of the electronic opera *Stacked Deck* I did at the 92nd Street Y, which I told you about in an earlier letter. Or the various kinds of "literary" presentations at Cooper Union that I put on together with Mura, Geraldine, Norman

Shelley, and others, or the various unusual events, including a staged concert reading of Valéry's *My Faust* that I directed for Theatre for Ideas, which I shall go into in a later letter. But wasn't I also, by the same token, experimenting with life? Back in Madison, of course, Mother and Father were still hoping (and probably praying) that I'd settle down and become a lawyer, a doctor, or even a professor of some sort.

Adventitiously, about that time, dear Nina, I fell into the orbit of The Cubiculo, which has come up at various times in these letters—intriguingly, I hope. For it proved a godsend of a new focus for me. (Maybe that's what I needed?) Phil Meister, the younger brother of Al Lewis (the ebullient cigar-chomping Grandpa Joe of TV Munster fame, whom you got to know out on Roosevelt Island, along with his charming wife, Karen), had met me at Lynne Michael's handsome theater on the busy East Village corner of 8th Street and Second Avenue, where Lynne was planning, in collaboration with him, to revive a play Piscator had introduced to America, Wolfgang Borchert's striking expressionist drama, *Outside the Door*. At any rate, Geraldine had recommended me to Lynne and Phil as an "expert" on German theater, and the three of us hit it off quite well, though, alas, that particular project never came to pass. Then one night several months later, I ran into Phil on my way to Theater DeLys on Christopher Street, where I was playing Peachum in *Threepenny Opera* and he was stage managing Tennessee Williams's *Summer and Smoke* at the nearby Circle on the Square Theater, on Sheridan Square where Christopher Street starts.

It was on that occasion that Phil invited me then and there—without any previous warning or talk—to help him and his actress wife, Elaine Sulka, to form an experimental theater center uptown, on West 51st Street, to be called "The Cubiculo," named after that little tavern frequented by Sir Toby Belch and Sir Andrew Aguecheek in *Twelfth Night*. And why the nod to Shakespeare for a modern avant-garde center? Because it was to be financed by the surplus, which Phil and Elaine's nonprofit, National Shakespeare Company, was bringing in from its tours, but, being nonprofit, had to be turned back into the Company's affairs. So The Cubiculo was to be, in effect, the pet child of the NSC. But it would also give the NSC a performing base in New York City itself. For some reason, it was never explained to me that the theater space could not be used for the NSC's Shakespeare touring shows! Or was it because these were performed by non-Equity actors only? Well, whatever the reason, it made no difference to me. On the contrary, it made The Cubiculo artistically independent of NSC, unless NSC tried to censor its work, which it rarely did while I was working with it.

The Cubiculo itself was lodged in the basement and first floor of a large five-story brownstone on West 51st Street off of Ninth Avenue, only a hop, skip, and jump from the heart of Broadway, with the National Shakespeare Company offices located on the second floor. Both parties shared the third and fourth floors. But the key area was its remarkable basement, with half of the ceiling carved out so that the first-floor ceiling became the top of the theater space. The part of the first floor that remained held the balcony, the entrance foyer, and the public restrooms.

Historically, 414 West 51st Street is an interesting site, for what now became The Cubiculo's theater space had once been the prime dance studio of the great choreographer-director-dancer Agnes de Mille—the place where she first worked on the dances for *Oklahoma* and many other shows and ballets. Before that time, the building had served as headquarters for a branch of the Knights of Columbus, which still retained a tiny office on the third floor to collect mail and count up memories! From time to time, one would bump into one of its still-living members, looking like an exile from a Coppola film, as he climbed the stairs, flourishing his cigar, only to disappear into that small, sturdily locked room.

Yes, those three years founding and then running The Cubiculo were among the most exciting in my up-and-down life, certainly more interesting, challenging, and stimulating than playing Reb Nahum, the Beggar (and occasionally the Rabbi and the Bookseller) in *Fiddler on the Roof*, eight times a week for three years on Broadway. Don't mistake me: *Fiddler* was a great experience, especially the rehearsals under Jerome

252

Robbins, and the professional lift of being in a hit show, and associated perks; but to do the same thing day after day, night after night, can be terribly enervating. Although, of course, I made ten times as much money doing so. And still get a little pension based on those earnings, plus that from the few other commercial shows I had been involved with. (My Off- and Off-Off-Broadway shows, even though Equity showcases, did not contribute anything to the pension fund: indeed, earnings from them barely covered one's transportation costs to and from rehearsals and the short runs for such shows.)

Fortunately, during my "Cubiculo period," the Brooklyn Philharmonic job was less demanding than it eventually became. Thus, in those earlier years, I was able to manage the basic, necessary BPO business during the mornings and early afternoons in Brooklyn, then take the subway to Manhattan to be at The Cubiculo at four or five o'clock, depending upon the schedules of both places. And leave generally about midnight! Gradually, of course, as I built up the orchestra's seasons, and the work load in Brooklyn increased accordingly, I would have had less and less time for The Cubiculo had I continued there—but that's another story involving other decisions, which I'll get back to you about in another letter, if you wish...

In any case, here we were, at the start of The Cubiculo's short history, ready to launch a brand new experimental theatrical enterprise. Each side of our four-sided, cube-shaped Cubiculo logo (technically a tetragon?) proclaimed another phase of the range of our actually more than four-sided, planned programming: theater, dance, poetry, and film. Somehow, music always spilled over into the other categories, and, at times, really took over more of the spots which film and/or poetry were meant to have filled. But the main point of The Cubiculo, and that which gave it its uniqueness, was that it was set up as a place to try out new ideas for plays, films, dances, music, etc., but always with the right to fail. This was the most important tenet or operating principle that Phil, Elaine, and I agreed upon from the very start. We had no desire to compete with any Off- or Off-Off-Broadway companies in launching "successful" productions. Not that we didn't want a project to succeed. On the contrary, every effort would be made to make a play work, or a dance float, or an opera soar. Did I ever mention that we premiered Tom Johnson's charming little *Four Note Opera*, built on four tones, reminding one of that remarkable French novel by Perec, in which he never employs the letter "e," not even once. But, of course, though successful artistically, it never made a cent for us. Nor for the composer! (Though in later years he may have had productions of it we were not aware of.)

In any event, The Cubiculo opened with a tried and true choreographer, Daniel Nagrin, the veteran modern dancer, premiering his most unusual work, "The Peloponnesian War," which he called a Dance/Theatre Collage, with a multitrack score by Eric Salzman and Archie Shepp. This was a significant start for us because it sent out a signal to young dancers and choreographers all over town (and to some not so young!) that here was a place that would help them try out new ideas, at no house costs to them. So Monday through Wednesday was given over to dance; Thursday through Sunday to theater, new plays or revivals of known plays done in often startling new ways, such as our once hosting a Columbia University drama workshop production of Büchner's *Wozzeck* that featured a huge watermelon into which *Wozzeck* plunged his knife to symbolize his murder of Marie. Poetry events, which were less frequent, would usually be scheduled on late Sunday afternoons and sometimes held in the smaller third-floor space that was gradually shaped into a secondary theater with skeletal lighting, where eventually we did the New York premiere of Brecht's *Roundheads and Peakheads*, among other plays. Film showings would usually be done on dark nights or as late shows between productions, in the main downstairs space, which was, of course, better equipped technically. Besides, film-goers are accustomed to weird hours.

Well, my dear, you can imagine what a complicated production schedule we had in those hectic days and nights—fitting in rehearsal times (using other floors for this), lighting times, dress rehearsals, tryout readings of new scripts, etc. Not to mention the advance planning involved: all those meetings with potential dancers, writers, poets, filmmakers, musicians. Then doing the publicity and mailings for these events. Thus, we would try to send out a monthly calendar card to our gradually growing audience. And, of course, since I had to bear the main load of supervising the overall production schedule, Elaine and Philip being mainly advisers and often heavily involved with money matters and keeping the NSC going, I couldn't direct plays as often as I had originally hoped would be possible. So we brought in some promising young directors, set and lighting designers, and, when necessary, technical assistants, though obviously sets had to be economically bare, but richly imaginative, due to the constant production turnover, and because the dancers for the most part wanted and needed a bare stage, where skilled lighting was more crucial than sets or props. So it's no wonder that some very talented people came to work with us. I recall especially a tall, lanky hippy type with a scratch beard, who came to be known as "Blue" because he used that hue so creatively in his lighting designs. He went on to become eventually quite successful in the commercial world. And kept that unusual moniker.

To get the theatrical phase started, I directed the first play we did at The Cubiculo, a strange but weirdly charming comedy, *Jenusia*, by René de Obaldia, one of the lesser-known French offshoots from the theater of the Absurd Era. It was well-received, for the most part, by the smaller press. Here, of course, I used Elaine for the leading female role of the enigmatic professor's wife who spoke only Jenusian! It was a good part for her, one of the reasons I chose that play in the first place. Fortunately, Elaine did not want to be in everything we did, and so finding right roles for her never really posed a problem.

No, that turned out to be something quite different. Namely, that as I took on more and more responsibility for running The Cubiculo, and was gradually gaining a greater proportion of the acclaim for it, Elaine and Philip began to worry about their being left out of the picture (though nary a word of complaint was ever spoken to me about this). Of course, Phil was not always around because he would have to spend considerable time on the road supervising and often rescuing his touring Shakespeare productions whenever they'd run into problems. Nevertheless, when, early in the game, *The New*

York Times wanted to do a story about The Cubiculo and intended to include me in the narrative, Elaine and Phil made sure that only they were to be featured in the picture, which accompanied the story. We got over that hump all right, as I recall, but a couple of years later, when the *Times* was ready for an updated story about more recent accomplishments at The Cubiculo, they tried to exclude me from its interview as well.

Of course, that didn't quite work either, with me being the major source of the information the *Times* wanted—which, naturally, didn't sit well with them. They were also upset that in between these two press benchmarks, numerous articles had appeared in other papers and magazines, most of which focused largely on my role at The Cubiculo, not theirs. Such as Jack Kroll, who, in *Newsweek*, called us a "dauntless little organization," and went on to report how "last season...it produced twelve new plays, three revivals, thirty dance programs, three new opera productions, ten poetry programs and fifteen film showings. All of this is coordinated by the 'Cube's' program director, a gentlemanly dynamo named Maurice Edwards. Not exactly a formal producing unit, nor precisely a workshop, the Cubiculo is a place where theater happens." After which he proceeded to favorably review my production of Joyce Carol Oates's one-act play, *Ontological Proof of My Existence*.

In any case, as was probably inevitable, this situation led to my eventual departure from the scene and the slowdown and near total eclipse of what had become in a few short years an exciting and important spawning ground for dance, theater, and music in blasé, always-looking-for-something-different New York. You can imagine how later it irked me when our precious, pioneering Cubiculo ended up being rented out for other people's productions.

At the same time, dear Nina, I don't want to overemphasize the differences between us; after all, there was far more that we agreed upon. For starters, Phil, Elaine, and I certainly shared the goals of The Cubiculo. How else could we have ever launched it together, and got the enterprise running and off to a great start with so little advance preparation? And, of course, both Phil and Elaine obviously

256

had great confidence in me, and allowed me considerable leeway in setting up our variegated programming. Nonetheless, I would go over all plans with them weeks, even months, in advance, depending upon the nature of a specific project. They both read most of the incoming scripts of plays and mixed media production proposals; and at least one or the other of them would sit in on important auditions with me. Certainly, budgets were closely watched and followed. Indeed, we had surprisingly few policy disagreements. And if one arose, it would be resolved by a vote between the three, and a two to one would carry the day. Later, when Al Schoemann was brought in as a production coordinator for the overall operation—both NSC and The Cubiculo—he would sometimes sit in for one or the other.

Philip was of medium, standard height; a taut, highly strung-out persona, with one of those interesting pock-marked, cavity-scarred faces that make you look older, more mature than you actually are. At times he almost looked like a shorter version of his elder brother, the tall, genial Al Lewis you knew, who also appeared to be older than he was, as Karen, his widow, informed me after his recent death. But there was a third brother, Henry, the youngest and shortest, sort of a meld of the two, but with a less "experienced" face. A rather laconic type, he was all business, and did quite well, they informed me, on Wall Street. In fact, so well that we rarely saw Henry on 51st Street; nor do I recall him ever attending any of our events. Nor did he ever make any financial contributions, as far as I know, to The Cubiculo or its various projects.

While Phil had done some acting early on, he was primarily a production person as well as a pretty good director, judging by the plays he put on the road with his National Shakespeare Company and its all non-Equity actors. (That was how he could outbid potential competition: his salaries were below Equity miniumum.) Though by the time I joined the cabal, he was already farming out two of the three plays he had chosen to go on tour to outside directors, favoring in particular Gene Frankel, apparently an old colleague of his. Even after the latter's Broadway successes, such as *The Great White Hope* and others, Frankel (the "snorter," we called him

257

in private, for he had a peculiar tick, emitting a sort of "ahem" type of snort which punctuated almost every other sentence he uttered) would still consent to do a bargain-basement show for us, i.e., for the NSC tours, from time to time. Sad to say, by the time his "star" waned, when he would have craved such a job, Phil was no longer with us to hire him. You see how easily I fall into the "us" language; for, while I didn't work directly for the NSC, I always felt that the NSC and The Cubiculo were one little family.

Yet, strangely enough, much as I tried, I could never get Phil to direct one of our more modern, experimental plays, even though I thought that that was one of the *raisons d'être* of The Cubiculo and one of the reasons he and Elaine had recruited me in the first place, to give them both a chance to experiment, and to do something other than their daily dose of Shakespeare. For example, with Phil's wry sense of humor, he might well have come up with a quirky *Way of the World*; a really stark, nasty Middleton "city comedy"; or possibly an Americanized Molière. On occasion, he would be tempted to take a chance, and Elaine and I would cross our fingers, but somehow he never crossed that threshold. Which is a shame, for I'm sure he would have added plenty of spice, plus a unique bittersweet sauce, to The Cubiculo menu.

Apropos of this postulate, it was Phil who first introduced me to the great potential of the Sweeney Todd story. He had long been thinking, or so he told me any number of times, of launching it as his own special project; naturally, I encouraged him to do so at The Cubiculo, the perfect spot for such a tryout. Remember, this was before the big revival of interest in Sweeney Todd had developed in London, especially with the Christopher Bond version of the story which came out in 1973. Now, whether Phil had dug the 1847 melodrama by George Dibdin-Pitt, subtitled *The Fiend of Fleet Street*, out of the Drama Research Library at Lincoln Center, or had seen the 1936 British film *The Demon Barber of Fleet Street*, or just heard about those rarities over drinks with visiting British players, I'm not sure. (I fondly remember having post-performance drinking sessions with the British players from *Marat Sade* when that

258

production played next to us in *Fiddler on the Roof.*)

Well, the gist of what I remember now is that I was intrigued by what Phil told me about Sweeney Todd, excited by his enthusiasm over it, and accordingly kept urging him to go ahead somehow with *Fleet Street*, to try out a few scenes from it at The Cubiculo and to see where that might lead. Even if it didn't turn out quite as successfully as he might have hoped, Phil would surely have made a mark for himself by being the first American to touch Sweeney! Look where the idea has gone since! In due time, Hal Prince hired Hugh Wheeler to adapt the Bond play as a musical, and Sondheim to write the score. The rest is theatrical history (as well as cinema lore).

But, no, Phil would either get side-tracked with planning the next season of NSC tours, or running out to Kalamazoo, Dubuque, Pike's Peak, or Seattle to fix a play in trouble. For there was always something unexpected happening on tour. Once I myself had to fly up to Maine to take over one of the conspirator parts in *The Tempest*, when the NSC actor playing it suddenly got too sick to go on, and the company was too small to carry understudies. I learned the role on the flight there and the subsequent connecting bus trip!

I could also count on Philip to make a good critique of a play in progress. He had a sharp eye, and real theater smarts. That he didn't make more of those talents is a shame. After all his braggadocio, and frequent conquests as a ladies' man, I think that when it came down to brass tacks, he was perhaps a little shy, or even scared, to make the big leap into the bigger professional arena. Whatever the deep-seated reasons may be, alas, he was never able to show us what he could have done on that level. Moreover, his life was short: not long after I left The Cubiculo he was felled by a sudden heart attack on the road with his cherished NSC troupe, somewhere in the Midwest, I believe.

Elaine, on the other hand, wanted to be, and often was, more involved with The Cubiculo than Philip, except at the very start; and she enjoyed aiding and abetting our various projects, although she rarely participated personally in anything but one or two plays per season. Otherwise, her zest for our tumultuous schedule had its various ups and downs.

Indeed, she showed more enthusiasm, generally, with the poetry readings, partly because, I think, she was writing poetry on the side; and seemed, probably, to have a real talent for that genre. Elaine Sulka was also blessed with a certain kind of Slavic beauty, though strangely mixed with a touch of tomboyishness. Somewhat like Garbo's Queen Christina, her intelligence was of the type some call masculine; she was definitely a tough business woman. At times she even contemplated going back to school to become a lawyer. She would have made a good one, which is why it's a shame she never played Portia, except in a few of her monologues, which she incorporated into her one-woman Shakespeare show. And it follows, "as night followeth the day," that she developed into a pretty outspoken and determined feminist and was an active member of several of their organizations. Her mother, who came from Russia, was also quite intelligent and served on the board of the NSC. She, too, was supportive of The Cubiculo, I was led to believe by those close to her.

This was important, because I'm sure there were times when, behind the scenes, Phil and possibly others on the Board would have liked to do away with The Cubiculo as an unnecessary burden for the NSC, even though it helped bring in considerable support for the overall NSC enterprise through the city's Department of Cultural Affairs (DCA) and the New York State Council on the Arts (NYSCA), by virtue of its strong track record of productions and its growing reputation. This, in turn, strengthened the NSC's standing as a non-profit organization and made it all the more eligible for foundation grants. I imagine that even Elaine Sulka at times might have vacillated between the pros and cons of continuing The Cubiculo, her business side admonishing her artistic side. But, in the long run, she stood by our goals and agenda, I'm fairly sure. Al Schoemann hinted at one such crisis, and implied that after some initial hesitation, that time, she did indeed help save the Cube. (I'm sure there were several more that Al never bothered to tell me about.)

How was Elaine as an actress, you are probably wondering? Well, here her intelligence and a certain sense of authority that she exuded helped, combined with her good looks and a sultry sexiness (the name Sulka may have underlined all that). Such traits made it possible for her to take on the roles of Lady Macbeth, Cleopatra, the shrew Kate, perhaps Portia as we noted above, and certainly Goneril or Regan (I think she may have played one of these cruel women); and, of course, she was ideal for Medea. She did land a role as Leader of the Chorus in one of the Broadway revivals of *Medea* and understudied the tempestuous lady herself on its subsequent road tour. Later, she played Medea at The Cubiculo. When younger, she was said to have made a good, haughty Olivia in *Twelfth Night*. But what prevented her from essaying a greater range of parts, especially in the modern vernacular repertoire, or even Ibsen, Chekhov, or Strindberg—any of which, one would think, should have been her cup of tea? Possibly she had difficulty projecting a sense of gentleness or vulnerability. Moreover, it was hard to rid her of a slight self-consciousness. I finally found out by trial and error a good way to do so during the second or third show I directed her in. We would usually go to a nearby French bistro up the block a bit on 51st Street during the break between a late afternoon rehearsal or an early evening one, or before the show itself. For, though definitely not an alcoholic, Elaine needed a drink before going on! It helped soften her responses. Yet if she drank too much, her dialogue would lose its edge. If not enough, she remained stiff, and looked unnatural. So, by experimenting, I found that precisely half a Manhattan—not an ounce more or less—did the trick! At which time I would tease her, and call her the Divine Sulka. And she would smile and sail smoothly onto the stage.

You see, my dear Nina, there were many ups and downs in the overall Cubiculo enterprise; and, as with so many other things I've done, I don't want to bore you with the full story. For example, how it led directly to my own involvement with the Classic Theatre. (Actually, the complete Cubiculo saga would take at least a long monograph or a short book.) But suffice it to say, for the moment, that it was a thoroughly engrossing project and proved to be a constant, worthy challenge.

Moreover, it was wonderful to work with so many, for the most part, talented people who came our way. I still cherish memories of some of the dancers who later went on to bigger things: Phoebe Neville, Toby Armour, Roy Rogers, Kei Takei, Rudy Perez, Remy Charlip, and Aileen Passloff; also older veteran dancers who wanted to try out new ideas or freshen their repertoire, such as Katherine Litz and Daniel Nagrin; plus specialists like the great Hindu dancer, Ritha Devi, and the wonderful Chuck Davis who did refreshing things with the varied African styles of dance and is now considered a major *griot* in that field. Or the group of young mimes we fostered, including Peter Lobdell, who graduated to solo shows and teaching. Not to mention the countless actors who trod The Cubiculo boards. The great Meryl Streep made her first New York stage appearance at The Cubiculo, when her mentor at Vassar College, Clinton Atkinson, brought his student production of Tirsa da Molina's original Don Juan play, *The Trickster of Seville*, to us; and we gave them a weekend to showcase it. Among the many other fine actors who played The Cubiculo were Vera Lockwood, David Tress, Gubi Mann, Arlene Nadel, Joanne Joseph, Angus Cairns, Floyd Curtis, Gretel Cummings, Owen Rackleff, Dan Lutzky, Michael Graves, and countless others. Indeed, for a number of years after the Cubiculo era, I kept running into Cubiculo veterans and participants in the downtown theatre area or up at the offices of Actors' Equity or around the Village, who would reminisce with me nostalgically about their experiences at The Cubiculo. It happens occasionally, even today...

Perhaps the least known of the Cubiculo's varied enterprises was the Poetry Series, which our dear friend, the poet Daniela Gioseffi—the Ariel who brought us together, as you'll surely recall—helped me set up. Though, of course, even before The Cubiculo days, the early seventies, I had been thinking how great it would be to work with poets and help them make more of their poems when they read them to poetry program audiences. Surely, the most sympathetic and predisposed audience you could ask for, these people very much want to hear those poems: you can almost see them lean toward the poet to catch his or her meaning. But too often the poet does not accommodate them. He or she may be almost inaudible at times, speak too fast and/or drop the last two or three words of a crucial phrase or the upcoming line break. Too often, as you are well aware, dear Nina, from some of the readings we've attended together, many will fall into a kind of monotone chanting pattern that they think enhances the hypnotic power of verse over prose, without realizing that they are thereby turning off the potential listener, and instead, hypnotizing the audience into boredom, or, worse, growing restlessness.

In fact, some years earlier, around the time I did *Stacked Deck* at the 92nd Street Y, I was approached by Galen Williams, who was then running the Y Poetry Center, out of which she developed that quite useful organization, Poets and Writers, Inc. (and whom you know through your mutual friend, Barbara Davis), to give a class for poets on "The Technique of Public Reading for Poets," as we called it. We had some minor success with a few poets in getting them to read more effectively, but unfortunately the idea did not catch on in sufficient numbers to sustain the class economically. Poets for the most part are so in love with their own melody they find it hard to believe anyone else could help them read their poetry better. As authors, they think they have the magic key. Yes, but while they certainly know their own works better, that doesn't guarantee their knowing how to get their meaning across vocally in the cold, cruel spaces in which most readings are usually given. They also tend to rush from one poem to the next without sufficient breathing space between pieces. This is especially hard on short poems, which pack a lot of meaning into a short space of time. (As you know, I often advise repeating a short poem to give an audience time to adjust to a new idea, a new voice, a new phrasing.)

Of course, when Daniela reads, it's another story. Also, when you, dear Nina, read your poems. You are both blessed to belong to that rare breed of poets who instinctively project the full scope of what your poem is trying to say. In D.G.'s case, certainly the fact that she started out as a professional actress helped. Remember, she played Gertrude, Hamlet's mother, on a tour with the National Players Classical

Rep Company and also did some singing of jazz standards around that same time, if not earlier. In later years, she began setting her own poems to music, accompanying herself on an African lyre. Though, interestingly enough, what brought her to The Cubiculo was not the "Poetry" slot on our cube-shaped logo but rather the hope of getting us to stage a mixed media opus she had been developing, based on her poems "The Sea Hag in the Cave of Sleep" and "Care of the Body," which required a good actress and a dancer/choreographer to perform them adequately.

Her work sounded intriguing; here's an excerpt:

> Down by the water
> silver-haired witches are dancing,
>   down by the water,
> tossing their curls.
> Their breasts are eyes
> from which the sea rises.
> In their mouths the sea cries.

So we decided to go ahead with the project. We were lucky to interest that excellent dancer, Ken Rinker (at that time a member of Twyla Tharp's core dance company, but who also had a budding little company of his own), in choreographing Daniela's "Care of the Body," and found a fine character actress whom you know personally—none other than our dear friend, Dina Paisner—to recite and embody the sultry, saga-like "Sea Hag" poem, with its alternating narrative and rhapsodic stanzas. Then to fill out the program, we had Daniela read a few other of her poems. Well danced, beautifully lit, it turned out to be a quite interesting and different evening. And, dear Nina, that was not so easy to bring off at The Cubiculo, which was already burgeoning with many very capable and original artists. I believe Daniela got a Creative Artist Award from the State Council for the playlet poems.

During the course of rehearsing and preparing this production, I often had serious discussions with D.G. about poetry in

264

general and my feelings as to how it could be best presented. These led to our scheduling a series of monthly poetry events, some of which ended up as straightforward readings, but more often our poets wanted to be experimental, and this led to a richer menu. Indeed, that was one reason most of them were attracted to The Cubiculo in the first place. Some actually came up with fragments of plays in verse that they were working on, some of which we would let them try out on their various individual poetry programs.

One of the more memorable of such evenings was that devoted to the poet Arthur Gregor, which featured two short one-act plays of his with a longish poem in between read chorally, using several actors. The first play dealt with two men on a beach. Though written in a poetic prose style, it was performed realistically, achieving its poetic effects through the easy melding of speech, action, and lighting. The second play, "The Door Is Open," was ostensibly a romantic duo for a man and a woman, and perhaps more lyrical in style. Yet the actors remained down to earth, totally believable. For, in the best acting, as I'm sure you've observed through the years, both in Bucharest and here in New York, the more true you are to the conflict or essence of the play (or the poem), the more truly "poetic" it will turn out to be.

A week or ten days after the presentation, Gregor was thrilled to get a complimentary note from the famed, retired *New York Times* drama critic, Brooks Atkinson, on that poetry/drama evening. And we didn't even know he had come! Here is part of what he wrote: "I came away with a feeling of great respect for a beautiful occasion. The plays and the poem have an exalted spiritual tone and great human sensitivity. And I thought the productions and the performances were imaginative, professional and moving. I thought the whole occasion, including the audience, had a purity that has been missing from the theatre for a long time." Even more rewarding for me personally was the little note that the beautiful dean of America's acting teachers, Stella Adler, with whom, you will recall, I studied following the Dramatic Workshop spell, sent me after her visiting the Gregor night: "Dear Maurice: It's splendid to see you working in top form—

`A True Artist'—Here is an affectionate (note?) wishing you happiness (some)—success (some)—and joy—Stella." The idiosyncratic punctuation is hers, of course!

Well, as you know, Shakespeare badly played can be almost boring—though it's tough to kill him! That's why most school productions, and even the less successful summer park professional productions, never fail completely. Think of it: why do almost all Shakespeare companies somehow succeed? And so our more theatrical poetry evenings would be alternated with more conventional poetry programs as well as various combinations of poetry and music.

Among the many poets featured that season were Daniela's mentor, the remarkable John Logan; her friends, the poets Bill Knott, Isabella Gardner (of the famed Boston family), James Wright, and Harvey Shapiro; plus Edward Field, Michael Benedikt, Dick Higgins, Ruth Krauss, and many other notable practitioners.

Working closely with Daniela, both on her own "Sea Hag/ Care of the Body" choreographed program, and in setting up the new series, we gradually got to know one another better. That process was helped along by the fact that we both lived in Brooklyn Heights and often took the train back there together, which, in turn, led to her inviting me to her charming apartment on Henry Street, only about a block and a half from mine on Remsen. This took place during the period of Ann's third hospitalization, I believe, by which time, as you might well understand, poor Ann was really no longer a wife, or companion, to me: she had retreated almost totally into herself. And with our son, Jacob, in boarding school, she was no longer even a "Mommy" presence in the house.

Of course, this must have been the most difficult thing for Ann to bear when she came back from the hospital—Jacob's absence, once we had settled him in at Green Chimneys. Yet how do I know for sure? At this stage of her schizophrenia she would never, and probably was unable to, articulate such thoughts to me, let alone herself. She had become almost a ghostly figure whom I had to feed, clothe, and put to sleep; and worry about what dangers might befall her when she would leave the the house from time to time and wander aimlessly about the neighborhood. For, had I not kept the household going and abandoned her instead, as some friends said I should have done(!), she would surely have become another one of those sad street persons we still encounter in New York.

So you can imagine how welcome was Daniela's invitation; especially from such a beautiful young woman, so *simpatica*, congenial, in tune with so many of my plans and ideas, and to all appearances, single, living alone with her child. No husband hiding in the closet! (Though it turned out he was not so many blocks away in the Park Slope section of Brooklyn; they hadn't divorced yet, for tax purposes.) Well, I could not help but take up that invitation and began to visit her in her third-floor apartment. Whereupon, it seems that one night, as she used to put it, I "leapt across" the living room sofa where we were seated as usual. Then things took a more intimate turn...

Daniela, for her part, was lonely because of her, by this time, almost complete separation from her husband, Richard Kearney, a theater designer she had met while on tour with that National Players' production of *Hamlet* I referred to earlier, and now teaching in the theater department of Brooklyn College. So here she was, trying to bring up their beautiful daughter, who had inherited her mother's good looks, alone, by herself; anxious to work on and promote her poetry; and at the same time finally achieving her master's degree so that she might teach. Her thesis happened to be an excellent adaptation for the stage of Turgenev's *Fathers and Sons*, of which I helped her get a good professional reading done on Station WBAI, with sound effects and music.

Around this same time, being perhaps unduly worried that she might be putting on too much weight, Daniela took up Mid-Eastern dance for exercise with Anahid Safian, who had studied it in Syria and Egypt. Inevitably, with Daniela, words began to sprout, this time associated with the dance movement she was learning. This resulted in her writing an ode to Mid-Eastern dance, called simply "Birth Dance: Belly Dancer," which by good

267

fortune appeared before long as a centerfold in *MS Magazine*!

I remember her reciting it, while beating out a dance rhythm on a hand-held dumbek or Moroccan drum, as a prelude to the actual dance that would follow. Thus, though she hadn't planned it that way, what had started out as an exercise program led to some paying dance and poetry concert engagements at college campuses around the country. This, in turn, encouraged her to dig deeper into the origins of belly dance, where she learned that what is commonly called the belly dance was in reality a ritual birth dance performed by women to assist at and celebrate the birth of children. Performed by women for women, the birth dance was not witnessed by men until the early 19th century, when it began to degenerate, in a sense, from primitive ritual purity to private entertainment of a pasha, to eventual commercialization in vaudeville and the nightclub scene. This research, in turn, resulted in Daniela's book *Earth Dancing: Mother Nature's Oldest Rite*, a serious study of the subject, which, of course, owed a lot to the rise in feminism and to earlier anthropological studies of the Earth Mother by Neumann, Joseph Campbell, Havelock Ellis, and others.

Yet Daniela's belly dance studies—both physical and intellectual—did not hold back her poetic development. On the contrary, they may have given it an added touch of "earthiness" and a welcome specificity. Luckily, this fell in line with her other influences, such as Walt Whitman and, above all, the curious French poet Francis Ponge, from whom she learned the potential rewards of particularization. Thus Daniela was soon able to turn almost any raw material she discovered, or almost anything she did, into poetry. Of course, all this made for some fascinating evening discussions but also sparked some esthetic disagreements here and there. And since, along with her mixed Italian and Polish heritage, Daniela was also endowed with a healthy temper, I remember one of those arguments getting slightly out of control, though at this point in time I don't recall what that particular scuffle was about. Nevertheless, it ended with her throwing a frozen chicken across the room, barely missing yours truly, en route to the wall behind me where it spattered. (I think the poor chicken was one she had been planning to cook for me, as she often did, being our master chef.) What would Ponge have made of that scene?

Of course, this altercation, like other lesser *malentendus*, would be followed by a quick calming down and a tender, mutual making-up. Before long, we might be back to talking metaphysics or analyzing Allen Ginsburg or discussing something quite neutral. In any case, we had to go quietly into the night because we didn't want to wake her little Thea. Moreover, getting back to my own place late at night was not a problem, since I lived practically around the corner. This was a *factum* which led to my sometimes teasing her about our relationship, maintaining it was based on G.D., i.e., geographic desirability, though still in the hands of the gods, inasmuch as G.D. was a reversal of her initials, D.G. Besides, didn't Romeo, too, and his infinite progeny, have to leave before dawn?

What was also salutary about our *entente* was that through D.G. I met many poets and writers, providing a heathy relief from having to deal primarily with musicians and composers at the Brooklyn Philharmonic, and with a constant flow of actors and directors, dancers and choreographers, at The Cubiculo. Among the more interesting characters I got to know was a tall, whimsical baseball lover, Marvin Cohen, who wrote wryly amusing dialogues on almost any subject, not just baseball! Something of a modern Mark Twain, his books were better received in England, I think, than here. (And where he used to go almost every summer.) At that time, his reading partner—for these were always dialogues—was the young Wallace Shawn, whose own future writing undoubtedly owes a great deal to this "Apprenticeship" with Mr. Cohen. Also amusing about Marvin was his obsession about getting himself invited to almost every book-launching, painter vernissage, and poetry club reading in town, where he could dip into the hors d'oeuvres and drinks in between meeting the host and his or her hosts of friends (who, admittedly, were often mutual friends of all concerned).

Daniela also had an eccentric neighbor on the floor above her flat, the frustrated, late-start conductor, David Aurelius, who was only then trying to make up for lost time by intensely studying and devouring music scores, leading church choirs, working on organ pieces by Bach and Buxtehude, and eventually becoming an assistant to our own Lukas Foss at the BPO, mostly for choral concerts. Among other unusual denizens of that odd brownstone on Henry Street was the enigmatic Herbert Hunke, hailed by some as a hippy guru because of his once-close companionship with Ginsburg and his entourage. Hunke lived one floor above Daniela with two young acolytes, one of whom used to climb down the fire escape to peep in on her rehearsing her dance program...

Then there were the many interesting, visiting "firemen," i.e., Daniela's bevy of literary friends, which included the poets Galway Kinnell, James Wright, Daniel Halpern, and the wan-looking Rochelle Ratner, with her remarkably adept and kind, blind husband. Daniela proved to be an easy, natural hostess for them all. Indeed, I sometimes wonder why none of these people or prototypes ever seemed to enter her poetry or prose. What do you make of that, dear Nina? Should we try to steer her that way? It's curious, now that I think back on it, that our dear Geraldine played a rather similar hostess role, though minus the hors d'oeuvres, with the original hippies of her day—about a half generation earlier than Daniela's crowd—although there could have been some overlap. For example, I remember once meeting Ginsburg, Gregory Corso, and another member of that well-publicized tribe chez Geraldine one dusk when she still lived on Hudson Street.

To get back to Daniela's motley crew, I suppose one of them, the iconoclastic poet Bill Knott, could be said to have been generically a close relative of the hippy crowd, although he was a much more private person, more of a loner, than them. Like Daniela, he was a student of the magnanimous John Logan, who also fostered Robert Hass and one of the better translators of some of your poems, dear Nina, namely Naomi Lazard. Then, somewhat later, there appeared on the scene a lesser, would-be hippy writer, Matthew Paris, who, before long, seduced Daniela off to Paris, where their differences led to a notorious vocal *malentendu*, or should we say in plain English, "shouting match," on the Champs Elysée, which probably both amused and shocked the French. (Which reminds me of something I read in a *Times* book review recently about how in Vienna two Americans in "animated conversation" is considered the "definition of a riot.") But, of course, these diversions did not exactly propel our friendship into a more lasting *entendement. Au contraire,* I should say. Though to be fair to D.G., she was hardly happy that, after Ann's sudden, fatal heart attack, I did not rush into marriage with her, once I was freed by the Fates of that earlier attachment.

Before leaving Daniela, I should tell you a bit about her excellent, and supportive, poet friend, the fascinating Isabella Gardner, direct descendant of the great art collecting and museum building Gardners of Boston. After her bitter divorce from the renowned poet/critic Allen Tate, this Isabella seems to have settled in at the Chelsea Hotel, where she often held forth with friendly, relaxed matinées and/or soirées for poet and musician friends and artists. Somehow or other Daniela became her confidante and part-time secretary for awhile, and so helped set up these events (to which I'd be invited, of course), the closest approximation to Gertrude Stein's matinées that I experienced in New York. One night Isabella surprised us all by announcing that we would be going upstairs one flight to the apartment of the octogenarian composer, Virgil Thomson, who lived directly above her, for a special, private, unrehearsed reading of Plato's *Symposium* with Thomson himself as Socrates and Isabella as Diotima. One couldn't have cast a more perfect Socrates; even at his advanced age, Virgil didn't miss a beat—or a potential laugh. And no cuts were made! Several other good poets participated, including, I think, Nina, your good friend, William Jay Smith. (Or was it on another occasion that I first met him chez Isabella?)

So it's quite understandable that Daniela and I have remained good friends down through the years; indeed, as you know only too well, it was she who tried to play matchmaker between you, dearest Nina, *et moi-même* during your first years in this country. And it was she who introduced us to Harriet Zinnes, our other matchmaker. Daniela is, after all, a warm, good-hearted, generous soul. Witness her extraordinary care of the older gentleman she finally settled down with, Lionel Luttinger, a quiet, intellectual, left-wing chemical scientist, who enjoyed camping and hunting to get away from it all. That she successfully nursed him through several serious health crises and operations over the years ought to be sufficient proof of the pudding, if any were needed. But to be fair also to Lionel, Daniela seemed to mature in some ways under his wing. For it was during the Lionel period that she produced her two excellent, substantial anthologies: *Women on War* and *On Prejudice: A Global Perspective*, both with prize-winning introductions.

Well, it's probably time to move on to other memories, but I know you did want me to tell you more about the Daniela era. I only hope I haven't repeated too much of what I may have already covered in our talks about her. Though perhaps I should add how grateful I am to her for having helped me survive those last years of Ann's decline, when poor Ann would identify me with Satan, call herself the Queen of Israel, and proclaim Jacob as destined to be the new Messiah. Who was it who said: when you start to think about God, you get combustion of the brain? I say: Amen to that.

Miltonically yours,

M.

June 18, 2008

Dear, patient Nina:

Perhaps I was really a little too hard on Ann toward the end of my last letter. To make up for that, I should try to recall for you, from time to time, some of the happier, more pleasant moments of our life together before she slipped into deeper madness. For example, once on a walk we were taking with Jacob when he was four years old, along Fifth Avenue's "Museum Mile," I remember our stopping to admire the exterior of Frank Lloyd Wright's then brand new, ovoid Guggenheim Museum. This was only a week or so after it had opened. Jacob had one word to say, "Space," and nearby people smiled and nodded, yes. Isn't that one of its strongest attributes—the way it defines space?

One of the favorite spots Ann often chose for little gambols with Jacob in Central Park was that picturesque cliff and surrounding grounds topped off by Belvedere Castle, with Turtle Pond below, which later became the site of Joe Papp's Shakespeare in the Park. There Ann used to take intriguing photos of Jacob winding in and out of the sculptures and crags and shrubbery. She had a way of making the resulting pictures come out looking like fairy haunts, with shadows falling a certain way, or through the angle at which she would shoot the "scene." Thus a bush might seem to harbor tiny *Midsummer Night's Dream*-like Cobweb, Peaseblossom, and Mustardseed figures spying on our little Jacob. Later, she might transfer the resulting scenes to her drawing book. Or incorporate them into little playlets she was working on. Talents she was never able to fulfill. Just as Jacob, alas, never fulfilled his...

Interesting how recollection of the Belvedere scene somehow revives memories of some of the quite contrasting walks I took with your faithful, devoted friend, Dragosh, exploring, among other areas, that hilly, picturesque old section of Bucharest above long, rectangular (King) Carol Park. I found the older buildings especially inviting, with their clever employment of trees and vegetation in often very cramped spaces. And, of course, with "form following function" much in evidence, they were, for the most part, often quite beautiful—even those beginning to fall apart. For, as with most sections of towns anywhere in the world, architecture is all the more interesting when faced by challenges from the surrounding terrain, isn't it? Take the incredible structures of Yemen, some built right into the mountains. Or the way those white, yogurt-looking buildings seem to have carved themselves into the rocks of the Aegean Islands. Compare these to the wide variety of cave dwellings created by the different Indian tribes of the American Southwest. But even with the more conventional, bland architecture of most of the States, outside the deep South, it's only when it has to cope with a series of rolling hills, or some other special geographic feature, as San Francisco has had to do, does something unique result. Of course, New Orleans remains, because of its many layers of history and culture, *sui generis*. The closest comparable rival to that great city that I've seen is the waterfront and downtown section of Port-of-Spain, Trinidad, a site with perhaps even more layers of different cultures (and races) than New Orleans, but not blessed with as defining a history, nor as focally important a geographical location, and not leading to any Louisiana Purchase!

As you well know, most of Bucharest is flat, built on an alluvial plain. Yet it probably has a greater number of trees, spacious parks, and odd-shaped lakes within the city proper than any of the other capitals of Europe I've so far visited. Berlin's are for the most part just beyond the city on the way to Potsdam. Vienna's are, of course, far beyond its famed "Ring," quite out of town. Similarly, in St. Petersburg, with its splendid estates, parks, castles, and forests you encounter as you move westward into the suburban spread along the Gulf of Finland. Of course, Bucharest is a much younger city than these capitals, and less compact than those older capitals—Paris, London, Brussels, and Copenhagen. So it had space galore to play with, and has done so handsomely. Then there is the late-19th-century series of long, wide, majestic tree-lined boulevards in imitation of Paris. Wasn't Bucharest called Little Paris from that time on, even to the extent of erecting its own Arc de Triomphe? (Of course, we have our fairly decent imitations in Washington Square in Manhattan and at the glorious entrance to Brooklyn's Prospect Park.)

Ah, yes, I've fond memories of your most unusual city. Remember how I once tried to write up some of these impressions? Would you like me to dig up my notes and quote a few passages here? Especially those about Bucharest's once-notorious Dog problem, which I tentatively entitled "City of Dogs and Trees!" To refresh your memory, here goes:

> Having spent several mornings this past, unusually cool summer walking—even wandering—the fragrant streets and boulevards of Bucharest, I was saddened meeting so

many sad-looking, homeless stray dogs, but gladdened, greeting so many verdant trees and other kinds of bounteous greenery. So much so that at one of my Romanian lessons with a young medical student, to and from which these walks led me, I baptised Bucharest "*Oraşul de câini şi copaci*" ("*The City of Dogs and Trees*"). Of course such appellations sound more romantic when couched in another language than one's own. But not at all romantic for the more than 200,000 stray dogs of Bucharest! Nor for the innumerable beggars, stray gypsies, and the occasional physically and mentally handicapped who flourish among those many trees, and here and there on street corners of those once-elegant but now-shabby boulevards, especially where a wide *Strada* crosses an even wider *Calea* or *Bulevard*. Some stand mute, others squat moaning, a few lunge at you lazily, but most curl up dog-tired on the sidewalks. Most unforgettable of all was a long, thin, bony creature who, when I first espied him from a distance, looked like a large dog bounding toward a car. But no, as I drew closer, I realized that he was no dog at all but rather a tattered, deformed, rickety-boned young man who actually crawled, or at least covered ground, using his hands as front feet like a four-legged animal, stretching his front paws/hands out to drivers of passing cars in eloquent, twisted, acrobatic beggary.

Understandably, I returned terribly depressed to my host [who was, of course, you] that night, and tried to describe these impressions without offending her Romanian sensibility. But it would have been impossible to get her to fully comprehend what I experienced unless I went the whole hog with my report, and so I decided to temper it somewhat—asking, for example, why there were so many stray, homeless dogs in Bucharest, who fed them, where did they sleep, etc.

I'm glad I did temporize, because the next day, which

was prematurely hot, with an almost unbearable sudden summer heat spell, there wasn't a dog in sight! I did nearly as much walking, traversing more or less the same routes and alley-ways without running into a single dog, and encountering almost no beggars. Where were the dogs? Where had they disappeared? Could they all have found refuge in the city parks, which are large and plentiful in Bucharest, snuggling under trees or near ponds and lakes? Perhaps to escape the heat? And what about the beggars? Had they, too, moved into more shaded areas, or possibly hidden in basements? Most peculiar, even somewhat eerie...

However, on the following day, which was still fairly hot, I did encounter two or three stray dogs but also a few others that somehow looked cleaner, evidently not homeless, one which could even have had a bath, another on a leash, and indeed one that probably had been to the veterinarian's, his body swathed in something like a little white, surgical jacket. All seemed better fed, and most actually looked happy, which was hardly the case earlier in the week. And while the beggar population had increased a bit, it seemed somehow more quiescent, looked less scraggly, and acted nowhere near so aggressively as heretofore. Or was I just getting used to all this?

True, this time I took a rather different route, strolling down wide, impressive Blvd. Stefan cel Mare toward former Revolutionary Square. This time around, the people I encountered were more fascinating than the dogs—and infinitely more varied! It would be hard to single out any one type and say it was pure Romanian. The women are generally more beautiful than those one would encounter on a similar walk in Paris or London; but one saw not just Latin types, as in Italy. The very mixed heritage that is Romania's battered history shows up in these wonderfully individual people—touches of Slavic ancestry, German stance, Hungarian cheekbones,

Bulgarian eyebrows, Turkish tawniness, Greek macho, and probably whatever the old Dacians looked like—who peer at you as you pass by. On this day, and perhaps because there were about three or four hospitals within several blocks of each other, one also saw doctors, nurses, patients, sales people, truck drivers, noncommissioned Army officers, an occasional white-collared clerical worker (no clergy, however!), and even one horse-driven wagon, coaxed on by a young farm couple bringing produce in from the country, the horse distinctly disliking the hard macadam-paved road, the noisy motor traffic, and the squalid urban heat. In this quarter, the mid-boulevard lawns had fewer trees.

And plenty of other colorful types as well: two gypsy teenagers trying to buy cigarettes in one of those peculiar Romanian tobacco shops, shirtless, but otherwise neater than the gypsies I encountered on Day One! Most peculiar were a group of what looked like nuns in towering Dutch hats, dressed in wonderful white and blue outfits, the large white panels of which seemed to be covered with fancy graffiti! I figured they were probably nurses wearing the uniform of the hospital they were emerging from. A little further down the block, and across the street, I passed a long, large, low-lying but beautiful children's hospital, with spacious grounds and well-tended greenery. Could this have been one of those supported by American and European money that flowed into Romania after that notorious orphan scandal some years back? Finally, I sat down on a rare bench to catch my breath, only to be suddenly surrounded by a flock of voracious pigeons. But all big cities have these!

Moving on, I was tempted to board one of those long, double-car streetcars that still run quite efficiently through Bucharest, but got sidetracked by a domestic dispute taking place in a bio-farm produce store around the corner: Romanian macho seemed to be at stake. Yet it was not the first little store I saw being run by women. Including a little second-floor restaurant two women were setting up on otherwise stately Calea Dorobanț. (Could this be the new Romanian street-wise capitalism at work?)

Well, this time when I returned to my lodgings, my host was entertaining a few friends to whom I was duly introduced, and who, of course, were pleased to learn how much I liked Romania and, especially, Bucharest. (I had not yet been to the Delta of the Danube, nor Transylvania, nor North Moldavia with its unique, late 15th/ early 16th-century monasteries, the beautifully painted frescoes on their exterior walls still amazingly fresh, and, for the most part, remarkably well preserved.)

So, after reporting something of what I had just seen along Stefan cel Mare, I felt safe about going into the "Dog and Tree" story reported above. At first, they were slightly taken aback, but, regaining their polite aplomb, explained how they, too, lamented the situation of the dogs, advancing a plausible answer to the origin of this problem. Apparently, many dogs were left homeless during that dreadful period when Ceaușescu had large swaths of the old city demolished to make space for his extremely wide, landscaped Unity Boulevard that leads up to that unbelievably ugly monstrosity which he christened his *Casa Poporului* (House of the People), since turned into an enormous state office building of sorts, said to be second in size only to the Pentagon outside Washington, DC.

But the people of Bucharest did not want to kill the dogs. And these first homeless creatures bred more homeless dogs. With each passing year, the problem became more and more acute. So it seems that gradually an unofficial, almost unspoken, system for semi-sheltering and basic feeding of these dogs developed among the many large Soviet-style block complexes that dot the city, plus, of course, thousands of independent, individual handouts. I was also informed that a documentary has been made by Alexandru Solomon of this monumental disaster, called "A Dog's Life," with commentary by Mircea Cărtărescu, and inspired by a Charlie Chaplin film. In any case, one must doff one's hat to the quiet way Bucharest seems to be dealing with this problem.

Yet no one there that night could quite figure out why one day I should have seen so many dogs and the next day none at all!—"Where are the clowns?"

To which I later added this Postlude, 8/15/97:

Here, back in the States, I've been shown an article, "Dogs of Bucharest," which appeared in Română Liberă on August 11th, almost exactly two months after my visit there, and the writing of my impressions inscribed above. It confirms much of what I had to say, echoing many of my thoughts and feelings on the subject, though, of course, the author couldn't possibly have seen my notes! Naturally, he goes into much more detail as to what Bucharest is trying to do to meliorate the problem.

It seems that that city's current, admirably humane, but obviously very ambitious, general Vice-Mayor (as he's called), in the hope of being re-elected, stepped into the limelight two years ago with a campaign to sterilize the dogs of Bucharest, under moral pressure also from the European Animal Rights Movement, one of whose leaders is the estimable and still very charming Brigitte Bardot.

However, as Romulus Ruşan, the author of this article, points out, though never doubting the good will of the Vice-Mayor, "until now no one knows if and when his promised sterilization ever took place. From time to time, some chief sterilizing officer declares that he lacks space, personnel, tools, or, in general, material conditions to accomplish this, but nonetheless leads us to believe that the work is going on. Yet, during this same period, hundreds of thousands of Bucharestans complain that they can't go out into the streets at night because of the dogs, or can't leave their windows open during the summer months because of the noise and uproar from packs of fighting canines."

But public opinion, he maintains, and above all much of the Romanian press, still has not come to terms with the basic inhumanity of this decision, whose "terribly distorted snobism goes against the grain of reality. Breeders or not, the number of dogs is disproportionate (about one to every ten Bucharestans), and cohabitation with them is promiscuous, and, in the long run, inhumane." He goes on to complain colorfully, and surely hyperbolically, that the dogs' barking sometimes wakes up the suburbs: "dogs in the courtyards respond, ready to break their chains; those in apartments drive their masters out of their minds... roosters are quick to echo their sounds; so that this city of over two million people begins to resound like thousands of reverberating villages." [And sleep deprived, besides; tempers could rise.]

Perhaps because I'm a sound sleeper, I was never kept awake by this choral masterpiece, nor was I ever attacked or overwhelmed by any of these poor creatures during my admittedly short stays over the past several years in Bucharest, but my heart goes out to them. After all, they did not create this mess! Like Ruşan, who also feels sorry "for these innocent dogs without a master," I am dismayed that a humane solution seems to be continually stalled by bureaucratic and political fumbling and hypocrisy.

Footnote (2/11/98):

> Still stalled? Apparently, yes. Though perhaps Brigitte Bardot's imminent visit to Bucharest with the Commission on Animal Rights will help turn the corner—and finally something will be done!

*

Well, dear Nina, as you know only too well, now at long last the dogs are almost gone from the streets of Bucharest, and the relieved city has calmed down considerably, so much so that on our last visit I found that I missed them somewhat. No more would we see a proud dog board a streetcar and sit down on the floorboard next to a passenger. No more *caveat canem* in Bucharest!

Yes, those were among my initial impressions of your beloved Bucharest, with which, as you'll recall, I was initially quite thrilled. I wonder why, with subsequent visits, and getting to know the city better, it gradually enchanted less? I don't think it was because one sometimes lost patience with the slow rate of clean-up after Ceaușescu. On the contrary, moving too fast in that direction might have erased some of the older, more fascinating spots. Of course, I still found, and expect to continue to find, your people charming, natural, friendly, and helpful to us foreigners. On each subsequent trip I seem to discover new places and quarters to explore, including some totally unexpected corners. So I guess that Bucharest has already begun to feel like an old friend—pleasant, comfortable, but also a mite predictable. Surprises come easier with fresh acquaintances. Or maybe I just missed the dogs after their eventual, inevitable expulsion!

Then there is also the question of chance that shapes one's attraction to, interest in, love for, and appreciation of, a city. For example, did I ever tell you the story of my one-day forced stopover in Milan that turned into a whirlwind of unexpected sight-seeing and unpredictable accompanying events? It gave me a unique feel and almost affection for that formidable city in a very short span of time—was it just ten hours? It all came about on my return trip from Venice after that assignment Mario Fratti had arranged for me at Teatro Ca' Foscari, namely, to advise them in their production of a play of his that I had already staged at The Cubiculo in English, *The Academy*, an amusing satire about a "school" for Venetian men, designed to teach them how to cope with American women tourists! Its Italian title, of course, is surely more seductive: *I Seduttori*.

It was also an amazing situation in itself, this being the first time any of Fratti's plays was to be staged in Italy, even in his native Venezia! By the way, somehow I've never been able to get him to tell me why he, a budding playwright, left Italy so young, when, of course, he naturally wrote in Italian. Who did he expect would be his audience? How in the world did he think he could crash the American theater scene? Well, how he managed that would surely make an interesting Odyssey in itself. Could there have been political reasons, as I suspect? And why was there such a long delay before anyone would do any of his plays in Italy? Why did he have to become a success first in America? And, as far as I can tell, why are there not more Italian premieres of his plays, other than productions of the musical *Nine*, since that first venture in Venice that he sent me over to aid and abet?

This "hit," *Nine*, is based on an original dramatization of Fellini's film *8-1/2* (something, my dear, you may not have been aware of), which Fratti had made in trying to turn it into a musical. Like the so-called "book" (or libretto) of so many Broadway musicals, it was much reworked in rehearsal by other writers and by the director himself, the very talented Tommy Tune. Yet the core idea was, and remained, Mario's, and he was obviously smart enough to have protected his authorial rights by insisting on a percentage of the royalties on signing his original contract, whatever that was. And so, because the musical was so successful—and is indeed still being done around the world—Mario flies off to each opening. Our progenitor is now living very comfortably (and pridefully) on the musical's so-far unending royalties. Which I would be the last to begrudge him...

Mario continues to write his odd little plays, now always in English, I think, none of which, though clever and almost always politically timely and aware, has ever quite caught on like *Nine* has, or even as *The Academy* did, before *Nine*. So I say: "Bravo Mario: you got me to Italy in style. As you were later able to get me to Russia, then still the USSR. Thank you. *Mille grazie!*" Yes, dear Nina, that Russian trip for six Off-Off-Broadway directors and producers that Mario concocted and convinced the Soviets to finance is worth a later letter in itself, as does, perhaps, that spell in Venice while working on his play, *The Academy*, with that Italian company.

But to get back to the Milan stopover. Alitalia, which flew me to Italy originally, had gone on strike during my sojourn there. So I had to take a plane to Milan to connect with British Airways, which was taking over Alitalia's flights. This involved a long, half-day wait in Milan.

Though this hopping around from one airline to another is always tiring and cumbersome, nevertheless, I was delighted to be able to get at least a glimpse of Milan before leaving Italy. In that sense, the strike was a break for me, for I hadn't planned on including Milan in my itinerary, and I was determined to make the best of it, now that Fate had stepped in to make this possible. So I started off with a quick tour of its enormous (some scoffers say "humongous") Gothic Duomo. Then I took a quick bus ride to the more intimate Church of Santa Maria delle Grazie to see Leonardo's "The Last Supper" and environs. Ah, this still-startling masterpiece is even more haunting in its now sad, paint-peeling state (which they are doing everything to stop and to preserve what's left) and is, of course, in the Refectory of the adjacent Convent, not in the church proper. On the way there, or the way back to central Milan, I can't remember which, I was able to spend an hour at the famed Rubens house, which the Sforzas had built near one of the great gates of Milano.

During the course of these sallies, I picked up a couple of Milan newspapers and found to my astonishment and delight that that extraordinary playwright/clown/politico, Dario Fo, was here in Milano and that very evening would be performing his latest play,

283

The Accidental Death of an Anarchist—but not at any theater, since at that time, he was forbidden to appear on the Italian stage and was banned from TV. Apparently, his last few plays and public statements had so disturbed the various governments (and you know how often they keep changing!)—and surely the Vatican—that he had become totally a *persona non grata*. (No one then could have dreamed that this renegade would win the Nobel Prize one day!) That's probably why, during my preceding sojourn, mostly in Venice, but also briefly in Parma, Florence, and Rome, with an even briefer stopover in Bologna, I would ask where I could find Fo, where he would be performing these days, if anywhere, what his status was? Nobody knew—or, in retrospect, maybe nobody dared tell me. So you can imagine, my dear Nina, what a relief it was to locate him unexpectedly on this last leg, albeit a forced one, of my *Italienische Reise*.

How did Fo manage to do the play then, there in Milan, without being arrested? Well, it seems he had hired, or perhaps had been given, a Union hall, which legally was not a commercial theater (from which he was then barred), but rather a place where he could lecture, which he proceeded to do, and then seamlessly sequeled from that talk into a performance of his play. The magical way he did this I'll describe to you shortly.

Now, first, you're probably wondering: why this great interest in Dario Fo, long before they gave him the Nobel prize? The answer takes us back to The Cubiculo and had nothing, originally, to do with Fratti, certainly not the trip to Ca' Foscari on his behalf! (Although one might conceivably think that there would have been an affinity between these two modern, living Italian playwrights.)

Moreover, Mario was, and still is, I'm sure, a Far Left person, whereas Fo's Left-ism has always been, in my view, more truly his own personal Anarchism! In any case, I often wondered back then, when I first discovered Fo and presented him at The Cubiculo, why Mario was not more supportive of, or enthusiastic about, that venture—why, in fact, he seemed somewhat cool toward it.

What happened is that, early in The Cubiculo years, I was approached by a slightly eccentric, middle-aged British lady who introduced herself as an agent for Fo's plays, claiming she had already paved the way for their production throughout Europe. (Which makes me wonder, my dear, why you don't recall Fo having been done in Bucharest?) She had also managed to get some of the plays translated, though unfortunately not always into colloquial English but rather into what we might call too "British English" for American audiences. True, the large plays (and don't you love these titles?), such as *Archangels Don't Play Pinball*; *Isabella, Three Tall Ships, and a Con Man*; *He Who Steals a Foot Is Lucky in Love*; and *This Lady Should be Thrown Out*; though tempting, were obviously beyond the limited means of The Cubiculo, both financially and spatially.

However, the shorter plays, mostly one-acts, which Fo called "Farces," and certainly not as original nor form defying as the larger opuses, were far more accessible and easier for us to produce. Some of these were already published in a volume of his one-acts, which included *La Marcolfa, Each in His Own Tailcoat*, and *Not All Thieves Are Mischievous*. Written in a sort of modern-ish *commedia dell'arte* style, with dabs and touches of Pirandello, and leaving room for some improvisation, they were delightful comedies with universal appeal. So I re-worked the translations Adrienne Douglass had given me (for that was the agent's name), and put on two evenings of them at The Cubiculo. They worked beautifully and provoked several good reviews, including an interesting one by Marilyn Stasio in *Cue Magazine* (since merged to become *New York Magazine*), in which she called Fo "an articulate champion of the proletariat—sort of the Arnold Wesker of Italy." Not a bad comparison, though Wesker certainly lacks Fo's divine madness.

Unfortunately, the *Times* didn't cover it, which is a shame, since we had, in effect, been the first to mount a Fo play in America, and this would have put us on the record. (In the USA, my dear, unless the *Times* reviews it, it seldom goes down in history—or these days, even onto the Internet.) Again, another example where luck plays such a part in destiny. For, in my bones, I felt some sort of kinship with Fo and probably should have persisted in pursuing his star. Of course, it would have meant trying to re-work the translations of those larger works and adapting them to the American scene, doing workshop tryouts of them, and eventually attempting to get them produced. Yet it might well have been too great a gamble to be worth taking...

Indeed, those who actually did, mostly lost out. Somehow or other, Fo's plays haven't worked on either the British or American stages to the degree they have in Europe. His is, after all, a more continental humor, full of earthy irreverence. And, as you know, comedy is the most difficult of all genres to transfer into another language, a different culture. Thus Kleist's *The Broken Jug* doesn't seem very funny in English, while the Danish Holberg just sounds dull. Even Wedekind loses much of his bite. Of course, Molière usually makes it, being the exception that proves the rule. Also, perhaps some Brecht, although his plays are a more mixed bag: none are really comedies. And it's difficult for us English-speaking people to capture the subtle humor in Chekhov, for example. Or the dark humor of Gogol. The sprightly humor of Goldoni. And what about Capek?

But how strange that Fo's plays were not being done in Romania during the Sixties and Seventies when you were still there, and when they were performed all over most of Europe. After all, Fo was called by some "the dramatic apostle of the proletariat." You'd think that the Communist overlords of your National Theater would have welcomed him. Though they may have been turned off by, probably, his most noted play, *Mistero Buffo*, of which, remember, I told you I saw a quite good production in Mexico City when we were on tour there with the Philharmonic. *Buffo*, which Fo revised constantly, including several one-man versions, probably reached more people, a wider, larger audience than any of his other plays. Why? Perhaps because of the almost primitive religiosity at its core. For, although religious clichés are dissected, mocked, and often maltreated in it, with its farcical inversions of traditional folk tales and biblical morality lessons (after all, *Buffo* was originally inspired by Mayakovsky, one of Fo's great idols), he still comes off sounding like some sort of radical saint. Indeed, that universality may have been instrumental in his getting the coveted Nobel Prize. However, that was not how the Vatican saw it then, calling a televised version "the most blasphemous program ever broadcast in the history of world television." All of which did not stop Fo from running for Mayor of Milan in 2006! But, of course, our jester supreme lost out. After all, Norman Mailer once ran for Mayor of New York and he lost too, didn't he?

Sorry, my dear Nina, I've been diverted again from the main line of the story. Remember, I left off with my discovering that *Anarchist* was being done in the outskirts of Milan that very night and that I'd miss the curtain if I didn't rush. So after downing a quick, tasty supper at a small working-class *ristorante*, I caught the first streetcar headed that way. Then, at the end of the line, I grabbed the first taxi I could find. Here let me quote from the account of this trip I later wrote up for *The Village Voice*: "I was lucky to get a driver who was both articulate and knowledgeable—a militant Communist well-versed in the latest twists of the Party dialectic. Not exactly a fan of Fo since he went Maoist (he liked Fo's beautiful actress-wife better), the driver took me straight there, insisting en route that all American blacks were Communist and all American whites bourgeois, and that's where the American Revolution was at! He also advised me to pretend to be French when I asked for my ticket."

As I continued in the *Voice*:

> The taxi slowed down as it entered a narrow street off one of the larger squares. A huge crowd, mostly college-age kids, very American in dress, was gathered outside a long, low-lying warehouse type of building. "Is that it?" I asked, wondering if this was theater-in-the-street, and worried that the show might be cancelled because of the rain. "Just push through," the driver said. So I got out and did as bid. But when I reached the entrance, two members of the Commune (as Fo's new group is called) shouted: "No more seats, Comrades. Come back tomorrow afternoon." Desperate, wet, and frustrated that after all this I should miss Fo, I forgot my driver's advice and begged the student guard barring the gate to please let

287

me in, as I had to get back to America the next morning and this would be my last chance ever to see Fo. He relented quizzically and let me pass.

Whereupon I found myself suddenly frisked for weapons and led into a side room where I had to join the Commune Cultural Circle of Milan before I could buy a ticket. Of course, by this time all seats were filled, the aisles packed, and I had all I could do to squeeze into an opening at the top of the stairway that led down into the improvised auditorium.

Fo was already on stage delivering an extraordinary off-the-cuff discourse on the political situation in Italy today, presumably as introductory justification for reviving *The Accidental Death of an Anarchist*, first performed in November, 1971. Looking like a huge rabbit with figure, face, and stance of the late Fernandel, and the marvelous springy lope of Jacques Tati, Fo talked with the comic ingenuity and intellectual acuteness of the younger Zero Mostel. He had that enthusiastic audience of intelligentsia, college students, and factory workers in stitches as he described the incredible stupidities of police investigations and the strange ins and outs of courts and bureaucracies in conspiratorially preventing anyone from ever getting any sort of justice. Italy was still agog over the Feltrinelli case—that murdered millionaire publisher who wanted to play Castro by invading Italy from Sardinia—with screaming headlines every day announcing some new suspect or witness. But apparently no one ever saw Feltrinelli's body once the police laid hands on it. Then there were those unexplained bombings and shootings which the extreme Left blamed on the Right and vice versa. Fo took full advantage of all this to lay the groundwork for the play to follow.

The Accidental Death of an Anarchist is based upon the 1921 case of an American anarchist (a year before the

288

more notorious Sacco-Vanzetti case) who jumped from the 14th floor of a building in mid-Manhattan, supposedly a suicide. However, subsequent investigation gave reason to suspect the police themselves of having pushed him out during interrogation. Fo took this situation and transplanted it into modern Milan, himself playing the anarchist, ironically called "Matto" ("Mad"). [Not surprisingly, I since learned that it was more immediately prompted by the 1969 death of an anarchist railway man in Italy, Giuseppe Pinelli, which amazingly echoed the American case, even to the extent that Pinelli, too, was probably pushed out of an upper-floor window, but this time of his jail.]

For this newer version, with an amended title, *The Accidental Death of an Anarchist and other Subversives*, to make it cover the recent shootings, Fo had brought together what looked like a couple of older professional actors and younger, less experienced members of the Commune, some of whom I saw later selling drinks in the lobby. After that thirty-minute introduction, Fo went right into the play without further ado. No lights, no change of costume, no theatrical "magic." He simply walked onstage, stood for a moment with his back to the audience, turned around—and *ecco*! He was Matto. It was a fantastic *tour de force*. Just as in his political harangue, he could make the audience laugh over anything, so in his play, through a wide range of comic twists and inversions, Fo turned this essentially dialectical and rhetorical rhodomontade of a play into a rousing but mordant political comedy/satire. No one here but perhaps a Danny Kaye or a Zero Mostel in their heyday could sustain such a torrent of words.

So at last I had found the great Fo! My Italian trip seemed complete. But first I must go back and congratulate him. I plowed through the milling crowd, crept under

289

the ropes, squeezed through wings, and found Fo warming himself backstage over an improvised camp stove. I introduced myself in awkward, hesitant Italian, more tongue-tied than ever after Fo's cascade of fast, staccato speech. Sensing this, he graciously shifted to French to make it easier for me: "So why don't you put this one on in America?" [He knew that I had done those one-acts at The Cubiculo. That's why they let me backstage.] "Why not?" I replied.

*

Thus ended my little *Village Voice* article on that trip, but not my interest in Fo and his work. Of course, as the years rolled by, my hope of witnessing some genius bridge the seemingly impossible language/cultural gap to help make Fo sparkle in English as he surely does in Italian gradually lessened. The last attempt I saw took place a few years ago in the former Provincetown Playhouse in the Village (now run by New York University), a woeful staging of his admittedly difficult *Johan Padan and the Discovery of the Americas*, so badly done, I had to walk out at intermission.

Nevertheless, overall, the Fo venture was a considerable experience. I learned much from it, both theatrically and practically. It extended my range, and enabled me to bring more to my subsequent direction of comedy—especially of European masters. Hence, my production of that wonderfully clever 19th-century Austrian farce, Nestroy's *Love Affairs and Wedding Bells*, probably benefited from a "Fo"-inspired touch here and there, even though I never consciously applied it as such. (To be sure, Fo and Nestroy have/had a lot in common.) Similarly, with directing the Brecht/Weill opera, *Der Lindberghflug*, for the Brooklyn Philharmonic at BAM some years earlier, and turning the stage into a boxing ring—which was how it was first done in Weimar Germany. *Und so weiter...*

But, Nina dear, I'm afraid that this letter has already been overly swamped by theater talk and ventures; and since Shakespeare reminds us that "all the world's a stage," it's time for an intermission.

In the next letter, I promise to touch on other aspects of my life.

Your humble servant,

M.

My dear, patient, ever understanding Muse:

Your reaction to the last two episodes was encouraging. I'm glad my Romanian sketch seemed to make you grow a bit nostalgic again for your "Little Paris" of the Balkans, and that my remarks and observations hold up factually. No geographic or historical errors at all? Really? (Though I'm sure the dogs of Bucharest may have barked in dismay.)

Sometimes when I get involved recording a particular memory or episode, I wonder whether I'm giving you enough background to understand not only what's taking place but why recalling it seems important to me and therefore somehow carries a deeper meaning. Does that ambiguity register similarly with you from time to time?

Also, I presume you'd like me to fill in more about what was going on in my daily life during these various episodes or, rather, between episodes. Actually, I've focused on the latter, for the most part, because generally they were more interesting for me to have lived through than the humdrum routine of daily existence and therefore, I hope, should prove more interesting to you. In other words, building up The Cubiculo, making it a center of creativity in dance, theater, music, poetry, and film was a demanding, but also a rewarding, adventure. Just meeting the many talented artists involved, a number of whom have gone on to great accomplishments, was life-enhancing for me as well. Working with them and helping them try out their ideas was often very exciting in itself, even if some of those attempts "failed" or didn't quite come off. After all, the try-out itself was the important thing. That is why the "right to fail" became a basic tenet of The Cubiculo. Yes, it gave me great satisfaction to be able to have helped so many of these people begin to fulfill their ideas, their dreams, their aspirations—or, rather, helped put them on the road to achieving the same. So, you see why many of those episodes became part of my life, the past upon which I was "doomed" to build my future. Whether for better or worse, can be argued by Clio or whoever else spins my destiny!

Even the "bread and butter" part-time jobs I had to pursue to keep the ship afloat, especially during those first ten years in New York, were generally somewhat engaging, at least from one or more angles, depending upon the parties and tasks involved. Fortunately, most of the people I worked for, or with, proved to be quite interesting—some, as I'm sure you'll agree, often rather compelling—personalities. Otherwise I would not have described them to you, or made them, so to speak, part of my story, perhaps even in some cases part of my *Bildung*, as they call it in Germany (and in certain circles of Romania, too, as you well know). Forming, development, learning, shaping is what that word embraces, right? Plus which, of course, if one stays open and alert, one learns and absorbs from everything one encounters in life. Isn't that what the *Bhagavad Gita* and similar guides are all about?

Besides, my dear Nina, one never knows which or what encounter will lead to another. Thus, it was through a part-time, restaurant waiter job I pursued for awhile in Madison to help cover living expenses while attending the university there back in 1941 to 1943 that I met the brilliant and beautiful Rachel Frank, likewise waiting table at the same restaurant. Offering to walk her home one night after work, she brought me to her modest third-floor student apartment not too many short Madison blocks away and introduced me to her tall, intense, scholarly friend and apartment sharer, Joseph Frank, the great critic (to-be) whom I've referred to several times in earlier letters, author of that magisterial five-volume biography of Dostoevsky from which I've shown you some sample passages. I understand he's now working on a single-volume synthesis of that enormous, all-encompassing work! Of course, while I could hardly on that occasion have predicted precisely such a future for Joe, I sensed then and there that I was in the presence of two remarkable minds, which lessened the disappointment that this dark-haired waitress, whose aura and complexion evoked for me Rebecca in Scott's *Ivanhoe*, or even what the fabled French tragic actress, Rachel, might have looked like, was not predestined for yours truly.

Instead, the two of them, Rachel and Joe, became my intellectual mentors, even at times affectionate "god-parents," during the two and a half years I spent at the University of Wisconsin before trotting off to war. They certainly influenced me scholastically, more than any of my assigned teachers or professors in that fairly easy-going citadel of learning did. It was they who urged me to pursue literature primarily and to learn languages in order to read the greats in their original tongue. Thus, it had to be Racine in French, Goethe in German, Dante in Italian, Virgil in Latin (though they could tolerate Dryden's marvellous translation of *The Aeneid*), and so on! That's why I took courses in those languages and one summer actually moved "across the tracks" into the small Italian quarter of Madison to hear that language spoken, innocently not realizing at first that I was being confronted with a Sicilian dialect, not literary Toscano, when I tried to communicate with my tough landlord and his neighbors, whose wives were not allowed to go out shopping, even in the daytime, without a chaperon or two! (Many years later I had similar difficulties in Venice dealing with replies to my street-direction queries in that ultra-impenetrable Venetian dialect.) I had even started Russian classes, taught by an excellent Polish teacher; we were just starting to work on Tolstoy's delightful stories for children when this paradise of learning was cut short for me by my being drafted into the Army. Or enlisted? I'm not quite sure, at the moment, which. Immaterial, because I'd be sure to have been drafted anyway.

Joe and Rachel also introduced me to a remarkable circle of fellow writers, artists, intellectuals, and serious graduate students (quite flattering in itself, since I was just a much younger, humble undergrad) who seemed to have been drawn to them and their aura. Among these varied individuals were the solemn, loner poet, Peter Gilbert, or Pedro, as we fondly called him, who, after wrapping his coat about him so as to look like a hidalgo, would recite Quevedo at the drop of a hat; the formidable, rather quiet, stoic-looking, quite Amerikanisch-sounding, Gordon Sylander; and that precocious, enthusiastic pioneer translator of Lorca and Calderon de la Barca, a red-headed El Greco look-alike, Edwin Honig—as well as others whose names elude me at the moment. Though I do remember that one of them was working at that time on a critical study of the 19th-century Spanish master novelist, Galdos, for his PhD thesis, and hired me to type it. Which, in turn, enabled me to drop that dull waiter job and also opened my literary horizons to the fact that there were other formidable novelists in other cultures besides Dickens, Balzac, Flaubert, Dostoevsky, and Tolstoy...

This slight preponderance of Spanish friends or Latin American specialists was because these were the people Rachel got to know while pursuing a Master's degree in that department. But that did not limit the range of our readings and discussions to the Latin cultures! On the contrary. Among other subjects, I recall a heated argument over the literary status and importance of Hart Crane, sparked by Waldo Frank's biography of him, which had just come out; of much interest to all was what R. P. Blackmur was currently writing about Wallace Stevens (I'm sure Joe never dreamed at that time that he would one day become a Princeton faculty colleague of the great Blackmur); not to mention spiky dissent over the problem of how to deal with the mystic claims of Yeats and his unique *Vision*. Nor can we ignore politics: remember, as I told you in a much earlier letter, it was Joseph Frank who introduced me to Henry Bamford Parkes's remarkably prescient book, *Marxism: An Autopsy*, and the crucial Dewey report on the Moscow Trials, which I tried, in vain, to get our "pure, ever-faithful" communist friend, Becky Nathanson, to read. Joe also loaned me William Ellery Leonard's down-to-earth translation of Lucretius (Leonard was one of the revered elder-generation figures at Wisconsin) and raved about Santayana's prose and some of his sonnets. Not to mention ocean-jumping to Croce and DeSanctis in Italy on the one hand, and Saint-Beuve and Taine in France on the other. I still cherish their gift volume of Croce's collected critical articles, *Poesia antica e moderna*, with an "expecting great things" of me dedication from Joe and Rachel—what kind of great things, I'm afraid I haven't quite lived up to—on its title page.

Indeed, it was during that period that Joe was working on his refreshingly original and ultimately path-breaking essay, "Spatial Form in Modern Literature," which focused on Joyce, Proust, and Djuna Barnes as exemplars of his thesis—passages of which I was privileged to read in advance from the typed manuscript. This, in turn, guided me to Barnes's murky, hypnotic novel, *Nightwood*, which I might otherwise not have encountered until decades later when it became *de rigueur* to "do" so. Nor shall I ever forget the excitement that rippled through our circle when that long essay on "Spatial Form in Modern Literature" by a then-unknown critic was published by the distinguished *Sewanee Review* (I believe it came out in three successive issues). About the same time, Honig was finishing his influential study of Lorca. Sylander had a poem published in the *Partisan Review*, and, to everyone's surprise, was later hired to write the history of General Electric, or some comparable corporate giant, and then seemed to disappear from the literary scene. Pedro (aka Peter Gilbert) continued to astound us all with his abiliity to read the Bible in seven languages, including Mongolian! And Rachel was deep into writing scholarly treatises on pre-Golden Age Spanish literature, as well as her own lyric poems, in addition to preparing for her exams and quoting Gongora on the side. And then Joe would bring up Mario Praz... It was a heady time, indeed; I still reel from it when I think of it.

A sad footnote to the Frank saga is that some years later, after Joe and Rachel had settled in the Washington area—he had by that time become an editor for the NLRB (National Labor Relations Board) reports but was destined to go on to much higher challenges at Princeton and ultimately Stanford—Rachel seems to have had something of a mental breakdown. I never did learn all the details about this tragic, unexpected problem, this stifling of a most gifted intellect, but I do know that in spite of her valiant attempts to regain her mental powers, she was never quite the same again (though she did recover enough at times to teach in the New York school

295

system). Indeed, the one time I saw Rachel briefly during that late phase, some of her symptoms were eerily similar to what I would later experience in the mental demise of my own troubled Ann. For example, not long after that meeting, I received a card from her, inviting people to view the paintings of "Rachel, Queen of Israel" — exactly what Ann not too many years ahead would sometimes call herself and then threaten to walk down Remsen Street in Brooklyn Heights proclaiming our son, Jacob, the Son of God, and me, Satan. (Remember that earlier letter in which I told you about her illness and four hospitalizations? I understand that these days, ironically enough, the very practical, hard-headed, money-milking star, Madonna, considers herself to be the reincarnation of Queen Esther!)

Well, my dear, you can see how my meeting at such an early age these superior minds of Joe's remarkable circle no doubt helped prepare me for some of the encounters I was to have after the war with Gertrude Stein and her circle, as well as for meeting a modest smattering of the intellectual and artistic elite of Paris, whom, somehow, I met independently of Gertrude. This *embarras de richesses* was for the better, I think, because it gave me a wider perspective and was totally French. How else would a young, inexperienced reader—but not a writer—have been prepared to converse with a Blanchot, a Picabia, Jean Paulhan or Braque, Bernac or chère Claude-Edmonde, for that matter, even though the latter preferred to go dancing with him at Bal Nègre? But why did they want to talk to "unaccomplished" me, I often wondered. Sometimes I felt like a Hottentot being cross-examined by Voltaire and Diderot. No, that's unfair: that's my projection. They were all mostly kind, friendly, and civilized, rarely condescending. I think word may have got around that I had translated some poems of Mallarmé. Indeed, it was probably that which won over Blanchot. Though the fact that I was studying music and dance, plus taking in some lectures at the Sorbonne, was probably entrée enough. That, plus the uniform, of course! I still cherish a copy inscribed to me by Paulhan of his fascinating *Lettre à Jean Dubuffet de Jean Paulhan* that accompanied the catalogue to a showing of Dubuffet's latest paintings in March 1946.

None of my other part-time jobs led into quite such lofty realms, although many of them were challenging in themselves, even exotic, and occasionally uplifting. As was, for example, my work with Klara Roman, the inscrutable, exiled Hungarian gra-phologist, described to you in a much earlier letter. It was she who recommended me to the tall, distinguished, Dutch international copyright lawyer, Edward van Saher, with whom I also worked spo-radically according to need, i.e., when he was handling a case which made more "literary" demands on him and was couched in English, not Dutch, German, or French. He wanted me to polish up his prose and cut down on his legalese, or at least make it more readable for American eyes. I've already told you a little about him and his lovely wife, Desi, as I'm sure you'll recall. But, as I think I noted then, fate was to lead me to work later for his first wife, the rather outrageous, but tantalizing, Lilla van Saher.

Yet, strangely enough, it was not through him that I met Lilla (could her parents have been anticipating a Lilith when they named her?) but rather indirectly through wily Geraldine, whose intervention helped bring about this encounter. Let me explain. One morning, Geraldine phoned excitedly to say that the job agency, provocatively and aptly called the "Hard-to-Find" bureau, had asked her to help them lo-cate someone who could fill the bill for a very demanding client who had already turned down three applicants they had sent her—and she had the brainstorm of recommending me! Nonplussed, I asked Geraldine: "Why me? Hard-to-Find handles only women, doesn't it?" "You're right," she answered, "and they wanted to send me; but from what they said about this person, I wouldn't go near her. So I suggested that maybe a man would be a safer bet. She'd be less likely to throw him out than me or another woman!" She assured Hard-to-Find that I could answer that need—if anyone could!

Which is how I happened to meet Lilla van Saher—under pressure. She was the difficult person Hard-to-Find was trying hard to satisfy. And so I went dutifully, but a little reluctantly (for I didn't want to let Geraldine down), to this mystery woman's apartment in one of those somewhat dingy but once elegant buildings in the once tony Murray Hill district. I rang the bell, was yelled at to open the door, entered awkwardly, and saw a large, plump, quite flamboyant, but also stunning, middle-aged woman, stretched out horizontally, Maja-like, on her sofa, scrutinizing me sharply. She was clothed in a garish silk house wrap, which clashed with the elegant, colored reproduction of a Matisse of the Nice period perched on the wall behind her. Then, after I introduced myself as being sent by Hard-to-Find, she relaxed slightly, took a huge puff on the long cigarette attached to her even longer cigarette holder, and, in definitively B-movie style, snorted in a thick Hungarian accent: "Do you type?" To which I meekly nodded yes.

"Then sit down. There!" she ordered, pointing with that menacing holder to a chair and little typewriter table at the foot of that sofa, "and take down what I dictate to you." Whereupon she spat out in an irregular rhythm and in fairly short phrases (which fortunately gave me time to keep up with her dictation) a rape scene on a Key West, Florida, beach, reminiscent of one of those sultry Tennessee Williams Southern dramas. She continued in a slightly hostile, challenging style until, exhausted, she got stuck; inspiration failed her; and she had to take a break, during which time I handed her what I had typed, and she proceeded to read it.

What a change overcame her when she found out that I had not only kept up with her dictation but had apparently also managed to correct some of her grammatical errors. Suddenly she was all middle-European charm and began to ask a few personal questions, which I parried back, in wonder at her command of American slang. This little badinage seemed to win her over. She went on to tell me about her friendship with Tennessee himself, whom she said she saw frequently in Key West, and pointed to a paperback crime novel on the table, which she claimed to have written the year before. But with Tennessee's blessing (and endorsement, she implied), she said this new book was sure to be a best seller. Then, freshly inspired, she began dictating a few more pages, during which she grew increasingly seductive. Just when I began to wonder how I was to deal with this new phase—especially since, though surely sexy, she was not at all "my type" as they say, and also, as you know, dear Nina, that's not my style—a side door opened and out stepped a dark-haired, stocky but not fat, middled-aged, quite good-looking man. "My Swedish husband!" she cooed, and suddenly we all began to talk politics. (Though she might more accurately have described Riwkin as her Swedish/Jewish teammate.)

Well, these were obviously intriguing characters to meet and to converse with on a dark, dank autumn working day in New York, but since I was being paid by the hour, we had to forego that temptation. Nevertheless, during breaks, and in the course of our subsequent rush to finish her sultry novel, she would reminisce from time to time about her glamorous past in Europe. Among other tales, the most incredible one posited that she was the original leading lady in that great, pre-war French film, which I'm sure you'll recall, dear Nina, *La Femme de Boulanger*. That she could well have had that role was less in question—since she must have been quite a beauty back then, about ten or twelve years earlier—than just why she lost the part! For, according to her *Arabian Nights*-like tale, it seems that midway through the filming, she was afraid her pregnancy would show. This meant wearing very tight corsets. But one tempestuous afternoon, the pressure of the stays forced milk to flow from her breasts, and with the very revealing bodice she was wearing, everyone on the set could see the results! So, she claims, van Saher, who happened to be present and was most likely the father, indignantly whisked her off the set and also, evidently, out of the film.

The general outlines of this story may well be true, but it's unlikely that a shrewd director and filmmaker like Marcel Pagnol would not have known how to cover for such a situation. Moreover, he wouldn't have wanted to waste weeks of filming if she had been "up to snuff," as we say in the business. More likely, she wasn't, and so he had probably welcomed an excuse to change leading ladies.

That she could have been making such a film would not have been impossible. Lilla came from the illustrious Alexander family of Budapest, one of nine remarkable children. Her eldest brother, a truly outstanding psychiatrist and a favored disciple of Freud, became the Director of the Chicago Institute of Psychoanalysis and built it into one of the major such clinics in the United States. One of Lilla's older sisters had been a leading mezzo-soprano at the Budapest Opera; another brother was a famed historian; apparently each sibling had achieved some distinction. They remind me of the comparably famed, nine-membered Ito family of Tokyo, one of whom I worked with here in New York, in the Living Theatre's ill-fated production of Kenneth Rexroth's play *Beyond the Mountains* at the Cherry Lane Theater in the Village and later in one of Yeats's *Plays for Dancers* at the 92nd Street Y. (I'll fill you in later about this Ito and his eldest, most famous sibling, Michio, for whom Yeats wrote those plays, when I get to relate some of my experiences with Judith Malina, Julian Beck, and The Living Theatre.)

There were, of course, many tales told by Lilla, our modern Scheherezade, some more interesting, I thought, than the rather banal fiction she was trying to fashion into a best seller. I would have liked to encourage her to move her novel along such lines, but Mme. Riwkin (though somehow "Lilla van Saher" better fits her persona) was not given to self-criticism. Nor would she have brooked any from an underling like me. Still, I wager she would have welcomed a critique from Tennessee, or, indeed, from Jane Bowles, whom I only much later learned she had also met—probably through Williams?

There was actually something imperious about Lilla, which I fancied she probably inherited or learned through the examples of her eight talented sisters and brothers. Or perhaps felt that the weight of the mantle of her world-famous eldest brother, the lion-like Franz Alexander, might someday fall upon her. As it turned out, he lived a long, full life, while Lilla died only about fourteen years after him. Indeed, he was something of a legend in psychiatric circles: I'm sure she relished being part of the Royal Family, like one of the Barrymores, though she rarely referred to him and also rebelled against the family from time to time. Oddly enough, she rarely mentioned van Saher, whom I presume was her first husband, nor when and why they divorced. Nor did van Saher himself, whom I worked with later, as you know, ever mention her at all. And was there a child?

Ah yes, there was always a touch of mystery, something unspoken lurking about in their rather small, stuffy, but expensive, apartment on East 39th Street. Yet when we finished what I gathered was the first draft of that hoped-for, best-seller novel, we parted amiably— and I was well recompensed.

About a year or two later, however, when Lilla called me back for help on another project, I could never find out what had become of the Key West novel; she evaded all questions about it. In the interim, Lilla van Saher/Mrs. Riwkin had moved to a large, airy luxury apartment in the lower East 60s, where one now had ample space to breathe. There was also less pressure to finish a novel this time around. Instead, we usually dealt with Lilla's more mundane, day-to-day business, which, unfortunately, proved to be much less amusing than the novel, amateurish as it had seemed to me then. But how and why had her fortune swung east and north from good old Murray Hill to the pretentious Silk Stocking district? I presumed she must have made a good final divorce settlement with van Saher, most likely in her favor. The new apartment was handsomely decorated and appointed, with numerous sculptures from Indonesia, where the Dutch had once reigned, and where van Saher no doubt collected art. There were also other choice Oriental pieces, as well as a few rather good examples of the standard Impressionists, including a few Pissaros, Sisleys, and a Monet or two, I believe, dotting the walls.

Recent articles in *The New York Times* and other papers about settling the complicated disposition of the famed Goudstikker art collection, which Goering and his cohorts had run off with, much of which later went to various Dutch art galleries rather than to family survivors, have somewhat clarified for me how Edward van Saher (also called August), Lilla van Saher and Desirée Halban fit into that amazing story. It turns out that primary among the survivors of the Goudstikker estate, of course, was Desi, who, as we've seen, became the second Mrs. van Saher. The descendants of Desirée and Edward, the younger van Sahers, some of whom are now living in Connecticut, I understand, are pursuing more zealously than Desi

301

ever did a fairer restitution of what was once an enormous, highly coveted collection of over 1,800 prize paintings and sculptures.

These articles also inform us that at the start of World War II, our dear Desi Halban, then a rising singer from Vienna, was courted by Jacques Goudstikker, the wealthiest art collector in the Netherlands and the owner of a castle and vast estates near Amsterdam. Indeed, it was at a special *Viennese Night* concert at his castle that he first met her and heard Desi sing—and was immediately smitten and pursued her relentlessly. They were married within six months!

Too bad Goudstikker did not move that quickly on escaping the Nazis. Though he knew danger was around the corner, and he had made a thorough catalogue of his paintings and other arrangements about his businesses, Goudstikker unwisely procrastinated until almost the last moment about actually taking that urgent final step of getting out of the Netherlands. Thus, it seems that he and Desi escaped only a day or two before the Nazis swallowed up Amsterdam. Nor did they manage to properly hide or store away all of their vast art holdings in time. Instead, they hurriedly boarded at night a cargo ship bound for South Africa—Desi, Jacques, and their tiny baby. As they were nearing England, so the various news stories seem to agree on, Jacques went up on deck for some night air. When he didn't duly return, Desi grew anxious and called out desperately for help, burdened as she was with the child. At first, nobody could find Goudstikker. Apparently, while trying in the dark to get back to his family, he opened a wrong door and plunged to his death in the ship's hold. When he was finally found there, Desi collapsed: it was too much to face.

Yet this rich (probably spoiled), delicate young lady rallied strongly, so that when the ship stopped at Liverpool for supplies and re-fueling, she boldly disembarked and found another boat to take her to America, where ultimately she found refuge. But, the story goes on, she also found time to have Goudstikker properly buried in England to the music of Cole Porter's "Night and Day," his favorite piece, as he had once asked Desi to do should the time ever come.

That I never heard this amazing, melodramatic story from

either Desi or van Saher is not strange: they were both too proud, private, and reserved to talk about such things. It was obviously too painful for Desi to do so. But also for most survivors: I vividly recall how almost no one in those days wanted to tell us about his or her escape from the Nazis or the camps. An almost tacit silence prevailed. However, the articles state that in 1947 Desi went back to the Netherlands to try to clear up what was left of that once-enormous estate, not just the paintings. Fortunately, Goudstikker's last listing of his holdings, typed up in a small black noteboook, was found on him when they discovered his body in the hold.

Nevertheless, this perfect evidence notwithstanding, it seems that Desi received only a paltry, partial return of about 200 pictures and was probably forced into a too-easy settlement with the Dutch government over the rest. It was much more difficult in those days to stand up to the "authorities." That's why her son's descendants (Edward van Saher adopted her son, Edouard Goudstikker, who took on the van Saher name) are trying to make up for it. As to how Desirée first met van Saher, it's likely that she may have encountered him in her search for a lawyer to help settle these matters.

In any case, Desi was younger, arguably more beautiful, potentially richer, and certainly more suited to a Dutch grandee than the turbulent, unpredictable Lilla. Hence the divorce? There's material galore here for quite a novel, don't you think, dear Nina?

There is also the question as to why Desi discontinued her singing career after what strikes one as a rather good start. Remember my mentioning earlier her recording of Mahler's *Fourth* under Bruno Walter? Besides, she knew the elite of the European musical world through her illustrious mother, the great *coloratura*, Selma Kurz. Here, I think I can more safely venture, judging from some of our private conversations, that she was too modest a being, not driven enough. Also, she would have had to overcome the feeling that she could never live up to her mother's supreme example. Nor did she have that consuming passion needed to succeed in any branch of show business, even Lieder singing! But she loved beautiful singing. I recall her generously predicting great things for Leontyne Price after hearing her in the Broadway production of *Porgy and Bess*.

But to get back to Lilla: here I have less pleasant things to relate. Whereas during my first work period with her, we had developed a good, and, I think, mutually beneficial type of working relationship, and I was well paid for my labors, it was a quite different story during our second round at the more "palatial" Upper East Side residence. There, Lilla seemed colder, more distant, less spontaneous. We had fewer talks between layers of work and during breaks, about life in general, politics, plays seen or concerts heard, galleries visited.

Yet she could still come up now and then with amusing remarks or observations delivered in that inimitable mustard-thick accent of hers. For example, once when the typewriter in her bedroom needed fixing, she called up a local repair man, who, on arriving, turned out to be an amiable, not bad-looking Middle European, who also sounded a bit more cultivated than your average technician. She soon disappeared with him into the bedroom to show him the problem with the machine, while I continued working on the other typewriter in the living room. Emerging a few minutes later, she sighed: "Ah, European men are so different: they know how to appreciate women!" Though not enough time had transpired for extensive hanky-panky, obviously there had been time enough for our gallant Yugoslav to flatter her with a few compliments and leering looks, probably telling her how honored he was to work for such a beautiful woman, or remarks to such an effect, as she patted her ample breasts.

As to her change in attitude toward me, among other things, it translated into her becoming more niggardly, difficult, and irregular about paying me, a great contrast to the earlier Lilla, who sometimes generously insisted on giving me more than the called-for rate. The result was that I finished that second work period without ever being fully paid up, even after sending her three or four bills and making four or five phone call reminders. I finally had to take her to Small Claims Court, where she put on a performance not to be believed, convincing the much too gullible judge that I had betrayed her in some strange way, and counter-claiming that I had violated her confidences so that I didn't deserve to be paid—I can't even remember exactly what the full story was. Whatever it was, the astounded judge believed her every word! Unfortunately, I had only my little notes of time put in as evidence and, what I thought would be sufficient, my simple, frank openness. But that didn't work: the judge simply dismissed the case. I was probably too literate.

Now, after relating to you this rather morbid story of a rather wealthy woman's cold breaking of a trust that one would have thought had developed from our earlier work experience, I recognize again my fatal inability to detect a scam in a guileful lady's confidence games. Strictly speaking, shouldn't the Lilla fiasco have prepared me for the ultimately greater disappointment I experienced later with Mme. Piscator, a similar, though classier, intellectual charmer and brain-picker? Though, as you may recall, I actually was more suspicious of Mme. P. at first, but didn't maintain the skepticism, and let down my guard too soon, too much.

Or maybe Lilla's betrayal was the result of her possible disappointment in me, that I might not have lived up to her expectations, although she never complained or criticized me in any overt way. Or perhaps she had learned somehow that in between I had worked for her now arch enemy, van Saher himself, and suspected me of spying on her? Or was it simply that I didn't flirt with or flatter her enough? That she may have wanted me to actually fall down before her, at her feet? That she may even hoped originally that I might fit into her circle somehow. But what was that circle?

Looking Lilla van Saher up on Google last night, I was not too surprised to find entries indicating that she had indeed carried on some correspondence with Tennessee Williams (listed in his archives), but more surprised that Jane Bowles was also a recipient of her letters (listed in her archives). Then there was that photo with her sitting on a boat deck, seemingly in Key West, regaling both of them. However, I looked in vain for any notice of that Key West novel we had worked on ever having been published. Though there was a garish-looking cover for a romantic novel of the tropics, *Macumba*, dated shortly after my first working period with her ended. Could she have found a ghost writer to help move her Key West fabrication to more exotic Curaçao, that fascinating Dutch Caribbean island—or was it Brazil?—and change it accordingly into a mixed-race, romantic drama, featuring native cult beliefs and New World witchcraft? Not impossible.

Finally, quite peculiar, and perhaps most revealing of all, there is an entry showing that that fake Holocaust sufferer, the notorious Jerzy Kosinsky, had dedicated his best-selling novel, *The Painted Bird*, to Lilla van Saher; plus a footnote attributing this to the fact that supposedly she had been his Dominatrix for quite some time!... Will I ever learn?

Perplexedly yours,

M.

December 9, 2008

My dear, patient, overburdened, put-upon Muse:

So, you think I have learned somewhat from experience? That, for example, nowadays I would be more adept at handling another Lilla (or Dalila, as Milton spelled it in his *Samson Agonistes*—another real Lilith type?) and not let her take advantage of naïve, innocent me? I wonder... While, yes, we do accumulate a great deal of valuable "know-how" over the years, we know how to traverse a city, to shop expediently; we may learn how to respond charmingly in public to a *vis-a-vis* no matter how exacerbating he or she might be; even, from time to time, we might manage to open a recalcitrant wine bottle. Yet there are some levels of human behavior so tied to old responses and useless compunctions, so vulnerable to certain challenges colored by the uncertainties of childhood, so sheathed by subtle, imperceptible camouflages, I think, my dear, no measure of experience or learning can ever really prevail, or ever enable us to rise above it all.

But don't despair: I seem to know how to bounce back. Such contretemps do not defeat me. I just close the book, put it on the shelf, and clear the way for the next adventure. As you well know, fortunately life is abundantly stocked with new challenges and temptations. Malherbe put it rather pithily about four hundred years ago: "*Le temps est médecin d'heureuse expérience. Son remède est tardif, mais il est bien certain.*"

Besides, as I look back over those first eight or nine years of getting settled and finding my place in New York after World War II, they embraced, for the most part, a healthy mixture of some fascinating college courses; simultaneously parallel classes in theatrical techniques—voice, dance, acting; a series of often interesting and challenging part-time jobs to keep bringing in the bread and butter, as well as money to pay for those extra outside classes (the GI Bill covered only my college courses); and a gradually increasing number of actual theater parts. There was even a very early television special of Kurt Weill's *Knickerbocker Holiday* I was lucky to participate in because Anna Sokolow did the choreography for it, and I had just finished working with her in my first Broadway show, *Happy as Larry*, which I later christened "Unhappy as Larry," since it closed after three performances!

Again, my lack of shrewdness and shortage of good, old-fashioned chutzpah probably prevented me from making the most of some of these early "breaks." For example, I remember once getting up very early in the morning back in 1948 or 1949, when I was rooming on West 68th Street near Central Park in the same building as the ubiquitous Wayne Murray (did he recommend me for it?), running around the block, and drinking plenty of coffee to be in good enough voice to sing several high notes at 9:00am. in some kind of off-beat commercial that used semi-operatic vocal passages, and in which I did better than I expected. (Why not more follow-up?) You see, in those early days, I didn't trust my technique enough to be ready to sing adequately so early in the day. Though I was re-assured when I later found out that even some big stars objected to such early singing calls. Thus Dennis King, veteran leading man of many a Romberg or Victor Herbert operetta during the Thirties and Forties, and who played Peter Stuyvesant in that same TV version of Weill's *Knickerbocker Holiday* I just mentioned above, grumbled *mezzo forte* on the set, as we were preparing to shoot the "September Song" sequence: "It's absolutely obscene to have to sing at this hour in the morning; I can't even spit yet!" On the other hand, I remember hearing the great Flagstad sing full voice at a 9:00am dress rehearsal for Gluck's *Alcestis* at the old Met, which, you'll recall, I mentioned in an earlier letter, I was fortunate enough to be able to attend.

Another example of lack of chutzpah and follow-up: I certainly should have done more to get the right people to see my production of *Stacked Death* at the Y, especially when I managed to have it repeated at Cooper Union a year or two later, with the same cast, and had the good reviews from the Y version to promote it better the next time around. I seem to have naively thought that such people would come to such an event, especially its repetition, out of sheer curiosity and the wish to keep up with newer happenings. As it turned out, I did better in future years promoting The Cubiculo and later the Brooklyn Philharmonic than I ever did promoting myself, or my own productions.

Certainly I learned how others went about it when I was running The Cubiculo. Many actors would send me postal cards or similar notices every time they appeared in a play somewhere or on TV or in a film. For instance, that future star Herschel Bernardi (who followed Zero in *Fiddler on the Roof*) inundated me with monthly notices of whatever he was up to, even if it was still months away. As did that later Latino star Hector Elizondo, who used to flood me with a constant barrage of postal cards. Then there was a tough, little African American cafe singer who didn't make it as big as the other two, though she rivalled their persistence in sending out announcements, if not surpassed it. Also, of course, I would be deluged with scripts by aspiring playwrights, scores from musicians, and performance notices by dancers, choreographers, and stage directors. Modesty was rare...

Not to be dismissed is what I call the "snob" approach

to these matters of promotion. Here one has to find something that distinguishes oneself or makes one's work stand out from all others—Andy Warhol's moment of fame, Duchamp's Mona Lisa moustache, Mailer's *Advertisements for Myself.* Actually, my old friend the healthy, blonde, blue-eyed Midwestern beauty, dancer/choreographer/physical therapist and would-be intellectual Shirley Broughton, with her unique Theatre for Ideas—which she founded along with Eric Bentley, Mary Hivnor, and Joseph Marx—was a master at this approach. She capitalized on making whatever TFI was doing or promoting available only for the intellectual elite of New York. Ironically, by limiting her audience, she gained an audience! You'll recall my mentioning that showing of Brecht's *The Elephant Calf*, which I put on at her large but modest second-floor dance studio on West 21st Street, between Sixth and Seventh Avenues.

That was the home of Theatre for Ideas, with its high ceiling, huge windows, excellent parquet flooring, curtains galore, and theatrical lighting, plus a small kitchen. Next door to it, moving eastward, was the picturesque, historic third cemetery of the Sephardic Shearith Israel Synagogue, the very congregation that settled in New Amsterdam against the wishes of Peter Stuyvesant and has continued to flourish here in Manhattan for more than 350 years, its cemetery always having to move uptown along with its ever-growing congregation and consequently larger synagogue. (I think it now has four sites!)

Of course, Theatre for Ideas had nowhere near such longevity! Probably the only theatrical endeavor which could ever come anywhere near boasting such a record would be the Comédie Française or the Chinese National Opera or any given Hindu theatrical religious festival. In any case, during TFI's modest twelve- to fifteen-year reign, it was the hot private ticket of the *New York Review of Books* and related crowd. To the outside world, that probably made it look like a secret society, if indeed one had heard about it, much like the Masons of today or the Knights Templar of yesteryear.

Entry was controlled by la Broughton and her crew with charm and an iron hand, once it won the approval of her co-directors and their tiny, high-powered Board of Directors. TFI boasted a very special mailing list, or rather several special related lists within that master list, enabling them to vary the invitees according to the type of program being held. For it was not only theater that was presented. More often it would be a public symposium on an important current political issue, in which several of the leading minds of the day would be solicited to participate. Or it might be a reading of a play about the Congo problem by the brilliant Irish scholar and diplomat, Conor Cruise O'Brien. Or a heated discussion of the Columbia University student uprising, pitting leaders of the New Left against the old radicals. Such evenings might be alternated with recitals of new music, organized by co-producer Joseph Marx (no relation to the great Marx). Or co-producer Eric Bentley himself at the upright piano, singing in his unique Sprechstimme, Hanns Eisler's little-known, mordant, devastating, but still most entertaining settings of Brecht and other subversive Weimar poets. Less often, Broughton put on a program of modern dance, since that was the world she came from. (Alas, I remember an evening of short Broughton dances to Schubert piano music, where her choreography never quite measured up to her obvious love for Schubert.)

Shirley drew many of her participants from the intellectual crowd she met while summering in East Hampton and Amagansett, such as Harold Rosenberg, *The New Yorker's* brilliant, maven art critic who coined the term "action painting"; the eccentric and amusing ex-Trotzkyite, Dwight MacDonald, editor of *Politics*, but probably best remembered now for his perky film criticism; the eloquent, engaging Saul Bellow (whom you know better because of his connections with that Romanian lady scientist); Lionel Abel, critic and translator of some of Sartre's plays, and would-be playwright of some promise, having won an Obie with one of his plays); Joel Carmichael, pugnacious, stubborn editor of *Midstream* and an expert on the "historical" Jesus, who had the old Amagansett Lighthouse moved a little inland and turned into quite wonderful living quarters, with his amusing, loquacious, Polish-speaking housekeeper; and their motley friends and colleagues, including that polymath

310

conductor, mathematician, scholar, Stefan Bauer, to whom I wrote that funeral ode, which I reproduced in an earlier letter; plus some of the leading abstract expressionists and the not-to-be-forgotten Broughton mainstays from the *New York Review of Books*—Elizabeth Hardwick, Robert Silver, Barbara Epstein, and, of course, Robert Lowell. Important feminists, such as Gloria Steinem and Betty Friedan, would also be invited, especially when needed for setting up a balance of ideas and ideals. With such an array of talent, intellect, and often megalomaniac personalities, you can imagine how heated some of the post-lecture or post-performance discussions could be!

Perhaps Shirley's most notorious forum took place at Town Hall in 1971, among the last programs of TFI and one of the few times a TFI event was ever thrown open to the general public. The subject was Women's Liberation, where poor, beleaguered Norman Mailer, who had just written *The Prisoner of Sex*, had to stand up, the sole male on that stage, as Moderator of this intellectual circus. He was pitted against the glamorous, razor-tongued Germaine Greer, whose even more recent book, *The Female Eunuch*, had just created a new sensation; Jill Johnston of *The Village Voice* reading her infamous essay on the Bible's "BEGATS"; and several other "Amazons"—as Mailer christened them—including, I believe, Diana Trilling and Jacqueline Ceballos, then President of the New York chapter of National Organization for Women.

After reading her lesbian, feminist poetic manifesto, Johnston announced that "all women are lesbians except those that don't know it yet," and was joined on the stage by two women friends. As the *Times* reported it, the three "began kissing and hugging ardently, upright at first but soon rolling on the floor" of historic Town Hall's stage in rather awkward simulation of clothed lesbian sex. Whereupon Mailer chided them to a halt before they went too far, with a jokingly sputtered "Come on, Jill, be a lady!" Then the contest shifted to a series of verbal blows and provocative repartee between Greer, Mailer, and a few eminent feminists who emerged from the voluble audience, including Betty Friedan and Susan Sontag! I think a tape of this often lugubrious debate may be found at the Lincoln Center

Library, or maybe even on Google...

Unfortunately, instead of extending the life of the Theatre for Ideas, that spectacular evening seems to have served as the apotheosis that choked it. How could one top such madness? Or who would want to? Ultimately, it was not quite what the leading members of TFI saw as its proper future.

For they had already quite a record of striking intellectual presentations and off-beat entertainment. For example, I believe the first reading of Lionel Abel's play *Absalom*, which later won that Obie mentioned above, was done at TFI. Later, I staged Abel's short play about a modern Prometheus there, while a dramatized version of Saul Bellow's *Seize the Day*, drew a large audience. But perhaps the most engaging of these sallies (at least for me) was the staged reading I directed of Valéry's *My Faust* (in English, of course). Because of the intellectual density of this extraordinary poetic drama, I thought it would work better with Faust and the Devil read by brilliant writers or sharp critics familiar with that world of thought and aesthetics, and with what one might call its sometimes deceptively lucid Valérian atmosphere, where, as his Mephisto says, "philosophers are happy to understand each other just enough to keep alive their disagreement, which, in any case, is their only reason for being." (Unfortunately echoing these days the behavior of our U.S. Congress and New York State Legislature—but that probably keeps Mephisto happy!)

So we managed to line up the controversial and always provocative Leslie Fiedler, in those days sometimes dubbed the wild man of literary critics, to play Faust; and the wonderfully acerbic stage and film critic, John Simon, to take on Mephistopheles (whose cursing he did in his native Serbo-Croatian). The romantic poet figure was played by the young, handsome poet/critic Michael Goldman, while Mlle. Lust was embodied by a beautiful young actress with brains, Arlene Nadel (also, serendipitously, the daughter of a good newspaper theater critic!) The three devil creatures (two succubi & one incubus) were played by a dancer/actress, a plump ex-librarian with a cat-like squint, and a lanky, bearded, semi-retired opera *basso buffo*. To almost everyone's surprise, *My Faust*, usually dismissed as a purely literary drama,

312

"played" better than anticipated, so much so that Fiedler, who was then teaching at SUNY Buffalo, got his English Department there to invite us all up to Buffalo for a double showing. Again: popular success. *My Faust* also garnered an unexpectedly appreciative review in *The Village Voice*.

For me, part of the joy experienced in taking this so-called closet drama out of the closet and bringing it to life, was just that; proving what I had always felt about it (and Valéry in general), namely, that his work is far more human, humane, and searching in the Pascalian sense than most people credit it for. I certainly made no money out of the endeavor; nor did it advance my "commercial" theatrical future. However, it did lead to one potentially commercial project: I was asked to prepare a similar kind of staged reading of *Taking the Sun in the Twentieth Century*, a kind of satirical political play with music in semi-vaudeville style by two witty younger colleagues (or disciples?) of Fiedler, Abel and Irving Howe. While stimulating and often fun to work on it ultimately did not pan out because the authors, though multi-talented on several levels, couldn't stretch those talents to the telling degree, which that kind of theater demands.

Again, my dear Nina, I've gone into some detail about the Valéry venture because it is one of the better examples of the kind of purely artistic approach that was at the heart of Theatre for Ideas programming. Also, of course, it exemplified the series of programs I had been doing at Cooper Union, and some of the earlier concerts on the 92nd Street Y's New Music series. It was probably these experiences that led me to coin the formula we later used as our byword at The Cubiculo—"the right to fail." In other words, while each artist strives his best to make a new dance perfect, a new play work, a new opera sing, a new film transcend, he needs a chance to spread his wings first, especially when experimenting with a new idea, a different style, or a seemingly unconventional concept. That space and freedom was what we tried to provide at The Cubiculo, the importance of which had been impressed upon me by my earlier experimenting at the Y, Cooper Union, and the Theatre for Ideas.

Well, as you can see, before ever setting foot in The Cubiculo, I had already participated in a considerable variety of projects, theatrical and otherwise, most of which, I must say, proved rewarding in one respect or another, or for one reason or another. Practically speaking, they certainly served as a background apprenticeship for my future production days at The Cubiculo, The Classic Theatre, and even the Brooklyn Philharmonic, although each of those ventures came with its own complications. Nevertheless, when involved with any one of them, I never thought of it in such terms. Each project was always valued for its own sake: to each I gave my best efforts and my fullest attention. The main frustration or principal drawback in pursuing most of these try-outs and often extremely chancy projects was, of course, lack of funds. Also, the fact that I simultaneously had to carry on one or more of my part-time jobs while working on them created its problems. Yet they were, in a sense, my life's blood and couldn't be dropped. (And this was all before little Jacob arrived on the scene. You can imagine how much more complicated and difficult life plus projects then became!)

Fortunately, I have been blessed, as you've discovered over the years, with the ability and energy to carry on several projects at the same time by readily shifting gears according to need. Thus I might be working for several hours one morning with, say, Klara Roman on some definitions for her demanding *Encyclopedia*, then I'd have to grab a bite of lunch before taking off for a rehearsal for, say, Aristophanes' *The Birds* down at Cooper Union that afternoon and/or early evening. Following another swallow of a sandwich, I might then be off to see la Broughton about planning the next showing at TFI. However, while finding during this period how to shift focus completely from one venture to another, no matter how different each might be, in the highest sense, there were inevitably some situations within some projects that might suffer as a result. Nor can anyone, except of course, a G.W. Bush or le bon Dieu, presume to be ever ominiscient and omnipresent! From time to time, one project or another is going to get short-changed in one way or another. For example, did I always have enough time to reflect on project Y before breaking off from project X to work on Y, bearing in mind that project Z was lurking around the corner? Something of this getting about—or scampering or "squirreling" around, as you like to call it—has obviously persisted in my makeup through all these years. Isn't that why, early on, you nicknamed me your squirrel, or *veveriță* in Romanian?

Similarly, I wonder now how I can really do justice in these letters of remembrance to the many friends, relatives, family members, colleagues, projects, producers, and critics—and their multifold stories that I try to relate to you in an interesting way. I fear that here and there I may sometimes short-change one or another by not giving him or her (or it) adequate attention. For example, have I really done justice to my very complicated, fascinating, and dear, lifelong friend Geraldine?

First of all, while I think I've already given you a pretty good idea of her unusual intelligence and her uncanny sense of what was "in" at any moment, I may have neglected to emphasize the tremendous sense of "presence" this striking, ample-bosomed, redhead made whenever she would enter a room, or join a scene, or crash into a conversation. Actually, in some respects, dear Nina, the two of you were quite similar. In your case, it's more evident, of course, when you speak Romanian. Then the whole room comes to attention. This used to happen, also, with Geraldine Lust. Unfortunately, she never fully cashed in, so to speak, on this gift, though undoubtedly it helped in her work with the Open Theater and with her proselytizing what she thought was the gospel of Artaud.

What is particularly remarkable about this Artaud phase of her life is that apparently she only first learned of the Artaud mystique through her reading of Mary Caroline Richards's translation of his *The Theatre and Its Double*, and with whom, I believe, she may have had some seminal conversations. However, she had had no actual, kinetic experience of Artaud: she never saw or did any Artaud "exercises." Did he ever develop any? As far as I know, he just left tantalizing, cryptic, often poetic, phrases and hints that could be read in many directions, or dimensions. Nor was Geraldine acquainted

315

with his startling play about the Cenci. And I don't remember ever discussing with her, or marvelling over, Artaud's unforgettable performance in Dreyer's haunting silent film, *The Passion of Joan of Arc*.

No, she seems to have developed this "doctrine" on her own, though there were winds of change stirring in many circles—witness Grotowski and some of the first gyrations of the Living Theatre. I remember her writing me from London in the early or mid-Fifties, where she must have picked up Artaudian murmurs at theater parties and gatherings. But her immersion went back, I'm sure, to some of her early broodings about our desperate need for a communal, communicative theater, a collective movement of the spirit. All this no doubt festered in her unconscious, aided and abetted by her deep love and almost ritual respect for modern dance, most especially the primitive myth-like dance dramas of Martha Graham. Then, too, there was her even earlier work with Theatre Lab, Mary-Averett Seelye, and other pioneer experimental theater people in her native Washington, DC. Somehow, Artaud seems to have served as a kind of binding force or coalescing agent between these various strands of influence. Remember my noting back in an earlier letter her very sensitive antennae and her acute sense of what might be brewing around her.

Unknowingly, perhaps, Ms. Lust invested more of herself into Artaud than she was aware of. Thus it was something of a personal Lust/Artaud doctrine that she passed on to her Open Theater disciples. (Knowing her better than her auditors did, I'd opt for it being more Lust than Artaud with which she imbued them!) Indeed, she became a kind of founding figure for the group, as her friend, playwright, and theater critic, Arthur Sainer, pointed out in his *Village Voice* obituary for Geraldine Lust: "Ritual, community, the unconscious—these were key operative words for her. Artaud, the ecstatic Artaud, the impossible Artaud was her mentor."

Ironically, this was not always the Geraldine I knew. For she had another more bourgeois side to her—the girl brought up in a vaudeville, cinematic tradition (via her adopted family?)—who loved and admired Bob Hope and Fred Allen; adored Judy Garland

and Ethel Merman; who would never miss what to me was the boring Ed Sullivan show. The one play she finished writing, *Seed from the East*, which I helped her produce, was actually not in the least avant-garde and didn't have an iota of Artaud in it (it could have used some)! I remember also that years earlier when I took her down to the Cherry Lane to see the Living Theatre's production of Gertrude Stein's *Dr. Faustus Lights the Lights*—while I was rehearsing their next production, the Rexroth play, *Beyond the Mountains*, with them—that somehow, to my surprise, she didn't dig the Stein opus at all. In fact, on that occasion, I recall how she leaned over and whispered in my ear that Judith Malina and Julian Beck were crazy.

Of course, she confided that only to me, since I'm quite sure she already sensed deep down that those two were onto something. As witness her later thriving on my recommendation of her to them to direct a staged reading of Beckett's great radio play, *All That Fall*. That association led to them letting her set up her first Artaud workshop on their premises. That, in turn, led later to her work with the Open Theater, which, strangely, took place in another world from mine, other than the one I thought I shared with her. No, this was obviously her own realm, and even though I had helped lead her into it, she didn't want me to enter it. Was she worried that I would compete with her about it? Or try to take it over? Which, of course, was an insane idea.

Actually, my problem in that stage of our relationship was that up until then I had always, in a sense, bowed to her priorities. Hadn't I set up the Cooper Union project largely to give her a chance to direct? For, ever since our joint directing class under Lee Strassberg during the late phase of the Dramatic Workshop, I always felt that that was her strongest suit. After all, she had done so in Washington during her periodic returns to that city, and obviously with some success, since they kept asking her back. Most noteworthy were her productions there of Christopher Fry's *Sleep of Prisoners* and, above all, Pirandello's *Six Characters in Search of an Author*, featuring the young, then still unknown, George C. Scott, which led to later rumors that she had "discovered" him long before he became a star. Yes, George did continue to have respect for her, and she remained friends for years with his discarded first wife, Pat Scott (who in time managed to make a place for herself downtown in the corridors of City Hall), but I'm afraid that good old George discovered himself!

In fact, Geraldine introduced Norman Shelly and me to Scott when he first "invaded" New York, and we immediately cast him in a Brazilian avant-garde play, *A God Slept Here*, a competent but uninspired version of the overworked Amphitryon legend, which somehow jointly we mounted at the historic Provincetown Playhouse, which at the time, Geraldine lived next door to. Peter Donat (nephew of the noted film star, Robert Donat, remember?) and his then-wife Michael Learned (who also went on to big things in TV and cinema) were in it, too. Norman directed. All three of them were sharp and brilliant. But the play itself was something of a dud. However, that didn't stop George. He went right on to make his first big splash with Joe Papp's Shakespeare Company. Norman eventually became one of Scott's poker partners. And later, George got me a part in that short-lived TV detective series of his which used to be filmed here in Manhattan. Then Hollywood and stardom beckoned, and it was goodbye George…

But back to our ever-planning, plotting, busybody Geraldine. For every ten projects we brooded on together, probably only one ever got hatched. We wrote each other countless letters on such subjects, even when we were both in the same town. Of course, still more was discussed over the phone or in person. The problem sometimes was to get Geraldine to focus on just one such project long enough to bring it to fruition. (Of course, as in all such endeavors, most brainstorms have to be discarded anyway.)

Yet there were times when she really could—and did—get things accomplished. For example, she, along with her friend Trudy Goth, refugee daughter of one of the former big bankers of Hungary (who had a retreat on the Isle of Elba, and whose mother presided over a huge elegant suite on the corner of 58th and Park Avenue), formed the Choreographers Workshop, which flourished in the late

Forties and early Fifties, and helped launch some good young choreographers. That's where, for example, the very successful African American Donald McKayle got his start. Another project that intrigued Geraldine, but me less, was doing the British writer Ronald Duncan's *The Death of Satan: a Comedy.* To my mind, Duncan was a better theater critic than playwright; also better as a librettist for Benjamin Britten than a popular boulevardier. Nevertheless, Geraldine was able to persuade the dour, never-smiling Lynne Michaels to get involved. Remember, I referred to Lynne earlier as the catalyst who brought me together with Phil Meister and Elaine Sulka over that never-produced Borchert play (but which ultimately led to our setting up The Cubiculo together)? Lynne and her much more amiable husband, an excellent professional set designer, Harry Baum (who did most of the Yiddish Art Theatre's sets), had gained control of a very good piece of property on the second floor of the northwest corner of 8th Street and Second Avenue, then the epicenter of the East Village—where the action was moving as the West Village became too expensive for Off-Off-Broadway. They produced it, and Geraldine directed the Satan play with some skill, but alas not enough to save it. (I'm glad I stood this one out!) But even had she shown more panache with it, I don't think the play would have survived.

Nevertheless, the experience gave Geraldine a good base from which to operate in the future, and I believe it was with Lynne's and Harry's help and enthusiastic support that she went on to miraculously procure the American stage rights for Jean Genet's *The Blacks*, which was eventually produced in their theater. Or maybe not so miraculously, since she was an old friend of the translator, Bernard Frechtman. Of course, this was a project I fully encouraged her in, and advised her about, from time to time. This time around, she was wise enough to take on a very experienced director, Gene Frankel, who knew the Off-Broadway scene inside-out and who had already worked well with black actors. So with a few other wise hands on the production team, *The Blacks* turned out to be quite a big success. Unfortunately, since Geraldine was more of an enabler than a financial producer (she had no money to invest in it), she did not profit from it, other than in prestige terms. Besides, its success was more artistic than financial.

After this all-absorbing venture, there was, naturally, a bitterness that the Genet project hadn't launched her into the higher echelons of the theater world as she had hoped it would, while at the same time there was a corresponding dwindling of her "commercial" stage ambitions. Indeed, it may have been the turning point for her becoming more involved with Artaud and that side of the avant-garde adventure. Certainly, it energized her return to the non-commercial world. Much later, she did experience one more spurt of notoriety when she organized, along with Lynne Michaels, a Marat-Sade Forum, which was held in Lynne's theater. It was headlined by Peter Brook, with whom Geraldine had been in correspondence about Artaud—though the actual forum ended up being more about a fusion of Artaudian and Brechtian techniques than an homage to Artaud—along with several other important figures on the then-current avant-garde scene and/or participants in Brook's *Marat-Sade* production: Ian Richardson, Leslie Fiedler, Norman Podhoretz, and Gordon Rogoff from Yale as Moderator. Plus, of course, Brook himself and Ms. Lust. A transcript of this heady forum was subsequently published in the prestigious *Tulane Drama Review*. Perhaps Geraldine's concluding remarks in launching the subsequent talks and discussion summarize the best of her thought in this realm: "I have worked a good many years in theater, and I find that it is a communal experience. People may come together as strangers, but they must not go away as strangers. This kind of fear is a waste not only of our energy but also of our beauty. It's an Artaudian concept that all fear can be deposited in the theater. I also believe that theater can illuminate our death as well as our life."

Interestingly enough, for some time before this event, I had been trying to get Geraldine to formulate and write down her basic concepts about Artaud and the kind of theater those challenging insights could lead to, as well as leave room for her own independent ideas about ritual theater, some of which I knew had preceded her Artaudian epiphany. Though these drafts were never realized sufficiently to be published, parts of them served as a basis for her opening remarks and contributions to that forum, as the above quotation shows. Could my work with her have borne some fruit? Here are a few further samples, my dear, for your delectation. They'll also give you an inkling, I think, of the considerable potential Geraldine had, and why I always tried to encourage her to make more of it:

> Parochial theatre would take place within a community, within a neighborhood. It would perhaps perform the ceremonies of the day, of the area, of the heart of its audience...
>
> Artaud wishes people to come to a particular kind of place with a particular kind of expectation of theatre. My necessarily limited experimentation to date with Artaudian theories has led me to an attempt (among other by-paths, other trials, etc.) to require of an audience that they also come prepared to be naked—figuratively speaking, i.e., unadorned. In our culture, this is of course not fully possible. But I would ask them, for example, to put their personal belongings in small lockers and to don an outer garment which allows them both an anonymity and a common identity...
>
> [This is] particularly apt in a time when the life process is being tampered with by scientists who can, with hormones and other devices or chemicals, affect our sex, our learning methods, our memory, our entire being on this planet and in outer space. [G. wrote this long before the newer gene science broke out.]
>
> When Artaud spoke of the cruelty of life, he meant primarily that creatures eat one another and that the heavens belabor the earth—that beauty rises out of excrement and that no state of being or feeling endures. The mass of life which began in the ocean churns and turns, over and over again, slowing

changing form, always moving, seeking a consumma-
tion and not knowing ever what that might or will or
should be.

*

Or, as that enigmatic Canadian poet/scholar, Anne Carson, reminds
us: Artaud died "alone in his pavilion. Seated at the foot of his bed./
Holding his shoe./ His body did not burst into unforgettable fragments at his death, no."

Ah yes, and as Hölderlin said in one of his shorter poems,
"the lines of life are varied." And Geraldine's conceptual being was
yet to go through some fascinating variations, including her strange
self-imposed exile the last few years of her life to what she, who heretofore had never seemed drawn to Nature, called a "potato patch" in
the Berkshires of Western Massachusetts! But more about that in a
later letter...

Except to note that harking back to Hölderlin's "lines of life"
reminds me that usually before Geraldine would fly off to Europe, or
even to comparatively close Chicago, curiously enough, she'd take
time to ask my ESP-talented late wife Ann to read her lifeline, or
consult the tea leaves!

Alchemistically yours?
Maurizio

March 21, 2009

Chère confidante:

When I first started writing these letters of remembrance to you—
largely at your insistent urging, as you'll recall—one of the reasons I
hesitated so much in the beginning to do so was that I didn't think my
limited memory would be able to meet the demands of a memoir. But
to my surprise, memories have emerged better than expected; what

has been perhaps most exciting about it all is the way one memory seems to feed another, as does a meandering, otherwise-lost tributary to a river. Thus, just the words "elephant calf" sent me back to the days of Theatre for Ideas, associated flashback ideas sprang up spontaneously, and before long my memory became crowded with other things that happened at TFI.

I could have gone on and on, but then had to stop that fount short so that I could have space and time for other memories or happenings. Besides, there is always a problem in conjuring up memories of theatrical or musical events, things that take place in time: just how does one cover that most important aspect of a concert or play or dance recital, the temporal sense? As Suzanne K. Langer formulated it in her famed study of the arts, these events take place in virtual time (something akin to a time warp, just as a painting embodies virtual space. Actually, I was lucky to be in her class at Columbia when she was working on that book. At times we students served as guinea pigs upon whom she tried out some of her ideas...

Which leads me to try to summarize for you the recent remarkable "Poussin in Nature" exhibit at the Metropolitan Museum I so much wanted you to see—and to which I still hoped to get you to come along with me when I returned the next week for a repeat visit. For Poussin's great "Dance to the Music of Time" (though that painting, alas, couldn't be in this exhibit) could almost serve as a kind of refutation of some of Langer's tenets, since, in a certain sense, the greater Poussin paintings enthrall you precisely because they cross invisible boundaries—virtual time and space and the mystery of life. This is especially true of the late paintings like "Spring and Summer" and "The Blind Orion Searching for the Rising Sun," which somehow put you in touch with eternity, by putting eternity onto the canvas. As Diderot said: "When it pleases him, this one [i.e., Poussin] knows how to interject fear and trembling into the middle of a rustic scene." Indeed, "Blind Orion," with the huge, giant figure of Orion dominating the right side of the canvas, and little Cedallion riding high on his shoulders pointing the way to the sunlight, is terrifying on first viewing, only to be somewhat softened when you look up and see

323

an angel in a cloud above them echoing the stance of Cedallion. An incredible work.

As you've no doubt heard from others, as well as from me, this terrific show focuses primarily on Poussin's landscape paintings, though there are two self-portraits, some genre scenes, and many drawings and studies for the landscapes (almost a show in itself); and then the paintings themselves, with their overwhelming presence. Perhaps it's the masterful way these are selected and set up, with ample space and breathing room between paintings, superb lighting, and excellent compact notes, that makes them so immediate, so compelling, much more so than those I visited at the more comprehensive Poussin exhibit I saw in Paris about nine or ten years ago, where some canvasses seemed a little dry or academic, and most of them were piled too close to one another. Not this time! Or have I matured enough to meet them on their own terms? Can I read a picture now like I read a poem, which is what Poussin himself urged his viewers to do, adding: "I am decidedly not among those who always sing in the same key." Again, note how music, painting, and poetry merge in Poussin's mellifulous world.

Speaking of maturing, did you realize that Poussin was a late bloomer? As with Cezanne, who idolized him, the early paintings don't always fully come off. Both artists usually had wonderful ideas but couldn't always manage to totally bring them together fruitfully, or masterfully, on their canvases. From time to time, there were a few awkward moments en route, but, of course, ultimately they did master their concepts magnificently—and that's history!

The exhibit shows clearly how Poussin matured constantly. And just as he seemed to master one phase, you see him in the next few years, as you move into the next gallery, trying something else. As quoted on the wall of one of these rooms, Cezanne once wrote: "A Provençal Poussin—that would fit me like a glove.... Like Poussin, I would like to put reason in the grass and tears in the sky." Or Poussin's own provocative observation: "Colors in painting are a snare to persuade the eye, like the charm of verses in poetry."

These quotes I've given you, and which I copied down on

my museum guide as I traversed the show, turned out to be a more inspiring companion than those talkathon earphone guides or even the short essays one encounters entering succeeding galleries—although I certainly don't mean to denigrate the fine work of the organizers of this almost perfect show. Not being a Poussin scholar, I didn't know prior to reading it there that day, how racked with syphilis our great artist was most of his life, and how therefore even more miraculous those late drawings and paintings are, where we see how he struggled painfully, hardly able to hold the brush steady anymore. But with what skill he compensated for that shortcoming! Imagine what torture all that adjustment must have been for such a precisionist. One can just feel with what courage he undertook those enormous-sized paintings: "Pyramus & Thisbe," "Adam and Eve" and "Landscape with Three Monks." As he himself wrote: "It is said the swan sings more sweetly when death approaches. I will try to imitate him and work better than ever." And he did!

So after almost weeping my way through that last gallery, I retraced my steps back through the earlier rooms, and gained even more insight than I experienced in my first viewings. I understood better Delacroix's compact summary of these middle landscapes, how, as he noted, "the mixture of buildings and majestic trees... leaves in the mind an impression of grandeur but also of melancholy and constitutes a separate genre for which he had neither models nor rivals." Or the often incredible humanizing of these paintings, where, as Di Chirico pointed out: "The trunks and branches... make one think of certain nudes by antique sculptors or of certain perfectly muscled limbs!" Maybe I should go back and look for touches of Poussin in some of the late Di Chirico's—if they have any at the Met? More likely at MOMA...

Finally, we must also point out examples of Poussin's occasional sense of humor, especially in the drawings and that subsequent little painting, which has two *putti* battling each other astride little goats to the amusement of several charming nymphs. Or the surprising number of quite openly erotic paintings in the first two or three rooms. Though the late paintings certainly are not shy of a more mature eroticism. And, of course, there's nothing in this show like the dark, almost menacing "Hannibal Crossing the Alps" that's in the wonderful Frick Gallery here in New York, or the rough humor of the child Jupiter sucking a she-goat in that incredible "Nurture of Jupiter" canvas in the Dulwich in London… But you would have seen treasures enough! Actually, the Met could have boasted (and probably did) an exceptional *embarras de richesses* of extraordinary exhibitions those days. In addition to the Poussin, there was a very good showing of highlights from Courbet's oeuvre, covering quite well most aspects of that iconoclastic master's extremely varied life's work with all its strengths, quirks, and glories—but which dimmed somewhat next to the Poussin. Maybe because it tried to be too all-inclusive? Besides, you're not a real Courbet fan, as I recall. But I am, and sought to see it again.

Running simultaneously with these two giants, the Met devoted a well-mounted exhibit of Jasper Johns' "gray" paintings (along with some prints and drawings), more properly described perhaps as the "use of gray" in his paintings of targets, flags, maps, alphabets, and numbers. This made for an overflow of monochromatic, achromatic, and just plain gray canvases, which, in spite of the fact that Johns is generally considered our greatest living painter, I found quite monotonous and, for the most part, uninspired. "'Tis pity," as Polonius describes Hamlet's behavior to the King and Gertrude. "Pity 'tis, 'tis true," as Polonius goes on, and as we feel, as one felt going from one dull gray stretch to another. "More's the pity" because, of course, there was extraordinary talent and technique displayed here as Jasper J. takes a fragment or a motif and works variations on it through oil, encaustic, collage, even the use of sculpt medal. He also shows considerable skill with charcoal and ink in the prints and drawings.

To be fair, I'm sure you'd find, as I did, that a goodly number of the paintings certainly transcend the almost ubiquitous grayness and limited vocabulary into "enlightenment," shall we say? "False Start" does, the one colored canvas with the least gray, which started the show, as did its black, white, and gray companion piece,

"Jubilee"; then there was the strange, haunting "Tennyson" with its echoes of Rauschenberg; similarly, a few of the map and flag paintings really grabbed you; also some of the hatch-mark series with their varied schematics; and, above all, the later "Racing Thoughts" and several of the so-called Catenary Series, those with the sometimes playful, sometimes arbitrary, curved strings, also ensnared you. But the show as a whole left me rather depressed, if not a little melancholy, with its pervading sense of loss and emptiness. Yet I felt that few of the works rose to the level of "utter emotional isolation," which a highly regarded British critic seemed to have experienced. Or could this reaction be more credible coming from a more objective European viewer—and I, as an American, missed something? Incidentally, I do think that an extension or vast enlargement of one of these fertile "grays" might have made a better set for the current revival of Beckett's *Endgame* at BAM than the one it had!

Actually, don't you sense, my dear, that Jasper Johns hemmed himself in far too long by limiting himself to flags, numbers, and targets for so many years? Where is the inner life in these quiddities? Technically superb as they may be, many of them leave you hanging—even without the "catenary" string! As Johns says somewhere: "My experience of life is that it's very fragmented. I would like my work to... [show] those differences." Well, in any case, I'm sure this "gray" immersion will make me appreciate his next showing that much more!

But enough paintings for awhile—except to note that it's amazing how a single painting can strike a chord that resonates for centuries. Duchamp tried to stifle that sort of thing by wiping out Mona Lisa with a moustache. But a painting like "A Dance to the Music of Time" seems to have continued to haunt, inspire, and cheer people on in all the arts for over three hundred years. We know that Sir Joshua Reynolds revered Poussin, and that the 18th century produced a number of embarrassing little Poussins. But perhaps the twentieth century gave him one of his greatest tributes, namely, Matisse's glorious round dance painting that ended up in the Hermitage. And, in another art, Anthony Powell's remarkable twelve-novel sequence, bearing the same title, and England's answer, if any was needed, to Proust's *A la recherche du temps perdu*. Also think of that extremely well-made sequence of British TV dramatizations of Powell which engrossed us recently via DVD. One of the most telling tales of the series is how we watch the rise of a mediocrity—the inimitable Widmerpol—to a Lordship, and then his subsequent rapid descent into groupie madness. As we wondered how our painfully dull supreme American mediocrity—I should also say dangerous—George W. Bush (shades of the mad George III of England?) could have been brought low, long ago. Or am I being too vengeful? After all, haven't you been cringing at the sight of him on TV and calling him "Mass Murderer" for the past eight years?

With hopes that we can wipe the slate clean with our new promising president and start over again with renewed vigor and restored honor, I am

your still somewhat optimistic

M.

July 10, 2009

Dear, wise Athena:

I've just run into another piece of luck in piecing together these memories of my past! Today on leaving the Grand Army Plaza library, and on my way to catching a bus on Vanderbilt Avenue, someone called out my name in a tone of sudden recognition. As usual, in such situations, he remembered me better than I remembered him. It turned out that he was an actor from my days with the Gate Theatre down on Second Avenue fifty some years ago, whom I don't recall having seen since! Not only that, he seems to have caught me in a number of shows and concerts I had no idea he had attended. Had he been too shy to go backstage and say hello? But I didn't dare ask him that during our too-short conversation before the bus came along and whisked me away. I did learn, however, that he had heard me in the concert version of *Threepenny Opera* I did at Lewisohn Stadium with Lotte Lenya, and certainly in all the roles I played at the Gate, including my work on Boris Tumarin's *Merchant of Venice* , which I discussed in an earlier letter.

But what surprised me most was that he remembered seeing the little Haydn comic opera, *The Apothecary*, which I had directed in spring 1962 for Actors' Opera and which was put on in the same space at the former Women's Y on 50th Street and Eighth Avenue, where Alvin Ailey established his first home. I pause to tell you especially about this Haydn episode because of the extraordinary thing that happened on opening night. The tenor lead, Maurice Stern, a veteran of City Opera, had come down with laryngitis the night before and could hardly open his mouth the next day. What were we to do? In such a small, non-paying, Off-Off-Broadway scaled opera production, there's neither time nor money to train understudies. Luckily, the conductor had a tenor, David Bender, who was coaching with him at that time and who was most opportunely an excellent sight reader. We called Bender in at once, and that night he sang the role from the score, standing next to the conductor, Kurt Saffir, at the harpsichord, on the audience level below that small stage, though off to the left, as I mimed it on stage, mouthing the words our valiant lifesaver tenor was singing. After all, as director, I knew all the stage business, of which there was a lot, since I had staged it in a modified *commedia dell'arte* style that fit this charming piece of abracadabra.

And it worked! So much so that people came up at the end and congratulated me on my singing it so well. This was a real shocker: I hadn't sung a note! It was all what they now call "lip-synch." I could almost understand this happening with people who didn't know me personally. But with some of my friends who surely knew I was a bass-baritone, not a tenor, how could they have been so easily fooled? Incredible, isn't it, my dear? But they were. The power of the gesture over the word.

Also important to note: the opera was sung in a translation that fit the English text to the music almost like a glove, while managing to retain the humor and style of the Italian original. Remember my earlier vow to pursue opera in English? That was one of the main reasons I took on the project. What a pity, then, that the guiding spirit of Actors' Opera, the charming, but haughty, Naomi Ornest, who also sang the female soprano lead and had already achieved some success with her little company, including a passable revival of Handel's *Ezio*, suddenly gave up the whole admirable enterprise, lock, stock, and barrel. So down went Actors' Opera, Humpty Dumpty, and the redoubtable Mme. Ornest along with it. From neither of whom have we heard a word since!

Quite a shame for me, too, in a way, since directing opera might have been a better path for me to have pursued after that hectic decade of the 1950s during which, as you have seen, my dear, I did a little of practically everything, including a dance drama of Anna Sokolow's. It was her version of the classic Yiddish play S. Ansky's *The Dybbuk*, in which I danced/mimed the rejected bridegroom whose bride-to-be gets possessed by the soul of her dead husband, and its tragic aftermath. That's where I first met Siegfried Landau, who composed the score for it. I also directed the much more jolly *Bartered Bride* at Cooper Union a few years later; then produced Tom Johnson's *Four Note Opera* at The Cubiculo; and subsequently several operas at BAM with, and for, the Brooklyn Philharmonic. However, by that time, I was so busy running the BPO and The Cubiculo I wasn't able to "cash in" on these productions by following up properly what leads they might have provided into the extremely competitive world of opera...

That my old friend from the Gate had travelled all the way up to Lewisohn Stadium for the *Threepenny Opera* in concert form there on the New York Philharmonic's summer series was less surprising, even though at that time Lenya was nowhere near the big celebrity she was to become (at least in this country) after appearing in the musical *Cabaret* on Broadway and in that James Bond movie *From Russia with Love*, in which she frightened even those of us who knew her personally! Less well known, but surely more subtle, was her superb performance in Tennessee Williams's *The Roman Spring of Mrs. Stone*. Actually, my acquaintance with Lenya much preceded that concert or those films.

Remember my mentioning Anneliese Gellhorn in one of my earlier letters, the assistant to Felix Gerstmann who had recommended me to Mme. Piscator, albeit with a well-timed warning? I had met Anneliese during my Dramatic Workshop days. She, too, had studied there. Indeed, that's where she got to know Mme. Piscator. A fine actress, though afflicted with a not-too-bad German accent; quite good looking, but not a screen beauty; with a possible commercial potential for playing suffering European refugee widows and similar roles, but too shy to compete in the casting jungle of our theater and cinema. A "*Mischling*," which helped her escape Nazi Germany. But also may have made her too proud to use her connections with those members of the famed Gellhorn family who had settled in America before the war, long before her. Thus, the remarkable journalist, and third wife of Hemingway, Martha Gellhorn, was her first cousin. Walter Gellhorn, distinguished professor of law at Columbia University and a strong voice on the American left during the McCarthy days, was a caring, though somewhat remote, uncle. Yet honest, cautious, too-modest Anneliese—who also had a beautiful, sweet soprano and was a good musician—ended up working clerically in the office of that quite decent Viennese exile impresario, the ebullient Felix Gerstmann. If only she had had half the chutzpah and daring of her famed writer cousin!

Nevertheless, she proved to be an efficient, loyal Girl Friday to Gerstmann. (What is the German equivalent of our American slang "Girl Friday" nomer?) It was Anneliese who invited me to my first Sylvester Abend anywhere—a wonderful Viennese New Year's Eve concert at Town Hall back in 1951. Star and headliner of the event was Lotte Lenya, in her first public appearance since the premature death of her husband, Kurt Weill, eighteen months earlier. She brought the house down with each number. It was the first time I had heard those great Brecht/Weill songs in live performance, although earlier I had often heard them on recordings. Of course, never again did they sound as thrilling: for that occasion was emotionally laden with Weill friends, survivors, mourners—and an infinitude of memories. And, mercifully, it brought the great Lenya out of retirement.

Fortunately, I was to hear Lenya do these songs many times after this event in subsequent Weill/Lenya concerts at Town Hall and Carnegie Hall that Gerstmann produced. I was the bass voice in the male quartet that usually backed her up in the numbers from *Mahagonny*, *Threepenny*, and *Happy End*; down-to-earth and friendly an hour or so before a concert, she was almost preternaturally terrified and withdrawn just before going on. Also, it was interesting how her voice seemed to drop a half step at each succeeding concert, so that we had to keep changing keys to accommodate her! As you may recall, dear Ninotchka, in the Pabst film version of *Threepenny* she was a high soprano. By the time she paced the stage of the DeLys, she had become a female baritone! (You can follow a similar gradual lowering of voice range in the films and recordings of Paul Robeson, where his "Ole Man River" rendition kept sinking a quarter tone or more with each new appearance on film or on each new record.)

Riding the success of these concerts, Anneliese and I kept urging Gerstmann to produce *Threepenny* Off-Broadway, and tried to line up a possible American collaborator/producer for him. But Carmen Capalbo beat us to the wire with his wonderful production of the Marc Blitzstein translation at Theatre DeLys (now called the Lucille Lortel) on Christopher Street in the West Village, an ideal small theater space for it, and a perfect location for such a seedy drama, with our own colorful, native prostitutes, male and female, ranging the adjacent street and nearby environs! An interesting sidelight to this is how Lenya used to pace the space fenced off from the street to the backstage entrance as Jenny, queen of the whores, every night for half an hour, in preparation for going on that night. Or so I was told by veterans of the first-year run of the play while she remained in it, for I didn't join that production until its second year, first as the Reverend, understudying Peachum, and then later as Peachum himself.

That led to my being chosen to sing Peachum in a concert

version of *Threepenny* a couple of years later when it was presented by the New York Philharmonic on one of the summer programs it used to give at Lewisohn Stadium uptown on the City College campus (where I had taken my ASTP training in German before going overseas). But I'm sure I told you several times about that event, which I so much wish you could have attended—certainly one of my best performances in one of my best roles. At the end of that concert, as you may recall, I was congratulated backstage by Lenya's friend, the divine Dietrich, dressed in a scarlet, form-fitting knit dress, who kissed me after first asking: "Where did you get that feeling for Berlin?" and then adding, in her delicious, husky accent: "I've never before heard such diction in an Amerikan!" Of course, that left me walking on clouds for weeks afterwards—the very time slot when you were probably having your problems with the Writers' Union in Romania for not following Party guidelines, and never dreamed then that you'd be exiled one day in capitalist New York.

Fortunately, I was able to fly Mother in for the occasion—her only trip to New York, alas. I had hoped to do the same for her to see *Fiddler*, a few years later, but she died unexpectedly during the first year of that run. Unfortunately, Father was not in shape to make that trip to Lewisohn Stadium with Mother; and he had left this world before *Fiddler* ever hit the boards. How I still regret those losses and their unfortunate timing!

Between that Stadium concert and *Fiddler*, I did a later concert version of *Threepenny* at Carnegie, this time in German, with Polyna Stoska as Mrs. Peachum, Ralph Herbert as Macheath, and Ludwig Donath as Tiger Brown. (Though we missed that wonderful comedienne, Charlotte Rae, who did Mrs. Peachum for us at the Stadium.) Looking back, it strikes one as strange how seldom these two worlds—the exiled-German concert audience and that of the big Broadway stage followers—ever overlapped. Thus, once during the first two years of the run of *Fiddler*, when Gerstmann asked if I could get a night off (and up to then I hadn't missed one show) for one of his Weill concerts at Carnegie Hall, our producer Hal Prince was very surprised. He had no idea such events were taking place. But he did let me off for that night! Years later, as you know, he turned into a Weill aficionado himself and became much more knowledgeable about things Weimar/German/Weill than years earlier when I had asked for that very short leave.

Yes, New York is a mighty complicated city, with scores of special groups and unique interests, not just nationalities, each drawing its own audiences and needing its own theaters, concert halls, community centers, and college campuses for its own special events. Much like, as I sometimes tease you, dear Nina, my saying that in New York one could eat in a different country every night of the year, the range of restaurants is so great. So, similarly, one could end up sitting amidst a totally different audience as well, if not several different sites, every night of the year!

My noting above the appearance of Ludwig Donath in that original German version of *Threepenny* reminds me of the excellent intimate studio production that Uta Hagen put on and directed several years before that event of Tolstoy's heavy, searing, heart-breaking but much too rarely performed tragedy, *The Power of Darkness*, in which Donath played a major role. Prior to that, I had only seen him in a number of Hollywood films, many of which I'm sure you saw in Romania, where he played a variety of nefarious Germans or Nazi villains—roles which gave him little chance to display his wide range of considerable talents. But after the war, Hollywood had stopped making such films, and so he had settled in New York. Which is probably why he did this play for Uta (and no doubt, gratis); and why she did it for herself, for us, for the world.

Indeed, that's why all of us work from time to time in the obscure burrows of Off- and Off-Off-Broadway, and in even smaller venues such as Hagen's studio or Broughton's Theatre for Ideas, where we did Valéry's *Mon Faust* and Brecht's *Elephant Calf*, which I told you about in earlier letters, both of which took place before I met you. Or, only two years ago, why I participated in that concert reading of Milton's *Samson Agonistes* with Nancy Bogen's Lark Ascending group for even more highly specialized audiences, which you did see and hear. Or later, that still more intimate Wordsworth night with its "Intimations of Immortality" and "Lines at Tintern Abbey" moments. Could this be what Cioran meant when he said: "We grow wise when we ought to be depressed"? Or why many people think we toilers in the seas of Off- and Off-Off-Broadway, and sometimes even smaller venues—usually for little or no money—are mad?

Insanely yours,
M.

October 22, 2009

Dear, most empathetic Ninetta:

Strange how an off-beat incident in an obscure little restaurant can set off a memory moment of something only metaphorically related, which happened backstage in a concert hall in no way connected to that particular restaurant about thirty years earlier. Thus, yesterday, while savoring a quiet, peaceful, delicious lunch with seven different appetizers in a tiny Korean restaurant around the corner from my Brooklyn address, I was startled by a sudden, sharp altercation between the proprietor and his comparatively new waiter—at least I hadn't seen the victim there before. Not loud, not violent, probably not noticed by anyone but me. Yet humiliating for that poor young man. And most likely due to a simple misunderstanding. How was I to know?

However, it reminded me of how roughly the director of the Brooklyn Boys Chorus that was performing a difficult modern work with us, the BPO, at BAM some twenty-five years ago, treated one of his slightly more mature boy sopranos one night, just before the children were to go on stage. For, the way he was harshly and loudly berating this boy right then and there in front of his singing mates, I was afraid the choir master might strike him at any moment. So I rushed up, ordered him to take it easy, then cleared the way for all the boys, including the victimized one, to take their places peaceably on stage.

I tell you about this minor incident because, unbeknownst to me at the time, one of our conductor Lukas Foss's composition students, a tall, lanky blonde then teaching at Goucher College just outside Baltimore, but visiting the BPO on this occasion because of her interest in the program, witnessed this unpleasant and somewhat embarrassing backstage *contretemps*. The lady in question was later to become a very dear friend as well as an inveterate "fan" of my work in theater and music. And once, several years later, while we were sunning ourselves in deck chairs beside a swimming pool in lower Eastern Maryland where we had gone to escape the heat and stuffiness of summer in Baltimore, and reminiscing about how we had met, she told me it was my defending that little boy soprano at that crucial moment that convinced her I was someone she would want to know better!

Of course, you must have guessed by now about whom I speak? You've met her on a number of occasions, usually at concerts where one of her compositions was to be played: Faye-Ellen Silverman. Strangely enough, while I recall this incident quite clearly, as well as some of our earlier meetings and encounters in Manhattan, such as her inviting me to her apartment in the Masters' Institute on upper Riverside Drive for drinks with a small group of her music-making friends, but most especially to meet the very good violist with whom I thought she was involved romantically at that time, I can't pin down exactly just when I first met Faye-Ellen. Though I'm sure it was through some music-related matter. And there were numerous other such meetings before and after the viola soirée. For example, there was the time I recall singing one of the roles in an audition of her one-act opera, *The Miracle at Nemirov*, based on a favorite Yiddish folk tale by Peretz, which we did for the new conductor and music director of the then-suddenly revived 92nd Street Y Opera. Indeed, Faye had come all the way up from Baltimore for the occasion; for by that time she seemed to have disappeared into Baltimore and environs, where she had been awarded a good position as a teacher of music history and composition at Goucher College, a job for which she was eminently well qualified.

In any event, I remember Faye coming back to New York to see one of my Off-Off-Broadway productions several months after that choirboy incident, and our having drinks after the show. I think that was the time I was startled by her inviting me down to Baltimore for a weekend, where I could stay at her apartment! Because, as she pointed out in her often rather charming school-teacher way, I needed a rest from the mad rush of my double life, my "Tale of Two Cities" existence, as I sometimes characterized that going back and forth to my work in Brooklyn and my other projects in Manhattan. Well, she was certainly right about the need, and, though skeptical about a stay-over in the apartment of a lady I had not exactly been courting, even though we were certainly good friends, I said to myself, why not? Besides, this was some time after my break-up with Daniela.

Well, the proposed weekend rolled around off the calendar, and I rolled into Baltimore's Union Station. There she was, Faye, prompt, well groomed, on time. She whisked me into her little Toyota, which took us to Towson, the northern suburb where she lived and taught, pointing out a few of the felicities of metropolitan Baltimore as we passed them en route. On later occasions, we would take more leisurely tours of the old, historic center of Baltimore, with its venerable music college, Peabody, the Baltimore Art Institute, and the superb Walton Gallery for Modern Art with its rooms full of Matisse paintings and sculpture collected by the justly famed Baltimore Cone sisters—a milieu you would very much enjoy. We also toured the then-just-completed, rehabilitated waterfront with its enormous new aquarium and colonial Fort McHenry looming out on the horizon over the large bay—the site immortalized by the lyrics for our national anthem by Francis Scott Key.

Since that first weekend was supposed to be a resting period for yours truly, I was treated to a specially cooked dinner, graciously served by my beautiful, new hostess. This was followed by a little music talk; some listening to passages from several of Faye's latest compositions; and a quick survey of her excellent music library. Then, at some point, apparently, we ended up on the spacious davenport, still talking a bluestreak, when, according to Faye's later recall of that evening, I must have moved or "hopped" closer to her, much as I seem to have done some years earlier on Daniela's sofa. Those pieces of furniture seem to be designed for such adventures...

Another memory I have of that first evening (or was it the second?), is that, while helping clear away the aftermath of her very special, self-prepared dinner, I gently stopped Faye from throwing out one of the more tasty leftovers and recommended a way to transform it into a new dish for the next day. Finding her quite surprised and skeptical that I knew anything about cooking, I assured her, donning my best French accent, that it was a recipe I had picked up after the war when I studied French *haute cuisine* for a magic spell at Fontainebleu. She was rather surprised at this sudden turn of events but also somehow impressed. Especially when, the next evening, after tasting my unique mélange (which turned out better than I expected), Faye was even more amazed. But it wasn't until I boarded the train back to NYC the third morning that, *sans* accent, I confessed that I never ever even visited Fontainebleu, to my eternal regret. Expecting her to be furious at my hoax, I was delighted she took it like the good sport she usually was.

Which she continued to be for several years at her place, which for awhile became my cherished Baltimore retreat. The train trip there, in itself, always proved a good way to unwind from the accumulated stress of the past week. Even this, Faye was able to treat with some of her dry humor. I remember a little mauve card inserted in one of her letters, inquiring: "Do you want visitation rights on the toothbrushes or do I get permanent custody?"

Faye also turned out to be an inveterate traveler, which I learned that she had been long before we met, she being one of the more respectable members of the hippy generation that roamed post-war Europe and the Middle East for years, with backpacks and nights in hostels. It will probably surprise you to learn that she even toured Romania before I ever set foot there. She would also take more conventional trips from time to time with her mother (also a teacher), who seems to have passed that traveling talent down to her daughter. So when I could escape for slightly longer periods—her college teaching schedule was much less demanding than my *Tale of Two Cities* one!—I'd join her on her *Wanderlust*.

At first, these trips would be short excursions to or through Maryland, Washington, DC, nearby northern Virginia, and the southeast corner of Pennsylvania, where we took in the standard sites such as reconstructed colonial Williamsburg; some of the historic Richmond spots; one of the Chesapeake Bay crab fishing islands where the native-born population still speak Elizabethan English; the surprisingly good Dupont museums and botanic gardens; and the verdant Andrew Wyeth area—plus, of course, catching major art shows in Washington, Baltimore, and Philadelphia. But I could rarely get away for long-enough periods to luxuriate for a week, say, in Europe or the Caribbean, although once we were able to fit in a long weekend in Guadeloupe. And somehow we did manage "flying down to Rio" for one great splurge—eight days below the Equator. In fact, isn't Rio exactly on the Tropic of Capricorn latitude line?

Ironically enough, it was in that beautiful tropical paradise of a city, with its inimitable fresh fruit breakfasts; its relatively calm bay which you could dip into at any time of the day or night; its fascinating grab-bag mixtures of architectural styles, including the wonderfully designed promenade tiles; its unique Samba schools with their weekly Saturday-night showcases, one of which we attended; and its own form of voodoo-like religion (the Brazilian name for which eludes me at the moment), which we sampled on another night; not to mention the incomparable beaches—I repeat—it was there where the first sputterings of disagreement between us seemed to well up, although we both tried to take them in our stride, not wanting to interrupt this Tropic of Capricorn idyll, and did so rather well for a while...

Had we stopped to analyze the situation, we probably would have realized earlier that the charm of our Baltimore weekends and our other little tours, which took at most a long weekend, had been gradually dissipating, and that the longer period together in Rio, where we were forcedly together all the time, and where, when one of us would want to go to Avenue A and the other to Boulevard B, it became a bit of a problem. It probably started the first night there, when I wanted us to explore the downtown center in the evening hours, and Faye was too tired to comply. This was climaxed on one of our last nights there, when she didn't want to take in the sights on Cross-Roads X, and so I went by myself, leaving her alone in the albeit friendly hotel we were lucky to have landed in, directly on Copocabana Beach itself. But, of course, it was much too dangerous for her to go out alone in Rio at night. It was even somewhat dangerous for me. Which made her rightfully worried about my taking off solo, but which strained the overall situation a bit more...

Well, as you know, my dear Nina, Nature usually takes care of these matters for us. What happened was that after the Rio episode, the weekend retreats gradually diminished in number and intensity, so that by the time Faye moved back to New York, we were already seeing one another less frequently. Moreover, with her now in the same city, the glamour, relief, and fun of a trip to a private retreat vanished.

Of course, there were other reasons why the original euphoria could not go on forever, as the old adage goes. Faye herself, being a very intelligent and perceptive woman, summed up one aspect of it quite succinctly, and actually charmingly, in a letter to me during that period, wherein she reminded me: "I realize that you, the secret romantic who brought me flowers but left them on the train, are afraid of commitment..."

No doubt the major stress on the relationship had been her growing need for just that, and, even more difficult for me to bear, her related desire for a child, something for which I felt I could never again take on the responsibility, especially being so much older than Faye, plus the past and present burden of poor Jacob I was still carrying. How could I dare have another child? How could I take on those exhausting physical tasks of raising a baby and later playing games with it as it grew into a lively, scampering child, now that I was already an ancient specimen myself? Also, how could she, though considerably younger than me, manage all this, plus keep up with her heavy teaching load and total inexperience raising children? So I would challenge her: are you prepared for an around-the-clock child-looking-after schedule for at least two or three years?

Most of this, I think, she certainly understood. As she went on in that letter: "Perhaps what has changed is that we both entered the relationship not wanting to be 'involved'; no real letters, no expensive presents, independent decisions, etc. But now I've re-evaluated my life and realize that, having truly lived alone, I now want a network of love and emotional support. The child (one only, at most) is only part of what I want. You probably sense this, and hence your fear is understandable."

Well, as you can imagine, my dear, it was a slow, sad, difficult parting of the ways. Nonetheless, as you also know and understand—and sanction—Faye and I have remained good friends ever since and see and/or consult one another from time to time. I go to her concerts; she comes to my events. *Et voilà: c'est la vie.*

Ironically enough, I need hardly remind you, next weekend you and I will probably be getting a good taste of American academic life (somewhat like those excursions I used to take to Towson, Maryland, to see Faye), when we'll be staying on the campus of Rhode Island University in Kingston, near Providence. There you'll be reading your poetry for the Ocean State Poetry Festival in the late afternoon and attending a concert that evening devoted solely to your own music, which they have sponsored in your honor. Hooray! Finally, Americans will be hearing your music. Then we'll spend the next day in nearby Providence with your dear friend, Marguerite Dorian, that wonderful schoolmate of yours from that extraordinary "ghetto school" in Bucharest that you both attended over seventy years ago, with a teaching staff of elite Jewish origin, drawn from members of the University, who had been forced out of their college positions by the Nazi controlled regime! Right? Are you set to go? Yes, yes, we'll soon be on the train heading east to New England, along that beautiful Atlantic shoreline. Don't you look forward to it, too?

Love,

M.

February 23, 2010

Dearest Nina:

I don't know why, but somehow during these last few days, my thoughts seem to have been going back often to my brother Lester, who, alas, was taken prematurely from us before you ever had a chance to meet him. Maybe they were further prompted by that recent call from Minneapolis from Uncle Meyer's branch of the family, telling me that Sylvia, his daughter, and probably my favorite cousin, had just passed away. In these last years, ever since Lester's death, she had been the only relative really interested in maintaining our family tree, as it were, and watering it occasionally. (Grand-nephew Allen seems to have lost interest in the project.) Before that, it was Lester who served as the go-between among our various relatives, visiting a different branch every year, if he could manage to fit it into his perennially busy teaching schedule. Fortunately, dear Sylvia, with the wonderful natural smile, passed that mantle on to one of her daughters, Anne, before she left us. (I've never seen Anne, only talked with her on the phone; does she have the same smile?) Reminder: we should send copies of some of these letters to her and the family left in Minnesota!

Now, how to go about describing Lester to you, and giving you a more rounded picture of him? Well, first of all, let's consider his physicality. If you had seen the three of us together—Lester, Jacob, and me—you would have thought Jacob was his son, not mine, because as you could see from that photograph of him I once showed you, Jacob was built more like Lester than me; they both had a heavier, wider bone structure and both were taller. And, alas, both were prone to putting on too much weight. (They were both definitely rounder.)

But Lester certainly had less melancholy in his nature than Jacob. His was an optimistic soul: he was a militant idealist and a natural teacher. He was also a scholar, a strong union member, a faculty organizer, a New Deal/Fair Deal liberal, as well as a wonderful

342

human being, one whom everyone warmed up to. Hence the love his pupils had for him, and the respect and affection his fellow teachers also had. As cousin Marvin, Sylvia's twin brother, said at Lester's Memorial Service in Buffalo back in 1994, "Politically, we saw eye to eye on the important issues of the day (Marvin is, or was, a professor of political science at Maryland University), both of us being unabashed liberals. Lester was then, and remained until the end of his life, a champion of the underdog and the dispossessed." Indeed, it was on one of his "good deed" missions—showing his troubled young nephew, Glen, whom I told you about in an earlier letter, the sights and wonders of ever-dynamic, expanding Toronto—that he was felled by a sudden cardiac arrest comparable to that which Jacob recently suffered, though in his case, I think Lester had had more warning from his doctor of danger ahead. He, too, was then in his early fifties.

Dozens of similar tributes were articulated that day. For it seems that Lester effortlessly made each friend feel uniquely his. What was so extraordinary was the way he embraced everyone—students, fellow teachers, ex-colleagues from all over the country with whom he had worked either academically or in politics. His mailing list was national, nay, international. And the recipients all became part of his ever-growing family. Moreover, there was never anything sanctimonious about Lester—certainly nothing saintly! His earnestness was saved by a rare, innate sense of humor, which he no doubt inherited from our wry, witty father, who, even from a hospital bed, could still find the paradox that sets life into a spin. (Remind me to tell you more soon about my dear father, whose last years were full of suffering and pain.)

But in his obsessions, Lester could also sometimes be a little trying. As one of his women colleagues said at that Memorial: "Lester was smart, funny, kind, concerned, dedicated—and a pest! He was always wanting us to fix things just because they ought to be fixed. He wanted people to know about things just because knowing them was right and reasonable. He wanted everyone's ideas to be represented just because that was morally proper. What a pest!" Yes, indeed, he was also the kind of pest who wanted to fix the world as well. "We don't have to have poverty, war, inequality, crime," he would passionately proclaim. World fixers almost always get on someone's goat! Can you imagine how impossible Thomas Bernhard's world fixer (remember that play of his, *Der Weltverbesserer*, which I translated?) would have been, had we met this "world improver" in real life instead of in a German theater in the former East Berlin? Yes, I suppose Lester was in some ways the kind of pest you call in Romanian a "*pacoste*." What a wonderful word: *Pacoste*! After all, Ghandi was also a *Pacoste*, a great pest to the British. As was Tolstoy to everyone...

So abundantly generous with his time, talents, and energies was this "pest" that it's a wonder he accomplished as much as he did. Of course, it also meant burning the midnight oil way past midnight. I used to worry about him leaving his office often as late as 2:00 or 3:00 in the morning. (Most of our phone calls took place around 1:00am) For he always had to catch up! Perhaps he had given a student too much time. Or perhaps he had had too many deadlines to meet that day because he couldn't say "no," and so his workday spilled over into a long worknight.

That's also why Lester's legacy was more that of a top-notch teacher than that of the writer or scholar or even the politico he might have become, although I tried many times, and in many ways, to persuade him to cut back on some of his public life and to devote more of his talents to setting down his ideas in a lasting form. I was convinced he did have a contribution to make that way. And, yes, actually he sometimes came near achieving such goals, or skirting them, such as when he served for a few years as the book review editor of *Publius* and also as a longtime member of its Editorial Advisory Board. He was one of the original members of a pioneer workshop in American Federalism from 1955 to 1964, which he joined after his stint as an officer with the U.S. Army Transportation Corps in France. (Unfortunately, his command post was just outside complacent, bourgeois Bordeaux rather than near anarchic, cosmopolitan Paris.) This led him to co-editing a book on "Cooperation and

Conflict" and later got him a job in the Minnesota state government, which, in turn, led to his deep involvement with Hubert Humphrey's presidential campaign of 1962. Had Humphrey won, Lester's life may well have gone the political route. Indeed, he was so involved politically that he was checked out by the F.B.I. I know this for a fact because one day, out of the blue, one of its solemn, unsmiling, black-suited investigators quizzed me about him for about an hour and a half at the Municipal Building in Brooklyn. As a friend of his from that Washington period remarked at the Memorial Service: "Had Lester chosen the easy course and stayed in his Federal Government position in the Sixties, there is no doubt he would soon have become a secure top bureaucrat, probably in the Senior Executive Service, with a very comfortable income. Instead, he gave up what he saw as a lesser contribution and returned to the lower rungs of the academic world in order to add to human knowledge, teach, and serve."

Hence, disappointed and discouraged by Washington, Lester returned to the academic life. His teaching engagements were such that he got to know almost every part of this big country of which you, my dear Nina, and indeed most Americans, have seen only one tenth as much as him. I won't go into a long tale of his many different teaching posts; suffice it to say that he taught at numerous colleges and universities, especially in the South: San Antonio, Texas; Tallahassee, Florida; Atlanta, Georgia, among others. Plus his two State government jobs in California and Minnesota!

But there was one factor—his Achilles heel, one might say—that prevented him from becoming a big-time professor or scholar-in-residence at one of those colleges: namely, that he never completed the doctoral thesis he had started at the University of Chicago before he went overseas with the Army. True, he would try over and over again to use whatever his current position was as a practical, take-off point from which to finish a survey project he had started back in Chicago, adjusting it to his current position (and usually in consultation with his old Chicago teachers). How I remember that repeated struggle. How often I'd beg him to take time out, to request leave from one of these colleges in order to finish that doctorate. But

I got nowhere with him about this. I also recall urging him from time to time to go into therapy for help in overcoming that blockage. He was so close to achieving the doctorate, and Chicago was being very patient and liberal about giving him time to do so. Yes, for a long time, I felt guilt over not being able to help Lester make that leap.

Well, my dear, I'm convinced that it probably all goes back to our family traits, both environmental and via the genes. Think back how often I, too, managed not to fulfill certain potentials. Then there was the age difference between Lester and me. I was ten years old when he was born. In other words, he was my baby brother! So that six years later, when I left home in New London to go to the University of Wisconsin in Madison, he was only six. That means I was not around to help him during his adolescent years in Madison, to which I had persuaded the family to move as soon as they could (and they did) while I was overseas with the Army. (Father served on the civilian staff of the large Army base there.) And sending Lester advice from Europe in those little Army V-letter forms was hardly an effective tutorial. So that when I got back to the States, he had already graduated from high school and entered college. Hence, I would only see Lester when he visited New York, or I visited Madison. Otherwise, we communicated primarily through letters and telephone calls. Also, I didn't want to nag him into action. Besides, at other times, I realized he was already doing interesting things and seemed to be leading a full, productive life. So I would sometimes ask myself if he really had to have a PhD after all? Yet, academically, he could not advance further until he got that damned PhD, as he used to call it.

Well, fortunately, in due time, he came upon Empire State College, that unique college where one doesn't need a PhD to move ahead. Here, the teacher works one-on-one with the student, who, in turn, does most of his preparation at home, by himself or herself. It's a most unusual student/mentor relationship. There are none of the usual lectures and standard class hours. The mentor, in effect, teaches the student how to teach himself.

Lester started his long tenure with Empire State first as a

visiting associate professor at its Long Island Center in Haupage (near Islip) in 1979. During that period we saw each other more often, since geographically he was not so far from Brooklyn, especially as I lived near the Brooklyn final stop of the Long Island Railroad. then. But by 1982, he was promoted to associate professor at the big Niagara Frontier Center of Empire State in Buffalo, and progressed to full professor in 1987, which meant he had to move upstate to Buffalo. During this period with the College, he was also a member of the College Senate, chaired several of its important committees, and participated in the creation of its graduate program. In addition, he served as the college's SUNY representative (Empire is part of SUNY, the State University of New York) on a national level. In other words, he spent his last years teaching in an atmosphere he very much enjoyed—and which he was perfect for—and for which he did not need a doctorate. Perhaps even more important: in a college where he was appreciated and where he was doing the kind of work, both tutorial and administrative, he enjoyed.

Are you out of breath like I am, from just talking to you about this heavy teaching load and related responsibilities Lester carried out and fulfilled? Wait, that's not all! Somehow, he found time to fly down to New York from time to time to catch major theater and concert events, even some of the more important plays and concerts I was either in or somehow involved with. Of course, I'd often fly up to Buffalo or Toronto to join him at the Stratford-Ontario Shakespeare Festival or the Shaw Festival at Niagara-on-the-Lake. Sometimes we'd take in both during a summer. Much-needed respites for Lester, they also gave me a chance to get to know my "baby brother"—now a full professor—better. More exhausting, but certainly even more stimulating for him, were the longer voyages he took to Europe, Russia, and China, from which he always returned loaded with gifts for us, his family, and also, I'm sure, some of his colleagues at Empire State.

Maybe I should give Lester the last word in this short summary of his unusual teaching career, from a talk he had with one of his students: "Learning has not just been a one-way street in our relationship. As a mentor, I have learned from you.... We have also learned to be a bit humbler about ourselves in the face of your perseverance, love of learning and continued willingness to inquire." And he concluded by quoting Anonymous: "Education is an ornament in prosperity and a refuge in adversity."

So you see, dear Nina, our Lester by his very nature could not help but be what you might call a *"pacoste"* in Romanian. Yet, I'm sure that even you would have been won over by his charm and affability, his kindnesses and sincerity, as were his students and fellow faculty; not to mention his passion for building a better, new world, with room for everyone, according to his ability, to shine and fully realize himself or herself. He certainly believed in, and sought to fulfill, a socialist, egalitarian, free-thinking ideal—the kind of world you had hoped was going to come out of Romania's initial plunge into Communism—an ideal much too often falsified and broken by dictators and their stubborn, usually stupid, narrow-minded apparatchiks...

Yes, we could use my brother Lester in today's government—where we sorely need him. I'm sure, were he alive, that he would be quite excited over the possibilities and scope of Hope in these grim days, as envisaged by our most promising Barack Obama.

So, hopefully yours,
M.

June 30, 2010
Dear Nina:

As a leftover of our "Hope" theme from the last letter, I hope it has led you back to your writing desk to start work on your own new "Eternal Remembrance" project, a sort of Obituary Dictionary of your best-remembered Romanian friends, family, and professional colleagues you recently outlined to me that you had in mind. Correct?

Alas, now I, too, probably have almost as much reason to

work on a similar project, commemorating my own lost friends and colleagues. Just in the last two weeks, two wonderful souls have passed on: Chris Gampel, a fine Canadian-born actor and longtime friend of Norman Shelly (whom you've already "met" in some of these letters, and who himself left this world about six years ago); and the ever-effervescent Frances Gaar, also of the theater, but perhaps better known as a swimming expert. She had coached and helped choreograph the water ballets in those MGM films starring Esther Williams, and, I think, may have been her standby in one or more of them. Both Gampel and Gaar appeared in productions of mine at The Cooper Union and The Cubiculo. There will no doubt be memorial gatherings soon for each of them, like the one I put together for Jacob, but, of course, on a much larger scale...

Yes, as I noted in the last letter, there is still much more I'd like to tell about my father, glimpses of whom I've already given you in some of my first letters, such as his tossing me into the cold waters of Lake Superior so that I simply had to swim—or go under! Whereupon I immediately went into a sort of doggy paddle (remember)? and somehow managed to plow my way back to his waiting arms, where I was also able to stand up straight on the sand floor of the lake without sinking. In a way, that "tough" act on his part was a deviation from father's usually gentler treatment of me; for, while I was not exactly spoiled, neither he nor my mother were ever quite strict enough with me, their first-born child: I could usually work my way around them with certain children's wiles when asked or ordered to do something I didn't feel like doing. Also, my dear Nina, in my boyhood, my father's business was at its height: he was generally too busy for us kids—my younger sister and me. It was the Great Depression that brought him and the family down with a thud, but also much closer to one another.

Father (whose fully anglicized name ended up as Henry Samson Levine)—starting off with what in England was apparently transcribed from the skimpy immigration records of those days as "Evans" for his last name, which probably became "L'Evans" or "LeVin" in Montreal, and later "Levine" or "LaVine" in the States—

was born in Linkova, a small village near Kovno, Lithuania, then part of Imperial Russia. Recall my relating to you even before we were married, my having to drop the Levine part of my name when I joined Actors' Equity because the Union already had a member with that name? And how I substituted my second name, Edward, adding an "s," ending up as "Edwards"? Nor did I feel any guilt about doing so, since by then I knew we weren't dealing with my real family name, anyway.

Father's native village was probably something of a small, ordinary shtetl; and though the "Evans/Levines" were not farm people, I could never get a reasonable story from my father as to just who our family forebears actually were, or even just what his father and grandfather did for a living, or exactly what the original family name was. Though Uncle Zavel once told me that his father, my grandfather, was a very learned man, and quite pious. It seems also that their sister Anna married a man who became quite successful in business—but this was after her brothers had already left for America. Whatsoever, there is absolutely no doubt that back then the whole family was desperate to get out from under the cruel, regnant Czarist regime, which lorded over them and the thousands of other "peasant Jews" of Russia. Above all, neither father nor any of his brothers wanted to serve in the Russian Army. In fact, they dreaded the prospect; although I think the eldest (Joseph?) actually had to give over two years to it. The other brothers would have had to do the same had they remained in Russia/Lithuania. It seems, however, that Uncle Zavel managed to escape that duty just in time; a relief to them all, since I do remember father telling tales about how one of their cousins had had a tortuous time serving, back in those days, under a Cossack captain. Then there was always the fear and possibility of another pogrom haunting them, hammering away at the back of their minds. No, there was no shortage of reasons to escape from that country, or to think of it as their "homeland." Shades of similar stories by Isaac Babel in Russian; Peretz and Sholom Aleichem in Yiddish?

In any case, one by one, all the brothers followed each other to the Golden Land, America. The eldest, Joseph, seems to have settled eventually in the Baltimore area, with tentacles of the family reaching down to North Carolina, which is where, I think, his few grandchildren still reside. After him came Zavel, whom I told you about in an earlier letter, our family's voluble anarchist/socialist, with his two beautiful daughters, Lee and Belle, whom you met, and whose granddaughters you also know and like—Valerie, now living and working in California, and Stephanie in Florida. Zavel landed first in Montreal or Quebec, I'm not sure which, but somehow ended up eventually in Chicago during the 1920s, where he met Eugene Debs and other less renowned socialists and anarchists. However, before the big Depression hit us all, he and his immediate family moved to New York City, although some parts and limbs of them stayed behind in Chicago and/or Detroit.

Several years after Zavel left Lithuania, it seems, my father and his younger brother, Meyer, following his lead, emigrated together via the Baltic Sea to England and thence directly to Montreal, though there was apparently a fifth brother, supposedly my father's twin, who somehow ended up in some sort of an asylum in Peoria, Illinois! Just how and when he came over, I was never able to find out. All I know is that his fate was something my parents would taunt each other about whenever a particular quarrel grew too heated. That was a danger sign I had come to recognize, whereupon I would run into the room of the conflict and try to separate them. Deep down, I sensed that they didn't want me to know about the mysterious brother, the black sheep of the family. In those days, one didn't talk about disturbed or missing relatives! Asylums and madness, especially, were taboo. (I later learned that Uncle Meyer once told his son Marvin that he had a brother, Louis, in a hospital in Illinois.)

I rather suspect that somehow poor Louis must have tagged along with brothers Henry and Meyer on their original migration to Canada, especially since he may have been my father's twin and, probably, in his condition could not have travelled alone. Then, I think, that after caring for him all those years, first in Canada and later in Michigan, he became too much of a burden for Henry and Meyer; and that finally they felt they had to confine him to a home or asylum for the seriously disturbed. Father must have made side trips to Peoria during the Amasa period to check up on poor Louis, whenever he went on a merchandise buying trip to Chicago (usually annually or semi-annually). In fact, I recall how sometimes when dad's conversation with mother would suddenly drop very low, all I could recognize was the word Peoria.

But as for the brothers' beloved sister, Anna, who, according to the original plan, was to follow soon after my father and Uncle Meyer got settled in America, she remained in Europe—alas, until it was too late to get out! Remember also how, in an earlier letter to you, I described my vain efforts to get all the brothers (i.e, all of my uncles) to join forces and bring Anna and her family here to the States as soon as possible?

To get back to Henry's and Meyer's coming to the States, I think that Zavel probably paved the way for the two of them (possibly the three of them?), just as Joseph probably did years earlier for Zavel. Meyer and Henry were only thirteen and fifteen years old at the time. (Could Z. have loaned them money upon their arrival in Canada?) It's amazing how these two young "greenhorn" teenagers, in no time at all, seem to have become more and more self-sufficient. Cousin Marvin (Sylvia's twin brother) in a letter to me, recalls his father, Meyer, having talked about "carrying trinkets on his back which he and your father, Uncle Henry, sold to farmers near Montreal. With the proceeds they were able to buy a horse and cart instead of doing business on foot. Many of the farmers were anti-Semites and threw stones at them. But every so often a kind one would offer them a meal and lodging for the night." Probably then they began to buy and sell larger items, from which they earned enough to start buying and selling furs. Certainly that would have netted them more money. Moreover, I know that father knew how to handle furs from our later experience in Wisconsin. He also talked at times about selling furs whenever I asked about his Quebec experiences, at which time he would sometimes speak in the French Quebec dialect, which I had a hard time understanding with my meager school French. In any case, the two brothers managed quite remarkably to survive and advance themselves in a country totally foreign to them, where they had to learn both French and English, as well as a totally new geography and strange, new customs.

In time, they somehow worked their way across the province of Ontario until they reached Upper Michigan. There, Marvin informs me, his father, Meyer, was employed by a store owner named Goldberg in a very small town, Stephenson, "at the princely sum of one dollar a day. He worked there for seven years and ended up purchasing the store from Goldberg." Meanwhile, my father, Henry, had settled, as far as I can determine, in a different town, Amasa (about the same size as Stephenson), and after some years was able to purchase the rather large building which ultimately became his general store and retail business. By the time I was old enough to understand such matters, it had become a flourishing business, and the upper floor became our spacious home of ten rooms, where we were ensconced until the Depression hit us. When I was about five or six, I remember father occasionally taking us, my mother and my sister, Millicent, to visit Meyer and his wife, in a larger, not-too-distant town, Iron River, where they, too, had a store, which Marvin does not recall, because he wasn't born yet, though I find it strange that his father never spoke of it. I also remember that Meyer and family made many more moves than we did, both around the Upper Peninsula and also southward in Wisconsin. Thus, Marvin and his twin sister, Sylvia, were actually born far away from us in Wausaukee, Wisconsin, near Milwaukee, where his father and mother ran a grocery store. Eventually, they ended up in Marinette, on the border with Michigan, where Uncle Meyer went into the livestock business, and where, among other things, he also served as cantor in the local synagogue. Finally, in 1952, they settled in Madison, where, as you know, my mother and dad were already living.

Perhaps I should explain, dear Ninicuța, that in the 1920s, the Upper Peninsula was flourishing "pioneer" territory, of almost early Gold Rush proportions and comparable lures, due to the ever-growing demand for iron ore or hematite (as I recall it being called by the miners themselves) by the steel industry. It was mined there and sent by railroad to Duluth, Minnesota, that big harbor on the western end of Lake Superior, where it was loaded into huge boats, along with the even larger output of Minnesota mined iron ore, and shipped across Lake Superior to either Lake Huron and thence down to Lake Erie and the steel factories of Ohio, or else through Lake Michigan to similar plants in Illinois and Indiana. To accomplish the hard labor of mining itself, immigrant miners were brought in from Italy, Sweden, Finland, and other European countries. And since the Upper Peninsula was quite sparsely settled then, there was an immediate demand for retail stores to meet the consumer needs of the new settlers as well as the relatively few farmers and the "ruling gentry," or property owners, already established there.

So that my father and his brother Meyer settling down in nearby mining towns in the center of the western half of that long peninsula-shaped section of Michigan in the very early Twenties made sense, even though their fortunes later diverged, as I noted above, with Meyer making more moves than my father. In any case, it was up there in that tiny hamlet—remember, with that wonderful Indian name, Amasa?—that I was born and spent the first ten years of my life, there where father ran a huge general store, stocked with every kind of hardware, household furniture, utensils, clothing, and boots. It was a cavernous space, with side balconies for additional display of drygoods, and with a large drive-in loading platform set up for receiving merchandise at the rear side entrance to the store. Indeed, it was in that partially enclosed platform space that I put on my first "theater production" ever at the age of nine and a half: excerpts from *A Midsummer Night's Dream*, with my little sister, Millicent (one and a half years younger than me) playing Titania, of course, and me filling in the missing parts whenever one of the cast didn't show up or forgot his or her lines, which, as I recall, I had laboriously transcribed on brown wrapping paper solicited from the store for them to learn! The fairy costumes were devised from cheesecloth and other fabrics "donated" by the business. Nor will I ever forget our intense audience of grazing cattle, one or two of whom might amble over to the stage at the end of a rehearsal and moo mildly! (How did they know the play had ended?) Above the store were the ten rooms I told you about for our little family—my father, mother, sister, and myself. Brother Lester didn't arrive on this planet until shortly before we moved southwards to Wisconsin.

You might well ask how a nine-year-old happened to "happen upon" Shakespeare for so primitive a stage, though nowadays, in certain circles, such a "set" might be considered "cool" or "chic." After all, while the few teachers at our small elementary school in Amasa were always enthusiastic and helpful, they had to deal with a very mixed body of immigrant and native children. They certainly had no time to introduce Shakespeare to us, let alone teach him, even had they wanted to, deemed it advisable, or been capable of doing so. No, I had started to devour Shakespeare from the moment I happened upon the wonderful set of his plays in seventeen elegant little volumes with brown and gold leather covers that crowned Mother's well-stocked living room library, where I also encountered many of the great classics, tempting me to premature dippings into Emerson, Montaigne, and Plato, and first readings from *The Iliad* and *The Odyssey*. (The Aeneid had to wait a few years—and, only then, via Dryden!) More accessible was a modest, pocket-sized, gray set of selected poems by the then-most-popular "serious" English and American poets, including, of course, Longfellow, Tennyson, Browning, and Poe—note, no Hardy or Whitman in that set, though there was an Emily D. and a Whittier. It was in the adjacent modern, newly-bought book section of that cozy library where I later discovered, as I mentioned in an earlier letter, mother's uncannily prescient purchase of *Vienna: City Without Jews*, incongruously present among the Book of the Month Club (to which mother subscribed) selections of those years. I think that Dorothy Canfield Fisher was one of the reigning heads of that Club during that period.

But to get back to Shakespeare. I was so overwhelmed by my first readings of him, of which mother very much approved, although I don't think she herself dared touch him (but she did read Scott, Dickens, and Thackeray; the Bronte sister and Jane Austen rages were still to come), that I had to go ahead and see how one of these plays would sound if those amazing speeches were spoken aloud. Instinctively, I soon came to realize that only something like the fairy and worker scenes from the *Dream* could possibly be done by us kids. As to the late romances, of course, I had more difficulties understanding them myself and passed them over. Yet the power struggles of monarchs and their beholden nobilities and cliques in the history plays were, I dare say, somehow a little easier for a preadolescent to partially comprehend. Thus *King John* was easier for me than *Measure for Measure*—or *Julius Caesar* than *All's Well That Ends Well*. And I'm sure no one in the Upper Peninsula ever read, or even knew of, the wonderful late romances in those days.

Which leads me to ask: when, where, and how did you, dear Nina, first meet Shakespeare? Though I presume you must have been exposed to Eminescu and other classic Romanian writers before him? As you can see, I was fortunate, as were you, to have parents who wanted us surrounded by books and a piano. Music and poetry. Except, of course, you were brought up in a really big city, Bucharest, in a cosmopolitan atmosphere, whereas I was reared in a little hamlet, up there in our isolated private "castle" in the midst of thick, primitive, evergreen virgin forests, not far from the blueberry- and gooseberry-laden Porcupine Mountains, as one approached majestic, lucid—and ice-cold!—Lake Superior.

Nor did it seem incongruous to my parents that, naturally, I had to learn how to play the piano. But who was there in little Amasa to teach me? I believe that my ever-resourceful mother was able to find a teacher for me through one of the local churches (which, of course, we did not attend, except for funerals and Christmas parties and the like). After five or six months, however, doodling around on that stolid, black upright, hoisted upstairs with such difficulty, I no longer had the patience, as I recall, nor the motivation to practice, and the lessons were discontinued. Nevertheless, one Saturday afternoon about four or five years later, after we had migrated south into Wisconsin, as I was lounging about that house, bored, I somehow drifted back to that first easy practice book, still sitting there on the piano, opened to where I had left off, and started to play. Which I proceeded to do, encountering no problems. I was amazed: everything was now so much easier! Of course, I was four years older. Things made more sense. Mother was overjoyed, and before the week was out, found a teacher for me in the slightly larger town of Elroy, Wisconsin, where we had moved and were living by then—but I'll go into that story a little later. (By the way, in those days, every decent bourgeois household had a piano; contrary to what you Europeans usually think of, or even know of, when you voice your impressions of what you all assumed of the deprived American cultural scene.)

Now back to Amasa, where I grew up in a kind of primitive *nouveaux riche* atmosphere, except that it was a tiny frontier town and not very rich! The few "aristocrats" around were the local WASP bankers, lawyers, property owners, real estate speculators, and other professional people whose parents, grandparents, and relatives had founded it. Yet they welcomed father and our family—exotic, strange, and non-Christian as we might have looked—probably because they very much needed a general store in that town, and father somehow convinced them he had the know-how to run one. (Where he acquired that skill, who knows? No doubt largely through instinct, developed and honed during his dreary, early peddling days and later fur trading experience, plus his being a smart, quick learner.)

Fortunately, father was also an amiable, cheerful, intelligent man, who could get along on both sides of the fence, as it were. His European background made it possible for him to handle the immigrant influx with comparative ease; and his natural intelligence, generous nature, and an ingrained sense of humor enabled him to deal with the older wealth—limited, to be sure, since some of them took on the airs of a landed gentry. With the latter, especially, he was helped by my mother, who was a born "lady," innately gifted at livening up social affairs and blessed with instinctive good taste and the best of manners (and also happily endowed with a quick brain). Her adaptabiliy was all the more remarkable in that she had no roots at all, or any prior experience, in this or any gentile community. Though born in Racine, Wisconsin, her family life had been with the Jewish community there and later in Milwaukee, where her family had moved. Or, at least that was the story I was told as a boy. Indeed, it wasn't until the summer before I was set to go to the university that the true story spilled out one day while visiting my Rotter relatives in Milwaukee and one of them suddenly spurted out, during a slight argument we were having, "Well, so what? You aren't our real cousin, anyway!"

So, quite belatedly, and painfully, I learned that my mother and her sister Edith were orphans who had been adopted by those wonderful people I thought were my real grandparents—which also helped me better understand why my mother and her sister were so close, and loved each other so much: they probably never felt truly at home with the Manhoff's, in spite of Grandfather Manhoff's natural, ingrained kindness. (Father's parents had died in Europe.) And our generous Milwaukee hostess over these many years, dear Aunt Sarah, was not a blood relative, not my real aunt after all, but my mother's older step-sister, who raised a large family, of first four girls and then four boys! To make matters worse, shortly after this episode, I managed to locate the Hellers in Milwaukee, who proved to be my mother's true blood relatives, but once found out, did not want to have anything more to do with her or her offspring. They were probably afraid that we might start making financial demands on them. It was one of my first experiences of that kind of social hypocrisy, from which it took me some time to recover. Even so, as you surely realize, that kind of scar is never totally healed: thus, I still find it difficult to understand and come to terms with such behavior whenever or wherever I run into it—as one certainly does from time to time in this best of all possible worlds, and more often than one would like! Don't you agree, dear Nina?

Compensatorily, I was relieved to learn that my beautiful Aunt Edith was mother's true sister, she whom I would so much have liked to have known and loved. Unfortunately, she died of tuberculosis when I was about two years old, yet I always felt that I did know her, since almost daily I'd pass by her handsome full-length photographic portrait that mother had enlarged for our living room. Besides, mother always talked so vividly about her, although each time she usually ended up in tears. Moreover, the fact that Edith had sung in night clubs to the chagrin of some of her adopted family, only made her that much more glamorous and interesting to me.

Indeed, I realize now that she was likely evidence of musical and possibly theatrical strains in the family genes, especially on my mother's true blood side. Then, too, there was their real father, who hailed from Odessa in the Ukraine, and was said to have practiced trumpet in the attic of his home there, so as not to disturb the neighbors. Plus which, there was also a musical strain on my father's side: his brother, Uncle Meyer, was a part-time, untrained cantor, who supplemented the income from his various enterprises by singing at high holiday services in Upper Michigan towns and nearby larger Marquette, Wisconsin, which I noted earlier in this letter. And then there was Cousin Lee, Zavel's daughter (whom you met once, Nina, as you'll surely recall), who, as I wrote in an earlier letter, had succumbed to that bland Christian Science faith, nevertheless kept up her often inconsistent "good life" as best she could in this jungle of Manhattan. Thus, after retiring from her *New York Times* secretarial job, she taught piano for years in her Stuyvesant Town apartment, though never once crossed the East River to hear any of our Brooklyn Philharmonic concerts, to which I offered her the best seats. And my dear departed sister, Millicent, turned out to be a pretty good French Horn player, having graced her high school orchestra, and later some community orchestras in Wisconsin and Illinois. Brother Lester, however, was tone deaf!

Uncle Zavel, in a letter my mother squeezed out of him in 1963 had this to say: "As for the family tree, I knew all of them, cousins, and uncles, as I used to go to visit them often. We lived in a town called Linkova while the family tree was rooted in a city called Binezze. There was quite a flock of them at that time. They were all very well learned in Scriptures and some of them worldly education [sic] also. They were very good-looking people also and talented. There were artists among them, one a great one. Many of them played several musical instruments. That great artist he played violin, piano and had a great baritone voice. His name was Bernard Michelson. Our mother had two sisters and one brother. His name was Chatzkele Lean. He was also an artist and played two instruments. In later years my sister wrote me that the family tree has increased to about 250 members and they were all economically well-set so they were saved for the Nazis. They all perished."

Back again to Amasa and the Upper Peninsula! Luckily, father was blessed with a wonderful sense of humor and was an excellent storyteller. He had your talent, dear Nina, that of an almost computer-sized memory library of jokes. This proved invaluable in helping him gradually gain the confidence and respect of his customers, fellow businessmen, and friends in that small town of Amasa. Father was also a good sport at community events, one of which, I recall, was an evening "drag show" version of one of the then-popular Romberg-style operettas, put on by the town's businessmen, in which men played all the female roles, and father had to wear a dress decorated with long beads and loud spangles, which completely won over the audience. (At first sight, my sister and I didn't recognize him in that new guise.) Could that event, coupled with my readings of plays (there was no television then, only limited radio, but silent movies galore, followed by the first awkward talkies on which I grew up) have kindled the theatrical spark in me? Was that the source of my "*theatralische Sendung*"—or would it have happened anyway?

How fascinated I was by those early films! The town's one little movie house, not much more than a simple, large wooden shed (probably once a farm supply station), was only half a block from our store, and when I was very small, my parents couldn't keep me away from it. Had I had my own way, I probably would have spent the whole day and night devouring cinema in Amasa's tiny shed of a movie palace.

And how I wondered where the sound came from! Don't forget: I was only about six or seven years old then, and I was sure the actors were carrying on behind the screen on the platform upon which the screen itself was mounted, and around which I would often sneak to try to find them. It was as if what was going on in front was a huge shadow play, like many Oriental societies still present to this day on festival occasions. But whenever I managed to elude the big, scary ushers and got back there to that holy place behind the screen, the actors would never be there. Where had they gone, I wondered, and was so disappointed... Of course, as I gradually matured, and after many patient explanations by my parents, I finally understood what was really going on. Yet I was still saddened: it would have been so great to have had real actors there, with a real drama taking place behind the screen.

That little Shakespeare attempt of mine on the store's rear loading platform described above came somewhat later—shortly after sound pictures had arrived. Incidentally, among other things, I forgot to mention that I had to teach all the participants how to speak that srange Elizabethan tongue. But where did I learn how?

In any event, as you can see, things went swimmingly for our entire family until the Great Depression landed in the Upper Peninsula like a gigantic clap of thunder. Suddenly, all the mines were shut down. The banks stopped all loans. People were desperate. There was no social security in those days, and guaranteed bank deposits had not been heard of yet. Amasa was a tiny town with no industry other than its one iron ore mine. So the poor workers had nowhere else to turn. Though some managed to get part-time jobs with the local farmers, many began to leave Amasa and move to larger towns and cities in the Upper Peninsula, or, more often, south to Wisconsin, even though it had no mines.

Of course, I was too small to really understand all that was happening around us, even though my parents tried to explain—as much as they themselves could comprehend the frightening losses, uncertainties, and turmoil that ensued. However, one thing soon became devastatingly clear to them: hardly anyone had enough money left to buy anything except absolute necessities. And Dad's spacious emporium was not a corner grocery store. Hence, business trickled down to almost nothing. Father's stock didn't move: it stayed on the shelves. For he didn't deal with the perishable basics, only with things people could postpone buying. Cash flow was running down to almost nil. What were they to do?

While much of all this was still a mystery to me, I couldn't help but sense that something terrible was afoot. What I did witness, and was now old enough to be horribly worried about, were the more and more frequent arguments, disputes, and *malentendus* between my parents that emerged from the tension and strain under which they were living, and trying to function. Finally, they painfully realized that they, too, had no choice but to abandon Amasa, business, home, and all. They were forced to sell off our ten-room house and most of its furniture, the huge store, and the remainder of its still large stock—all at bargain prices (though I still have the beautiful mahogany living room table you admired on one of your rare visits to Brooklyn, with that gilt-edged mirror designed to hang above it, and one lone, dark blue, wicker-back mahogany armchair from those days). With the big sale money they acquired a big truck, and one dramatic day, early in the morning, shortly after the once-family rooster crowed "Wake up!" we all bundled up for a long, brutal expedition of several hundred miles down to a small town in Central Wisconsin called Elroy, only a little larger than Amasa, but where none of us knew a soul. Apparently, one of my father's business associates from Milwaukee or Chicago (to which cities he used to make annual or semi-annual buying trips) must have given him a lead to a fellow "*Landsmann*" in or near Elroy, who wanted to sell out his mixed metal trade and junk business there to anyone who'd buy. And father felt he had no choice but to take up that offer.

By the way, the name "Elroy" must ring a bell with you, dear Nina, doesn't it? That's where your first and best American friend, Barbara Davis, came from. But she probably hadn't been born yet during our family's brief stay there, so our paths couldn't have crossed. It's also interesting to note that Elroy is close to Baraboo, the town where the famed circus giants, the Ringling Brothers, came from and spent every summer there (and with whom our niece, Stephanie, worked for quite a few years). Then, between those two towns, there were the beautiful Dalles—Wisconsin's miniature answer to the Grand Canyon! But during that difficult post-Depression period, our poor family could only make one little sight-seeing trip to these sites; nevertheless, it whetted my aptitude for future travel!

How my poor father—he was already in his late fifties—managed to learn that new business (new to him, of course) from the ground up practically overnight still amazes me. Yet after just two years in Elroy, he accumulated enough to move us about a hundred miles northeast to a larger Wisconsin town, New London (about 5,000 people), in the Fox River Valley, a more industrialized part of the state, hence with a better potential for the scrap metal trade. Moreover, during the winters, when the metals part of the business became too difficult or impossible to deal with, father was able to revert to his earlier fur trade experience, with which he obviously felt much more competent and at home. It was also less physically demanding on him. Unfortunately, so much change and adaptation was no picnic. Among other obstacles, father encountered more competition in New London than he had expected. There was a slick, shifty fur trader ensconced on a large farm/estate about ten miles out of town. Also it must have been difficult for father to face the only other Jewish family in town, who ran a big store (though not as large as his in Amasa) on the main street, a place he would have loved to take over (and which he would probably have run better); but he had nowhere near the capital needed to do so. On the contrary, his business, indeed most everybody's business, grew worse and worse. For the Depression in that section of the country did not lift until World War II, when Army orders began to come in and bolstered the economy.

Unfortunately, as mother used to complain to him about—or accuse him of—father was not shrewd or cunning enough in dealing with the big-time buyers, wholesalers and middlemen from Milwaukee and Chicago who used to come through Wisconsin once or twice a year on statewide buying trips to bargain with him and buy up his accumulated metals and furs, then resell them in the larger cities. Even I, who by then was in my early teens, began to realize that while father was a good businessman when times were good, and knew how to handle the normal trade, he was probably not tough or hard-headed enough in his dealings with some of those visiting, often quite dishonest middlemen—"shysters" and "momzers," as mother used to call these buyers. Too often, they would leave father in the lurch by reneging on what he had understood was a done deal.

You can well imagine, my dear, what a tremendously difficult period it was for us all. Mother had to do the heavy housework, the laundry and the like, which a servant usually did for her before, back in Amasa—and that was when she was younger. We have to also remember that in those days one had only primitive household machines to work with and often had to revert to plain scrubbing. Mother certainly wasn't strong enough for such demanding labor. Plus which, I think it possible she may have had a miscarriage when I was about twelve or thirteen, after we had already moved to New London. For, I remember her once being confined to her bed for several weeks, the explanation for which was not too convincing from either parent. During this period my sister and I had to take on the household duties. I even learned how to cook the basics, and gained a certain "renown" in our nearby neighborhood for the stuffed goose I prepared for an otherwise depressing Thanksgiving dinner. (Dear Nina, shades of my "chef" trick on Faye in Baltimore, you remember?)

Of course, father was too overwhelmed by the gradually failing business to be able to help out on that score. And household demands on my sister and me grew only more complex and overwhelming, especially as I got older and became more and more involved with outside projects at school such as music, rhetoric, and sports. I played viola and oboe in the high school orchestra and band; I was on the oratory and debating squads; and, for a short time, also on the track team, where I surprised everyone (including myself), when earlier, still in the eighth grade, I defeated the high school champ (a larger, taller African American, the only one in town) in both the 100-yard dash and the broad jump!

But things changed a bit when my piano teacher, who was married to the school's track coach, persuaded him that I should spend more time at the piano than out on the track field (though I still paid for my lessons with her by tending their furnace in the winter and mowing their lawn in the summer). Yet ultimately, I justified my teacher's faith in me by winning, in my senior year, a 1939 national piano tournament at Lawrence College in nearby Appleton, where I had to compete with young virtuoso players from Milwaukee, Chicago, and even distant New York—for Lawrence's music school had a great reputation at that time—who had been studying piano for years with the country's best and most expensive teachers. The majority of them played dazzling concert showpieces by Chopin, Liszt, Rachmaninoff, even Ravel, while I had barely mastered and then humbly offered the first movement of Mozart's superb, crafty *Sonata in F Major, No. 15, K.533*, and the first movement of Brahms's *Sonata No, 3 in F minor, Op.5*, neither of which were too formidable technically. I'll never forget how everyone's jaw fell—theirs and their parents—when I was awarded first place because, as Lawrence College's wise headmistress explained to the audience, and, in particular, to the horrified and disappointed parents of my big-city competition: "Why, the boy's playing was more 'musical.' "

Unfortunately, I was sorry to disappoint that admirable woman later when I had to turn down the Lawrence College music scholarship I had won in order to accept a different, general scholarship to the University of Wisconsin in Madison—among other reasons, because I couldn't see myself practicing piano seven hours a day for the rest of my life! Nevertheless, the whole experience of developing a viable piano technique, taking part in such a competition, learning new music so fast, and doing so with a minimum background stood me in good stead in subsequent years...

But to get back to father: where was he to go with that forlorn business? Especially, as I noted before, now that times were getting worse and worse, and there was no other trade he could go into at that time and place. He and the family could hardly endure still another move on the geographical business chessboard. Besides, he was too old to start afresh, even if he had had sufficient capital to do so. Instead, he was humiliatingly reduced to having to borrow money sometimes from mother's brother-in-law in Milwaukee, Uncle Louie. Of course, my father was not a "fromme Yid," a religious Jew—nor was your father, correct? But having been brought up in the faith, and having been Bar Mitzvah-ed himself, my father, unlike yours, felt he had to do something about his son getting a religious schooling.

So it ended up that father would drive me every Sunday morning to Appleton, where I would spend several hours learning the essentials of Judaism from a cultivated and philanthropic middle-aged woman, Mrs. Louis Marshall, wife of the owner of a major paper-manufacturing plant in Appleton. But it was all in English, which meant, alas, as I was to discover later, as in most translations, there was a lot missing. Mrs. Marshall knew neither Yiddish nor Hebrew, nor really much Jewish history (some of which she actually picked up, I'm quite sure, while teaching it to me), because, of course, I had read ahead in the texts and knew what was coming next! Besides, much as I enjoyed these lessons and her charming company, I was unhappy not so much about not learning Hebrew, but at missing the chance to learn Yiddish. (Strange: because later I was to reverse that wish and opt for Hebrew.) Hence I would try to get father to teach me Yiddish on our trips to and from New London for those classes, or to at least practice some conversational idiom with me en route. But, as in other Jewish families, as I later learned from brethren Jews, he preferred to keep Yiddish as a secret, private language between him and my mother, even though her Yiddish was quite limited! Besides, father always wanted to talk politics with me on those trips.

At any rate, while I was revelling in Jewish history lessons, learning about the major Jewish holidays and the nature of Jewish monotheism, and gaining a limited look at our people's customs and special distinctions, father would be hobnobbing with his Appleton synagogue friends. So these trips were not that much of a burden on him after all: they gave him a needed relief from family problems, domestic business, and fixing up the house back in New London.

Yes, I did get a good beginner's foundation in many of these matters, but without the rote learning of those rote passages from the Torah and Haftorah required for a Bar Mitzvah in Hebrew, the essence of which I learned in English. I still think it a shame how that old custom of rote learning persists to this day in even some of the more sophisticated synagogues of New York. How dare we mock the Muslims for doing the same thing with their Madrassah boys, where they don't bother about the meaning of what they're reciting by rote from the Koran, either? Or what about the Catholic church's rote use of Latin? True, the last few decades have seen belatedly something of a change in parts of the New York religious scene. Some women have even concocted a feminist Haggadah for Passover, I understand! The Catholic Service is now in English. It is, after all, "cool" nowadays to study other people's customs and religious practices, especially those of exotic, distant foreigners. We pretend to be scientific about all this but usually end up like amateur anthropologists. It goes back, don't you think, to the infectious writings of Malinowski, Margaret Mead, and more recently, Levi-Strauss? Not to mention *The Golden Bough*.

However, even back then, young as I was, I would sometimes feel that something was missing in what I was being taught, and sought glimpses of what that might be in other Jewish history books I would have liked to peruse and study. I often wondered about those fascinating hidden paths and byways of Philo Judaeus and the neo-Platonists; the medieval cults and the beginnings of Kabbalah; then later the incredible stories of Sabbatai Zvi, the false Messiah, who ended up a Muslim; and still later, his 18th-century imitator, Jacob Frank (Yakov Leib Frank), who also assumed the role of the Messiah. But later he actually became a Christian, selected his own twelve apostles, and settled down in Brno after gaining the patronage of Maria Theresa. Finally there was the rise (and fall?) of Chasidism. Esoteric, but most fascinating aspects of Judaism, hardly ever touched upon in the more elementary texts I was assigned, if indeed it was mentioned at all. Unfortunately, English translations of Buber's marvellously accessible versions of the major Chasidic tales had not yet been made (or, if so, hadn't yet reached us). And Gershom Scholem's exhaustive writings on the Kabbalah and Jewish mysticism were not to come out until much later in English.

Besides, when the standard histories did talk about the Kabbalah, it was usually in somewhat demeaning terms. In fact,

I was told that most rabbis wouldn't let their pupils even touch the Kabbalah until they were thirty-five or older. But, remarkably, my late Ann, with her propensity for the occult, had found one of those early, popularized versions of excerpts from the Zohar some forty years before Madonna and her tribe latched onto them! Only recently, I learned that one of the many names of God tattooed on the nape of another pop star's neck, Britney Spears's, is misspelled! In any event, Mrs. Marshall, who was at best an amateur scholar, was hardly inclined to pursue such exotic paths. I'm sure she wasn't the least curious about the amazing Sabbatai Zvi and the strange Yakov Frank I was to encounter with much excitement in some of my future forays. I wonder now if she even knew what a Chasid was, or had ever seen one. Certainly not in Gentile-preponderant Appleton, Wisconsin! (Nor would her family likely have welcomed that of the four-year-old immigrant child, Houdini, when it first settled in Appleton toward the turn of the century, only later to escape to possibly more hospitable Brooklyn!)

Perhaps the most avant-garde, or unorthodox, book Mrs. Marshall gave me to read was T. E. Lawrence's *Seven Pillars of Wisdom*, which was, indeed, a compelling compilation of eclectic, though sometimes seemingly elementary, approaches to religion and/or religious thought. Yet it was still an eye-opener and an adventure for me at that young age to read Lawrence, from whom I learned much, although it was hardly as absorbing a read as *Les Misérables*, which I had devoured a year or so before meeting Mrs. Marshall. So imagine my surprise yesterday, dear Nina, while reading up on Simone Weil in preparation for our attending the American premiere of *La Passion de Simone*, the big cantata-like opus about her by Kaija Saariaho, that very gifted Finnish composer, at Lincoln Center, I discovered that in spite of the much superior philosophic training she received in Paris, and her virtual "apprenticeship" with Alain, Weil was strongly affected and possibly influenced by the *Seven Pillars*, which she apparently first encountered in her teens! (Of course, I wasn't to meet Kafka and Kierkegaard until I got to the university in Madison.) But I was even more struck by the fact that it wasn't until

Weil was stranded in hostile Vichy France, while running from the Germans and their collaborators, that for the first time in her life she saw orthodox Jews in solemn prayer, and was duly impressed. Though that didn't seem to have solved the perennial problem she was facing then, again, as to whether she should be baptized or not!

Also I find it peculiar that a year or two after the Marshall period, I recall encountering a totally different kind of book, a strange volume I was only allowed to glance through, but never read, that employed an old German Gothic typeface, the title of which, alas, I can't seem to remember, shown me by an equally strange lawyer holed up in a cheap office in "downtown" New London, who looked like something out of a German expressionist film or painting—a comparison based on hindsight, of course, because at that time I hadn't yet met any of the Impressionists, let alone heard of the Expressionists. I now realize that this odd book was probably an attempt by some German pseudo-philosopher to transmute Spengler's *Decline of the West* into popular, palpable, almost mystical terms. Interestingly enough, I had already heard of Spengler even there and then, young as I was, in rural, backwoods Wisconsin, his *Weltanschauung* being known worldwide in the Twenties and Thirties. Though, as I look back at my adolescence in rustic New London, it could be that this unique older gentleman, who had an office next to the union leader I occasionally worked for on weekends (a disciple of Norman Thomas), may have been trying to lure innocent me into his lair. Just as I was quite shocked when around that same time I overheard the dark, middle-aged lady who supervised the entrance to the local town park and swimming pool, and who always wore the heaviest possible makeup, huskily implore our handsome, young lifeguard to let her soap him down while he took his obligatory pre-swim shower. Then there was that strange hush-hush talk about those two unmarried, one-time women schoolteachers who had been living together for thirty years in a small house on Montana Street, and were termed peculiar by their neighbors...

To get back to basic Judaism and Lady Marshall, I must say that, for the most part, those sessions with her were a rewarding experience and an ideal relief from the daily diet of New London life, to which I looked forward each week. Moreover, they helped me begin the long process of trying to understand what in the world being a Jew was all about, and what demands it entailed, something I'm still working at, my dear Nina, as you, too, must be doing! As Heschel said: "There's a high cost of living to be paid by a Jew."

This was a big step in my development, since, being brought up as the only Jew in one town, and later, one of the few in another, there was no one to help me see or realize how different I—and my family—must have appeared to the neighbors, colleagues, and friends (and possible enemies) who surrounded us. Except, of course, on rare occasions, such as that time the boys mock-crucified me at play, as I described in an earlier letter; or when some of the older boys might from time to time tauntingly call me a kike or a sheenie (the first time I heard these words I didn't even know what they meant!), but seldom with the malice with which the same thing might have been done at that same time in Milwaukee or New York, or, God forbid, in Europe!

This was also the period when, as I was maturing, I was gradually growing more and more aware of the dark times we were living in, and in particular the terrifying rise of Nazism and Fascism. (Our era gave us youngsters plenty to debate about in our intramural high school county and state contests.) There was even wild talk then about shipping all the Jews of Europe to Madagascar! Before long I would be involved, as I explained in that earlier letter, in trying to organize and persuade our family—that is, my several uncles and their families—to join forces with us in order to rescue our Lithuanian relatives from the mounting dangers they would be facing, before it was too late. In retrospect, for me the Marshall lectures and readings were a prelude to that ultimate realization.

However, need I add that I was always treated royally at the Marshall home, refreshed by being offered healthy breakfasts with nuts and fruit galore, and with the lessons taking place in a luxuriously appointed, comfortable study adjacent to a commodious living room? Though as I recall, her husband used to glance in occasionally to see what this strange, long-nosed, immature boy with tousled hair and cheap clothes was up to! These sessions, which went on for almost two school years—what patience my father showed through all this!—were climaxed by my being brought by Mrs. Marshall down to the major Reform Synagogue in Milwaukee for the confirmation ceremony (the Reform substitute for an Orthodox bar mitzvah). It was run by Wisconsin's leading Reform Rabbi, with whom apparently she had studied, and who individually coached me before my being "confirmed" along with his Milwaukee graduating class, in their enormous palace of a synagogue in the grand boulevard section of that city. All this preparation was topped by my short speech on "Why I am a Jew," which created something of a minor sensation among the Milwaukee regulars. "Did you hear that boy from New London?" "Where did he pick up those fancy ideas?" Of course, Mother, Father, my sister Millicent, and my baby brother Lester all came along, and were proud to see me up there on the platform—shades of future theater experience ahead?

I believe that we, the family, stayed overnight at the Rotter mansion—after all, we were about two hundred miles south of New London. And Mother's parents, who also lived in Milwaukee, and other relatives, including all the Rotters, as well as Mother's stepbrother, Bernard Manhoff and his colorful wife, Anita, who ran a somewhat risqué restaurant in the seedier, older section of downtown Milwaukee, all came to the ceremony and were duly impressed. Though, of course, my father and grandfather, as well as Uncle Louie, were naturally disappointed at it not being the real thing, that is, a genuine Bar Mitzvah with me reading and reciting the required passages from the Torah and the Haftorah in rote-learned Hebrew.

Now for a strange footnote to the Mrs. Marshall "saga": after that schooling period, she seemed to have lost interest in her protegé; or, as I had begun to sense toward the end, perhaps her husband didn't approve of her spending so much time with a nobody? Otherwise, one might think that she would have been proud some three years later, even if she weren't a music lover, to have her one-time pupil win a major piano competition at prestigious Lawrence

College—in her own city, walking distance from her mansion, and to which, of course, she had been invited to the awards presentation but did not come.

Ironically, about ten years later in New York, after my return from Europe, I was to become considerably better acquainted with the New York world of Jewry, so different from that of Appleton, so much richer, more colorful and variegated, and, of course, infinitely larger. Among other things, I partially supported myself by singing bass in the once-well-esteemed Silbermintz Orthodox Male Choir and later accompanied singing teachers at the 92nd Street Y's School of Music. When performing with Silbermintz, we would do concerts with many of the great chazans (cantors) of those days, a practice that nowadays has almost disappeared. I remember especially the golden-voiced Moshe Kussevitzky (no relative of the great conductor), with his superb musicianship and beautiful, tasteful improvised roulades, merging quarter-tone Middle Eastern themes with cadenzas borrowed from Verdi and Rimsky-Korsakov operatic arias. We also sang at many an Orthodox Jewish wedding and danced many a *hora* at fund raisers and celebrations during those heady first years of Israeli Independence (1948-1950). There, I learned willy-nilly much about the actual life of the *shtetl* as transposed to modern America long before entering the *Fiddler on the Roof* world, with its often overly sentimental evocation of that other world, through actual participation in some of its century-old customs and practices.

However, let me assure you, my dear Nina, that these experiences, mind-enhancing and culture-broadening as they may have been, did not turn me into a Zionist, on the one hand, nor entice me into any "born-again" Judaism, on the other. True, they may have made me more curious to explore from time to time the deeper philosophic roots of that religion. And often wonder at or marvel over how these daily customs and holiday rites rose out of them! Not to mention awe and wonder at the miracle of the maintenance of that faith and that spirit for over two thousand years. As I mentioned earlier, I was to find much to ponder and relish in the writings of Buber and his kind of "Jewish existentialism," especially as embodied in his book *Between Man and Man*, as well as in some of his later essays. (Only recently did I discover the excitement of his earlier work, especially *Daniel*.) I was also lucky to have heard Buber speak once, when, as a tiny, very old, white-haired patriarch (he was under five feet), he lectured at the Hebrew Institute, next door to the Stephen Wise Free Synagogue on West 68th Street, and in very good English! Unfortunately, that moment came before I had read any of his works, so that I didn't derive as much from his homily as I might otherwise have. However, just a few years later, I was to attend a few lectures by Eric Gutkind, who both knew and had studied under Buber and Moritz Rosenthal during the period when they started their pathbreaking translation of the Bible into a modern, poetic German that gets to the essence of the Hebrew original (or so I'm told by those who should know), probably better than the albeit powerful standard German translation by Martin Luther himself. Gutkind and his willow-thin wife, Lucie, had also been intimate friends of Walter Benjamin and Gershom Scholem, as I recently discovered in perusing Scholem's fascinating memoir of Benjamin.

Certainly, Gutkind was one of the more learned scholars I've personally encountered, a learning backed up by worlds of both lived and literary experience in Europe, Russia, the Far East, and ultimately, America, where he finally settled down and was teaching at The New School, when I met him. It was from his lips that I first heard the phrase extolling Hebrew as "*die Sprache der Sprachen*," which, I understand, served as a sort of byword for that brilliant group of German Jewish intellectuals of the period just preceding World War I and the first ten years of the Weimar Republic, who still maintained their faith but also tried to somehow make the deeper, more profound reaches of Jewish thought accessible to the best minds of our time, secular or clerical—or non-committal!

Yet one of my problems with these thinkers—not only mine, but yours, too, I'm sure, dear Nina, as we've often touched on it in past conversations—is their conviction that the Jews were and are the Chosen People, and that Hebrew was and still is, as Gutkind said above in German, "the language of all languages," plus all that implies. (What about Sanskrit, Egyptian, Chinese, and other great languages, most of which actually preceded Hebrew—or even the *Ur-Sprachen* that preceded them?) It's as difficult for me to justify this seemingly fundamental belief as I feel it should have been for, say, a Simone Weil to justify a comparable fundamental faith in the Trinity, or for poor Bergson, of all people, to ask for absolution on his deathbed, through Catholicism!

Of course, there were probably even more German Jews of that period, their contemporaries, who had been either fully assimilated into Christian or German laic cultures or in many cases even converted, who had no patience with such problems of Faith. Yet there were those among them who returned to that faith, or to some sort of religious thought, in the face of the precipitous and terrifying rise of Nazism. I'm thinking of Schoenberg as a prime example, an unexpectedly early re-convert, who returned to Judaism in the early Twenties. As you know, his enormous struggle in finding that faith again is brilliantly embodied in the tortuous score of his opera *Moses und Aron*, for which he also wrote the libretto, remember?

In any case, just when the Gutkinds made the leap, I don't know, but I'm quite sure it was before Schoenberg did; definitely before the Nazi threat emerged in full stride. Apparently, Scholem had arranged Hebrew lessons for them during World War I. But, of course, by the time I heard Gutkind speak, he had been long steeped in that culture. The essence of his thought is embodied in his book *Choose Life*, a copy of which, dear Nina, I must search out for you to imbibe. I loaned mine to someone, and it has never been returned. In spite of your reluctance to delve into that realm—as you'll recall, I can't get you to even skim the beautifully printed Romanian translation of Buber's *I and Thou*, which retains a dusty spot in your library—Gutkind's book might prove to be an easier entrée for you into that world. (Though perhaps Levinas in French would be better yet.)

Opportunely, I met the Gutkinds through Judith Malina and Julian Beck, when they took me to one of his private lectures at the Masters' Institute on Riverside Drive (given separately from his New

374

School classes) during the early days of my working with them in the very first phases of their Living Theatre project back in the early Fifties, even before they settled into the Cherry Lane. Among other things, we did a concert reading of Otway's *Venice Preserved* in a very un-Venetian second-floor studio on 101st Street and Broadway! It's not generally known, I think, that Judith's father was a distinguished rabbi. And I'm told that Julian's family founded the Beck shoe dynasty. Nonetheless, with the Becks, Gutkind's writings became a sort of Bible for their Anarchism, even though, admittedly, that takes some stretching to make sense—techniques at which, of course, both Judith & Julian were quite adept. But back to my family now, and more about the Becks later.

*

That I seem so far to have given relatively more attention to my father than to my mother is, of course, most unfair to her! She, too, was a wonderful parent, as I'm sure you've gathered from this account already, who I cherished and loved dearly. Indeed, in some ways, I was actually closer to Mother, and was no doubt more influenced by her, than Father; especially since she was always there on the scene, whereas he would be away tending the store, in the beginning, or in later years would be off on trips collecting scrap metals or buying furs, etc. Also, Mother, being American-born, seemed to fit in a little more easily than Father with the people and mores of the Midwestern towns described earlier; she was certainly more "at home" in Michigan and Wisconsin than Father, even though he had made, and was still making until his health broke down, a remarkable adaptation to this country and its customs. Yet less so, to be sure, than to our basically cruel, hard-hearted, money-driven, acquisitive society.

For that matter, have you and I done any better on that score? Indeed, in some ways the world seems more rapacious than ever, with our so-called free Capitalism running dangerously wild; with our old, often admirable, Protestant-American, ethical/moral restraints having practically disappeared; with not one Republican vote for the recent House passage of a very watered-down version of the health bill, and a Senate bent on draining it still further. While, dear Ninicuța, you've never been quite reconciled to the loss of your earnest hope for a future, truly benevolent Communist Utopia, which, of course, has appeared nowhere yet, nor ever will.

However, let's get back to my dear parents. You probably recognized from this and earlier letters that both of them, though neither had a formal education, were very intelligent, well read; and basically pragmatic, with Father being slightly more intellectual, and Mother more intuitively smart and quizzical. They knew the overall scene quite well, even if they may not have been able to verbalize certain aspects of it, nor face others, such as the fact that the World is a Jungle, as I think I've probably reiterated too often already in these letters. Hence, most of their worldly problems and occasional awkward adjustments (and probably some of mine!).

But dear courageous Mother, bless her, lacked totally a sense of humor. This, I realize in retrospect, may well have, from time to time, frustrated or annoyed Father who, bless him, was always able to laugh things off even after some of their worst moments. Mother was more "serious" and something of a worrywart. (Aren't you, too, dear Nina, a *prăpăstioasă*, as they say in Romanian?) Yet aspects of their two personalities, while often leading to more than a fair share of their quarrels and *malentendus*, would finally re-converge enough for them to be able to call a truce and carry on from there. Nevertheless, their last years, after I left home to go to college and later overseas, with Father having had, humiliatingly, to take on caretaker and watchman jobs, and Mother half-supporting the family by working as a saleslady in a department store in Madison, plus the burden of father's declining health, were most difficult for them to cope with—as stories and worried reports from both my sister and brother steadily reminded me. And likewise increased my guilt over not getting back to Madison more often to see them, at which times I should have tried to partially ease their suffering by taking their minds off it, and, by reassuring them of my love, convince them that I was still part of the family.

I'm particularly grieved, and indeed often angry with myself, for not having made a greater effort to make more of those later visits, when I knew time was closing in on them and that I would soon lose both of them forever. Of course, at first I was more concerned about Father, who was fifteen to seventeen years older than Mother. (There were no Russian or Lithuanian birth records which we had access to or could consult at that time.) We all certainly expected Mother to be around much longer. Alas, it turned out that her demise was horribly premature and unanticipated, most likely brought on, as my enraged sister, Millicent, claimed—and she was there, on the scene, at Mother's bedside—by excess anaesthesia administered to her in advance of her diverticulosis operation. (She died of a heart attack the day after.) I was playing in *Fiddler on the Roof* at the time and flew to Madison as soon as I heard from Millicent that Mother had taken a turn for the worse after her supposedly successful surgery. Alas, I didn't get there in time to bid her farewell. But upon my return to the show two days later, I learned that the cast, who had been extraordinarily supportive throughout this period, had left a memorial for Mother. Whereupon I wrote them this little letter of thanks, which I find that I've saved all these years:

Friday, July 29, 1967

Dear Fellow Anatevkans [*Fiddler* was set in Sholom Aleichem's fictional shtetl of Annatevka]:

Ever since my return from that sad, enforced pilgrimage to Madison, Wisconsin, I have been hearing little whisperings in corners and tantalizing rumors that some kind of memorial was afoot for my mother. At one point, it sounded like a tree! Whatever it was, and perplexed as I was, I was most touched that you, my *Landsmänner*, should be that concerned. But imagine my surprise when today I received notice in the mail from the Jewish National Fund that nine trees were being planted in Israel in my mother's name—in other words, practically a whole grove!

I hardly know how to thank you. All I can say is that somehow, some way—miraculously enough—you must have sensed something of her quality. Certainly Mother would have understood and appreciated this wonderful gesture. As some of you know, she left her eyes to the University of Wisconsin Medical Center for Research, some of her very limited resources to the Cancer Fund, and her clothes to the Sisterhood of Temple Beth-El in Madison. "A little bit of this, a little bit of that"—and now nine trees. Thank you, thank you, one and all!

No longer "beggarly yours," [I played the Beggar]
Reb Nahum   /s/ Maurice

*

Ah, among other things, I had hoped to have longer, intimate talks with each of my parents about what life meant to them here in this "best of all possible worlds," and to have taped such conversations, and whatever reminiscences I could evoke from them. But Father would keep putting me off with a gentle, "Later on, son, later on." And Mother would always be too exhausted from her job, and perhaps too modest and shy to talk about "personal" things. It's at such moments that I would lose patience with an Eluard, for example, who was able to lyricize mellifluously "Je n'ai pas des regrets"—even though we know very well he wasn't talking about the above! Ah, how can one not have regrets?

Also, I've shamefully neglected to tell you more about my poor, long-suffering sister, Millicent, she who, before puberty set fully in, had been a happy, smiling, alert, inquisitive, quite charming though somewhat shy young lady, who even managed to begin mastering that tough instrument, the French horn, and played it in the New London High School band (and later in community orchestras in Madison and Chicago). While not beautiful like her cousin Belle, she was an attractive girl, with harmonious features and a potentially good figure.

But then something none of us—Mother, Father, myself, nor close friends—were ever able to fully understand was what happened to dear Millicent during her transition to womanhood. The smile began to disappear; her front teeth started to protrude; her young back slumped a bit; too often she'd wax lethargic; seldom did the old curiosity bubble up as it did formerly. There was no longer any *joie de vivre*. And, of course, that made the always-difficult adolescent passage that much more difficult for her to elbow her way through. I still think this abrupt change may have been due to sudden shifts in the normal functioning of her neurological system, such as possible hormonal or glandular imbalances. Also, the sudden dental troubles may have been a contributing factor. In any case, I remember frequently urging mother way back then to have Millicent examined in one of the better hospitals in nearby Appleton. How ironic that she would end up choosing to become a nurse!

A profession for which she was really not tough enough; less so, indeed, since the change that overcame her. Nevertheless, she tried nobly, and, after graduation from high school, came down to Madison, where I was already attending the university, as you'll recall, and entered a nursing college not connected with the university. Once there, I tried to help her adjust to Madison (a big city for her), to go regularly to classes, to gain confidence, etc., as much as I could. For a time, we even shared an attic in one of those quaint boarding houses near the university. (This was before my parents also moved to Madison.) She set up house at one end and I settled into the other of that odd triangular structure, with its still-fresh-smelling, unpainted wooden railings and stairs. The stairwell was between the two sides of this ample attic, which somehow we managed to turn into a practical, livable space. Moreover, it pleased mother and father that both their son and daughter—after all, our Hebrew names were Moshe and Myriam, biblical siblings—were sharing a household. They also knew that Millicent needed help in adapting to a big city, a new environment with many new challenges. What a shame, then, that too soon I had to leave her alone to handle these things by herself, when I entered the Army in March, 1943. For she wasn't anywhere near ready.

Yes, Millicent tried valiantly but somehow couldn't make the grade in nursing. Again, strange, because she had done so well academically in high school, graduating second in her class. But she rationalized it all by saying it was a mistake: nursing wasn't for her. (Which was, of course, what I had tried to tell her before she took the plunge.) I don't know how she managed by herself for the next few years, because, alas, I obviously couldn't be there to help her deal with those unpredictable kinds of problems that always seem to come up to disturb day-to-day existence. For I was down in lower Mississippi crawling under barbed wire in basic training exercises, or making a long march burdened with a heavy backpack, or already slogging through Belgium and Germany. In any case, at some point, she decided to try her luck in an even bigger city and moved to Chicago, where we still had some relatives on my father's side. She found work there as a secretary in some business or other. Took up her French horn again. Went folk dancing, where she met her future husband, Arthur, a refugee from the Nazis. Probably doing the polka. If only all this had a happy ending...

No, the rest of her life is a very sad story, dear Nina, as you no doubt realize from some of the family incidents I've already related to you from time to time. Thus, even though their marriage was not ideal, the two had many things in common. Arthur was a talented silversmith, basically a warm-hearted person, and initially, I think, loved her very much. But whatever I suspected was wrong with Millicent physically seemed to worsen as she grew older; she was always having to go to the doctor about something or other, usually the heart or the digestion. Which led to further loss of confidence and self-esteem. This was bad enough in itself, but it was heightened by the tremendous problems she and Arthur faced in raising their firstborn, Glen, whose fate I've already discussed in the letters about Jacob, what with his even more serious mental problems than my Jacob's, and his total inability to focus on anything for more than a few scattered, consecutive moments. Remember my visit to him last year, when he was housed for awhile in that forbidding mental ward at Downstate Medical—a building that looked like a jail, as I described it in my letter about Jacob's premature death. Well, Glen was finally released, only to start roaming again. The last I heard, he was exploring the West. After seeking hospitality in San Francisco, he's now approaching new territory (for him) in remote Utah and Idaho.

Fortunately, Millicent and Art's younger son, Allen, managed to come out of this troubled household scene sane and healthy. He married an intelligent, though rather diffident, young woman, bilingual, with some experience in editing. Their son, Joseph, supposedly a near genius in science, is now a graduate research fellow in biochemistry at Harvard. Yet he always seems vaguely remote from this world, when I occasionally see him with his parents, and I worry a little about his ultimate happiness—especially bearing in mind the troubled genes of our family. Fortunately, grandmother Millicent did live long enough to see her grandson Joey graduate with honors from high school and receive a subsequent scholarship to Harvard.

Yet all this is but a brief outline of their family saga, which needs a modern-day Dostoevsky for the telling of it, as I realize only too well after writing this long, essentially family letter. And which I felt years earlier when I tried writing a sort of elegy for Millicent after her heartbreaking, early funeral in Chicago. She now rests next to her husband Arthur in a well-designed resting place, providentially set aside by some of Chicago's wealthier refugees from Germany and Eastern Europe for themselves, their families, and a smattering of fellow refugees with lesser means. Millicent qualified, of course, because of Arthur, who was a German refugee, remember? He had barely escaped the Nazis with his mother, first to England just before the war, and thence to Chicago after the war ended. (I think they may have been housed in one of those restrictive communities while in England.) Fortuitously, their funeral plot is not far from the section of Chicago where they lived for the last ten years or so. Here are a few excerpts from my modest attempt at a little requiem for poor Millicent, invoking her Job-like suffering, a longer version of which, you may recall, I once showed your hyper-critical eye:

Riding broken down the Chicago El
to the place you dubbed Hell,
I re-live your midnight phone calls,
despondent pleas heavy with tears,
and impractical demands, laced with
fears of death and suicidal doubt.
How many times, dear Sister, did you reiterate: "I can't go on.
I can't. O God, take me away. Let me not wake up tomorrow."—
"But your wounded son," I'd answer. "He needs you. So does his
brother and your brother's son (Jacob). You are, after all, the
sole grandmother. The end of the line. You must carry on."—
"But why? What's the point? Why didn't I give up the ghost already?
The sun has gone down; my days are done. I look for death, but it
doesn't come."
        —"But your friends?"
                        —"What friends?"
And you got your wish, dear departed sister:
you've been taken back, snatched out of this world.
        Yet at the service in the wake of the rain,
        between lovely droplets from the tall oaks,
        the Rabbi reminded us that one doesn't live
        until one gives, and called upon us one and all
        to remember the good will that ran beneath
        the rough bark of bitterness you couldn't cover up.
Nor dare we forget
how you hung on through thick and thin.
And that is how we shall record you
in the Book of Hours, O Sister Myriam—
O Light—for that's what your name means—
as we unveil this modest stone
at the New Light Cemetery

hidden away here
in deceptively calm
beatific suburban
Lincoln Wood.

Well, isn't it about time for me, dearly beloved Nina, to bring this ultra-long family epistle to a close, and to give you a breather from that phase of my life, even though, of course, I'm sure related episodes will return to my memory bank and we'll probably be making another retreat to the Midwest soon to recollect and record them? In the meantime, however, I hope these reminiscences have given you a better idea of what has helped shape my life, as well as a deeper understanding of the personage you now know (even when he turns into your triple animal Skipenko). In the next letter, certainly, we'll move into a different memory patch. Is that OK, *dragosteă-meă* ("my beloved")? Incidentally, one of Mother's favorite folk figures was Mrs. Wiggs of the Cabbage Patch!

> Suspendingly yours,
>> M.

October 11, 2010

Dear patient, understanding Nina:

I'm glad you found the Michigan/Wisconsin/Illinois episodes interesting. As I intimated at the end of the last letter, there will no doubt be other moments from that period that will come back to haunt me. Among other things, I've been wanting for some time to give you a better picture of what New London itself was like—just what kind of a city was it? what were its people, my townsmen, like? how did it really influence me, etc.? Why do I have such mixed feelings about it? Well, as you may recall, I revisited New London about nine years ago for our sixtieth high school class reunion—and it was indeed a rather strange, somewhat disappointing, but overall provocative experience. Fortunately, I had the foresight upon returning to New York to write up some of my impressions while still fresh, which, for some reason or other, I put aside before ever showing them to you. So here, belatedly, I'm making amends for that long delay:

NOTES on NEW LONDON REVISITED—
SIXTY YEARS HENCE—August 2000

The town itself is, of course, changed. Yet seemingly unchanged. Strange paradox. Previous visits to other old, once-lived-in sites usually revealed shrunken towns or landscapes, with everything looking smaller than I remembered it. But here, this time, just the opposite has happened. The town looks bigger. The streets seem wider. The bridges longer. The river deeper. Yet...

However, the small downtown area, especially its one main business thoroughfare, North Water Street, with gaps left by its many torn-down buildings, looks like a row of broken teeth. Nevertheless, the basic profile hasn't changed. And, fortunately, the wonderful old, late Victorian City Hall, on the corner of North Water and West Pearl, has been saved through being taken over by some large business firm; and, lo and behold, the old Op'ry House has been restored. In fact, this was a great surprise for me, since I never suspected way back then that the old shambles of a run-down cinema we used to attend had once been the town's grand old Op'ry House—with, I'm sure, a nice, bawdy history of its own.

Moreover, with the remarkable fluorescence of the Fox River Valley, not-too-distant Appleton has grown into a near metropolis—New London and its sluggish Wolf River site have profited mightily therefrom. Thus, a promising landscaped waterfront is now being fashioned along both sides of the river. Already, there is a small-craft boat station at the middle of North Water Street, where tours up and down the Wolf River are sold. Little antique shops are springing up with gourmet eateries on the way. The most one could ever get in that area sixty or more years ago would have been a dry hamburger or an even drier, duller frankfurter! *Tempus fugit*... [Interpolation: since first writing this, I'm sure there has been even more modernization.]

But, alas, all the heavy, dull shopping these days seems to be done behind and north of North Water Street in a mini-shopping-mall site dominated by a gigantic supermarket. Smaller retail shops cannot compete with this Behemoth. Accordingly, while looking for a liquor store to buy some scotch for my host, I saw a sizable building with a huge liquor sign, which, upon reaching it, I found to be boarded up and in a state of partial demolishment. But two hundred yards beyond was the liquor compartment of the Behemoth itself, which had obviously eaten up that individual store's once-considerable business (judging by the size of its corpse). Hence the sad decline of North Water Street itself.

As to the town proper, most of the old structures, i.e. homes, churches, and schools, seem to be standing stolid, still intact, except down near the waterfront, which had been something of a slum anyway when I was a boy, as I recall. However, a number of buildings have been enlarged or modified and occasionally given modernized facades. Before long, one reaches the newer, large ranch houses. You know when it's a new section of the town because the sidewalks disappear. Does anyone walk anymore, anywhere—even in a small, compact town like New London?

A new City Hall and administrative center, both with fairly good architecture, have sprung up a block or two northwest of North Water Street, but don't register as good as they really are because they're not well placed, nor landscaped to advantage. Sorry to say, the one lonely, old hotel the town once boasted has been demolished, and nothing put in its place. Only rather dreary-looking motels for occasional travelers seem to be left, or probably more recently constructed.

Since my visit, I've learned that guided walking tours of New London have been started for tourists, showing off some of the splendid older buildings that have survived all these years, a few going back to the 1880s and 1890s and built in a variety of styles, including largely Queen Anne Victorian, but also some examples of American Foursquare, Italianate, and Carpenter Revival (American Gothic). I wish such tours had been set up earlier, so that I could have taken advantage of one of them on that trip of mine—a trip not likely to be repeated, I'm afraid.

As to meeting and recognizing my old classmates, it was mighty difficult to remember who was who, even after seriously studying the graduation yearbook. Indeed, I would probably have near-recognized only three or four of them without the help of the individual passport-like identity photo tags derived from the yearbook, which we were all given at the entrance to wear for that evening's festivities. In general, except for a few schoolmates, they seemed to me older than yours truly, although that was probably due to one's near-sighted inability to ever see oneself as what one really looks like to others.

However, many of them still struck me as rather spry, some of the men quite hale and hearty advanced septuagenarians, and the women almost all too bubbly. Indeed, most everyone looked in comparatively good health for his or her age. Oddly enough, not one was obese, with perhaps only one or two obvious beer bellies in sight. Just a few of my once-agile schoolmates needed canes or walking sticks. Only two ladies required wheelchairs. Not bad for a group of seventy-seven- to seventy-nine-year-olds. But we must also bear in mind that about 40 percent of the original class were now no longer with us on this earth, and probably another 10 percent did not show up because they were not in condition to make the long trip to get back to the old homestead. Nevertheless…

Again, gradually, as we talked to one another, aspects of different personalities would emerge more clearly, so that I began to place them better in my memory file. Generally speaking, as I told my host for the weekend, schoolmate Don Huber, the women remained a little more of a blur; that is, after awhile, they all seemed to sound the same, to have retained less of their original personalities, and become something of the "Little Biddy" stereotype of an older woman. Thus, after being introduced to, say, Mrs. A, and talking to her for a spell, then seeing her again ten to fifteen minutes later in another spot and in a different context, attached to another couple, she had merged into Mrs. B, and I'd almost have to start all over again to reconstruct her personality. Whereas, the men, for the most part, were easier to pin down and remember, once I found the hook. Many had retained more identifiable traits and personality quirks left over from those early school days—yes, more so usually than the women. Besides, I seemed to be able to retain their names and identities once pinned down comparatively longer than the women's. Yet it was still quite a strain sorting out thirty or more vaguely recalled personalities. I was truly exhausted at the end of that evening!

That's where I left this account—unfinished, really just a first sketch. For I was planning to work up a suitable ending and then send it to the local New London paper as a kind of memento of that sixtieth class reunion. I even harbored, rather foolishly, I suppose, the hope that my report might in some way spark similar recollections from other attendees. But when I wrote Don Huber, who had been a most friendly, generous host, about this plan, and asked him to look over my manuscript before submitting it to the paper (counting on him to catch any errors about New London), I got absolutely no reply. Also, the morning of the day I left, Don had arranged a short interview with a young reporter from that paper, with whom I had left a few old photos and some press clippings from my years at the Brooklyn Philharmonic and some On- and Off-Broadway shows I had been in, from which he could choose passages if he needed them to supplement his article, a copy of which he had promised to send me, along with an envelope returning that material. Well, nothing of all that ever reached me. I never saw any article. I got no reply from Huber. Finally, I wrote the young reporter himself, begging him to return the material, parts of which were my only copy. No response. No apology. No mention of whether he ever actually wrote the article. No return of anything whatsoever. Later, I left several phone messages for Huber. Again, no replies. I returned two tapes of his little jazz band, which he still kept up after all these years, along with a thank you note for his hospitality. Again, silence. I still wonder what was amiss. What had happened? Could I have inadvertently offended the group, or maybe two or three influential members of their reunion committee? In any case, I never heard from any of them again. Nor was I invited to the sixty-fifth (they have these reunions every five years); nor have I been invited to the upcoming seventieth. I guess I always was, and obviously still am, something of a foreigner to these people. Maybe I had been too open with them, talked too freely, wasn't quite quiet and dignified enough. I know I shocked a few of the more conservative Republicans there that night with some of my stronger Democratic positions. But good Lord, reunions are supposed to be fun. People are expected to enjoy themselves, right? In any case, I don't want to depress you with more of this almost incomprehensible reminiscence.

*

High time to shift gears. To go to another compartment of my brain. For there's still considerable catching up to do in recounting more of my theater adventures, especially after the *Fiddler* and

Cubiculo periods. And these, I can assure you in advance, will be much more varied. Fortunately, I just located a copy of a proposed article I sent to *The Villager* in the late Seventies (not to the *Voice*, since they wouldn't print such a lengthy report) about the origins of The Classic Theatre to which I was then devoting more of my time, especially after leaving The Cubiculo and before my work at The Brooklyn Philharmonic grew so time-consuming. Well, this piece was never published: *The Villager* suddenly underwent one of its annoying shifts in emphasis and wouldn't allow space for such a long article about just one theater company. But I think that with a little editing, I should transcribe it for you here and now because it covers the first phases of my post-Cubiculo period, and, besides, will give you a better idea of the incredibly difficult circumstances in which we Off-Off-Broadway producers and directors had to operate in those pioneer days. Also, you'll meet another interesting woman in my growing gallery of strikingly unusual female figures, Sala Staw. She's someone you probably would have got along with better than you would have with either Sari Dienes or Mura Dehn—or surely Lilla van Saher. And you'll learn more about our unique friend, Nick Stathis, whose untimely death last year we all lament, and who played a most important role in this phase of my life. After all, he was the Santa Claus behind our Classic Theatre!

So, here goes—you'll see why I designed it for *The Villager* and why I'm resurrecting it now for you. I called it:

THE CLASSIC THEATRE RETURNS TO THE VILLAGE

Somehow one always comes back to the Village. The Classic Theatre started there, on East 9th Street, to be exact, only a few doors down from the second office of *The Villager*; and now it is back again, this time on West 14th Street, a block away from the current site of *The Villager*. [This was written in early summer, 1977.]

Within that circuit of time and space lies the saga of trying to establish an Off-Off-Broadway theater, of finding a home terrain, a stepping stone to the future. Of course, the nomadic nature of The Classic Theatre is not necessarily so unusual. Nowadays, or a thousand years ago. Medieval jousters went from town to town, from one village square to another. Think of Bergmann's film evocations of such troupes. Similarly, early American theater was 90 percent itinerant. You could see and hear Shakespeare in Salt Lake City and San Francisco in the mid-19th century, and hear opera in New Orleans in the 18th century. Jumping to the twentieth, the Bread and Puppet Theatre has had many homes and covered many terrains. Even giants like the Canadian Stratford Festival and the Royal Shakespeare Company of England spend a great deal of their time on the road. And Broadway shows go east, west, north, and south. (Though, alas, with the advent of TV much less than they used to.) Nevertheless, to find the right home base is most vital for any theatrical company. And we of The Classic Theatre hope that now that we're back in the Village, we can make a good fresh start in that direction.

But where did it all begin? Sala Staw, who founded The Classic Theatre (which at one time she wanted to call the Theatre for the Poor, pace Grotowski, and years before he came to the fore), had been an itinerant actress/sculptor of some note. Her main problem was that she looked too much like Judith Anderson and, indeed, in her prime was said to have had some of the same power and vitality as that often-overwhelming Australian-born actress. (Sala once sculpted a bust of Miss Anderson that is quite superb.) But, with time, Miss Staw turned her energies more and more to directing.

It was probably her production of Sean O'Casey's *Within the Gates* for Equity Library Theatre around 1948 that started her on her first big innovation—doing plays in the libraries of Greater New York. In any case, that was where the initial productions of The Classic Theatre (its name obviously describing the nature of its repertoire) were presented, starting with the Hudson Park branch library on lower Seventh Avenue and moving from there in a circuit around local libraries of Manhattan, the Bronx, Queens, Brooklyn, and Staten Island. This took place during the late Forties and early Fifties.

I first became acquainted with Miss Staw when she called me in to replace a Rodrigo in one of her traveling *Othello* productions, probably the winter of 1949. It was amazing to discover how high-powered her condensed versions of *Othello*, *Macbeth*, Molière's *The Learned Ladies*, could be in their plain, stark stagings, almost totally bare of furniture and props, with the actors dressed simply in black chinos and white polo shirts and the actresses in black skirts and white blouses. The swirl of Shakespeare, and later the splendor of Racine, the pathos of Euripides, and the rowdy fun of Molière and Goldoni spilled out onto those little raised platforms in the tiny, otherwise often God-forsaken, auditoriums of the damp, gray library basements of Greater New York.

But, of course, Miss Staw had a larger "vision." She wanted all America to have full productions of such classics, with all the proper accoutrements, touring all over the country like a truly national theater. This was her *cause célèbre*. She became notorious anually for rising up from her seat or bench at Actors' Equity union meetings to spout forth eloquently her vision of a "National Theatre for the Poor." Unfortunately, hardly anyone took her seriously. For this was during what I call the Dark Ages of American theatre and dance, before the rise of state arts councils, national endowments, Ford philanthropy, and Mellon munificence. If only Equity had rallied behind her vision, appointed committees headed by stars, and provided initial partial financing, something might have

391

been launched earlier—roots of which, once the Lincoln and Kennedy Centers mushroomed, would have been there—a tradition already in the making with a corps of dedicated actors ready to be tapped.

However, before meeting Miss Staw (Ms. had not yet entered the English language), I had been following another path. Younger than she, I was in that stage of wanting to do primarily new works, break new trails, start new styles—all this, in turn, before the eruption of the experimental theater groups of the late Sixties. Back in 1958, for instance, I had staged the first electronic opera at the 92nd Street Y, repeated later at Cooper Union, along with another mad new sound piece, "Two Sounds," by LaMonte Young, which almost caused a riot: the police had to be called in to quell it. [More fully covered in an earlier letter, as you'll recall.]

But, of course, I was never against working, or, better yet, re-working the classics. On the contrary, I had by this time already staged Aristophanes' *The Birds* and his *Congress of Women* at Cooper Union with meager means, and had even mounted a staged reading of Dryden's stark answer to Shakespeare's *Antony and Cleopatra*—his underrated *All for Love*. [Also partially covered in earlier letters.] So, by the time I met Sala Staw, I was ready to join forces with her in trying to establish a more far-ranging Classic Theatre. Unfortunately, sickness on her part and my landing a role in a hit show, *Fiddler on the Roof*, delayed implementation of that plan.

Nevertheless, in the meantime, I tried to help her begin to launch productions somewhat more full-scaled than her basic library-type showcase, for which we found a temporary home at the Second Moravian Church on 30th and Lexington Avenue, where she put on quite competent productions of Racine's *Britannicus*, Goldoni's *The Fan*, and Euripides' *The Trojan Women*. It was also during this period that Sala staged a shoe-string production of Maeterlinck's *The Bluebird* for a settlement house on the Lower East Side, which turned out to be one of her best shows and which certainly deserved more attention than it received.

Here we come to perhaps the chief among the many problems of doing Off-Off-Broadway theater: when you finally do get something on the boards that you consider a good example of what you're aiming at, it's usually next to impossible to get the press coverage it cries out for. Or, if you do manage to interest someone, it's already too late. The show has come and gone. [This idea is also partially covered in my earlier letters. Remember especially the one discussing my *Notes from the Underground* production.]

But to continue the Sala Staw saga: after she lost her space at the Moravian Church (to social services and drug addiction work), Cooper Union (at my behest) invited her in to put on several plays, including Molière's very early comedy, *The Blunderer*. These, in turn, led to her first grant from the New York State Council on the Arts and two showings at La Mama; where she repeated *The Blunderer* and added Strindberg's *Dream Play*. Alas, it was just at this point that she was struck by some undiagnosed illness and shortly afterward passed away.

I was the production coordinator at The Cubiculo Theater during this last phase of her original Classic Theatre repertoire, when she was finally beginning to gain some recognition and contributions were starting to come in, and so could only help peripherally with advice and occasional appearances. But when she died, she left the paper past and airy future of The Classic Theatre to me; and I felt I had to try to carry out something of her dream.

So I persuaded a benevolent, arts-loving, theater-

393

struck patent and copyright lawyer, Nicholas John Stathis, who had financed several of my productions at The Cubiculo, including two new plays by Joyce Carol Oates [again discussed, you will recall in earlier letters], to assume the presidency of the newly constituted Board of Directors of The Classic Theatre. Of course, that in itself didn't mean clear sailing, though we subsequently owed much to his generosity and guidance.

For there were plenty of problems to be solved. First of all, I was still basically tied to The Cubiculo, the multi-arts center I had helped Philip Meister and Elaine Sulka of the National Shakespeare Company to establish on West 51st Street. So we tried first to present Classic Theatre productions jointly under the latter's aegis. This worked fairly well for awhile.

One of the first things we produced under this new arrangement was an experimental staging of Euripides' *Alcestis*, with a wondrously simple but eloquent set by Donald L. Brooks, and with choral vocal and group work in alternating Greek and English that anticipated much of what Andrei Serban was to do later in his famed Agamemnon cycle at La Mama, though, of course, on a smaller, more modest scale. Our *Alcestis* started in total darkness, which was then punctuated with torches, primitive percussion effects, and the chorus spread throughout the theater space intoning passages in the original Greek, alternating with English (not, however, in a motley of other languages, and even nonsense syllables, as Serban did, for a more mysterious effect, I presume). Then on into the play proper, in English, of course, although the choral passages would still use the alternate languages from time to time. Sala Staw would have applauded both productions. In any case, Nick Stathis's friend, the great Canadian soprano, Teresa Stratas, brought a colleague, the then on-the-rise English poet and opera librettist,

Tony Harrison, to see it; and it was even rumored about that our show may have influenced him in penning his upcoming Agamemnon cycle at the National Theatre in London (though I'm a bit dubious about its accuracy).

Other Classic Theatre plays produced jointly under the aegis of the The Cubiculo included the American premiere of *The Dogs of Pavlov*, a new play based on the obedience-to-authority experiments of that period, by the Welsh/English poet (and doctor) Dannie Abse; and a double bill of two delightful Shaw one-acts, The *Music Cure* and *Press Cuttings*, the latter a brilliant, neglected satire on women's liberation, dealing with those early suffragettes who chained themselves to No. 10 Downing Street in the early 1900s, to attract the Prime Minister's— and thereby Parliament's—attention, and force them into action. Numerous other companies have since put on versions of *Press Cuttings*: we started a vogue.

However, before long it began to become clear to us that if The Classic Theatre were to fully establish its own identity, it could not go on forever under the aegis of The Cubiculo. People began to think of our productions as The Cubiculo's, but not vice versa. And since a true marriage of minds and means finally proved impossible, we decided that The Classic had to move on. [A prescient decision, since only one or two years later, I resigned from The Cubiculo, and its activities were drastically curtailed, alas.]

And so The Classic Theatre's odyssey was resumed: we were out on the street again. Through Saylor Creswell, who had acted in our *Press Cuttings*, we were led to the New York Society for Ethical Culture, that stalwart bastion of free thinkers on Central Park West and 64th Street (an unusually classy address for Off-Off-Broadway!). Because a faction there at that time wanted a resident theater of ideas, they offered us their huge hall of worship rent-free. But what could be done in such a place, with its tiny platform for the Leaders (their term for ministers) and its total lack of theatrical facilities? However, since The Classic Theatre had by this time a long history of adapting to various sites, including the most simple, like those library stages in its beginnings, this did not stop us. On the contrary, it led to some interesting choices of plays for production.

Thus, sensing that the hall looked surprisingly like one of those 19th-century French etchings of Paris's *Chambre des Deputées,* we thought to ourselves: what about staging *Danton's Death* here, Büchner's remarkable epic drama in epic style, that should have the barest of sets anyway, what with its constant shifting of scenes, as in Shakespeare, and with many of those taking place in that historic chamber?

So *Danton's Death* it was—and it worked magnificently in that space. We used various sections of the hall for disparate scenes, shifting a spotlight to follow actors en route to new locations, or back to old ones. And the big crowd scenes in the Chamber of Deputies, with the eloquent exhortations of Robespierre and St. Just from the rostrum, using the Society's elegant lecterns, gained unexpected verisimilitude (which was aesthetically justified, since Büchner took those speeches practically verbatim from the public record). We even found a striking substitute for a guillotine—a heavy metal door that separated the hall from the adjoining school, which we clanged shut each time a head had to be lopped off!

But what other play(s) could fit such a space? No sets could be built, because the architecture could not be altered, nor the wood paneling disturbed. Moreover, anything special, like folding furniture and props, or screens substituting for walls, had to be removed for the weekly services. The Society did not want another epic production so soon, successful as *Danton's Death* had been, with the largest box office The Classic Theatre had had to date (and probably Ethical Culture as well)! Their Leaders hoped that we would try next a more conventional kind of drama. So we decided upon Duerrenmatt's *The Physicists*, which, with its European-type interiors, looked somewhat at home in this beautiful authentic hall, where the wood itself smelled musty and the benches exuded age. But, alas, the hall turned out to be too large and overwhelming for the kind of intense psychological focus that play needed, and so this production, while reasonably well done, and with respectable results, did not fare quite so well.

However, even had we solved the problem of sets, staging, dressing-room space, etc., we found ourselves suddenly confronted by a much more serious problem when we wound up the run of *The Physicists*: the faction that had brought us in had been, in the meantime, overthrown by rear-guard diehards who did not want theater to spoil the "ethical" ambience of their holy meeting hall (unconscious shades of Danton's revolution?). The alternative space offered us beneath the hall would have engendered even more problems to solve, of storage, constant shifting of props, costumes, etc. It would also have conflicted frequently with the social functions of the Society, which took place down there from time to time. So, in effect, we were unceremoniously forced out—thrown out, to be more exact, since we were given only one night's notice! Not very ethical behavior, one might say, by the much-vaunted Ethical Society of New York! Once again The Classic was on the move....

Ironically, we found another church space directly across Central Park on 64th Street and Park Avenue. The Central Presbyterian Church there was renting its basement (a former church gym of good dimensions) to groups such as ours, the tail-end of their formerly

397

ambitious arts program, which had recklessly used up much of the church's capital, instead of functioning on the income from that capital alone. Nonetheless, we signed on and immediately went ahead with staging Ben Jonson's rarely performed comedy, *Epicoene*, although up until the 19th century, it was his most popular play. I like to think of it as the venerable grand-uncle of *Charley's Aunt*. In any case, we had a rousing success with it, drawing almost as big an audience as we had for *Danton's Death*. This was in late May, early June, 1975. We were invited back for the following season.

Nevertheless, here again it was not easy going. This time, we had to share the space with another group by alternating productions. Moreover, again we had the problem of identity. Was the production to be known as The Classic Theatre's or Central Arts's? And would our shows be confused with those of other groups on the alternate dates? Still, the space itself was so multifunctional, lending itself to so many different kinds of theater (especially after the limitations of the Ethical Culture space), that we decided to try to weather the storm and show the Church that we could also be of service to them and their community needs—particularly since the plays we were doing had moral stature and substance, even when as bawdy as *Epicoene*.

Our first production that fall was a revival of Victor Hugo's strangely still-moving drama, *Mary Tudor*, not exactly a true historical play, since Hugo took great liberties with Mary's life and fate, but a good example of the power of that kind of melodrama, if well performed, to make history live and vibrate. We did it in homage to the great French group, Théatre Nationale Populaire, which had presented its *Mary Tudor* here in New York with the divine Maria Casares as the Queen back in 1957 (and who I had seen in Paris twelve years earlier in a Cocteau play; also, of course, in Marcel Carné's film *Les Enfants du Paradis*, among others.) Surprisingly, it worked in English better than expected, with the excellent Linda Barnhurst as Mary.

But shortly after this success, we heard rumblings that the Church might have to be torn down to make way for the Rockefeller's expanding Asia House next door. So when we were invited by the Armenian Cathedral at 34th Street and Second Avenue to do *Badvi Hamar* (*For the Sake of Honor*), a 1905 Armenian classic by Alexandre Shirvanzade, a sort of mélange of Gorky, Chekhov, and Ibsen, we decided to try out their space. But this was a one-shot deal and created another problem—that of losing followers by such frequent shifts of location. However, it was wonderful how many of our fans followed us from one site to another, and would continue to do so in subsequent moves, as I shall soon describe.

So back to Central Arts, where we wound up the season with three more productions: an adaptation of Kafka's story, *A Report to an Academy*; an unusual modern Italian fantasy/drama about Rousseau and his ideas, Apollonio's *The Apocalypse according to J.J.*; and the avant-garde Polish painter/playwright Witkiewicz's offbeat *Tropical Madness*, an absurdist treatment of the colonial question, East/West psychology, and metaphysical heroics, almost as if it were a take-off on Joseph Conrad via Bernard Shaw by a fellow Pole! Actually, the main protagonist may have been a cross between Witkiewicz himself and the great anthropologist, Malinowski, the two having spent some time together in the Dutch East Indies, where the play is set.

These last two productions were surprisingly well received by the Fathers at the Church, if not by all the Lords of the Press, though they did elicit some excellent reviews. However, they did not draw the typical

Central Arts audience the way Ben Jonson or Victor Hugo did. Yet that was not the main problem. We could have weathered smaller houses. We could even have endured the inordinate heat (the place was not air-conditioned). Indeed, for *Tropical Madness*, we furnished the audience with Chinese fans and seated them cafe style, serving cold drinks during the show. But what we could not survive was the Church's economic plight: they had reached another crisis, now that the sale to Asia House was voided by the courts, namely, plain economics—the upkeep of the Church. Though we were paying them a hefty rent for the premises, plus bringing in our own lighting and sound at considerable expense (their lighting and sound systems having been systematically ripped off during the past years by a variety of predecessor groups), the new president of the Synod had persuaded the presbyters to shut down the church, except for services, in order to save money. And so The Classic Theatre was out on the street again. (Several years later, the space was turned into a private health club, I think, thus, via poetic justice, returned to its original status as a gym!)

However, not being prepared to do street theater—though some of our plays might possibly have been adapted to that genre—we spent that summer scouring the town for a place we could finally and truly call our own, namely, a loft or floor of a building that could be leased only to us, where we could be autonomous, not subject to the shifting whims and unreasonable demands of boards of directors, presbyters, community leaders, bankrupt churches, conflicting ethical factions, or jealous arbiters—all those problems attendant upon any "guest" status.

But now we found ourselves transported, in effect, from Lilliput to Brobdingnag! Renting or leasing property in Manhattan takes you into another kind of nightmare, involving greed, duplicity, misrepresentation, rent gouging, and other economic hurdles. Even with City property, we encountered many problems; mostly bureaucratic, to be sure, but frustrating and difficult to deal with. We had to abandon a most promising prospect, partly because we discovered that the City wanted to make money on it! Also, because everything was kept in limbo, including the plans.

Then there were the empirical problems of physical dimensions, accessibility, faulty staircases, and bad wiring. We explored scores of lofts. If accessible, with good structure, there would be pillars obstructing sight-lines. If free of pillars, the ceiling would be too low for lighting fixtures or for the heads of tall members of the audience perched on back risers. And if everything else seemed right, then the rent would be sky-high. Finally, we began to consider taking over plants of other theater groups that were failing or that had given up because they couldn't bear the wear and tear of nonprofit theater any longer. Whereupon we faced the problem of determining whether it was worth buying them out. In one case, for example, the space itself was quite desirable, with a Fifth Avenue entrance no less, and rent not out of the question, but the departing group wanted an extra $5,000 for the "plant" they were leaving behind—old lumber, a poor grid, fairly good seats, but no lights! Five thousand was excessive, when we would also have had to rebuild almost everything but the seating platforms, plus make a big investment in lights.

Finally, we found our haven back in the Village in the hospitable but small Spanish theater, Caras Nuevas, housed in a fourth-floor loft on West 14th Street. The group had done some fine work, and had even won a grant or two, but was discouraged from going on because Spanish audiences did not respond, and so they decided they should try something else. It was November, we were exhausted, the place was promising, our Spanish hosts amicable, and we had to get our program going. We took it on a year's sub-lease, agreeing to buy them out at the end of the year, provided things worked out well.

Did we have problems? Of course, we did. On the opening night of our first production there, the American premiere of Yuri Olyesha's sharp, brilliant, Soviet 1926 satire, *Conspiracy of Feelings*, two reputable critics came, but the elevator was not functioning, and they had to climb up three flights of stairs, along with the rest of the audience. That hardly put them in a receptive state of mind. Then, midway through the run of our second play there, O'Casey's *Shadow of a Gunman*, there was a power shortage, although that created some auxiliary excitement! The heat failed entirely during the dress rehearsal for our third play, Pirandello's *Each in His Own Way*, and it was in midwinter. Finally, actors in 19th-century woolens suffered through the extraordinary heat wave that occurred last spring, during our fourth play, Ibsen's *Rosmersholm*.

Though we're now preparing for the coming season's productions here at hospitable but problematic Caras Nuevas, we fear that our Odyssey may not be over yet. [It wasn't.] They may lose their lease! So, dear Reader (and potential Playgoer), double check the listings this fall to make sure that The Classic Theatre has not moved once again. In the meantime, does anybody know of a Perfect Space or a Magic Loft? If so, please inform us where. Could the Law of Eternal Return be operative here? [End of proposed *Villager* article.]

*

As I said at the beginning of this letter, change of management at *The Villager* probably left this article sitting in some lonely back drawer: it was never published. Bad timing—and a pity it was—because I think it might well have given The Classic Theatre the boost in public notice it so much needed at that point in its growth and development. But that didn't stop us from moving ahead. No, the next season was already on the planning boards.

This time, luck was on our side: a comparable-sized space opened up two floors down from the Caras Nuevas space in the very same building—on its second floor—which meant that an audience would have to walk up only one short flight of steps to reach us.

It was also an easier move for our lighting fixtures, costume collection, prop-room items, and the limited stage furniture we had by this time collected. There was a further welcome advantage to this loft over the last: its ceilings were higher, better for lighting and seating purposes as well as many other theatrical factors and features.

In any case, we soon said "*adios*" to Caras Nuevas. The new space became our longest-lasting home, at which site we were able to build up quite a large following, almost enough to guarantee an automatically good-sized audience for the three weekends allowed each show by our Equity Off-Off-Broadway showcase rules. Here we did any number of fascinating plays, including Massinger's *A New Way to Pay Old Debts*; Sardou's *Tosca*, which, as you know, Puccini turned into perhaps his tautest opera; *Love Affairs and Wedding Bells*, a delightful frolic by the wonderful Austrian comedy playwright, Nestroy (Vienna once had a theater devoted solely to reviving Nestroy plays); and Dostoevsky's *Notes from the Underground, Part I*, which I described in an earlier letter. But after that long tale of our earlier Classic productions in *The Villager* article, I think maybe you've had enough theater to mull over for awhile!

However, from time to time I'll want to return to the theme and to describe a few of the more interesting shows that transpired in that space on 114 West 14th Street, next door to one of the larger Salvation Army centers in Manhattan. All I might add now is that while we mounted some of our best productions there, it was not without its jarring ups and downs, unfortunately aggrandized by an unwise "downsizing" imposed upon us by the more conservative faction of our rather small board of directors. This, in turn, led to the eventual abandonment of a basically satisfactory space and the beginning of the end of a fundamentally worthy project. All the more galling when we have now lived to see our name and concepts taken over quite successfully by two other theater groups now functioning Off-Off-Broadway—The Classic Stage and the Pearl Theatre. I'm tempted to go into the problems we went through with boards of directors at The Classic Theatre and the Brooklyn Philharmonic—but that would end up as almost a "treatise" in itself!

And so, melodramatically, or fatalistically, yours,

M.

December 19, 2010

Dear Nina:

What an unexpected saga that *Villager* article turned out to be, followed by my brief coda about The Classic Theatre's long residence at 114 W. 14th Street, and a hint of its sad denouement to come, which I certainly wouldn't want to weigh you down with now.

Or weigh me down! For I'm exhausted reliving those eventful, often very exciting and rewarding yet also often extremely stressful, years, simply by recording them. Remember, during this period, I continued holding down my Brooklyn Philharmonic "civilian job." At the same time I was putting on these plays in order to keep me and the family afloat. In any case, as you have seen, my "*theatralische Sendung*" turned into a veritable theatrical Odyssey. But its lengthy and sometimes perilous ups and downs recall another odd, totally different, odyssey in my life which somehow I failed to write about in any of the earlier letters that dealt with my Army comings and goings, namely, a short Land Voyage that turned out to be, in its way, a sort of prelude to that other odyssey that was my life in the Army, though seemingly unrelated to anything else that touched my existence during that crucial maturing period; or even to my much longer theatrical odyssey, and on to Life itself, as well. Ah yes, we have here another example of the quixotic unconscious Exquisite Corpse game that Life plays with us from the moment we leave the womb.

Have I aroused your curiosity? Well, that unanticipated Odyssey was the long, *langsam*, laboriously drawn out, four-day railroad trip that took me from my Ides of March 1943 enlistment into the U.S. Army at Madison, Wisconsin, to my first basic training at Camp Roberts near San Luis Obispo in sunny California, halfway up the Pacific coastline between Los Angeles and San Francisco. Consigned to a drab old passenger car, wearing a drab-colored, ill-fitting uniform, along with a small ad-lib unit of enlistees from the Madison area, we, a truly odd assemblage, were first transported to Milwaukee, then on to Chicago, where we were transferred to another train puffing westward into Iowa and Kansas, soon sidelined for a long spell, after which we continued westward, we thought, but were never quite sure, since our west-bound train had to switch over to other lines from time to time to give civilian passenger trains priority. This meant that sometimes we went backwards, other times seemingly sidewards, then surely westward again, we hoped, eventually chugging up, down, and through dismal passes in the Rockies, stopping at towns we had never heard of, but weren't permitted to get out of the train to savor or explore, and then again, most discombobulatingly, when our car would be disengaged from one locomotive to be hitched to another, only to be pushing ahead again, but then suddenly backing up for another spell, in a frustratingly bewildering zig-zag pattern none of us guys could predict or confidently interpret, since we were never once told where we were or where we were headed next. The result was a hooded mystery voyage to the West Coast—yes, somehow we did learn that our destination was California, but not where in that huge state. It was a trip, which in peacetime would have taken little more than two days, that lasted four and one-half dark, dank, and uncomfortable days and nights interrupted and interspersed from time to time by the sudden changes of direction and constant shifting of positions described above, harbored in dirty, drafty cars and regaled by terrible, stultifying meals. For me, it was also a scary plunge into a world I never dreamed I'd ever inhabit. I knew no one personally in our little, heterogeneous Madison group, which ipso facto limited discussions and "socializing" with them. For I had yet to develop the limited talent I later discovered I had for talking to total strangers. In any case, many members of that unit seemed unduly sullen, even somewhat hostile; but they probably felt the same way about me. So what choice did I have but practically to withdraw to my sleeper area for 90 percent of the time? And what did I do to while away that time? After all, there were no Circes or Calypsos circling around to seduce us, nor a terrifying Cyclops or an impetuous Aeolus to worry about, not even a nice Nausicaa to ogle or transpose into a Gypsy Rose Lee.

But luckily I had had the foresight to have taken along a still (for me) unexplored, magic book, Joyce's *Ulysses*, a perfect choice for such a voyage, even if it was land-bound, and ideally needed an amenuensis, some kind of reader's guide or gloss. And yet what an adventure even alone, unaided, it proved to be! While at the university, I'd only had time to dip occasionally into that formidable tome, for it was never part of the curriculum of any of my classes. However, I managed to read short excerpts from time to time, skim through the later chapters, and poke my nose here and there into that challenging volume, searching for the "ineluctable modality of the visible" (a locution which continued to haunt me for years)… Of course, I had had some previous Joyce experience in absorbing his *Portrait of the Artist as a Young Man*, reading *Exiles*, and cherishing *Dubliners*. But here on this God-forsaken train I had all the time in the world to plow systematically through this amazing, all-embracing book from start to finish, to stop and go as I might choose, to turn back and re-read passages I didn't grasp the first time through, some of which still remained obscure (of which, as you know, my dear, there's an overabundance, even in the Romanian translation that you assure me is superb). And since I was alone, and no one cared a damn what

I was doing, although a few snickered at their fellow eye-glassed, bookworm soldier, I paid no attention to any of that, or to them, the perpetrators, and simply plowed ahead. Not surprisingly, the more I read the easier it became. So that by the time I reached the Nighttown section, I was passably Joyce literate! Besides, Nighttown, being more or less a play, was a cinch. And while I surely missed a goodly portion of the double meanings or just what Joyce was satirizing or which English style he was doing a take-off on for which chapter, and, due to youthful inexperience, certainly missed some of the rich gusto of Molly's great soliloquy finale, I found myself swept along by the book's miraculous narrative flow, its fresh, bubbling diction, the eloquent cadences, and much of the humor which I did get. I also caught the smell of the Liffey, the charm and bustle of Dublin, the incomparable lilt of the Irish-accented English dialogue of an incomparable cast of characters, led by Bloom, Molly, and Stephen, with Bucks Mulligan and all the rest of the crew chiming in. Enchanted, enthralled, exhilarated, fascinated, stimulated, enlightened—I was tied down, held captive, and truly spellbound for four and one-half days and nights. Thus Joyce's masterpiece became my private odyssey, my unexpected salvation. Hallelujah! How else could I have survived that hideous, almost surrealistic, voyage?

Looking back on it now, the first time I've mused over this incomparable, solitary intellectual feast for some years (although it continued to nourish me ineluctably for a long time still to come), I see how this unplanned, unbidden personal Railroad Odyssey also served as a prelude to my three years in the Army and the events that accompanied that stint in time, which, in its way, turned out to be another far-longer, infinitely more variegated odyssey for me, personal, impersonal, communal; private, public and international; encompassing many lands, rivers, lakes, seas, harbors, and islands; towns, villages, cities, zoos, plains, peninsulas, and mountains; peoples, animals, insects, and birds; cathedrals, hovels, slums, and temples; shanty towns and palaces, Reichstags and Parliaments; ruins, catastrophes, sufferings and storms; mud, dead animals, cemeteries and death camps I was to visit and explore, to cohabit and share, to learn from and take pity upon, to devour and derive sustenance therefrom, for a long time ahead. This double heritage of two odysseys, in turn, undoubtedly influenced, enhanced, hopefully enriched, and maybe occasionally impeded, the sixty-plus years of Life that followed, highlights from which I've scribbled down for your delectation in this hodgepodge sequence of letters, critiques, quotations, and reportage. And perhaps even influenced the telling of what happened in my childhood and youth, which pre-dated those odysseys?

Of course, a lot has been left out. I could go on filling those gaps, retrieving past memories, and further exploring my Self and my Life while trying to figure out what that life adds up to, for weeks, months, years to come—at the same time, making it interesting and hopefully also amusing. But where and how would I stop? Otherwise, I might end up feeling like that Middle Eastern poet Adonis, who once confessed "I am living my death every day." A most difficult question, indeed.

That is why, my dear, I sense that Fate, or what someone once called "the droll dispatch of nature," has intervened again in leading me to this point, this summing-up imperative, "for as long as I am entitled to be"—as Frank Kermode put it at the end of his memoirs. Is it saying that we should bring this series of letters, much as I enjoy writing them, and you, I trust, relish reading them, to a sensible close? We have a lot to prepare for, what with your writing deadlines and our upcoming trip to Romania, where at last they will be giving your inimitable life work its due, and will honor you with the reprinting of two volumes of your voluminous oeuvre. Agreed? Let me know soon.

In the meantime, with a fond "until the next time, my beloved" vocalized in your melodious Romanian: "*La revedere, iubită-meă*"!

Retrospectively yours,

M.

P.S.: And, of course, upon the return from our Balkan retreat, we could always pick up where we left off, if you should so wish! As you know, there are any number of strands of reminiscence I've left dangling: special memories, incidents, and/or people I had promised to take up in later letters and now feel a little guilty not keeping my word to you about, indeed, by leaving them lost in space, searching for a landing spot.

P.P.S.: One final point—a question I raised at the start of one of my earlier letters. May I quote myself? Here goes: Why am I dredging up these seemingly unrelated mementos of my past? Is it to entertain you, to justify my existence—in your eyes, in the eyes of others, in my own eyes? Or is it to answer some higher order, some pressure of conscience? Possibly even a hitherto unrecognized teleological urge?—"Fate" mentioned above?—No, nothing so grandiose! I think it's simply that I'm trying to make sense of my life: finally to understand myself—surely, as Socrates said, the most difficult of all endeavors...

Accordingly, I ask myself, who am I?

Birthday Poem 2010 (for Maurice)
by Nina Cassian

You are the Man among the men,
You are my M, I am your N.
If I'm a rose, you are my stem.
I am your N, you are my M.
You keep me vertical indeed.
You are my song. I am your Lied.
If I'm a pearl, you are my gem.
I am your N, you are my M.
You are my book, I am your pen.
You are my M, I am your N.

Amen

MAURICE EDWARDS has been involved in many aspects of the theater and music—as performer, director and producer—and translator. Featured in the original casts of *Fiddler on the Roof* and *The Golden Apple* on Broadway, he appeared in the original DeLys *Threepenny Opera* production, *The Fantasticks*, Brecht's *A Man's a Man*, Turgenev's *The Bachelor*, and many other plays Off- and Off-Off-Broadway. He also staged a number of lesser-known classics for The Classic Theatre, including *The Jew of Malta*, *A New Way to Pay Old Debts*, Hugo's *Marie Tudor*, Jonson's *Epicoene*, and Dostoevsky's *Notes from the Underground*, Part I. Co-founder of the experimental theater, The Cubiculo, he has served as Executive and Artistic Director of the Brooklyn Philharmonic, where, among other things, he produced with Lukas Foss nineteen years of Meet the Moderns concerts at BAM and Cooper Union, staged several new operas as well as a concert version of Duke Ellington's *Queenie Pie*, and a Weill/Brecht cabaret for Marianne Faithful at BAM, followed by a rich variety of festival programming there under Maestros Dennis Davies and Robert Spano. In between acts, Edwards performed his own cabaret programs of Weill/Brecht songs and a Noel Coward anthology. Retired from the Brooklyn Philharmonic, he now serves as its Archivist; his history of the orchestra, *How Music Grew in Brooklyn,* was recently published by Scarecrow Press. He is also consultant to the Interfaith Concerts of Remembrance at the Cathedral of St. John the Divine. In addition, Edwards is known for his translations from the German of plays by Grabbe, Sternheim, Marieluise Fleisser and, most recently, Thomas Bernhard's *Der Weltverbesserer*, as well as from the Italian, several of Dario Fo's *commedia dell' arte* one-acts.